To Peter Haas,

The International Politics of the Environment

Andrew Hurrell

THE INTERNATIONAL POLITICS OF THE ENVIRONMENT

Actors, Interests, and Institutions

Edited by Andrew Hurrell and Benedict Kingsbury

CLARENDON PRESS · OXFORD
1992

Oxford University Press, Walton Street, Oxford OX2 6DP
Oxford   New York   Toronto
Delhi   Bombay   Calcutta   Madras   Karachi
Petaling Jaya   Singapore   Hong Kong   Tokyo
Nairobi   Dar es Salaam   Cape Town
Melbourne   Auckland
and associated companies in
Berlin   Ibadan

Oxford is a trade mark of Oxford University Press

Published in the United States
by Oxford University Press, New York

British Library Cataloguing in Publication Data
Data available

Library of Congress Cataloging-in-Publication Data
The International politics of the environment, actors, interests, and institutions/
edited by Andrew Hurrell and Benedict Kingsbury.
p.   cm.
Includes bibliographical references and index.
1. Environmental law, International.   2. Environmental policy–
International cooperation.   I. Hurrell, Andrew.   II. Kingsbury, Benedict.
K3585.6.I584   1992   341.7'62—dc20   92–2806
ISBN 0–19–827365–7
ISBN 0–19–827778–4 (pbk.)

Typeset by BP Integraphics Ltd., Bath, Avon
Printed and bound in
Great Britain by Biddles Ltd.
Guildford & King's Lynn

ACKNOWLEDGEMENTS

WE would like to thank the Nuffield Foundation, the Cyril Foster Fund, the Astor Travel Fund, and Nuffield College for financing this research project. Institutional support and hospitality was provided by Nuffield College, Oxford; Exeter College, Oxford; and the Cornell Law School, Cornell University. We thank Sarah McGuigan, Leah Adams, Winnie Young, and Vivian Lee for their invaluable assistance in helping to assemble the final typescript. For their time and advice in helping us to plan and organize this project we are indebted to Adam Roberts, Lucy Butterwick, Dennis Anderson, and Tim Barton.

A. J. H.
B. K.

September 1991

CONTENTS

viii Contents

ABBREVIATIONS

AJIL	*American Journal of International Law*
CFC(s)	chlorofluorocarbon(s)
CITES	Convention on International Trade in Endangered Species of Wild Flora and Fauna
CLC	IMO Convention on Civil Liability for Oil Pollution Damage 1969
CO_2	carbon dioxide
EC	European Community
ECE	United Nations Economic Commission for Europe
ECOSOC	United Nations Economic and Social Council
EEC	European Economic Community
EEZ	Exclusive Economic Zone
EFZ	Exclusive Fishing Zone
FAO	Food and Agricultural Organization
FOE	Friends of the Earth
GATT	General Agreement on Tariffs and Trade
GDP	Gross Domestic Product
GHG	greenhouse gases
GNP	Gross National Product
ICJ	International Court of Justice
ICRW	International Convention for the Regulation of Whaling
ICSU	International Council of Scientific Unions
ILM	*International Legal Materials*
IMF	International Monetary Fund
IMO	International Maritime Organization

IPCC	Intergovernmental Panel on Climate Change
ITTO	International Tropical Timber Organization
IUCN	International Union for the Conservation of Nature and Natural Resources
MARPOL	Convention for the Prevention of Pollution from Ships 1973 (amended 1978)
NGO	Non-Governmental Organization
OAS	Organization of American States
OAU	Organization of African Unity
ODA	Official Development Assistance
OECD	Organization for Economic Co-operation and Development
PCB(s)	polychlorinatedbiphenyls
PCIJ	Permanent Court of International Justice (predecessor to the ICJ)
SCAR	Scientific Committee on Antarctic Research
SCOR	Scientific Committee on Oceanic Research
TFAP	Tropical Forestry Action Plan
UN	United Nations
UNCED	United Nations Conference on Environment and Development, Brazil, 1992
UNCHE	United Nations Conference on the Human Environment, Stockholm, 1972
UNCLOS	United Nations Convention on the Law of the Sea, 1982
UNDP	United Nations Development Programme
UNEP	United Nations Environment Programme
WCED	World Commission on Environment and Development (the Brundtland Commission)
WMO	World Meteorological Organization
WRI	World Resources Institute, Washington, DC
WWF	World Wide Fund for Nature (formerly World Wildlife Fund)

SOME MAJOR MULTILATERAL ENVIRONMENTAL TREATIES

Transboundary Atmospheric Pollution

Geneva Convention on Long-Range Transboundary Air Pollution 1979, *ILM* 24 (1985), 484.

Protocol for Long-Term Financing of Monitoring 1984, *ILM* 24 (1985), 484.

Protocol on the Reduction of Sulphur Emissions or Their Transboundary Fluxes by at Least 30 Per Cent 1985, *ILM* 27 (1988), 698.

Protocol Concerning the Control of Emissions of Nitrogen Oxides (1 November 1988), *ILM* 28 (1989), 212.

Protocol on the Reduction of Volatile Organic Compounds 1991.

Stratospheric Ozone Layer

Vienna Convention for the Protection of the Ozone Layer 1985, *ILM* 26 (1987), 1516.

Montreal Protocol on Substances that Deplete the Ozone Layer 1987, *ILM* 26 (1987), 1541. Amended and Adjusted at London 1990, text in Carter and Trimble (eds.), *International Law: Selected Documents* (Boston: Little, Brown, 1991), 731.

Transboundary Movement of Hazardous Wastes

Basel Convention on the Control of Transboundary Movements of Hazardous Wastes and Their Disposal 1989, *ILM* 28 (1989), 657.

Bamako Convention on the Ban of the Import into Africa and the Control of Transboundary Movement and Management of Hazardous Wastes within Africa, concluded under the auspices of the OAU, 29 January 1991, *ILM* 30 (1991), 773.

Transboundary Standing and Environmental Impact Assessment

Nordic Environmental Protection Convention 1974, *ILM* 13 (1974), 511.

Espoo Convention on Environmental Impact Assessment in a Transboundary Context 1991, *ILM* 30 (1991), 800.

Nuclear Tests and Accidents

Treaty Banning Nuclear Weapon Tests in the Atmosphere, in Outer Space and under Water 1963, *UNTS* 480, p. 43.

Paris Convention on Third Party Liability in the Field of Nuclear Energy 1960, *AJIL* 55 (1961), 1082, with supplementary Convention 1963, *ILM* 2 (1963), 685.

Vienna Convention on Civil Liability for Nuclear Damage 1963.

Convention on Early Notification of a Nuclear Accident 1986, *ILM* 25 (1986), 1370.

Convention on Assistance in the Case of a Nuclear Accident or Radiological Emergency 1986, *ILM* 25 (1986), 1377.

Antarctica

Antarctic Treaty 1959, UNTS 402, p. 71.

Protocol on Environmental Protection 1991, *ILM* 30 (1991), 1455.

Convention for the Conservation of Antarctic Seals 1972, *ILM* 11 (1972), 251.

Convention on the Conservation of Antarctic Marine Living Resources 1980 (CCAMLR), *ILM* 19 (1980), 841.

Wellington Convention on the Regulation of Antarctic Mineral Resource Activities 1988 (CRAMRA), *ILM* 27 (1988), 868.

Space Objects

Convention on International Liability for Damage Caused by Objects Launched into Outer Space 1972, *AJIL* 66 (1972), 702.

Outer Space

Treaty on Principles Governing the Activities of States in the Exploration and Use of Outer Space, including the Moon and Other Celestial Bodies 1967, UNTS 610, p. 205.

Marine Pollution: Global

International Convention on Civil Liability for Oil Pollution Damage 1969, *ILM* 9 (1970), 45.

Brussels Convention Relating to Civil Liability in the Field of Maritime Carriage of Nuclear Material 1971, UKTS, MISC 39 (1972), Cmnd. 5094.

International Convention on the Establishment of an International Fund for Compensation for Oil Pollution Damage 1971, *AJIL* 66 (1972), 712.

London Convention on the Prevention of Marine Pollution by Dumping of Wastes and Other Matter 1972 (London Dumping Convention), *ILM* 11 (1972), 1294.

Convention for the Prevention of Pollution of Ships 1973 (MARPOL), *ILM* 12 (1973), 1319, Amended by Protocol 1978, *ILM* 17 (1978), 526.

London Convention on Civil Liability for Oil Pollution Damage Resulting from Exploration for and Exploitation of Seabed Mineral Resources 1977, *ILM* 16 (1977), 1450.

UN Convention on the Law of the Sea 1982, *ILM* 21 (1982), 1261.

Marine Pollution: Regional

Oslo Convention for the Prevention of Marine Pollution by Dumping from Ships and Aircraft 1972, *ILM* 11 (1972), 262.

Helsinki Convention on the Protection of the Marine Environment of the Baltic Sea Area 1974, *ILM* 13 (1974), 546.

Paris Convention for the Prevention of Marine Pollution from Land-Based Sources 1974, *ILM* 13 (1974), 352.

Barcelona Convention for the Protection of the Mediterranean Sea Against Pollution 1976, with Protocols, *ILM* 15 (1976), 290.

Kuwait Regional Convention for Co-operation on the Protection of the Marine Environment from Pollution 1978, with Protocol, *ILM* 17 (1978), 511.

Lima Convention for the Protection of the Marine Environment and Coastal Area of the South-East Pacific 1981, UN doc UNEP-CPPS/IG. 32/4 (1981).

Jiddah Regional Convention for the Conservation of the Red Sea and Gulf of Aden Environment 1982, with Protocol, *Envt'l Pol. & Law* 9 (1982), 56.

1

The International Politics of the Environment: An Introduction

Andrew Hurrell and Benedict Kingsbury

IN addressing the international politics of the environment this book is concerned with the processes by which inter-state agreements on the environment are negotiated; with the rules and regimes established to facilitate environmental co-operation; with the international institutions that have been, or need to be, created to implement those rules; and with the conflicting political forces on whose resolution any successful regional or global environmental initiatives must depend. The global environmental issues discussed in this volume include climate change (chapters by Richardson, Beckerman, Cooper, Shue, Susskind and Ozawa, and Maull), ozone depletion (Bramble and Porter, and Maull), marine dumping (Stairs and Taylor), deforestation (Hurrell, Myers, and Bramble and Porter), and biodiversity (Myers). The objective is not to provide detailed scientific treatment of the nature of the major environmental challenges facing the world, but rather to explore the international political forces that work to complicate the negotiation and implementation of rational environmental policies between states, to analyse the strengths and weaknesses of various institutional mechanisms by which states have sought to co-operate in managing environmental problems, and to assess their relevance for the future. Underlying this analysis is a central question: Can a fragmented and often highly conflictual political system made up of over 170 sovereign states and numerous other actors achieve the high (and historically unprecedented) levels of co-operation and policy co-ordination needed to manage environmental problems on a global scale?

The international dimensions of environmental problems have

long been apparent, whether cross-border industrial pollution, the degradation of shared rivers, or the pollution of adjacent seas. Yet the scale and extent of these problems have increased dramatically as a result of the triple processes of population growth, rapid industrialization, and increased fossil fuel consumption. As one recent report points out:

Since 1900, the world's population has multiplied more than three times. Its economy has grown twentyfold. The consumption of fossil fuels has grown by a factor of 30, and industrial production by a factor of 50. Most of that growth, about four-fifths of it, occurred since 1950. Much of it is unsustainable.[1]

The tremendous increase in the scale of human impact on the earth wrought by these developments, together with our increased, although still highly imperfect, understanding of ecological processes, means that the environment can no longer be viewed as a relatively stable background factor. Rather the interaction between continued economic development and the complex and often fragile ecosystems on which that development depends has become a major international political issue.

Not only has the number and scope of transborder environmental problems increased, but a new category of global environmental issues has emerged; it is this global character that is the most distinctive feature of the present era. First, and most obviously, humanity is now faced by a range of environmental problems that are global in the strong sense that they affect everyone and can only be effectively managed on the basis of co-operation between all, or at least a very high percentage, of the states of the world: controlling climate change and the emission of greenhouse gases, the protection of the ozone layer, safeguarding biodiversity, protecting special regions such as Antarctica or the Amazon, the management of the sea-bed, and the protection of the high seas are among the principal examples. Second, the increasing scale of many originally regional or local

---

[1] Jim MacNeill, Peter Winsemius, and Taizo Yakushiji, *Beyond Interdependence: The Meshing of the World's Economy and the Earth's Ecology* (Oxford: Oxford UP, 1991), 3. In 1990 the UN Population Fund estimated that the then population of 5.24 billion would grow to over 6.2 billion by the year 2000, with 94% of the projected increase to take place in developing countries. The estimate of 6.2 billion was 124 million higher than the 1984 projection. See UN doc. A/CONF.151/PC/38 (26 Mar. 1991), 5.

environmental problems, such as extensive urban degradation, deforestation, desertification, salination, denudation, or water or fuel-wood scarcity, now threaten broader international repercussions: by undermining the economic base and social fabric of weak and poor states, by generating or exacerbating intra- or inter-state tensions and conflicts, and by stimulating increased flows of refugees. Environmental degradation in diverse parts of the developing or indeed the industrialized world can in this way come to affect the political and security interests of the developed countries.

The third, and in many ways most important, aspect of increased globalization derives from the complex but close relationship between the generation of environmental problems and the workings of the now effectively globalized world economy. On the one hand, there is the range of environmental problems caused by the affluence of the industrialized countries; by the extent to which this affluence has been built upon high and unsustainable levels of energy consumption and natural resource depletion; and by the 'ecological shadow' cast by these economies across the economic system (a theme addressed by Hanns Maull in his chapter below). On the other, there is the widely recognized link between environmental degradation, population pressure, and poverty, given prominence in the Brundtland Report and at the 1992 United Nations Conference on Environment and Development (UNCED) in Brazil and highlighted below in Peter Thacher's examination of the present and future roles of the UN system and in Norman Myers's discussion of the 'shifted cultivator'. The environmental problems created by both affluence and poverty have focused attention on the need to develop new understandings of sustainable development and new mechanisms for implementing the shift towards sustainability. Sustainable development has become a global issue both because of the high levels of economic interdependence that exist within many parts of the global economy and because it raises fundamental questions concerning the distribution of wealth, power, and resources between North and South.

As several of the chapters in this volume demonstrate, it is no longer possible to treat ecology and international political economy as separate spheres. The institutions that matter most are not specifically 'environmental', but rather are the core institutions that govern (or at least seek to govern) the workings of the world economy: such institutions as the World Bank, the IMF, the GATT, the Group of Seven, and to some extent the OECD. A major contemporary focus is the integration of environmental concerns into the sphere of economic planning and policy-making, rather than the development of an entirely separate and thus inevitably somewhat peripheral sphere—this point is developed in Kenneth Piddington's chapter on the World Bank.

Why should the international political aspects of environmental issues be a distinct object of study? Why, given the seemingly obvious incentives to co-operate, should inter-state co-operation by viewed as problematic? The most basic answer lies in the striking dichotomy between the seamless web of ecological interdependence on the one hand and the fragmentation of the international political system on the other. A single, complex and highly integrated ecosystem has to be managed within the constraints of a political system made up of over 170 states, each claiming sovereign authority within its territory. It is, moreover, a political system which has historically been prone to violent conflict and in which co-operation has been difficult to achieve.

For many (including the self-styled 'Realist School' of international relations), the absence of any central authority—the existence of anarchy between states—is the defining principle of international relations and the source of inevitable insecurity and conflict. The existence of anarchy fuels the inescapable logic of the security dilemma: the foreign policies of states are dominated by the need to survive and to accumulate power in order to guarantee their survival. This creates a vicious spiral of insecurity and mistrust that makes sustained co-operation all but impossible. As Robert Jervis puts it:

Because there are no institutions or authorities that can make and enforce international laws, the policies of co-operation that will bring mutual rewards if others co-operate may bring disaster if they do not. Because states are aware of this, anarchy encourages behavior that leaves all concerned worse off than they could be.[2]

[2] Robert Jervis, 'Cooperation under the Security Dilemma', *World Politics*, 30 (1978), 167.

On this view, the prospects for effective global environmental management are modest indeed. Anarchy and conflict are the rule, order and co-operation the exception.

Even if this image of a Hobbesian world is rejected as overdrawn, and it is recognized that a great deal of co-operation does in fact take place, the difficulties of inter-state co-operation must still constitute the starting-point for any study of the prospects for global environmental management. There are many collective action problems in which states would clearly stand to gain from co-operation but are unable to do so—situations in which (in the language of game theory) instrumentally rational actors have an incentive not to co-operate, even though mutual co-operation would be the collectively optimal outcome. Why is this? Most centrally because of the weakness or absence of the institutions required to stabilize expectations, to prevent defections and free-riding, and to encourage and channel domestic pressures for international co-operation. Although international co-operation is required both to manage global environmental problems and to deal with domestic environmental problems in ways that do not place individual states at a political or competitive disadvantage, states will not participate in such co-operative efforts unless there is some guarantee that other states will do likewise. This assurance problem is exacerbated by the pressures on states and state representatives to place a high priority on their immediate short-term interests and on relative gains and losses; by the large number of deep-rooted historical conflicts that exist between states; and by the cultural, political, and economic heterogeneity of the international system. Moreover, although interdependence both generates collective action problems and creates incentives to co-operate, it also creates new elements of instability (because of the increased susceptibility of domestic politics to external shocks), leads to new sources of conflict (because the costs and benefits of managing interdependence have to be distributed between states), and opens up new sources of power and leverage (because it exposes states to external vulnerability, is rarely symmetrical, and introduces new connections between international and domestic politics).

Managing the environment also demands high levels of co-operation and policy co-ordination. The forms of co-operation that emerged historically between states were largely concerned with elaborating minimum rules of coexistence built around the mutual recognition of sovereignty and the corollary norm of non-intervention. Co-operation was built around the rights of states to independence and autonomy and the creation of certain minimalist understandings designed to limit the degree of conflict that naturally occurred within such a pluralist and fragmented system. The classical state system was therefore a 'practical association' which did not embody any overarching set of common purposes or any common vision of the good life.[3]

This minimalist picture of circumscribed international co-operation has of course been recast in the twentieth century, through the extension of economic interdependence, the growth of international institutions, and the emergence in international law of customary and treaty norms establishing rights and duties for individuals.[4] Yet despite the changes that have occurred, the structure of both the international political and legal systems continues to rest heavily upon the independence and autonomy of separate sovereign states and the pluralism which this entails. Collective environmental management poses a severe, and therefore politically sensitive, challenge because it involves the creation of rules and institutions that embody notions of shared responsibilities and shared duties, that impinge very heavily on the domestic structures and organization of states, that invest individuals and groups within states with rights and duties, and that seek to embody some notion of a common good for the planet as a whole.

The clash between the character of the international system and the necessities of rational environmental management has often led to acute scepticism about the suitability of the state system. One such sceptical position was summarized by Richard Falk, writing at the time of the first wave of global environmental concern in the early 1970s:

A world of sovereign states is unable to cope with endangered-planet problems. Each government is mainly concerned with the pursuit of

[3] Cf. generally Terry Nardin, *Law, Morality, and the Relations of States* (Princeton: Princeton UP, 1983).

[4] See Wolfgang Friedmann's discussion of the evolution from an international law of co-existence to an international law of co-operation, in *The Changing Structure of International Law* (New York: Columbia UP, 1964); and e.g. Michel Virally, 'Panorama du droit international contemporain', *Recueil des Cours de l'Académie de Droit International*, 183 (1983), 9–382.

national goals. These goals are defined in relation to economic growth, political stability, and international prestige. The political logic of nationalism generates a system of international relations that is dominated by conflict and competition. Such a system exhibits only a modest capacity for international co-operation and co-ordination. The distribution of power and authority, as well as the organization of human effort, is overwhelmingly guided by the selfish drives of nations.[5]

For some the only logical answer to this conundrum lay in curtailing the sovereign powers of states and in moving towards a greater degree of supranational authority: 'Thus the already strong rationale for a world government with enough coercive power over fractious nation states to achieve what reasonable men would regard as the planetary common interest has become overwhelming.'[6] However, the prospects for extensive supranationalism and world government are inevitably remote, and are open (at least with regard to the short or medium term) to several objections that are well known but deserve brief restatement.[7] First, the nation state remains extremely resilient as a focus for human loyalties and as a structure for the exercise of political power. There is little or no consensus amongst the leaders of states or amongst populations that a move towards supranationalism is desirable. This is particularly true of the developing world. For many peoples of the post-colonial world, the achievement of statehood was the condition of political emancipation. Second, claims to autonomy and sovereignty have a moral validity that has to be set against the increased stridency of cosmopolitan moral claims. Many states, although by no means all, fulfil purposes and represent values that deserve respect and may require protection from the power of

[5] Richard Falk, *This Endangered Planet: Prospects and Proposals for Human Survival* (New York: Vintage Books, 1971), 37–8. For a more recent negative assessment of the states system's capacity to manage the global environment see John Dryzek, *Rational Ecology* (Oxford: Blackwell, 1987), esp. ch. 6.

[6] William Ophuls, *Ecology and the Politics of Scarcity* (San Francisco: W. H. Freeman & Co., 1977), 219. For a discussion of others who view the centralization of power as the solution to collective action problems see Elinor Ostrom, *Governing the Commons: The Evolution of Institutions for Collective Action* (New York: Cambridge UP, 1990), 8–10.

[7] For a classic discussion of the difficulties of transcending the states system see Hedley Bull, *The Anarchical Society: A Study of Order in World Politics* (London: Macmillan, 1977), esp. Pt. 3.

some global authority.[8] Once power is given over, it is not easy to limit it to a particular sphere. Third, claims about the need to abolish or limit sovereignty have to be thought through in the context of all the other issues and problems of international life. The environment, although important, cannot be viewed in isolation. Fourth, it is far from clear that the creation of some supranational authority would in fact lead to more effective environmental management. The negotiations over the nature of a new political authority would be enormously difficult and time-consuming and would generate much conflict. This would almost certainly divert attention away from devising environmental agreements and could all too easily postpone the implementation of necessary environmental policies. Distributional conflicts between different parts of the world would still remain to be resolved within the new political structure. Local political authorities would still be required to implement effective environmental policies, and the current weakness of such authorities in many parts of the world would be reproduced within a broader political system. Finally, there is the basic paradox that if there were sufficient consensus to move beyond the state system, there would also be sufficient consensus to ensure a degree of inter-state co-operation that would make such a move largely unnecessary.

An alternative radical solution argues not for the creation of a global Leviathan but rather for the decentralization of power and authority.[9] For its proponents such an approach would weaken

---

[8]   The case was put forcefully by two legal counsel in the Bush Administration in the US: 'Internationally, a command and control emphasis is simply not feasible . . . Creating a supranational organization to monitor the process would have dubious benefits. In advocating such an organization, many environmentalists tend to denigrate the value of the nation-state. At best, they see national sovereignty as an inconvenience, and at worst, an all but insurmountable obstacle to effective global environmental policy. However, environmentalism is not the only value worthy of protection. Being environmentally responsible does not require abandoning other important values, such as national self-determination. The modern nation-state is a manifestation of the bedrock principle of national self-government . . . National sovereignty is especially important to the developing countries. Many of these countries have only recently achieved their own independence. They are not likely to welcome suggestions that their interests should again be subordinated to ''metropolitan'' concerns. Any global program that does not take into account the legitimate value of the nation-state is doomed to failure—and rightly so.' C. Boyden Gray and David B. Rivkin, Jr., 'A ''No Regrets'' Environmental Policy', *Foreign Policy*, 83 (Summer 1991), 63–4.

[9]   Such a vision is implicit in the campaigning goals and priorities of many environmental pressure groups. See also Dryzek, *Rational Ecology*, esp. ch. 16.

the competitive drives of the global economy that intensify the depletion of natural resources and the degradation of the environment and in which environmental 'management' is often no more than the displacement of a problem from one sphere or locality to another. It would empower local communities which have a greater understanding of the specific ecosystems on which their economic livelihood depends. And it would build on the experience of those groups that have historically been able to create small-scale and sustainable forms of economic development. Whilst there are powerful arguments in favour of greater decentralization and empowerment of local communities, there are also important limitations: that empowerment of local communities and rational ecological management are not always consistent; that it neglects the broader functions of the state system in the many other fields of human activity; that the costs of disrupting the global economic system would be enormous and would also prove a potent source of conflict; and that there would continue to be a need for some degree of global co-ordination either for effective ecological management or out of considerations of social equity, but that such co-ordination would be infinitely more difficult in such a system because of the increased numbers of communities.

It is perfectly possible, indeed likely, that new forms of co-operation will be required, and that some further constraints on state sovereignty will emerge. Nevertheless, environmental issues will still of necessity be managed within the constraints of a political system in which sovereign states play a major part. This starting-point, recognized and adopted (albeit with differing degrees of enthusiasm) in all of the chapters in this volume, is a fundamental from which the present analysis of the international politics of the environment proceeds.

Clearly international negotiations and agreements are only one aspect of the management of the global environment. A great deal will depend on reform at the domestic level: on the growth of environmental awareness and changing individual attitudes and life-styles; on the reform of public policies that encourage unsustainable forms of development such as inappropriate agricultural or energy subsidies; on internalizing the costs of environmental damage by means of new taxes or the creation of new markets; on the implementation of new forms of 'environmental accounting' that reflect the true value of natural capital; and on unilateral policy reforms adopted irrespective of the behaviour of other states.

Equally, international action is not limited to formal inter-state agreements, and states are by no means the only important actors. The attitudes, investment decisions, and capabilities of companies play a major role in determining how environmental problems are defined and dealt with by governments. Political pressure from business and concern about the impact of environmental regulation on economic activity, competitiveness, and specific industries can often lead states to obstruct international action. However, as Maull points out below in discussing Japan, market and competitive pressures can be a powerful 'transmission belt' leading to changes in states' environmental policies. The diffusion of green thinking through the workings of the global media, informed and spurred by environmental NGOs, is an additional, and insufficiently studied, aspect of environmental politics. The activities of environmental NGOs have assumed an important place in issue identification, agenda setting, policy formation, normative development, institution building, monitoring, and implementation.

Yet, while formal inter-state agreements are not always needed and certainly do not provide a complete picture of global environmental politics, they form the centrepiece of international efforts to deal with global environmental problems. Indeed the number and range of established or emerging rules and legal regimes in this field is striking. [10] Moreover, the distinction betweeen regulatory and market-based approaches to global environmental management, while philosophically important, is often drawn too sharply. Regulatory approaches may well require far more detailed sets of rules, but rules are also indispensable to market-based approaches: in expressing fundamental principles, in establishing and defining property rights over common resources where they do not currently exist, and in creating the

---

[10] As environmental issues have grown in prominence and importance, the number, range, and political significance of international agreements has increased enormously on a bilateral, regional, and global basis. UNEP's *Register* lists 152 multilateral agreements (including Protocols and Amendments) on environmental issues up until 1990, of which 102 were concluded in the preceding 20 years. (*Register of International Treaties and Other Agreements in the Field of the Environment* Ref n (Nairobi: UNEP, 1991), UN doc. UNEP/GC.16/Inf.4.)

structure of the market itself and the mechanisms by which it will be monitored.

In order to lay out the issues involved and to provide a framework for evaluating the progress that has been made and the considerations which may influence or constrain future developments, the chapters in this book (and the main sections of the Introduction) are organized around three broad themes: first, the processes by which environmental rules and regimes have been and will be created, and the problems connected with their implementation; second, the past and future roles of formal international institutions in the international protection of the environment; and third, the nature and significance for international environmental protection of the conflicts between states over power, over the distribution of the costs of environmental management, and over questions bearing upon state sovereignty and freedom of action.

A. Standard Setting and Implementation

Inter-state environmental co-operation is increasingly directed toward agreeing upon, and implementing, international legal standards. Standard setting is necessary to define the general principles of collective management of the global environment and to formulate precise rules of process and of mandatory, permitted, or proscribed conduct. At the same time standards stabilize, reflect, and give contractual expression to the results of the underlying bargaining process between conflicting state interests. The strengths and limitations of existing international law and of the rule-making, implementation, and enforcement mechanisms presently available are examined in the chapters by Patricia Birnie and Elliot Richardson.[11] A slightly different

---

[11] See also A. E. Boyle, 'Saving the World: Implementation and Enforcement of International Environmental Law through International Institutions', *Journal of Environmental Law* 3 (1991), 229–45; Peter Saud, *Lessons Learned in Global Environmental Governance* (Washington, DC: World Resources Institute, 1990): Oscar Schachter, *International Law in Theory and Practice* (Boston, Mass.: Martinus Nijhoff, 1991); and Patricia Birnie and Alan Boyle, *International Environmental Law* (Oxford: Oxford UP, forthcoming).

12 Andrew Hurrell and Benedict Kingsbury

approach, increasingly emphasized in international relations literature and espoused in this volume by Martin List and Volker Rittberger, focuses on the role of regimes in managing conflicts and solving collective action or common interest problems. Regimes include legal rules, but are defined more broadly as 'sets of implicit or explicit principles, norms, rules and decision-making procedures around which actors' expectations converge in a given area of international relations'.[12] Although international law provides the principal frame of reference for those involved in inter-state negotiations, at the theoretical level there is a degree of complementarity between international law and regime theory. Regime theorists have tended to neglect the particular status of legal rules, to downplay the links between specific sets of rules and the broader structure of the international legal system, and to underrate the complexity and variety of legal rules, processes, and procedures. On the other hand, theoretical accounts of international environmental law have often paid rather little explicit attention to the political bargaining processes that underpin the emergence of new norms of international environmental law, to the role of power and interest in inter-state negotiations, and to the range of political factors that explain whether states will or will not comply with rules.[13]

[12] Stephen D. Krasner, 'Structural Causes and Regime Consequences: Regimes as Intervening Variables', in Stephen D. Krasner (ed.), *International Regimes* (Ithaca: Cornell UP, 1983), 2. For a survey of regime theory in general see Stephan Haggard and Beth A. Simmons, 'Theories of International Regimes', *International Organization*, 41 (1987), 491–517. For its application to the environment see especially Oran R. Young, *International Cooperation: Building Regimes for Natural Resources and the Environment* (Ithaca: Cornell UP, 1989). Further references are given in the chapter by List and Rittberger below.

[13] An interesting example of an enforcement regime not intended to establish new normative standards is the Paris Memorandum of Understanding on port state control, concluded in 1982 among the 11 coastal EC states plus Finland, Norway, and Sweden. The general objective is to promote and harmonize efficient port state inspection of vessels in accordance with the standards laid down in six major maritime conventions, to which the participants are expected to become parties. Vessels found to have deficiencies 'clearly hazardous to safety, health or the environment' shall not be allowed to put to sea, except in very limited circumstances e.g. to proceed to a port capable of making the repairs. A Port State Control Committee is established, together with a computer centre in France in which results of inspections are stored and which can be accessed on-line and used for inter-port communications. The Secretariat is provided by the Dutch government. It is a low-cost arrangement, envisaged as 'a formal co-operative regime on enforcement issues but not as an international regime creating new legal rights and obligations for its parties.' See George Kasoulides,

1. *The creation of environmental law and regimes*

The general need for legal or other regimes if major global environmental problems are to be adequately addressed is scarcely in question. The attainment of even basic agreement on what arrangements are required is, however, much more complicated. One major reason for this is that global environmental issues are typically characterized by high levels of uncertainty in which the *definition and boundaries* of the 'problem', the *costs* of alternative policy responses, and the *identity* of the actors and their *interests* are all far from self-evident. This has a number of important consequences.

(i) *Research co-operation.* A great deal of international co-operation, especially since the Stockholm Conference in 1972, has been concerned with gathering information and promoting research on the character and extent of environmental problems: UNEP's research and monitoring activities are discussed in Peter Thacher's chapter, and other examples include the work of the Group of Experts on Scientific Effects of Marine Pollution (GESAMP), Unesco's Man and the Biosphere programme, the International Council of Scientific Unions' International Geosphere/Biosphere Programme ('A Study of Global Change'), and ICSU's Scientific Committee On Problems of the Environment (SCOPE).[14]

(ii) *Problems of scope.* The complexity of the science, together with the close links between environmental problems and economic processes, means that a great deal of negotiating time is spent deciding which aspects of a particular problem should be included in negotiations and which states should be involved. Thus, for example, the range of human activities that contribute to the greenhouse effect is extraordinarily wide, their relative weight varies from country to country, and the scientific evidence is far stronger in some areas than in others. In such a case, fixing the boundaries of the negotiation, the identity of the parties, and

---

'Paris Memorandum of Understanding: A Regional Regime of Enforcement', *International Journal of Estuarine and Coastal Law*, 5 (1990), 191. See also A. V. Lowe, 'A Move Against Substandard Shipping', *Marine Policy*, 6 (1982), 326.

[14] Ronald Brickman, Sheila Jasanoff, and Thomas Ilgen, *Controlling Chemicals: The Politics of Regulation in Europe and the United States* (Ithaca: Cornell UP, 1985), discuss the tendency in relation to toxic chemicals to share research findings but regulate unilaterally.

the range of their admissible interests becomes a central element of international negotiations. The criteria for such decisions may in part be technical. States might seek, for example, to include those aspects of a problem that are best understood or that can be most effectively monitored. But such decisions are also highly political given that they influence the distribution of costs and benefits and affect the extent of states' bargaining power and leverage. Such considerations may lead states to try and broaden the range of issues—as in the attempt by the developing states to link global environmental negotiations with both present economic inequality and their future development needs. But it may also lead states to exclude issues. Indeed the power of the North has been particularly visible in focusing attention on 'environmental' issues—and on the narrower category of global environmental issues—and in moderating, perhaps even minimizing, the concern of the South with the human development dimensions of the same agenda. International negotiations over a complex issue such as global climate change, with its multiple causes and global implications, can also readily be made into a symbol for, and entrée to, debates about appropriate development models, duties of technology transfer, and the structure of development assistance.

The merits and demerits of such linkages are discussed in several chapters in this volume. The problems of striking the balance in structuring such negotiations are addressed by Susskind and Ozawa. The relationship between issue linkage, bargaining power, and justice forms a central theme of the argument developed by Shue that poor nations not be required to sacrifice their own development to prevent the climate changes set in motion by the process of industrialization that has enriched the North.

(iii) *Adaptability and flexibility.* The perceived seriousness of many environmental problems (especially climate change, ozone depletion, loss of biodiversity, protection of forests) pushes states towards co-operation and collective management even though there continue to be very high levels of scientific and economic uncertainty. This in turn means that international agreements must be structured to provide scope for new regulations as new data becomes available, and to promote improved data collection and further scientific research. Typically such agreements call for regular review in the light of changing scientific knowledge, and provide for close collaboration between rule-makers and research scientists.

The experience with control of substances depleting the stratospheric ozone layer constitutes a useful illustration. The 1985 Vienna Convention, which established general policy goals but no quantitative reductions, was almost immediately shown to be inadequate by evidence of ozone layer depletion over Antarctica.[15] The response was to adopt the Montreal Protocol, but even before its adoption Mostafa Tolba asked the negotiators pointedly: 'Have we compromised so much that we have emasculated the agreement? Have we compromised so much that the ozone layer will continue to deteriorate?'[16] The answer soon proved to be affirmative, as research established both that many of the substitutes envisaged in phasing out CFCs contributed seriously to the newly documented greenhouse effect, and that several substances not controlled under the Protocol were ozone-threatening. The 1990 London Amendments added a new Annex B to stabilize and eventually reduce emissions of carbon tetrachloride, methyl chloroform, and fully halogenated CFCs not covered in Annex A, and Adjustments hastened reductions in production and consumption of Annex A CFCs and halons, although not to the extent wished by thirteen OECD countries (joined in 1992 by the US) which unilaterally undertook to proceed more quickly. The damaging effect of substitutes was not, however, addressed beyond a general resolution to use them with great care and to seek more environmentally benign alternatives.[17]

The character of many environmental issues renders flexibility essential. Rigid and detailed sets of rules are likely to become

[15] J. C. Farmer, B. G. Gardiner, and J. D. Shanklin (British Antarctic Survey), 'Large Losses of Total Ozone in Antarctica Reveal Seasonal ClOx/NOx Interaction', *Nature*, 315 (1985), 207; R. S. Stolarski *et al.* (NASA), 'Nimbus 7 Satellite Measurements of the Springtime Antarctic Ozone Decrease', *Nature*, 322 (1986), 808.

[16] Quoted in Jamison Koehler and Scott A. Hajost (US EPA), 'The Montreal Protocol: A Dynamic Agreement for Protecting the Ozone Layer', *Ambio*, 20 (1991), 84.

[17] See David D. Caron, 'Protection of the Stratospheric Ozone Layer and the Structure of International Environmental Lawmaking', *Hastings International and Comparative Law Review*, 14 (1991), 770. The text of the Montreal Protocol as amended at London is conveniently reproduced in Barry E. Carter and Philip R. Trimble (eds.), *International Law: Selected Documents* (Boston: Little, Brown, 1991), 731.

quickly outdated, and their effectiveness thereby undermined. For this reason, international environmental negotiations have increasingly led to agreements that put in place continuing, fully- or semi-institutionalized multilateral rule-making frameworks. Several related regulatory techniques have evolved to meet these demands for flexibility. One method is to include amendment procedures within the treaty and to list detailed 'technical' regulations in annexes to the treaty, which are made subject to regular review and can in many cases be amended by majority agreement. A further refinement is introduced by provisions that amendments become binding upon all states parties except those which specifically oppose them. Variants of this technique have long been used in Conventions adopted by the International Maritime Organization (IMO), such as the London Dumping Convention,[18] and have also been employed in, for example, the 1989 Basel Convention on the Control of Transboundary Movements of Hazardous Wastes and Their Disposal.

A second, and increasingly common, technique is to begin with a framework treaty containing a statement of agreed general principles, together with mechanisms for promoting further research and strengthening data collection, and the establishment of a forum and timetable for subsequent negotiations on specific issues. Out of these negotiations emerge separate protocols covering in detail a specific aspect of the problem, and themselves subject to formal mechanisms for regular review and revision. The Geneva Convention on Long-Range Transboundary Air Pollution of 1979 provides a good illustration.[19] It established monitoring stations, requirements for national reporting of emission levels, and general commitments to gradually reduce transboundary acid rain emissions. Subsequent Protocols, adopted as and when the necessary research had been completed and the requisite level of political agreement attained, provided for a 30 per cent reduction in sulphur dioxide from 1980 levels,[20] and for certain limitations on and reductions in emissions of

[18] See Nagendra Singh, 'The United Nations and the Development of International Law', in Adam Roberts and Benedict Kingsbury (eds.), *United Nations, Divided World* (Oxford: Oxford UP, 1988), 184–5.
[19] Printed together with the 1984 Protocol for Long-Term Financing of Monitoring, in *ILM* 24 (1985), 484.
[20] Protocol on the Reduction of Sulphur Emissions or Their Transboundary Fluxes by at Least 30 Per Cent (9 July 1985), *ILM* 27 (1988), 698.

nitrogen oxides.[21] This group of acid rain agreements has been criticized, *inter alia*, for focusing on emission levels rather than on ambient air quality, for not providing for international trade in emission permits so as to encourage least-cost reductions, and for failing to charge polluters. Nevertheless, the basic format appears to have worked well. Certain improvements have been made in the similar format adopted under the 1985 Vienna Convention for the Protection of the Ozone Layer. The Montreal Protocol, which established the first quantitative reduction commitments, provided for amendments which bind only those states accepting them, and for adjustments to reduction levels for controlled substances which can be adopted by a qualified majority of the parties but bind all parties.[22]

The Montreal Protocol, especially as enhanced by the 1990 London Amendments, applies pressure to participate by restricting and eventually prohibiting parties from trading in controlled substances with non-parties. Incentives were also formalized in agreements reached at London for commitments to technology transfer, and (pending the creation of a permanent Financial Mechanism) for the establishment of an Interim Multilateral Fund of some $160 million (rising potentially to $240 million) contributed principally by developed states to aid the implementation of the Protocol through non-ozone-depleting development in developing countries which are parties. The Fund is to be administered by UNEP but controlled by an Executive Committee comprising seven developing and seven non-developing countries party to the Protocol as Amended;[23] approved projects will be implemented by UNEP, UNDP, or the World Bank. Limited provisions are included for trade of quota production among parties to facilitate 'industrial rationalization'. Trade in controlled substances among parties is permitted, both to promote 'economic efficiency and

---

[21] Nitrogen Oxides Protocol (1 Nov. 1988), *ILM* 28 (1989), 212. See also the Volatile Organic Compounds Protocol (Nov. 1991).

[22] Adjustments require a two-thirds majority. Under the Montreal Protocol this must include states consuming at least 50% of the total consumption of the controlled substance, but under the 1990 London Amendments the two-thirds majority must include both a majority of developing countries (as defined in Art. 5, para. 1) and a majority of non-developing countries. Only states parties count in these calculations.

[23] See generally Caron, 'Protection of the Stratospheric Ozone Layer', 755–80; and Sylvia Maureen Williams, 'The Protection of the Ozone Layer in Contemporary International Law', *International Relations*, 10 (1990), 167–78.

free trade'[24] and to ensure that non-producing consumers are not spurred into beginning production in the period before suitable substitutes or alternatives are available. Developing-country parties with 1986 consumption levels below 0.3 kg per capita are allowed a ten-year grace period whenever they wish in the implementation of all reductions.

While variations and improvements on these precedents are being sought in the emerging climate change regime, the general format of framework convention and protocols appears to be, as Elliot Richardson points out in his chapter below, a much more viable model than, for instance, the single package deal approach embodied in such instruments as the 1982 Convention on the Law of the Sea. There are, however, potential drawbacks to the Convention-Protocol approach as currently practised: a number of these are discussed by Susskind and Ozawa.

A third and long-established technique is to provide for regular meetings of the parties to a fundamental instrument, to review the implementation of the basic arrangements and to make modifications or draft additional instruments. The International Whaling Commission has been setting catch limits since 1949, and more innovation was introduced under the Antarctic Treaty: regular and special meetings of the Consultative Parties produced several separate agreements, such as the 1972 Convention for the Conservation of Antarctic Seals, the 1980 Convention on the Conservation of Antarctic Marine Living Resources, and the ill-starred 1988 Wellington Convention on Antarctic Mineral Resources, as well as the Environmental Protocol to the Antarctic Treaty. Indeed the Conference of the Parties has become an established institutional feature in recent environmental instruments, including the 1989 Basel Convention on the Control of Transboundary Movements of Hazardous Wastes and Their Disposal, the 1991 African Convention on hazardous wastes,[25] the 1985 Vienna Convention for the Protection of the Ozone Layer, the Montreal Protocol, and the Montreal Protocol as Amended (although the latter two do not make formal provision for such a Conference, meetings of parties take place as subsets of the

[24] Koehler and Hajost, 'The Montreal Protocol', 84.

[25] The Bamako Convention on the Ban of the Import into Africa and the Control of Transboundary Movement and Management of Hazardous Wastes within Africa, concluded under the auspices of the OAU, 29 Jan. 1991. *ILM* 30 (1991), 773.

Vienna Convention meetings). Such institutions are often supplemented by intersessional working groups (for example, the open-ended working group established by the parties to make recommendations on modifications to the Montreal Protocol), and by informal meetings or initiatives often promoted by particular states or by the secretariat. It is notable that such specialized mechanisms have been preferred even where the Convention was adopted within an existing institutional framework such as the IMO or UNEP.

The character of specific international environmental regimes is heavily dependent on the nature of the issue, the level of knowledge about it, and the costs of alternative policy options. Several analysts have come to lay particular emphasis on knowledge as a core factor. Thus Richard Cooper has stressed the importance of there being a widely shared scientific consensus on the nature of the problem and its solutions. [26] Peter Haas has pointed to the role of 'epistemic communities' of scientists and specialists and to the critical role that these transnational communities play in promoting 'environmental learning'. [27] Haas defines epistemic communities as 'networks of knowledge based communities with an authoritative claim to policy relevant knowledge within their domain of expertise'. [28] However, as Stairs and Taylor point out, scientific communities are by no means necessarily consensual nor necessarily impartial. It is important to pay attention to the conflicts and tensions that occur *within* epistemic communities— to the sociology of scientific knowledge. It is also important to recognize the problematic relationship between the nature of scientific knowledge and debate (often characterized by high levels of uncertainty) and the kinds of knowledge (readily communicable, and accompanied by at least an aura of authoritative certainty) needed to spur public or political action.

[26] Richard Cooper, 'International Co-operation in Public Health as a Prologue to Macroeconomic Co-operation', in Richard Cooper et al. Can Nations Agree? Issues in International Economic Cooperation (Washington: Brookings Institution, 1989), 178–254.

[27] Peter Haas, Saving the Mediterranean: The Politics of International Environmental Co-operation (New York: Columbia UP, 1990); and Haas, 'Do Regimes Matter? Epistemic Communities and Mediterranean Pollution Control', International Organization, 43 (1989), 377–403.

[28] Peter M. Haas, 'Epistemic Communities and International Policy Co-ordination', in Peter M. Haas (ed.), Knowledge, Power and International Policy Co-ordination. Special Issue of International Organization, 46 (Winter 1992).

Several other factors implicated in international environmental law and policy formation and in the development of international regimes are often undervalued and merit particular attention. First, there is the increasingly important role of environmental NGOs, analysed in the chapters by Bramble and Porter and Stairs and Taylor. Environmental NGOs have played a major role in shifting public and political attitudes towards the environment and placing environmental issues high on the political agendas of an increasing number of states; in publicizing the nature and seriousness of environmental problems; in acting as a conduit for the dissemination of scientific research; and in organizing and orchestrating pressure on states, companies, and international organizations. Bramble and Porter trace the growth of US NGOs and evaluate their success in exploiting media attention and in lobbying the US government, the Congress, and Washington-based multilateral financial agencies. Their chapter highlights the obvious fact—but one neglected by those who seek to model international negotiations in game theoretic terms—that states are not unitary actors with clear sets of ordered interests and stable preferences. Rather state interests and international policy objectives with respect to the environment derive from a complex range of often-conflicting domestic pressures and forces within the government bureaucracy, within the legislative process, and within the broader political system. This provides environmental NGOs with ample scope for effective lobbying. The chapter by Stairs and Taylor on maritime waste disposal illuminates another aspect of NGO influence, namely the increasing extent to which NGOs are involved in the detailed process of rule-making and regime formation: influencing the drafting of agreements, providing input to scientific or policy working groups, supporting 'friendly states', mobilizing publicity, and seeking to shape the law-making process itself.[29]

Second, there is the role of individuals in highlighting a particular problem (for example Norman Myers's work in drawing attention to problems of deforestation); in shaping international responses to environmental problems (the role of Maurice Strong); and in facilitating successful negotiating outcomes. Oran Young gives the examples of Tolba, Lang, and Benedick in

[29] See also Philippe Sands, 'The Environment, Community and International Law', *Harvard International Law Journal*, 30 (1989), 393.

the case of ozone negotiations.[30] In their chapter in this volume, Stairs and Taylor point to the role of individual scientists in shaping the direction of debate and the formation of a scientific consensus.

A third factor of particular importance is the impact that the broader foreign policy context can have on the process of environmental negotiations. On one level, attention must be paid to the relationship between environmental policy objectives and the range of other foreign policy goals. The chapter on Brazil illustrates how this interaction can work at times to facilitate and at times to hinder progress on environmental issues. More broadly, the prospects for international environmental negotiations will be affected by the overall climate of international relations. It was not accidental, for example, that international concern about the environment in the early 1970s coincided with a period of *détente* and with a more general shift away from the Cold War and regional security issues that had previously dominated the agendas of major states. In the 1990s there are many who suggest that the end of the Cold War will be followed by a new period of sustained concern for both development and the environment. Whilst there are factors pointing in this direction, it is far from pre-ordained. Political or military crises in, for example, the Middle East or the former Soviet Union rapidly divert political and media attention away from global environmental issues.[31] It is also important not to overlook the possibility that the end of the Cold War might lead the United States towards a retreat from global involvement, to a period of introspection, and to an attempt to further disengage itself from the manifold problems of the developing world.[32]

---

[30] Oran Young and Gail Osherenko, 'Testing Theories of Regime Formation', in Oran Young and Gail Osherenko (eds.), *The Politics of International Regime Formation: Lessons from the Arctic Cases* (forthcoming); and Oran Young, 'Political Leadership and Regime Formation: On the Development of Institutions in International Society', *International Organization*, 45 (1991), 281.

[31] Many apparently 'diversionary' issues such as the 1990–1 Gulf War may trigger environmental problems of regional or global proportions.

[32] Compare, e.g., the contrasting perspectives of Jessica Tuchman Mathews, 'Redefining Security', *Foreign Affairs*, 68 (1989), 162–77; and Stephen van Evera, 'Why Europe Matters, Why the Third World Doesn't: American Grand Strategy after the Cold War', *Journal of Strategic Studies*, 13 (1990), 1–51.

2. *The limits of international environmental agreements and the problem of compliance*

The fact that large numbers of international environmental agreements have been reached and numerous environmental regimes created is important and encouraging. But it does not in itself answer the sceptics. Analysing the conclusion of agreements and the formation of legal or other regimes is interesting and important, but it does not get to the heart of the matter and to the two central questions. First, to what extent and why do states actually implement and comply with the principles and rules to which they have agreed? Second, even if compliance is secured, do these agreements contribute appreciably to securing effective environmental management? In other words: to what extent, and in what ways, do legal instruments, customary international law rules, and international regimes matter?

The difficulties of reaching adequate agreements, and the weaknesses often found in such agreements as are concluded, are discussed in several chapters in this volume. States often prefer to agree only to non-binding guidelines or principles which they view as targets rather than firm obligations and which they are usually free to implement (or not) at whatever pace they see fit. Of the environmental treaties that have been concluded, many (although by no means all) relate to issues that do not engage core state interests, and the lessons from them are not necessarily transferable to other and more important issues. Treaties bind only those states that become parties to them, and under some instruments states are permitted to make reservations to specific articles. Treaties may contain deliberately ambiguous language designed to secure consensus and to paper over continuing disagreements or conflicts between states. Very few environmental treaties contain inescapable requirements that states resort to binding third-party procedures for the settlement of disputes, and sanctions for non-compliance only infrequently extend beyond polite if vigorous disapprobation. States are keen (and usually successful) in maintaining firm control over reporting, inspection, and monitoring procedures. The need to base rule-making and regime creation on consent or consensus means that many agreements reflect the ambitions of the slowest and embody as targets the lowest common denominator. This can actually impede the efforts of those states anxious to implement tougher environmental standards, by legitimizing feeble compliance and opening free-rider and comparative advantage problems.

Many 'environmental' regimes (including some of the regional fisheries regimes) are portrayed by critics as users' clubs that reflect the self-serving economic interests of limited groups of states, rather than necessarily serving broader environmental purposes. The process of negotiation and regime creation is often extremely time-consuming and laborious (even the success story of ozone took nearly a decade), and further delays occur because of the need for treaties to be ratified (which may involve lengthy domestic processes) and because they can only come into force after ratification by an agreed number of states. Domestic legislation is often required to render treaties effective, which may add considerably to the lead time before effective entry into force. All these points reflect the abiding constraints of the state system and the fundamental facts that, in a decentralized legal system, no obligation can be imposed without consent and that states continue to be extremely resistant to the creation of any coercive mechanisms for enforcement.

In light of these features of the international system, it is important to consider the means by which implementation can be achieved and compliance may be secured.

(i) *General reasons for compliance.* In general states agree to, and commonly comply with, international environmental agreements because it is in their interests to do so. Agreements both reflect the shared interest in the collective management of a particular environmental problem (and especially in avoiding the often unknown, but potentially disastrous, costs of non-agreement) and embody a stable outcome to the underlying bargaining process between states over the distribution of the costs of collective action and other politically divisive issues. As the chapters in Part III illustrate, the resolution of this bargaining process is far from easy and will often require recognition of the special interests of particular states or groups of states. To meet the range of interests and to persuade states to participate, 'side payments' are needed which may take the form of differential obligations, financial inducements, mechanisms to facilitate the transfer of relevant technology, or market access. Agreement may also require that states act 'counter-preferentially', focusing not just on short-term interests but taking into account considerations of equity, fairness, or some sense of the 'global common good'. But the central point is that, once agreements are reached, they are likely to be implemented because they reflect the interests of the states concerned.

The fear that others will formally agree but then subsequently defect and fail to comply remains a fundamental obstacle. However, international law and environmental regimes can play an important role in helping to overcome the assurance problem and to provide incentives against defection.[33] Legal regimes do this in various ways. In the first place, states generally comply with international obligations and choose to co-operate even against their short-term interests because of their broader concern with their reputation as reliable partners and their long-term interest in a rule-governed (or at least rule-structured) international system. Moreover, formal legal rules have a particular status because of the role of international law as constitutive of the state-system and therefore of the very identity and standing of the parties to an agreement.

Second, legal and other environmental regimes stabilize expectations and institutionalize the fact that states are involved in long-term co-operation and in negotiating over an increasingly wide range of issues—they are not just concerned with bargaining over a single problem at a single point in time. The need to negotiate and co-operate over a wide range of issues is characteristic of high levels of interdependence (leading to so-called 'issue density') and increases the interests of states in the predictability provided by rules and the salience of reputation. Such a picture also casts doubt upon characterizations of global environmental bargaining in terms of a one-off Prisoners' Dilemma game in which it is rational to defect. As game theory suggests, reiterated games and 'lengthening the shadow of the future' increases the likelihood of co-operative solutions.[34]

[33] On the role of regimes in facilitating co-operation see esp. Robert O. Keohane, *After Hegemony: Cooperation and Discord in the World Political Economy* (Princeton: Princeton UP, 1985); and Keohane, *International Institutions and State Power* (Boulder, Colo.: Westview, 1990).

[34] See Robert Axelrod, *The Evolution of Co-operation* (New York: Basic Books, 1984); and Kenneth A. Oye (ed.), *Co-operation Under Anarchy* (Princeton: Princeton UP, 1986), esp. Pts. I and IV.

Third, environmental regimes facilitate communication and learning, and contribute to a greater degree of transparency, which has two important effects. It undercuts the 'realist' position that anarchy inevitably generates mistrust and forces states to base policy on worst-case assumptions. Further, it leads to modifications in perceptions of state interests, with states coming to be more aware of the dangers of environmental degradation and the costs of non-agreement. In sum, environmental law and environmental regimes facilitate co-operation because of the functional benefits which they provide in the form of an order based not on coercion, but on the co-ordination of interests and of patterned expectations. This is not to suggest that satisfactory co-operation is easily achieved in the environmental sphere: in many cases it is not, and the instruments and regimes already in place are imperfect in many respects.

The prospects for compliance will also depend on the detailed nature of the environmental agreement. General declarations of principles and goals can be useful for generating a broad base of international acceptance for environmental objectives and for creating and maintaining forward momentum. They can also, as the chapter by Bramble and Porter illustrates, serve as a rallying point for NGO pressure and domestic political action. But their necessarily vague and general language makes it difficult even to assess the subsequent record of states, let alone to enforce compliance.

(ii) *International law techniques for implementation.* Several different sets of approaches to implementation and compliance are evident in existing international law. The first set of approaches rests centrally upon concepts of liability. Unless the state is able to rely upon some exculpatory defence, responsibility in principle attaches for any breach imputable to the state of an international legal obligation binding upon that state. In practice, however, liability in the environmental field will usually only flow from physical damage outside the state attributable to causes within the jurisdiction or control of the damaging state. It has been suggested that at least in the case of damage resulting from particularly hazardous activities such liability may be strict (or even absolute): that is, the damaging state is liable even where it is not otherwise at fault. Such liability has been imposed upon private parties (subject to upper limits) by international instruments concerned with civil nuclear installations and with maritime oil transportation, and upon states parties directly in the 1972 Convention on International Liability for Damage Caused by Objects Launched into Outer Space. In general, however, liability attaches only where the damage results from breach of a substantive primary obligation, such as conduct expressly prohibited by treaty, or conduct falling below an accepted standard of care. In addition to compensating innocent victims, a liability regime shifts costs to those responsible for potentially harmful activities, and encourages both care and internalization of these costs. Liability contingent upon actual damage may have a deterrent effect, but such regimes on their own generally do not do enough to prevent environmental degradation and protect ecosystems from *future* damage. In practice there are only a limited range of activities and types of damage where formidable problems of defining and assessing actionable harm, victims, causation, and unacceptable risk do not occur. States have in any event been very reluctant to include liability provisions in environmental treaties, and to make claims against each other asserting the liability of other states. State liability regimes have a place, particularly in relation to single damaging episodes or hazardous activities known to entail long-term risks to identifiable victims, but they are unlikely to be of use in relation to damage with multiple causes or arising from widespread and not highly hazardous activity.

A second set of approaches emphasizes justiciable legal duties of an important procedural character. Thus in the *Corfu Channel* case the ICJ found Albania liable for breach of the duty to inform other states at least of an acute and unusual hazard, and the 1991 ECE Convention on Environmental Impact Assessment in a Transboundary Context establishes duties to conduct environmental assessments and to consult affected states about proposed or completed projects, together with an obligation to allow the public from all affected areas to participate in the assessment procedure. These procedural duties are important but insufficient to address many substantive environmental concerns.

A third set of legal approaches casts obligations in the form of a right of individuals or groups to a clean and sound environment, borrowing and extending concepts from human rights law. But these 'rights' remain vague and it is difficult to derive specific sets of obligations and even harder to decide against whom such rights should be upheld.

The fourth, and most widely employed, set of approaches sees compliance and implementation in terms of establishing regulatory and supervisory frameworks, often with a permanent institutional basis. The myriad examples of this approach include the London Dumping Convention, the Vienna Convention and Montreal Protocol, the Convention on International Trade in Endangered Species, and the International Whaling Convention. The focus here is on elaborating detailed sets of rules, standards, and procedures; creating mechanisms for data collection and scientific assessment; and establishing a system of regular meetings to review state performance and to amend regulations in the light of changing circumstances. These regulatory frameworks can assume different forms: the institutional structure can be provided either by regular meetings of the parties to an agreement, or by establishing a permanent secretariat, or by establishing a formal commission made up of the representatives of the parties. Similarly, data collection can be achieved by requesting states to make formal periodic reports of the steps they have taken to secure implementation, or by establishing procedures for inspection and monitoring (although few environmental agreements presently allow for compulsory inspection, the Antarctic Treaty being an important exception).

Given the continuing limits of coercive enforcement, this approach draws its power from the elaboration of specific regulations against which state performace can be assessed, from the generation of the information needed to make such assessments, and from the transparency of, and publicity attaching to, the process. It lays less emphasis in practice on formal mechanisms of legal settlement (mediation, conciliation, arbitration, judicial settlement), instead favouring ongoing and institutionalized bargaining between the parties at both a technical and a political level. It relies heavily on the extent to which publicity and 'community pressure' will persuade states to improve compliance.[35] Moreover, this kind of approach can gradually be tightened as (or

[35] Cf. Michel Virally's analysis of the authorizing and legitimating function of international law, and of the central role of 'pression sociale' in securing compliance ('Panorama du droit international contemporain', 183 RCADI 9). See also the excellent discussion of legitimacy and justification by Thomas Franck, *The Power of Legitimacy Among Nations* (New York: Oxford UP, 1990).

if) consensus develops: by moving towards compulsory and more independent inspection and monitoring procedures, or by creating a complaints procedure. The difficulties of doing so, however, are illustrated by the experience in the ozone regime. The Montreal Protocol (Article 7) requires parties to report to the Secretariat (UNEP) on amounts of controlled substances produced, imported, and exported (to parties and to non-parties), and, under the London Amendments, on amounts destroyed or recycled as feedstocks. The reports are available to NGOs and news media, but some parties have failed to submit reports or have submitted only incomplete reports, and an *ad hoc* Working Group was established at the 1990 London meeting to try to enhance the effectiveness of the reporting system.[36] The 1985 Vienna Convention establishes obligations to refer disputes to negotiation, good offices, mediation, and conciliation, but the choice as to whether to accept an obligation to resort to binding third-party settlement is left to individual states.[37] The 1990 London meeting agreed that the concerns of any state party about another state party's fulfilment of its obligations could be raised in writing with the Secretariat, which would investigate and refer them to an Implementation Committee with a view to amicable resolution.[38]

(iii) *Developing enforcement techniques.*   It is widely acknowledged that implementation and enforcement has been the weakest part of international environmental law and related regimes.[39] The enforcement mechanisms already referred to comprise 'enforcement' of a rather soft sort. But the range and effectiveness of techniques for enforcement of international environmental norms has gradually been increasing, as Patricia Birnie demonstrates in her chapter below. First, legal enforcement is frequently possible within domestic legal systems. Whether they establish obligations of conduct or obligations of result in which the choice

[36] Caron, 'Protection of the Stratospheric Ozone Layer', 771–2.

[37] See Article 11. Sixteen states recorded their regret that compulsory procedures were not included—see *ILM* 26 (1987), 1535.

[38] See Peter Sand, 'International Co-operation: The Environmental Experience', in Jessica Tuchman Mathews (ed.), *Preserving the Global Environment* (New York: W. W. Norton, 1991), 271.

[39] 'In general the record of enforcement and compliance with international environmental legal rules has, for a considerable time, been thoroughly disappointing.' E. Somers, 'The Role of the Courts in the Enforcement of Environmental Rules', *International Journal of Estuarine and Coastal Law*, 5 (1990), 195.

of means is left to each state, environmental treaties often in effect oblige states to enact the necessary national laws and to enforce them against their own nationals and within their own territory. As Birnie points out, this obligation is a central part of the enforcement system. In addition, local legal remedies made available to non-nationals and non-residents may provide an important means of dealing with transborder or even other environmental harm. The 1974 Nordic Convention on the Protection of the Environment allows nationals of each Nordic country to bring proceedings in the administrative tribunals or courts of the state from which transboundary pollution emanated,[40] and the European Community applies a similar rule.[41] The extension of local court jurisdiction to activities of nationals carried out offshore or in zones of contested jurisdiction is essential to, for example, the regime established by the Antarctic Environment Protocol.[42] The traditional flag-state jurisdiction over vessels has been supplemented in the case of marine pollution and maritime standards by extensive port-state jurisdiction, by plenary coastal state prescriptive and enforcement jurisdiction in the territorial sea (indeed, the coastal state must enforce its anti-pollution laws against all vessels under Article 4 of the 1973 MARPOL Convention[43]), and by coastal state inspection jurisdiction (rising to powers of arrest if the coastal state is threatened by major damage) in the EEZ in the event of substantial discharge threatening the environment.[44]

Second, obvious failure to comply with important environmental agreements may well lead individual states to exert pressure. Decentralized and in some cases extra-legal sanctions continue to play a role in the international legal system.

Third, and of particular importance, the information gathered

---

[40] *ILM* 13 (1974), 591.

[41] *Bier* v. *Mines de Potasse d'Alsace*, [1976] ECJ Rep. 1735, a decision of the European Court of Justice. In 1977 an OECD Council Recommendation urged member states to apply a similar policy to transfrontier pollution suits—text in *ILM* 16 (1977), 977.

[42] See also the national legislation adopted in relation to deep sea-bed activities, and the legislation adopted by e.g. the UK before the effective demise of the 1988 Wellington Convention.

[43] Reprinted with 1978 amendments in *ILM* 17 (1978), 546.

[44] See the 1982 Law of the Sea Convention, Pt. XII; and, for commentary, Alan Boyle, 'Marine Pollution under the Law of the Sea Convention', *AJIL* 79 (1985), 363.

under such regimes, their transparency, and in certain cases their forums all provide opportunities for pressure by NGOs. This may well prove to be the most important element of 'coercive' enforcement of international environmental agreements. As Stairs and Taylor point out, states are often very reluctant to criticize or condemn each other. The resources and influence of NGOs provide them with the capacity to publicize non-compliance by states, to establish and fund their own monitoring and investigation, and to employ their own (not necessarily totally disinterested) scientists to evaluate the claims made by states.

(iv) *Problems of state capability.* The capacity of states to implement international agreements presents further difficulties. In the case of many weak states in the developing world, effective compliance may be hindered by the lack of efficient domestic institutions, by a severe lack of appropriate human, financial, and technological resources, by deep-rooted economic problems, by the absence of a stable political coalition in favour of implementing environmentally more rational policies, or by civil unrest and ethnic strife. These problems reinforce the centrality of the link between environment and development. Without continued economic and political development, the ability of many states to translate international obligations into coherent and effective domestic policy reforms will remain limited. This has been recognized by many states and international institutions, and is one of the priorities of, for example, the UNDP's technical assistance programme within the Global Environmental Facility (GEF).

B. Institutions

Many intergovernmental institutions play important roles in such activities as international environmental rule-making, policy-making, research, monitoring, training, project financing, and supervision. Three of particular significance are examined in this book: the United Nations system (especially UNEP), the World Bank, and the European Community.

The major intergovernmental institution created specifically to address environmental issues is the United Nations Environment

Programme (UNEP). UNEP was established as a subsidiary organ of the General Assembly by GA Res. 2297 (XXVII), following a recommendation of the Stockholm Conference.[45] The principal decision-making body is the Governing Council (elected by the UN General Assembly), which hitherto has comprised 58 states although proposals for expansion are under discussion. The Secretariat comprises some 200 people, based mainly at UNEP headquarters in Nairobi but with operations also in Geneva and New York. UNEP has had only two Executive Directors: Maurice Strong of Canada (1973–5) and Dr Mostafa Tolba of Egypt (1976–). UNEP is not a Specialized Agency of the UN, and plays a monitoring, co-ordinating, and catalytic role rather than a large-scale directly operational role. Co-ordination between different bodies within the UN is the overall responsibility of the UN's Administrative Committee on Co-ordination (ACC), at which UNEP is represented. In the environmental field co-ordination is also pursued through the DOEM (Designated Officials for Environment Matters), which brings together representatives of UN specialized agencies and other UN bodies (although not the World Bank or the IMF), and through the Committee of International Development Institutions on the Environment (CIDIE), which brings UNEP and the UNDP together with representatives of the World Bank, the regional development banks, and other intergovernmental financial bodies.

UNEP has been seriously underfunded in relation to the scope of its mandate ever since it was established, although since 1989 the states members of the Governing Council have begun to try to improve the position. It was intended that the costs of the Secretariat and Governing Council would be met from the UN's regular budget, and that all other UNEP activities would be financed by voluntary contributions to the UN's Environment Fund. In fact the financial difficulties of the UN, arising particularly from non-payment of dues by member states and from limited budgetary growth, have extended to UNEP, and the Environment Fund has perforce been used to meet some regular expenditures. More seriously, most states were singularly parsimonious in their contributions to the Fund, so that over much of UNEP's history the purchasing power of the Fund has been

[45] Report of the Stockholm Conference on the Human Environment, UN doc. A/CONF.48/14/Rev.1 (1972).

lower even than the 1973 base level. Receipts for 1989 were estimated at $39.17 million, rising to $52.33 million in 1990. In 1989
the Governing Council set a target of $100 million for contri-
butions to be reached by 1992, and in 1991 the target for 1995 was
raised to $245 million. Spending on Programme Activities was
estimated at $68 million for the biennium 1990–1, rising to a pro-
jected $180 million for the 1992–3 biennium.[46] UNEP was also
administering 13 general trust funds and 26 technical co-operation trust funds at the end of 1990, with a total projected expenditure in 1990 of $14 million, up from $8.2 million the previous
year.[47]

UNEP's mandate is threefold: the global environmental assessment programme ('Earthwatch'), environmental management
activities, and supporting measures. It has focused its limited
resources mainly on the assessment function, to considerable
effect. The Global Environment Monitoring System (GEMS), the
Global Resource Information Database (GRID) satellite-fed geographical information system, and the Infoterra data system are
prominent examples, but UNEP has engaged in an immense
range of co-operative ventures with such bodies as the International Council of Scientific Unions (ICSU), the OAU, the OAS,
and the World Bank. It publishes the International Register of
Potentially Toxic Chemicals, supplying detailed information and
policy proposals on over 80,000 chemicals. The management
activities have been on a much smaller scale, with UNEP mainly
playing a catalytic or consultative role, as exemplified by the
Regional Seas Programme, or contributing to training and institution-building.[48]

UNEP suffers somewhat from isolation, being one of the very
few global international organizations to have its headquarters
outside Europe and North America, although the symbolic and

---

[46] The projected percentage allocations among the 13 programmes or budget
lines were: environmental assessment (21.7), terrestrial ecosystems (17.5), environmental awareness (13.2), technical and regional co-operation (10.6), oceans
(10.3), energy, industry and transportation (6.4), environmental management
measures (5.8), water (5.0), atmosphere (4.0), human health and welfare (2.1),
human settlements and environment (1.9), lithosphere (0.9), peace, security, and
the environment (0.6). These were the Secretariat proposals—see UN doc. UNEP/
GC.16/23 (24 Jan. 1991), 2.

[47] UN doc. UNEP/GC.16/24 and Corr. 1 (1991).

[48] See generally Peter Thacher's chapter below; also Thacher, 'Multilateral Co-
operation and Global Change', *Journal of International Affairs*, 44 (1991), 433–55.

perhaps the policy-input value of the Nairobi location is considerable. Much more acute, however, has been the lack of state commitment to the pursuit and implementation of the principles set out in the Declaration and Plan of Action of the Stockholm Conference. The Nairobi Declaration, adopted at the 10th anniversary conference in 1982, noted bluntly that 'the Action Plan has only been partially implemented, and the results cannot be considered as satisfactory, due mainly to inadequate foresight and understanding of the long-term benefits of environmental protection, to inadequate co-ordination of approaches and efforts, and to the unavailability and inequitable distribution of resources'.[49] Although numerous environmental problems were addressed at regional levels in the 1970s and early 1980s, global standard-setting activity and policy initiatives only began to intensify in the second half of the 1980s. UNEP was centrally involved in the adoption of the Vienna Convention in 1985 and the Montreal Protocol in 1987, the conclusion of the Basel Convention on the Control of Transboundary Movements of Hazardous Wastes and Their Disposal in 1989, and (with the World Meteorological Organization) in the negotiations for a framework climate change convention. The Brundtland Commission took a positive view of UNEP's activities, although suggesting that more could and should be done. The UN General Assembly at last focused serious attention on institutional aspects of global environmental issues in 1989, supporting the 'further strengthening of the role of the Environment Programme as the central catalysing, co-ordinating and stimulating body in the field of environment within the United Nations system'.[50]

Proposals for the establishment of a new international organization to deal with environment or environment/development issues have frequently been mooted. The pre-Stockholm suggestion that an Environmental Security Council be established has been refloated, and other recent proposals include the creation of either a General Assembly environmental committee, a Sustainable Development Commission encompassing the entire UN system as well as treaty bodies, or a slightly less

---

[49] Report of the Governing Council, UN doc. A/37/25 (1982), 49.
[50] GA Res. 44/229 (adopted without vote, 22 Dec. 1989). See also the very detailed and carefully negotiated Res. 44/228 of the same date, dealing with UNCED 1992.

ambitious UN International Development Council.[51] Some proposals, such as the appointment at a high level within the UN Secretariat in New York of an 'environment supremo', or the Brundtland Commission's proposal for a UN Board for Sustainable Development chaired by the UN Secretary-General,[52] are relatively minor adjustments which involve only questions of efficiency, demarcation, and bureaucratic structure. Others, such as the convening of *ad hoc* intergovernmental or independent expert reviews similar to the IPCC, are likely to receive significant support, and UNEP has successfully initiated the establishment of a small-scale UN centre for emergency environmental assistance.

There is, however, considerable reluctance among states to embark on the creation of new institutions. Problems of duplication would be almost inevitable unless UNEP were incorporated into a new organization, and even then problems of overlap, turf allocation, co-ordination, and co-operation with existing organizations would persist and probably become more acute. The tortuous process of improving planning and co-ordination of existing UN economic and social activities and reforming and revitalizing ECOSOC has made little progress, reinforcing doubts about the addition of new institutions. The philosophical commitment to limited government and paring of bureaucracies in several major contributing states, while perhaps past its zenith, remains strong in their international policy-making. Funding remains highly problematic, and least-cost approaches are likely to be favoured. These elements are all evident in, for instance, the reluctance of the Antarctic Treaty parties to establish a permanent institution, and in the discussions about reducing the costs of the institutions contemplated in the 1982 Convention on the Law of the Sea. The preparations for UNCED, including the IPCC and the Intergovernmental Negotiating Committee, were undertaken by ad hoc secretariats of limited size and deliberately established

[51] Many such proposals are summarized in UN docs. A/CONF.151/PC/36 and A/CONF.151/PC/80 (1991). On proposals for an Economic Security Council, see e.g. Maurice Bertrand, 'Can the United Nations Be Reformed?', in Roberts and Kingsbury (eds.), *United Nations, Divided World*, 204–8. Note also the long-standing proposals for a special environmental disputes chamber of the International Court of Justice—e.g. P. C. Jessup, *The Price of International Justice* (New York: Columbia UP, 1971), 61–70.

[52] *Our Common Future* (1987).

for only a limited period. Specialist institutional frameworks in the form of Conferences of the Parties and more continuous working groups or commissions will continue to be established in conjunction with new instruments, and in some cases modest secretariats to support these may be established autonomously or within existing organizations. Beyond this, the dominant view among states is that to meet new environmental needs over the next few years UNEP should be strengthened, and perhaps the balance of its activities adjusted more to Geneva and New York, rather than a new institution of general competence established.

At least as difficult as the problem of creating or strengthening specifically environmental intergovernmental organizations is the problem of integrating environmental management considerations into the work of existing institutions. The World Bank has attracted particular scrutiny in this regard, partly as a result of the NGO campaign described by Bramble and Porter. Although its Washington location and other factors have perhaps earned it disproportionately more attention than other international financial and development institutions (including the Asian and African Development Banks, the OECD's Development Assistance Committee, and the European Community's Lomé Convention and other development operations), the Bank is a major lender, and its influence in the formation of general international development and project-financing policy is considerable, as is its ability to influence the policies of borrowing states. The problems of transforming a lending institution which had paid little express attention to environmental issues into one which is expected to take a leading role in such areas as project-wide environmental impact assessment, forestry policy, the implementation of biodiversity or global warming investment projects under the Global Environmental Facility, and the development of more environmentally sensitive economic analysis (reflected in a limited way in such concepts as that of sustainable net national product) are discussed from a personal perspective by Ken Piddington. Although material and human resource constraints and bureaucratic and other factors inevitably affect the Bank's performance, the most important determinant of the Bank's policies and impact is its relationship with its member states, which may be that of intergovernmental forum, lender, or aid conduit. The European Community is unique in the degree of supranational authority the member states have conferred on it. While it is for this reason most unlikely to provide a model for global environmental governance in the foreseeable future, the Community is an important actor in international environmental affairs both through its internal competence to set policies applicable within the Community and through its external competence to negotiate agreements and provide development assistance on behalf of the member states. The interrelations between these roles, and the complexities inherent in each of them, are addressed by Nigel Haigh. He draws particular attention to the potential difficulties of international environmental negotiation in situations of mixed or divided competence, where the Community is able to negotiate some aspects of a treaty but the member states retain competence to negotiate other aspects individually. While the Community may in some respects be a more difficult counterpart than a state in negotiations, in areas where it has internal competence its ability to develop and harmonize environmental standards, and to implement and enforce internationally agreed standards, among the twelve member states is a significant attribute.

C. Power and Conflicts of Interest

Environmental issues have the potential to generate various forms of conflict. At the extreme this can involve overt social/military conflict between states over access to, and control of, natural resources. In many parts of the developing world control over rivers and access to water resources threatens to emerge as a major source of tension (as in the cases of the Jordan, Litani, Euphrates, and Nile rivers in the Middle East). Social/military conflict can also occur within or between states when environmental degradation undermines the social stability or economic viability of a society and leads to political instability, a breakdown of political order, and increased flows of refugees.[53] This volume does not deal directly with such conflicts, nor with the analytical constructs to address these conflicts, such as the

[53] See e.g. Jodi L. Jacobson, *Environmental Refugees: A Yardstick of Habitability* (Washington, DC: Worldwatch Paper No. 86, 1988).

concept of 'environmental security'.[54] It is, however, important to recognize that the perceived need to avert such nascent or latent conflicts may influence the attitudes of states towards international environmental negotiations.

The two broad areas of conflict that are most directly relevant to international environmental negotiations are, first, conflicts over the setting of priorities and the distribution of the costs of managing the global environment and, second, conflicts over a variety of sovereignty-related issues.

1. The setting of priorities and the distribution of costs

It is true that ecological interdependence creates a powerful incentive to co-operate. Radical environmental degradation of the planet will involve losses for all and, more so than in the case of economic interdependence, states are locked into a situation from which they cannot escape. Against this, priorities have to be determined, and the costs of managing ecological interdependence and of finding effective solutions to major environmental threats have to be distributed between states. This provides both the primary focus for bargaining and a potent source of political conflict.

The capacity to determine the international agenda has rightly been identified as a particularly effective form of power.[55] The industrialized countries have successively focused international attention on those issues which affect them most directly: marine pollution, ozone depletion, global climate change, biodiversity, and deforestation. By contrast, the states and peoples of the South have had less success in securing prominence for environmental problems closely associated with development.

[54] For various approaches to issues of environmental security see Michael Renner, *National Security: The Economic and Environmental Dimensions*, Worldwatch Paper No. 89 (May 1989); Mathews, 'Redefining Security'; Norman Myers, 'Environment and Security', *Foreign Policy*, 74 (1989), 23–41; Daniel Deudney, 'The Case Against Linking Environmental Degradation and National Security', *Millennium*, 19 (1990), 461–76; Sergei V. Vinogradov, 'International Environmental Security: The Concept and Its Implementation', in A. Carty and G. Danilenko (eds.), *Perestroika and International Law* (New York: St Martin's Press, 1990), 196–207; Arthur H. Westing, 'Environmental Component of Comprehensive Security', *Bulletin of Peace Proposals*, 20 (1989), 129–34; and Westing, 'Environmental Security and Its Relation to Ethiopia and Sudan', *Ambio*, 20 (1991), 168–71.

[55] On this subject see Steven Lukes, *Power: A Radical Approach* (London: Macmillan, 1974).

The problem of distributing the costs of environmental management and the seriousness of conflict will depend on the character of the issue and the structure of state interests.[56] In some cases the costs of tackling environmental problems are relatively modest and the benefits clearly large,[57] in which case distributional problems are unlikely to be insuperable. Nor do such problems necessarily prevent agreement even on global issues, as demonstrated by the successful negotiation of the Ozone Convention and its amended and extended Protocol. In this instance the scientific evidence established the nature and general consequences of the danger beyond any reasonable doubt. The costs within the industrialized world of abandoning CFC production could be accurately assessed and were low relative to the expected benefits. Similarly, the costs of assisting developing countries to move away from CFCs were moderate and involved the creation of a fund of only $160–240 million over three years. Finally, the number of relevant technologies was limited and controlled by a very small group of companies, for whom the shift to CFC substitutes and the transfer of technologies to developing countries did not entail reduced earnings. Indeed, restrictions on CFCs would create a new market for substitutes in which the major companies had a strong lead.   Yet the ozone precedent is a narrow one. On an increasing number of environmental issues a discussion of the costs of international action is inseparable from broader debates about the character of economic development and about the need to promote more sustainable forms of development. Global action on the environment is therefore centrally concerned with developing new understandings of sustainable development and agreeing the changes in the pattern of economic activity needed to implement them. The need to move away from traditional forms of development characterized by high levels of energy use, the intensive exploitation of natural resources, and extensive environmental degradation will often involve significant economic and social costs that have to be distributed between states. As Cooper and Beckerman point out in

[56] See Scott Barrett, 'The Problem of Global Environmental Protection', and K. G. Mäler, 'International Environmental Problems', both in *Oxford Review of Economic Policy*, 6 (1990), 68–108.

[57] The 1976 Bonn Convention for the Protection of the Rhine Against Pollution by Chlorides involved abatement costs of $136 million. See Peter Sand, 'International Co-operation', in Mathews (ed.), *Preserving the Global Environment*, 245.

their chapters below, agreeing a fair and acceptable distribution between the industrialized countries will be far from easy. But the principal fissure is between the developed and developing world, and it is the potential for the global environment to become a major source of confrontation between North and South that renders it such a fundamental international political issue.

Three aspects of the problem are especially critical. First, there is the striking asymmetry between North and South in terms of both existing resource use and existing relative contributions to such global problems as ozone depletion and global climate change. With around 16 per cent of the world's population, the industrialized countries are responsible for 48 per cent of current greenhouse gas emissions. US per capita CO_2 emissions are 5.7 tonnes as against an average for the developing world of under 0.5 tonnes. On one estimate a US population of 230 million emits the same volume of greenhouse gases as 4 billion people in the South.[58] Second, the global environment will have to accommodate the future development needs of the South. The unavoidable need for continued economic development arises partly from the inevitable increases that are going to occur in the population of the developing world and partly from the pressing necessity to overcome the present appalling levels of poverty and deprivation. Third, the failure to promote more sustainable forms of economic development in the South may well work to undermine many forms of environmental action undertaken by the North. If Indian and Chinese per capita carbon emissions reached US levels, world emissions would treble.[59]

As Hurrell points out, the position of major developing countries has shifted substantially since the time of the Stockholm Conference in 1972. Developing countries have come to lay greater weight on the importance of protecting the environment and on moving towards more sustainable patterns of economic development.[60] But the stress on continued economic development

[58] Leiv Lunde, *The North/South Dimension in Global Greenhouse Politics* (Lysaker, Norway: Fridtjof Nansen Institute, 1990), 9.

[59] See Michael Grubb, *The Greenhouse Effect: Negotiating Targets* (London: RIIA, 1989), 17.

[60] For important position statements of developing countries see the Tlatelolco Platform on Environment and Development, 4–7 Mar. 1991, UN doc. A/CONF.151/PC/L.30, and the Beijing Declaration of 41 Developing Countries, 18–19 June 1991, reprinted in *China Daily*, 20 June 1991, p. 4.

remains dominant. Development cannot be sacrificed as a means of stabilizing the global environment—because of the enormous social and political pressures facing all governments in the developing world; because sacrificing growth would perpetuate the unjust division between rich and poor; because the rich countries bear the greatest responsibility for existing environmental problems; because poverty is itself a central cause of environmental destruction; and because the ability of poor countries to adapt to future environmental changes can only be increased by continued social and economic development.[61]

In addition to bearing the costs of solving environmental problems within the developed world, the rich countries are therefore being faced with various demands from the South. First, the South demands that the rich countries take the first steps in tackling global environmental threats (for instance, by reducing CO_2 emissions) and that, as the principal beneficiaries of past emissions, they bear a disproportionate share of the costs. Second, declarations from the South call for the rich countries to provide assistance to the South to cover the costs of specific measures to tackle global environmental threats so that resources are not diverted from development. As Peter Thacher points out, the central demand is for 'additionality', in other words new and additional assistance, whether in the form of financial transfers or the transfer of environmentally related technology on concessional terms. Third, the developing world is demanding assistance in dealing with the many serious environmental problems within their own countries which do not (yet) directly affect the North (desertification, water and air pollution in urban centres, etc.). Finally, there is the argument for additional development assistance unrelated to specific environmental projects, above all

[61] Not all of these positions are shared by representatives of all developing countries. Many are subject to critiques, including those from environmentalists in developing countries. Anil Agarwal, for instance, argues that 'development cannot be true development unless it is environmentally harmonious . . . The best and most immediate form of development for the poor is often the improvement and the regeneration of their immediate environment.' He argues for more local self-determination at community level, and criticizes over-consumption in Western life-styles and in those of Third World élites. 'The world-market system, as it grows, distorts local land-use systems in more and more subsistence communities and renders them environmentally unsustainable . . . It is not enough to say that the overuse of chlorofluorocarbons is destroying the global environment. Over-demand for bananas is also destroying the global environment.' 'The North –South Perspective: Alienation or Interdependence?', *Ambio*, 19 (1990), 94–5.

in the form of reducing both the burden of foreign debt and the level of Northern protectionism.

Many developing countries are demanding the linking of environment and development to serve as the basis for a 'new, just and equitable international order'. These claims are being made partly out of considerations of equity and justice, arguments that are carefully explored by Henry Shue in his chapter below. But underlying them also is the belief that the environment provides the South with a new source of leverage and bargaining power. This power is essentially 'negative' and derives from the ability of the South to undermine agreements on global environmental issues. Any reductions in greenhouse gas or CFC emissions agreed by the industrialized countries could be easily undercut by increases on the part of a few large developing countries (particularly China, India, and Brazil). The claims here need to be treated with some caution. The costs to many developing countries of undermining global environmental co-operation may well be substantial. For example, China, with around 25 per cent of the world's population, has access to only about 5 per cent of the world's water resources, which global warming could reduce to just 3.5 per cent. Environmental priorities differ between developing countries, and there may well be opportunities for the North to exploit divisions or to 'co-opt' or 'buy off' certain particularly important developing countries. Not employing environmentally efficient technologies will reduce the competitiveness (and even the right of entry) of Southern products in the markets of the industrialized world. Finally the leverage of the South has to be balanced against the far wider range of power resources available to the industrialized countries.

Distributing the costs of global environmental management is complicated by a number of other factors. First, the question of costs is complicated because of the high levels of both scientific and economic uncertainty. There is uncertainty amongst scientists over the nature, scope, and seriousness of global climate change. There is uncertainty over the future development of the technologies which may enable societies to adapt to future environmental changes. And there is enormous uncertainty over the assessment of the costs and benefits of alternative policy options. As Cooper and Beckerman argue, assessing the costs and benefits of abatement and adaptation responses to global

climate change is made extremely difficult by the high levels of
scientific uncertainty, by the range of economic activities involved, and by the fact that so many of the costs will arise only in
the future.[62]

Second, negotiations are complicated because the costs of
unchecked environmental degradation will not fall evenly. Some
countries may stand to make substantial gains as a result of global
warming, whilst rising sea levels threaten many low-lying, poor,
and often densely populated regions with destruction. According to the argument presented by Beckerman, the economic
impact for the industrialized countries of unchecked (or at least
only moderately reduced) greenhouse gas emissions would be
small, whilst radical reductions would be enormously expensive.
Moreover it is precisely these societies that are most able—in
technological, economic, and social terms—to adapt to such
negative environmental developments as may occur. On this
analysis, whilst there may be a strong case for cost-effective 'no-
regret' policies (for instance, in the form of greater energy efficiency), there is little incentive to embark on large-scale transfers
of technology or financial resources to the developing world.[63]

Third, the definition of sustainable development remains contested. State representatives from both North and South now use
the same lexicon of sustainable development, and both have
come to pay far more (if still far from identical) attention to environmental problems. In one sense negotiations are about the
means of achieving a common and agreed goal. But on closer
inspection the exact nature of the goal proves to be blurred.
Although it has acquired a very wide currency, the phrase
'sustainable development' does not have a generally accepted

[62] See generally William D. Nordhaus, 'A Sketch of the Economics of the
Greenhouse Effect', *American Economic Review*, 81 (1991), 146; Nordhaus, 'The
Cost of Slowing Climate Change: A Survey', *Energy Journal*, 12 (1991), 37–65;
David Pearce (ed.), *Blueprint 2: The Greening of the World Economy* (London:
Earthscan, 1991), esp. chs. 2, 3, and 4.

[63] See also Richard D. Morgenstern, 'Towards a Comprehensive Approach to
Global Climate Change Mitigation', *American Economic Review*, 81 (1991), 140,
pointing out several pitfalls in existing economic analyses of costs and benefits of
greenhouse gas emission strategies, and noting that while difficulties in obtaining data cause analyses to focus on the US (and other industrialised economies), there are 'very real possibilities that the damages of global climate change
may be greater and/or the marginal costs of emission reduction lower in developing countries', and that optimal controls on greenhouse gases for the global
economy may be tighter than for the US alone.

definition. A 'sustainable' economy has been defined as one 'using only renewable resources (and those only at a rate at which they are replenished) and producing only low, non-accumulating levels of pollution'.[64] However, such a radical approach is not what is contemplated by states as a policy goal nor what is proposed by most policy analysts.[65]

Once the notion of sustainable development is unpacked, conflicts over basic values can easily re-emerge. How much development is compatible with ecological rationality? What forms of development are to be promoted, and who is to decide? To what extent should questions of social justice and equity within developing countries be included in definitions of sustainability (as argued, for instance, by the Brundtland Report)? On what criteria should considerations of inter-generational equity be based?

Fourth, the competitive pressures of both the international political system and the global economy reinforce the natural concern of states with relative gains and losses. States are inherently self-regarding, and governments are expected by their constituencies to ensure that the state and the influential groups within it do not suffer a relative loss or bear a disproportioo-nate share of the environmental burden. States, represented by governments, are not concerned solely with maximizing their absolute welfare but also with their relative position within the international political and economic systems. Their utility is in this basic sense interdependent. They are 'positional' as well as 'atomistic' actors and are unlikely to accept schemes for envstironmental management that might have serious implications for the competitive position of their economies, that might undermine their long-term power positions, or that would increase their vulnerability to outside pressure.[66] The extent to which states are preoccupied with relative gains will depend on the particular issue, and a rather more optimistic position is taken in the chapter

[64] Ernst U. von Weizsäcker, 'Sustainability: A Task for the North', *Journal of International Affairs*, 44 (1991), 422.

[65] For further discussion of sustainabiliy, see WCED, *Our Common Future*; D. W. Pearce, E. B. Barbier, and A. Markandya, *Sustainable Development: Economics and Environment in the Third World* (London: Edward Elgar, 1990); and Peter Thacher's chapter below.

[66] See Joseph M. Grieco, 'Anarchy and the Limits of Co-operation: A Realist Critique of the Newest Liberal Institutionalism', *International Organization*, 42 (1988), 485–507.

by List and Rittberger. Nevertheless, the tendency of the states system to exacerbate concern with relative gains and losses remains an important feature of international environmental negotiations.

Finally, the broader political and economic context must again be emphasized. Thus, for example, US attitudes towards the consequences of unchecked environmental degradation in the developing world will not be based solely (or perhaps even principally) on economic, ecological, or moral considerations. Political and strategic imperatives mean that certain areas matter more than others. On the one hand, the current trends towards regionalism may well spill over into a greater willingness to make concessions to particular groups of states in the interests of the broader regional project. On the other, geopolitical concern for environmentally induced instability in, say, Egypt is far more likely to persuade Western policy-makers of the need for global action than the threat of still further human misery in, say, Bangladesh.

2. *Sovereignty issues*

From one perspective, differences between states over the protection and maintenance of sovereignty have been moderated by recent trends. Thus developing countries have come to accept that environmental degradation within states is a matter of legitimate interest to the outside world, being both of 'international concern' (suggesting that it is legitimate for other states to become involved), and of 'common concern to humankind'.[67] Recent declarations have also acknowledged the rights of NGOs both to involve themselves within the 'domestic' environmental affairs of developing countries and to participate in global negotiations.[68] They also accept the rights of individuals and of indigenous peoples to play a legitimate role in environmental management.[69] Finally, the development of international environmental law has reduced the autonomy (although, apart from the EC, not the legal capacity or 'sovereignty') of states and

[67] Beijing Declaration of 41 Developing Countries, para. 1.
[68] See e.g. the Tlatelolco Platform on Environment and Development, para. 21. UN doc. A/CONF.151/PC/L.30, 22 Mar. 1991.
[69] Tlatelolco Platform, para. 18.

provided for the international regulation of an increasing range of domestic environmental activities.

Despite these developments, sovereignty questions remain the focus of much actual and potential political conflict. One issue concerns the difference between those states and political groups who believe that greater authority does need to be vested in an international environmental authority and those who do not. Many states continue to be extremely reluctant to give up authority over the procedures of rule-making or rule-implementation. Even quite limited proposals, for example the use of majority voting for amending 'technical' annexes, have often met with considerable resistance. The Beijing Declaration restates the centrality of sovereignty for the developing countries: 'The developing states have the sovereign right to use their own natural resources in keeping with their developmental and environmental objectives and priorities.'[70] Moreover, the stress on sovereign rights is by no means limited to the developing world. Both on the environment and in several other areas of international law, the USA has manifested at least as much reluctance as any major developing country to accept constraints on its sovereign rights.

A second issue concerns the distribution of decision-making authority. How are decisions over the global environment to be taken? What voting procedures and decision-making structures should be adopted? For example, many developing countries are reluctant to see the World Bank entrusted with environmentally related development assistance because of the disproportionate influence over the Bank wielded by the major industrialized nations. For this reason developing countries have emphasized the importance of equality between states (and hence of one-state, one-vote voting procedures), and have tended to favour the creation of new institutions. Concerns over sovereignty often converge around the vexed issue of conditionality, in other words the attachment of environmental conditions to flows of trade, aid, investment, loans, and technology. Conditionality has been consistently denounced in recent statements by the developing countries and disputes have already arisen, for example, over the imposition of environmentally related conditions in World Bank project lending. Yet the Northern countries are united in believing that environmentally related resource trans-

[70] Beijing Declaration, para. 6.

fers should entail a significant degree of conditionality. Underlying this might be the determination to maintain political control, a desire to ensure that the resources are efficiently invested, or a wish to benefit particular groups within developing countries. Moreover, calls for environmental conditionality come on top of well-established forms of economic conditionality (common to many forms of IMF lending) and coincide with moves to apply conditionality in other areas—to support democratization and to press states to reduce levels of arms spending. In addition to increasing the sovereignty concerns of the developing countries, the mushrooming of conditionality raises complex questions of monitoring, enforcement, and dealing with problems of 'cross-conditionality' and the clashes that emerge between different sets of conditions. A different problem of conditionality relates to market access, where states restrict the import of products whose production infringes environmental standards set by the importing country, by the country of production or export, or by international agreement. The wider questions of the relation between environmental safeguards and the open liberal market trading systems embodied in the GATT and regional free trade agreements have not yet been adequately resolved.[71]

This leads to the third source of potential conflict, namely the broader, if still largely submerged, arguments about environmental management and non-intervention. The fragility of many states in the developing world represents one of the weakest links in the structure of global environmental management. It may well be possible to secure international agreements on global environmental issues. But even with substantial levels of external assistance many of the poorest or most politically divided societies in the developing world may well prove unable to implement effective environmental policies. Although this may have little impact on some global issues (such as global emissions of greenhouse gases), states with particular resources such as forests will be increasingly seen as managers of a global resource. Other states may fail to protect their own populations from disastrous environmental degradation, or to manage water resources in an efficient and equitable manner,

[71] See esp. the Report of the GATT Dispute Settlement Panel on *United States Restrictions on Imports of Tuna, ILM* 30 (1991), 1598.

damaging both themselves and their neighbours. Such a situation is likely to give rise to calls for greater and more direct outside intervention and, as is already evident within the broader debate over the future role of the United Nations, any such proposals are likely to become a source of significant conflict and controversy.

Conclusion

Can the existing international system, dominated by sovereign states but powerfully shaped also in relation to environment and development issues by multinational corporations, international institutions, and non-governmental scientific and political groups, respond adequately to the burgeoning environmental challenges? States have achieved the requisite degree of co-operation in relation to some of the less difficult issues, including marine pollution, Antarctica, the protection of the stratospheric ozone layer, and to a lesser extent acid rain and the transboundary movement of hazardous wastes. More complex and difficult problems have at least been accorded recognition on the international agenda, and new forums and institutional responses have begun to appear.

It would be wrong to assume, however, that the universal rhetoric of ecological interdependence translates readily into effective international action. Even in established environmental regimes, implementation and enforcement lag far behind the achievements of standard-setting. The potentially vast magnitude of the climate change issue, and the fundamental scientific uncertainties about it, render economic and social analysis and political decision-making deeply problematic, and threaten to exceed the present capacities of the system. The environmental issues whose roots lie in the absence of, or unsustainability of, development in the South and in eastern Europe are even wider in scope, and raise fundamental issues about the distribution of power, wealth, and resources, and about the values which should or will determine that distribution. Even where states are able to reach agreement on general principles in these areas, concrete measures and effective institutional structures may be much more elusive. It is with the means and prospects for developing such principles, measures, and structures that this book is principally concerned.

PART I. Standard Setting and Implementation

2

International Environmental Law: Its Adequacy for Present and Future Needs

Patricia Birnie

IT is generally accepted that our environment is now threatened by a wide variety of humankind's activities, ranging from its instinct to reproduce its kind, its restless urge to improve its standards of living, the ability of certain sections of society to develop technological solutions to this end, and the vast amount of waste, both natural and chemical, that these advances generate. Paradoxically, the results of this urge to grow and develop, which initially was uncontrolled, are now widely perceived to be threatening, if not the very possibility of development, then at least its maintenance on a sustainable basis for all peoples. As living and non-living resources are depleted at an alarming rate and life-support systems such as air and water become increasingly polluted, it has become more necessary to regulate these human activities to eliminate these threats.

Regulation is essentially a legal process since it implies an attempt to govern behaviour by the setting of rules or standards and the promulgation of principles. In this chapter, therefore, we shall examine the underlying concepts and techniques of the international regulatory processes and re-examine the sources of international law from the perspective of their usefulness in environmental protection. This will involve consideration of so-called 'hard' and 'soft' law approaches and their sources, the role of international, intergovernmental, and non-governmental organizations in the regulatory process, new concepts such as 'common heritage' and human rights to environmental quality, new principles such as 'the polluter pays' and the 'precautionary principle', and attempts to reformulate the doctrine of state responsibility, liability, and compensation. The institutions established and techniques used to formulate and prescribe, enforce, and monitor the necessary measures will also be scrutinized, as will methods of settling any disputes arising in relation thereto. The need for environmental regulation is necessarily identified in the first instance by the conclusions of scientific studies, and so the relation of science and law must also be taken into account.

A. 'Hard' and 'Soft' Approaches to Regulation

International regulation is one of the main and undoubtedly the most useful of the services law can offer for preserving the environment, since by this means the conduct of states and nationals can be controlled. Regulation can prescribe what shall be done, by whom, when, and where. It can also lay down the methods of enforcement and penalties for breach. This is essential since the development of environmental law generally requires that states restrict the customary freedom of their citizens and companies to conduct profitable economic activities. But regulation is neither the beginning nor the end of the process. A great many issues and conflicts of interest relating to them have to be resolved before the necessary majority support, consensus, or unanimity, whichever is by law required, can be built up to enable the adoption of a regulation which states will accept to be binding upon them. Even at this stage it is not likely—whether this approach is expressed by conclusion of a solemn treaty or emerges from state practice—that all states will have participated in the process, still less that they will ratify or acquiesce in the result. Even when they do so, they are often lax in applying or enforcing the regulation, and international law seldom provides any international body to scrutinize their performance in these respects. Frequently also states stop short of adopting binding regulations and prefer merely to set standards or lay down guidelines, criteria, principles, or recommendations which they regard as non-binding; failure to observe these does not expose them, therefore, to criticism, except from ever-watchful non-governmental bodies with a particular interest in the activity regulated. This method is particularly useful when the needs of environmental protection clash with those of developing states to develop.

Binding regulations, which are most often laid down in treaties, are generally regarded as part of so-called 'hard law' which imposes mandatory obligations on states which must then implement and enforce such law in their national legal systems. Observance of guidelines, standards, etc. depends, however, on the form and terms of the instrument establishing them and on the views expressed by states participating in their production. Generally these are set out in resolutions or declarations and do not bind; states can proceed at as slow a pace as they like in working towards implementation; indeed frequently they feel no obligation of implementation at all, treating the principles laid down as goals only. These instruments are thus often referred to as part of 'soft' law,[1] although they are not really law at all, *strictu sensu*; the term is paradoxical. None the less, it does express the element of strong expectation that states will gradually conform their conduct to its requirements, which may include that they enact binding national regulations to control particular activities. The so-called 'soft law' approach is, in the writer's view, best considered as part of the dispute settlement/conflict resolution process, indeed as an ongoing process for these purposes. It may serve this purpose at the global, regional, sub-regional, or even bilateral level, depending on the issue in question and the number of states involved. The technique should be regarded as 'soft settlement', rather than 'soft law',[2] since the vague and general terms most often used in such instruments permit states to continue the negotiating process and to develop acceptable interpretations of ambiguous terms or to comply in a variety of ways without exciting complaint. However, as 'soft law' is now such a

---

[1] For an excellent description and analysis of 'soft law' and its uses see T. Gruchalla-Wisierski, 'A Framework for Understanding "Soft Law"', *Revue de droit de McGill*, 30 (1984), 37–88. For a briefer account see C. M. Chinkin, 'The Challenge of Soft Law: Development and Change in International Law', *International and Comparative Law Quarterly*, 38 (1989), 850–66. She points out that 'the international legal order is an evolving one that requires a wide range of modalities for change and development, especially into new subject areas. Labelling these instruments (traditional and soft law) as law or non-law, disguises the reality that both play a major role in the development of international law and both are needed for the regulation of States' activities and for the incorporation of conflicting standards and goals and provide states with the room to manoeuvre in the making of claims and counter claims' (p. 866).

[2] P. W. Birnie, 'Legal Techniques of Settling Disputes: The "Soft Settlement" Approach', in William E. Butler (ed.), *Perestroika and International Law* (Boston: Martinus Nijhoff, 1990), 177–95.

commonly used term it will be used here. Its main characteristic is that the generality and vagueness of its requirements allows a large amount of discretion in its application, and this allows states to assume certain obligations that they might not otherwise have accepted. A more specific 'hard' form may inhibit some states from accepting the regulations in question. Some soft law remains soft; some may harden into binding customary law or be included in a treaty. The soft approach allows states that are prepared to co-operate in dealing with a problem to do so without unduly restricting their freedom of action, since they retain control of the extent of the obligation or regulation they will accept, and of its timing.

B. How Is International Legal Regulation Achieved?

1. *Sources of international law*

According to Article 38(i) of the Statute of the International Court of Justice, there are three primary sources of international law all of which are long standing and well tested, though they are not without certain inherent weaknesses given the nature of the international community, which is still composed of sovereign states jealous of their sovereignty, however much they may at the same time recognize the interconnections of environmental problems and their solutions. The main sources are treaties; custom; and general principles of law.[3] Decisions of international and national tribunals and the writings of eminent publicists provide secondary sources, related to these. Resolutions and declarations of international bodies and conferences are not in themselves a separate source but may become part of customary law, as discussed below.

(i) *Treaties.* Prima facie, treaties bind only the states which formally agree to be bound by them, normally by depositing an instrument of ratification or accession. As the texts of treaties are generally adopted by a majority vote, those voting against or abstaining are not likely to ratify and thus will not be bound by

[3] For an excellent analysis of these see I. Brownlie, *Principles of Public International Law*, 4th edn. (Oxford: Oxford UP, 1990), 1–31.

the treaties themselves, except to the extent that the treaty rules become part of customary international law or that such so-called 'third states' subsequently express in writing their consent to be bound. To avoid this result, the UNCLOS 1982 was negotiated slowly, over a period of ten years, by consensus in the hope (unfulfilled in the event) that its final text also could be adopted by consensus. The consensus process is not defined in any general treaty or customary law, but a useful guide is the procedure laid down in Article 161(8)(e) of the UNCLOS, which requires negotiation to continue if objections are raised to proposed articles until an article (including regulatory ones) acceptable to all emerges. The UNCLOS was also negotiated as a single interconnected package to encourage states not to press objections on other articles once they had secured an acceptable compromise on their main concerns. The resultant text thus contains much deliberate constructive ambiguity, which can be resolved only by state practice, and many provisions specifically require subsequent development, by diplomatic conferences or through 'appropriate' or 'competent' international organizations, in the form of promulgation of further measures, including standards and guidelines. Thus, remaining difficulties are postponed and their resolution is left to development of further legislation in the future, often through UN Specialized Agencies, such as the IMO, or regional agencies or *ad hoc* commissions, such as the United Nations Environment Programme (UNEP) Regional Seas bodies, or fishery or pollution commissions. This technique for negotiating the treaty text through political forums rather than leaving it to the International Law Commission, and for disposing of 'hard core' issues, resistant to acceptable solutions, has been heralded as a 'brilliant invention and a new contribution to the resources of diplomacy' by one writer and participant in the process.[4] It is always possible, however, to make reservations to specific articles in treaties, as long as these are not prohibited by the text or inconsistent with the object and purpose of the treaty.[5] Treaties may, however, codify custom, and that custom would continue to bind even non-parties to the treaty; a treaty may also

---

[4] P. Allott, 'Power Sharing in the Law of the Sea', *AJIL* 77 (1983), 1–30. See also Elliot Richardson's chapter in this volume.

[5] *Reservations to the Genocide Convention*, Advisory Opinion, ICJ Rep. 1951, p. 4; Vienna Convention on the Law of Treaties 1969, Art. 19.

lay down norms which, if sufficiently followed in subsequent state practice, may become binding as part of customary international law. Detailed rules for conclusion, interpretation, and for most other aspects of treaties have been set down in the UN's 1969 Vienna Convention on the Law of Treaties.[6]

As treaties can bind and can also deal with detail, they are a particularly useful vehicle for environmental regulation, despite the limitations referred to. A further drawback is, however, that, given the formal processes surrounding their adoption, and the need for all the states concerned to convene in an *ad hoc* diplomatic conference or one convened by a concerned international organization, such as the UN (including the UNEP), its Specialized Agencies (such as the IMO or FAO), or regional bodies (such as the EC, OAS, OAU, or Council of Europe), treaties can be somewhat rigid and inflexible. It may be difficult to change the substantive provisions, since this may require a further conference to adopt a formal protocol. To avoid this, treaties, especially those regulating environmental issues, now generally include amendment procedures. These procedures often distinguish between amendment of the major substantive articles of the Convention, which generally requires unanimity or a large majority, and amendment of practical regulations, set out in a separate schedule, Annex or Appendix, which will require only a simple or qualified majority. This is a common feature of conventions regulating fisheries,[7] marine waste disposal,[8] and,

[6] Concluded 23 May 1969 at Vienna; entered into force 1980. Text in *ILM* 8 (1970), 679; and in I. Brownlie (ed.), *Basic Documents in International Law*, 3rd edn. (Oxford: Oxford UP, 1983), 349.

[7] e.g. the International Convention for the Regulation of Whaling, concluded 2 Dec. 1946 at Washington, 161 UNTS 72. It followed the models provided by several pre-World War II fishing conventions: Convention on Future Multilateral Co-operation in the North-West Atlantic Fisheries, concluded 24 Oct. 1978 at Ottawa, UKTS Misc. 9 (1979), Cmnd. 7569; Convention for the Conservation of Salmon in the North Atlantic Area, concluded 2 Mar. 1982, at Reykjavik, UKTS Misc. 7 (1983), Cmnd. 8830; Convention on Future Multilateral Co-operation in North-East Atlantic Fisheries, concluded 18 Nov. 1980 at London, UKTS Misc. 2 (1980), Cmnd. 9474. There are now a large number of such conventions throughout the world, including several concluded under the auspices of the UN Food and Agriculture Organization (FAO).

[8] Convention for the Prevention of Marine Pollution by Dumping from Ships and Aircraft, concluded 15 Feb. 1972, at Oslo, *ILM* 11 (1973), 262; Convention on the Prevention of Marine Pollution by Dumping of Wastes and Other Matter, concluded 27 Dec. 1972 at London, *ILM* 11 (1973), 1294; Convention for the Prevention of Marine Pollution from Land-Based Sources, concluded 4 June 1974, at

more recently, the transboundary carriage of hazardous and noxious wastes.[9]

There is also a new trend, evidenced by UNEP's Regional
Seas[10] and Ozone Conventions,[11] to adopt first a framework
treaty expressed in general terms and establishing only general
duties, with provision for adopting subsequently, through the
Commission established by that treaty, detailed Protocols on
specific topics, laying down more stringent regulations. The
UNEP Regional Seas Conventions now have Protocols on dumping, offshore installation removal, land-based pollution, and
specially sensitive areas; the Ozone Convention has the Montreal
Protocol; and the Geneva Convention on Long-Range
Transboundary Air Pollution has several Protocols, including
that on sulphur emissions.[12]

(ii) *Custom.* Legal custom, based on observation of state practice, crystallizes into law, i.e. becomes legally binding, only if
accompanied by a subjective belief on the part of the state concerned that it is under a legal obligation to conform to the custom.
Although in certain circumstances custom can become binding
very rapidly, this is rare; generally it takes a considerable time for
evidence to accumulate that the practice is so widely and consistently followed that the necessary sense of obligation (the *opinio
juris*) is apparent and established. It is, none the less, possible for
custom to emerge on a regional basis, or even bilaterally.

It is difficult in a world of diverse cultures, policies, interests,
and legal systems to identify any universal practice. A wide variety of materials evidencing state practice has to be examined—
official statements, declarations, laws, court decisions, acts in

Paris, *ILM* 13 (1975), 352. See also the eleven UNEP 'Regional Seas' Conventions
which have similar Protocols on both of these topics, in P. Sand (ed.), *Marine
Environment Law in the United Nations Environment Programme: An Emergent Eco-
Regime* (New York: Tycooly, 1988); and the series of IMO conventions regulating
vessel source pollution, including the International Convention for the Prevention of Pollution from Ships (MARPOL) 1973, as amended by Protocol in 1978.

[9] See the Basel and Bamako Conventions, discussed below.

[10] For texts of these see Sand (ed.), *Marine Environment Law.*

[11] Convention for the Protection of the Ozone Layer, concluded at Vienna, 22
Mar. 1985, *ILM* 26 (1985), 1529; Montreal Protocol on Substances that Deplete the
Ozone Layer 1987 and London Amendments 1990, in Barry E. Carter and Philip R.
Trimble (eds.), *International Law: Selected Documents* (Boston: Little, Brown, 1991),
723 and 731.

[12] Convention on Long-Range Transboundary Air Pollution, *Environmental
Policy and Law*, 6 (1980), 37–40.

bodies concerned with environmental issues, which have pro-
liferated in recent years as UN Specialized Agencies take up the
issues and as new commissions are created by environment
treaties. Numerous conferences also produce a variety of relevant
instruments of varying degrees of significance for this purpose.
Particularly difficult to evaluate are unilateral acts such as
France's declaration that it would not conduct further atmospheric nuclear tests, which the ICJ in the *Nuclear Tests* cases
regarded as binding;[13] texts, resolutions, and declarations
adopted by consensus, as at the UN, the UNCHE and the
UNCLOS, and acts of individuals, especially when concerted
through NGO pressure groups such as Greenpeace or the World
Wide Fund for Nature that actually campaign for changes in the
law to protect the environment. In the case of the former, it is the
intention to be bound that is the determinant, in the latter the
adoption of the proposals by states.

It is not required that state practice be universally consistent, as
long as inconsistent conduct is regarded as an exception to the
rule, not creative of a new one. In the *Nicaragua* v. *USA* case the
ICJ stated that the fact that the parties knew of the content of the
rule was not determinative; the Court still had to satisfy itself that
the existence of the rule in the *opinio juris* of states was confirmed
'by practice'. Moreover, the ICJ added that the inclusion of a rule
in a treaty did not supplant its continued existence as a rule of
customary law, from which further relevant aspects of the
required conduct could be derived.[14]

There remain problems, however, concerning the status of
resolutions of authoritative international bodies and states' votes
(or acquiescence in consensus) in relation thereto, especially
with regard to General Assembly Resolutions (GARs), a main
vehicle for introducing global environmental concerns and standards, as in the case of the World Charter for Nature[15] or the GAR
expressing 'common concern' about the effects of possible
climate change and the actions required.[16] The problems arise
from the facts that the UN Charter prima facie accords GARs only

[13] ICJ Rep., 1974, pp. 253, 457.
[14] *Nicaragua* v. *United States*, ICJ Rep., 1986, p. 14.
[15] UN GA Res. 37/7, 9 Nov. 1982; *ILM* 22 (1983), 455.
[16] UN GA Res. 43/53 (1988), *ILM* 28 (1989), 1300; for discussion of 'common'
concepts, see J. Brunée, 'Echoes from an Empty Shell', *Zeitschrift für ausländisches
öffentliches Recht and Völkerrecht*, 49 (1989), 791–808.

recommendatory status; that they may be adopted by simple or weighted majority vote (unanimity is not required); and that increasingly no vote is taken and GARs are adopted by consensus. But resolutions, although clearly not generally binding *per se*, may become so on the basis of states' acceptance of them as such, either when adopted or in their subsequent practice in relation to them, a view confirmed in the *Nicaragua* v. *USA* case. Any abstention or negative vote has to be examined to ascertain the underlying *opinio juris*. Declarations of Principles, a more solemn form of UN Resolution, exemplified in the Stockholm Declaration,[17] as later adopted in a GAR, must be subject to similar tests. If such tests are passed they can be regarded as rules of customary law, and even of *jus cogens*, i.e. part of the body of customary law that is regarded as a peremptory norm, accepted and recognized by the international community of states as a norm from which no derogation is permitted and which can be modified only by the emergence of subsequent similar norms.[18] This concept is controversial but obviously of special relevance to environmental protection. We must ask what, if any, environmental norms can be so regarded: what is the status, for example, of the concept of the environment as a 'common heritage', of the proposed right to an environment of quality, or of an alleged general duty to conserve living resources?

General Assembly Resolutions are also important in so far as they can be relied on to justify conduct based upon them. States, though not bound to apply them, often cannot object if other states or international organizations do so. Resolutions are a popular vehicle for the adoption of 'soft' guidelines, standards, recommended practices; examples include the Stockholm Declaration of Principles on the Human Environment; UNEP's various sets of principles and guidelines, such as those for shared natural resources;[19] and the numerous IMO guidelines and codes

[17] Report of the United Nations Conference on the Human Environment, Stockholm, 5–6 June 1972; UN doc. A/CONF.48/14/Rev.1 (1973).

[18] Article 57 of the Vienna Convention on Treaties; see also articles 61 and 74. For an analysis of this concept see Brownlie, *Principles of Public International Law*, 512–15.

[19] UNEP Series on Environmental Law Guidelines and Principles, No. 2; 'Principles of Conduct in the Field of the Environment for the Guidance of States in the Conservation and Harmonious Utilization of Natural Resources Shared by Two or More States', UNEP IG 12/2 and UNEP/GC 6/17. See also UNEP, *Environmental Law in the UNEP* (Nairobi: UNEP, 1985).

of practice,[20] especially the International Maritime Dangerous Goods Code (IMDG),[21] which is widely observed. The legal status of each GAR has to be tested individually.

The formalities involved in amending the substantive articles of treaties, and the slowness and uncertainty of identifying the crystallization of new customs, make it difficult to change the law or to 'fine tune' it to rapidly changing environmental perspectives and emergence of new scientific information. Faced with these difficulties states often argue that initially they have to act unilaterally, breaking the existing customary law in order to modernize it to meet the need for urgent environmentally protective action. An example of this was Canada's Arctic Waters (Pollution Prevention) Act, 1970[22] by which Canada sought to control oil tankers passing outside its territorial waters, and the United Kingdom Petroleum Act,[23] giving the UK government the discretion to decide whether or not completely to remove oil installations at the end of their working life. The Canadian Act was protested against by the USA, *inter alia*, as an infringement of its right of innocent passage. The problem was resolved by, in effect, non-application of the Act pending the development of coastal state marine pollution prevention rights in EEZs through the UNCLOS negotiations. The UK Act was challenged during its passage through Parliament as being in violation of the requirement of Article 5 of the 1958 Continental Shelf Convention[24] that offshore installations be entirely removed at the end of their useful life. In both cases the states concerned alleged that they were leading the way towards better international laws. The UK in the latter case eventually instigated development of guidelines through the

[20] For an overview of some of these see T. Mensah, 'International Regulatory Regimes on the Carriage of Dangerous Goods by Sea', paper presented at the Ninth International Symposium on the Transport and Handling of Dangerous Goods by Sea and Inland Waterways (TDG-9), Rotterdam, Netherlands, 13–17 Apr. 1987.

[21] IMO doc. MSCG 497, 26 July 1988, Ref. T 33.06; the full code is published (as updated regularly) by IMO.

[22] Canadian Arctic Waters (Pollution Prevention) Act 1970, in S. Houston Lay *et al.* (eds.), *New Directions in the Law of the Sea*, vol. i (Dobbs Ferry, NY: Oceana, 1973), 199–210.

[23] Petroleum Act 1987.

[24] For the text of the Geneva Convention on the Continental Shelf see Brownlie (ed.), *Basic Documents in International Law*.

IMO,[25] giving effect to Article 63(3) of the UNCLOS despite not having signed it. Thus in both cases new treaties or guidelines were negotiated which helped to defuse the situation. More recently, a report commissioned by the Canadian Government suggested that to conserve the fish stocks which currently straddle both the high seas and the outer limits of Canada's 200-mile Exclusive Economic Zone (EEZ), Canada should unilaterally extend its fishery limit to 300 nautical miles (the consensus arrived at in the UNCLOS 1982 limits the EEZ to 200 nautical miles).[26] The report suggested that in the interim Canada should arrest on the high seas foreign flag vessels that are allegedly over-exploiting such stocks there and thus undermining Canada's efforts to conserve the same stock by adopting and enforcing regulations imposing quotas and other conservatory measures within its EEZ and in the NAFO 'Regulatory Area' (the area covered by the regulations of the North-West Atlantic Fisheries Organization established under the 1978 treaty). The Canadian Government is, however, more likely to seek a negotiated solution with the European Community than to resort to such illegal solutions.

(iii) *General principles of law.* Given the difficulties of formulating treaties and custom, it was thought by the drafters of the Statute of the ICJ that cases might arise in which neither was applicable. To avoid placing the Court in a *non liquet* (unable to decide) situation, this source, limited to principles 'common to civilized nations', was included. It is generally regarded as relating to procedural principles commonly followed in courts throughout the world to ensure a free and fair trial, but some contend that it could be used to invoke such basic principles as 'sovereignty' and freedom of the seas; and the basic principles concerning human rights and, nowadays, developmental and environmental rights. Others argue that these become principles of law only to the extent that they have been accepted into customary law. The ICJ and arbitral tribunals have seldom invoked principles other than procedural ones, although the principle of

---

[25] Guidelines and Standards for the Removal of Offshore Installations and Structures on the Continental Shelf and in the Exclusive Economic Zone, IMO doc. MSC 55/WP 11; reproduced as Annex I to G. Kasoulides, 'IMO Draft Guidelines for the Removal of Offshore Platforms', *International Journal of Estuarine and Coastal Law*, 4 (1989), 71–9 at 76–9.

[26] 'High Seas Arrest Threat', *Fishing News International*, 29. 2 (May 1990), 1–2.

restitutio in integrum was referred to in the *Chorzow Factory* case[27] and that of *sic utere tuo* in the *Trail Smelter* case. The ICJ and arbitral tribunals have invoked various equitable principles in recent maritime boundary delimitation cases;[28] equitable principles also are often referred to as a means of resolving certain kinds of environmental disputes, for example over shared natural resources, including watercourses,[29] and have been included in various UNEP guidelines.

2. Role of international organizations and bodies

(i) *IMO.*[30] It will already have become apparent that international organizations play an important role in the regulatory process. They provide forums for the political processes of negotiating conventions, can help with the drafting thereof, and can adopt guidelines, codes, etc. through their resolutions. Those that have permanent organizations, as do most of those of relevance to our purposes, benefit from the legal doctrine of implied powers, namely even if their constitutions do not specifically confer such powers, they can exercise those necessary to apply and interpret their constituent treaty so as to give effect to the purposes of the organization. The IMO, for example, must ensure safety of shipping and prevention of vessel-source pollution, and has taken a broad view of the definition of 'vessel', to include hovercraft and mobile and non-mobile offshore oil platforms; it has taken a similarly broad view of what it considers contributes to 'safety'. It can act through a variety of organs—including its Council, Assembly, Marine Environment Protection

---

[27] *Chorzow Factory (Merits)* case PCIJ, Ser. A, No. 17 (1928), 29.

[28] For a brief account of these see P. Birnie, 'Delimitation of Maritime Boundaries: Emergent Legal Principles and Problems', in G. Blake (ed.), *Maritime Boundaries and Ocean Resources* (Totowa, NJ: Barnes & Noble, 1987), 15–37.

[29] G. Handl, 'The Principle of Equitable Use As Applied to Internationally Shared Natural Resources: Its Role in Resolving Potential International Disputes over Transfrontier Pollution', *Revue Belge de Droit International*, 14 (1977–8), 40–64; see also the UNEP principles, n. 19 above.

[30] For details of the IMO, its structure, purposes, conventions, and other instruments, see its useful series of publications under the title 'Focus on IMO', obtainable from IMO, 4 Albert Embankment, London SE1 7SR.

Committee, Maritime Safety Committee—and has expanded these to meet the new needs of environment protection. It has concluded a large number of Conventions and Codes, which it continues to revise and augment in order to enhance environment protection. IMO provides a vital forum for resolving regulatory conflicts between the flag states and their shipowners, who generally seek to preserve maximum freedom for their vessels, and coastal states, which emphasize protection of their environment. Developmental issues work both ways here, since though a decade ago developed states were numbered among the major flag states (by virtue of the tonnage registered with them), and these, though often also coastal states, gave priority to their merchant shipping interests, now many more developing states have inaugurated extensive registries. This does not, however, necessarily mean that they have weaker regulation, since they have realized, in the light of growing concern for environment protection, that to attract shipowners to register vessels under their flag they must give that flag respectability. This they can do by becoming parties to relevant IMO Conventions. For example, Cyprus recently ratified the MARPOL Convention on Prevention of Marine Pollution from Ships 1973/78.

(ii) *UNEP*.[31] The United Nations Environment Programme is not an autonomous organization but an autonomous unit within the UN Secretariat. Its powers are more circumscribed, its budget more limited than IMO's; it does not have a permanent organization but a Governing Council of States that now meets biennially and which determines its budget and programme. None the less, it has been very successful in concluding (if not in making particularly effective) a series of so-called 'Regional Seas' Conventions and, using consultants and working groups of intergovernmental experts (as it lacks its own in-house experts), it has produced numerous sets of principles and guidelines. Though less authoritative than the IMO, which is both a UN specialized agency and very practically oriented, these are having an influence on state practice. The new Protocol to the Kuwait Conven-

---

[31] For an outline of UNEP's structure and activities, see C. A. Petsonk, 'The Role of the United Nations Environment Programme', *American University Journal of International Law and Policy*, 5 (1990), 351–92, and UNEP, *Environmental Law in the UNEP*.

tion on pollution from offshore activities, for instance, follows closely the relevant UNEP guidelines.

UNEP has also been successful in a comparatively short space of time in providing the impetus, text, and forum for negotiation of the 1985 Ozone Convention and subsequent Protocols, and the 1989 Basel Convention on the Control of Transboundary Movements of Hazardous Wastes and Their Disposal.[32] These agreements were achieved despite formidable political difficulties in both cases, deriving from divisions of interest and opinion between developed countries, which had benefited from the use of the substances involved in the former case and from freedom of disposal options in the second, and developing countries, which mainly (but not exclusively) saw themselves as being deprived of developmental options in the first case and as victims of a capitalist trick in the second. As a result the Ozone Treaty and its Protocols, whilst requiring developed states to reduce the use of certain gases considered to pose a threat to the ozone layer, allowed developing states to increase their use thereof, to make possible, *inter alia*, increased supplies of refrigerators in China. This solution raises some fundamental questions concerning the best way to regulate such problems. Both the UNCHE and the UNCLOS made concessions to the so-called 'double standard', by virtue of which developing states should not be obliged to conform to international environment protection requirements during their period of development. Instead, in these treaties the same obligations were imposed on all states, but cognizance was taken of the right of states to pursue their own environmental policies for achieving these, at their own pace and using the best practicable means available to them. A further important development has been the establishment by parties to the Montreal Protocol of a fund financed by developed states, to be used to assist developing states to move towards use of less damaging propellant gases. Developed states have also been asked to indicate how they can assist scientists in developing countries to seek better technical solutions to the problems involved.

(iii) *Other international bodies, including NGOs.* Although these

---

[32] Convention on the Control of Transboundary Movements of Hazardous Wastes and Their Disposal, concluded at Basel, 22 Mar. 1989, *ILM* 28 (1989), 657.

bodies have played a leading role in developing environmental regulation, there are, of course, many others that have played similar roles in environmental fields relevant to them. At the global level, WHO, FAO, UNESCO, the IAEA (International Atomic Energy Agency), the IUCN, and UNCTAD (United Nations Conference on Trade and Development) have all provided forums for negotiation of treaties and standards enabling conflicts of interest to be resolved—conflicts which have often, although not invariably, been between states from the developed and those from the developing world. The IUCN, the membership of which is a unique combination of states and conservationist NGOs, has tackled some issues that others have found too difficult politically, including the controversial 1979 Convention on Conservation of Migratory Species of Wild Animals, though this remains poorly ratified, starved of funds, and thus relatively inactive. It also produced a draft convention on Preservation of Biological Diversity which influenced negotiations on this topic in the run-up to UNCED 1992.

At a regional level, the OAU, OAS, EC, ECE, Council of Europe, Nordic Council, and similar bodies have provided forums for negotiation of environmental rules, regulations, and standards. NGOs, whilst not usually providing forums for inter-state negotiations, can put forward technical advice, and draft articles etc. for interested states to use, and can attend meetings as observers when the treaty or its parties permit this. Both the International Whaling Commission and the Conference of the Parties to the Convention on International Trade in Endangered Species provide examples of this role; many NGOs have observer status in UN bodies, but ad hoc commissions, such as the Oslo and Paris Convention bodies, are more cautious. NGOs also play an important role in raising public support for regulation, and in monitoring its progress. By concentrating on particular issues such as preservation of birds or whales, or control of waste dumping, they can often convince governments of the need for particular provisions or amendments. Many countries now include representatives of relevant NGOs on their delegations, and NGO representatives, if permitted, attend drafting conferences, meetings of the parties, etc. As many as fifty NGO observers now regularly attend meetings of the International Whaling Commission, for example.

C. Regulatory Techniques: Reinforcement of Regulation *per se*

1. *Liability and compensation*

International law has relied, as one of its most important techniques for inducing good behaviour, on the concept of state responsibility, based on the principle that violation of an international obligation gives rise to a right on the part of the victim to compensation and reparation for damage. However, there are serious difficulties with the effective application of state responsibility in the field of environmental law. There is a lack of refinement and specification of the concept in customary law; the customary doctrine of state responsibility requires a breach of a clearly established specific 'obligation' before responsibility is enjoined, and has failed to clarify whether fault must be proved or whether liability is strict, i.e. whether the breach of the obligation *per se* is sufficient to give rise to liability to compensate without need for proof of negligence. Few treaties—and those often have limited scope and membership— have provided the necessary specification of, for example, the nature of the violation giving rise to liability or the nature of the liability (strict or absolute). Some of those that do so, moreover, such as the 1969 IMO Convention on Civil Liability for Oil Pollution Damage (CLC), [33] in return for accepting strict liability, channel liability to particular private operators (in this case the shipowners), limit the definition of damage, and set a limit to the maximum amount of compensation payable (this limitation of liability being the quid pro quo for the specificity). Although the principle of state responsibility is necessary, since compensation or reparation should be made if obligations are not observed, for purposes of controlling behaviour it is a much weaker technique than positive regulation by means of treaty or established custom. Indeed, it is often forgotten that Canada and the USA were well aware of this point, and asked the tribunal in the *Trail Smelter* case to lay down regulations for the future control of the emissions from the smelter, as well as to determine liability for the damage that they were

---

[33] International Convention on Civil Liability for Oil Pollution Damage 1969, concluded at Brussels, 29 Nov. 1969, *ILM* 9 (1970) 45; see also the Convention Relating to Civil Liability in the Field of Maritime Carriage of Nuclear Material, concluded at Brussels, 17 Dec. 1971; UKTS, Misc. 39 (1972), Cmnd. 5094.

already agreed had occurred. None of the conventions relating to environment protection, whether concerning pollution or species conservation, does more than state that principles of liability should be developed. This includes the UNCLOS, although it does specify that states are responsible for fulfilment of their international obligations concerning preservation and protection of the marine environment and that they 'should be liable in accordance with international law'.

The question now is how far further to expand the application of the principles, especially concerning the means and extent of reparation for injury to the environment: does willingness to apply the view of the Permanent Court of International Justice in the *Chorzow Factory* case, that 'reparation must, as far as possible, wipe out all consequences of (an) illegal act and re-establish the situation which would in all probability, have existed if that act had not been committed', require the British, as some environmentalists suggest, to slaughter all sheep and annihilate all heather in order to re-establish the great forests that once covered their island? Should present generations not merely hand on to their descendants a land as they themselves inherited it, but be under a duty to right the alleged wrongs of their ancestors and restore it to its Neolithic condition? A United States Appeal Court, faced with the decision of courts in Puerto Rico that a shipowner should pay the full cost of replanting a mangrove swamp damaged by a massive oil spill and compensation for damage to all the organisms, down to the smallest diatoms that formerly existed there, decided on appeal that only 'reasonable' actions need be taken and that costs of the damage should be estimated on a reasonable basis, although the local court had found that the shipowners should pay all costs since Puerto Rico was in a *parens patriae* relation to its environment.[34]

2. Regulatory measures

As has been noted earlier, almost all treaties regulating activities potentially damaging to the environment, be it emitting noxious fumes, transporting or discharging hazardous wastes, over-exploiting living resources (whether of the sea, air, or land), now follow a similar pattern. The main convention establishes a regime. It empowers and requires its parties to adopt measures of

[34] 456 F. Supp. 1327 (1978); USDC, D. Puerto Rico.

various kinds. The law fulfils a constitutional role in instituting a commission, council, Meeting of the Parties or other bodies in which the parties can negotiate the necessary measures on a continuing basis. The substances (as in the Ocean Dumping Conventions and Protocols), the species (as in the whaling and other fisheries conventions), the sea and land areas (as in the Wetlands Convention),[35] or buildings and sites (as in the UNESCO World Heritage Convention)[36] to be controlled are listed in Appendices to the Convention, which the parties can amend annually or biennially by a vote determined by the Convention. In the case of fisheries conventions, the required measures—species quotas, gear used, time, place, and intensity of fishing—may be included in a Schedule of Regulations, amended annually by the Commission composed of states parties to the Convention, and supported by a Scientific Committee, usually composed of scientists nominated by (and generally also employed by) their governments. The advent of the EEZ has resulted in many fishery commissions renegotiating their constituent conventions in order to take out of their Regulatory Area the coastal states' EEZs. The coastal state then has only to seek advice from the Commission in relation to conservation in its EEZ. It is no longer bound by its regulations. This can work both ways: the coastal state may regulate either more or less strictly than the multilateral commission; it is likely, given the extent of overfishing, to regulate more strictly. Problems remain concerning straddling stocks, incidental catches of one species taken in nets used for other species (the dolphin problem), and drift nets more generally: the latter were the subject of a UN General Assembly Resolution[37] paving the way for the conclusion of a regional convention curtailing their use.[38]

All these conventions[39] also address to some extent the other

[35] Convention on Wetlands of International Importance Especially as Waterfowl Habitat, concluded 2 Feb. 1971, at Ramsar, *ILM* 11 (1971), 963.

[36] Convention for the Protection of the World Cultural and Natural Heritage, concluded 16 Nov. 1972, at Paris, *ILM* 11 (1972), 1358.

[37] UN GA Res. 44/225, 22 Dec. 1989.

[38] For a summary overview of the driftnet problem see *Ocean Policy News*, Dec. 1990/Jan. 1991, 4–5. The first convention to seek to ban driftnet fishing completely in its area of application is the South Pacific Forum's 1989 Wellington Convention for the Prohibition of Fishing with Long Driftnets in the South Pacific, with 1990 Protocols, *ILM* 29 (1990), 1449.

[39] S. Lyster, *International Wildlife Law* (Cambridge: Grotius, 1985), includes the texts of 12 major wildlife conventions concluded between 1940 and 1980. This collection of texts and commentaries facilitates useful comparisons.

legal problems relating to regulation: dispute settlement; enforcement; liability; scientific research; and monitoring, as appropriate to the subject matter. We should, therefore, look briefly at these aspects of regulation, apart from liability, to which reference has already been made.

3. Dispute settlement

Most conventions either do not provide at all for dispute settlement (for example, the ICRW), or refer to the choices set out in Article 33 of the UN Charter, or provide an article or Protocol giving the option of resorting to arbitration, if the parties so agree, in any particular dispute.[40] The ICJ, the UN's organ of judicial settlement, has no compulsory jurisdiction. In any case, no environmental treaty, other than the UNCLOS and the Antarctic Environmental Protocol, *requires* that its parties resort to binding settlement. Given the cultural, economic, social, scientific, and developmental issues that are involved in environmental issues, this is not surprising. Such disputes are more appropriate to political settlement by the protagonists, either in the forum provided by the meetings of the organizations, or by postponing the conflict or transferring it to other forums, or by resorting to the 'soft' settlement technique of resolutions and codes, or directly, through bilateral or other negotiations. No pollution or wildlife cases have been decided by the ICJ other than indirectly in the *Anglo-Icelandic Fisheries* case;[41] in the light of the ICJ Chamber's dismissive treatment of environmental factors in the *Gulf of Maine* case[42] this may be a matter of some relief to that court. It is, however, now considering the case brought by Nauru against Australia[43] concerning mineral exploitation, and cases concern-

[40] For the range of methods available see Brownlie, *Principles of Public International Law*, 708–36; and L. Bjorkbom, 'Resolution of Environmental Problems: Use of Diplomacy', in J. E. Carroll (ed.), *International Environmental Diplomacy* (Cambridge: Cambridge UP, 1988), 123–37.

[41] *Fisheries Jurisdiction* case (*Jurisdiction*), ICJ Rep., 1973, p. 3; (*Merits*), ICJ Rep., 1974, p. 3. See also *Nuclear Tests*, ICJ Rep., 1974, p. 253, 457.

[42] *Gulf of Maine* case (US v. Canada), ICJ Rep., 1984, p. 246.

[43] ICJ Communiqué No. 89/7, 22 May 1989. The Republic of Nauru instituted proceedings on 19 May 1989 against The Commonwealth of Australia concerning rehabilitation of certain phosphate lands mined under Australian administration before Nauruan independence, on the basis of state responsibility for damage, claiming restitution or the appropriate reparation.

ing a right to an environment of quality may be brought before the
European Court of Human Rights in Strasbourg, if that right is
ever added to the European Convention on Human Rights. At
present that convention does not secure such a right; nor does the
UN Covenant on Civil and Political Rights; thus alleged breaches
of such a right cannot be subject to either set of complaints procedures. It should be noted, however, that the American Convention on Human Rights (by Protocol) and the African Charter of
Human and Peoples' Rights both include such a right, though this
has not been activated through dispute settlement procedures.

It should be noted that developing states have been suspicious
of the ICJ, alleging Western bias in its composition; they also lack
experts and funds to take cases to court. However, much has
been done to meet these objections. The membership of the
Court has broadened and a legal aid scheme for developing states
has been introduced.

4. *Enforcement*

This remains one of the major problems of effective regulation.
Clearly, regulations that are not observed are ineffective, but
none of the conventions referred to establishes any form of international inspection or observance that is in effect (see below).
Within their territories and territorial sea and on their registered
ships and aircraft, states are empowered to enforce the international law by any means legally available to them. On the high
seas and in airspace beyond their territorial sea they have few
powers over foreign craft, unless this is conceded under international agreement, as it was in some fisheries agreements.
Terrorism and hijacking conventions also allow some national
enforcement of international offences.

(i) *Inspection at sea.* Some fisheries conventions (notably
NEAFC, the North-East Atlantic Fisheries Commission, and
ICNAF, the International Commission for North-West Atlantic
Fisheries), before the advent of 200-mile EEZs, had limited Protocols on Joint Enforcement. Parties could mutually inspect each
other's vessels and report any violations of regulations to their
flag states, but they could not arrest them. As most of the high
seas areas to which they applied have now been incorporated
into the EEZs/EFZs of their parties, these schemes have lapsed.

The parties to the Whaling Convention, by a subsequently negotiated Protocol, have established an Observer Scheme, [44] but this too is limited by the fact that it requires states parties to agree bilaterally to exchange observers: for example, the USSR and Japan entered into an agreement to exchange observers on each other's vessels. The observers are nationals of the other state concerned, paid by them but appointed formally by the IWC. They report to the state whose ship they are on, to their national state, and to the Commission, and their reports can be discussed at IWC meetings in its Infractions Committee. (A similar scheme is emerging in the ozone regime.) The temporary cessation of commercial whaling means that the schemes have lapsed pro tem; the 'scientific' whaling currently taking place is not subject to observation since approval of licences for this purpose is entirely within the discretion of the states concerned.

Here again, it is the EC that leads the way. It has a small corps (15) of inspectors who police its members' fisheries activities at sea, in addition to any exercise of national powers of inspection within the 200-mile zones, but this is too small a corps to prevent the continuation of overfishing, which has now reached crisis levels. [45] The EC Council has recently agreed that this corps should be enlarged. Landing controls and checks can also be made, facilitated by specification of the ports at which fish must be landed. The EC Commissioner concerned has expressed the view that national licensing systems restricting the number of vessels and their catches would be a more effective method of enforcement. [46]

(ii) *Port state inspection.*   The role of ports in enforcement of environmental standards concerning vessels is becoming increasingly important. Some IMO and ILO (International Labour Organization) Conventions have developed the possibility of at least limited port inspection to offset the weaknesses of flag state enforcement, since vessels rarely visit the ports of their state of

[44] For further details of the enforcement problems of the ICRW over its entire history see P. Birnie, *International Regulation of Whaling*, 2 vols. (New York: Oceana, 1985).
[45] See R. Churchill, *EEC Fisheries Law* (Dordrecht: Nijhoff, 1987), *passim*; and 'Scrap Europe's Quota System', *Fishing News International*, 30. 2, (Feb. 1991), 1.
[46] 'Fishy Business', *The Times*, 19 Dec. 1990, p. 13; see also letter in reply from John Gummer, 'Safeguards for U.K. Fishing Interests', *The Times*, 20 Dec. 1990, p. 11; see also n. 45 above.

registration. These Conventions permit the port authorities of states whose port a vessel voluntarily enters to inspect its oil record book and its certificates and other relevant documents to see whether the ship conforms to these. Inspection of the oil tanks, which enables the port state to ascertain whether the vessel has illegally discharged oil, can be carried out if another state in whose jurisdiction the vessel is reasonably suspected of illegally discharging so requests, or if the coastal state so suspects. Inconsistency of the ship's equipment etc. with its certificate, and any violations discovered, can only be reported to the flag state; the vessel cannot be detained unless it presents a serious safety hazard or threat to the marine environment, when it can be required to visit a repair yard before being released.

These provisions have been utilized since 1978 in a novel scheme of 'port state control' based on a Memorandum of Understanding (MOU) concluded between the administrative officials of the fourteen North-West European states concerned.[47] They agree to inspect a target number of vessels (up to 25 per cent of those entering their ports in a given year) to see whether they conform to certain IMO and ILO Conventions and regulations in force (as listed in the MOU). Any deficiencies are merely reported to the flag state; vessels are not detained unless they pose a safety or environmental threat, as above.

The port state's potential role has been taken a stage further in the UNCLOS (Part XII, Article 211). If a ship that voluntarily enters a port is found to have discharged oil on the high seas in violation of international standards (MARPOL etc.) it can be detained by the port state, which can institute proceedings against it unless the flag state itself wishes to do so. The port state, on the request of the state concerned, can take similar action against vessels that have discharged in the territorial sea or EEZ of another state. Coastal states can arrest vessels contravening the international standards in their territorial sea (subject to specific safeguards spelt out in the UNCLOS) or committing frequent violations with serious damaging consequences in their EEZs. Unfortunately, the UNCLOS is not yet operative, and such a

[47] G. Kasoulides, 'Paris Memorandum of Understanding: A Regional Regime of Enforcement', *International Journal of Estuarine and Coastal Law*, 5 (1990), 180–92; the Conventions include e.g. the IMO's OILPOL 1954, MARPOL 1973/78, and ILO Convention No. 147 on Minimum Standards for Seafarers.

scheme cannot be effective without the backing of a widely accepted convention.

(iii) *Enforcement by national means.* Most conventions leave enforcement to the parties, which must enact the necessary national laws and enforce them on their own nationals or vessels and within their territory or maritime zones, following the accepted jurisdictional rules concerning such powers. The obligation to enact such measures is a vital part of the enforcement system. States parties generally do enact the necessary domestic legislation—many states have extensive fisheries and pollution control statutes and subordinate legislation covering highly specific details, such as when and where fish can be taken, by whom on what conditions, in what amounts, or precisely which pollutants can be discharged in what quantities or levels and on what conditions. Enforcement, however, remains a weakness. The extension of coastal states' jurisdiction in EEZs of 200 nautical miles has increased their rights and duties to enforce regulations—on fish, energy, offshore platforms, marine environment protection (including disposal of wastes), and scientific research. But it is more difficult for national states to regulate their own fishermen than foreign ones, for political and socio-economic reasons.

Control of trade in endangered species under an international permit system is a technique employed in the CITES and other treaties, but the United States has introduced unilaterally, through its national legislation, [48] economic sanctions applicable against states which undermine conservation treaties to which the US is party. These allow the US to ban the import or export of fish or fish products emanating from states determined and certified by the relevant US Secretary of State so to have undermined a treaty, and to deny access to fisheries in the US EEZ to such states; if the states concerned do not conform to the treaty any quotas previously allotted to them are automatically halved the first year and cancelled thereafter. This has had some effect in inducing members of the IWC who had formally objected to the ban on commercial whaling to withdraw their objections, though it gave rise to rancorous political and diplomatic protests and allegations of assaults on sovereignty—not without some justifi-

[48] Packwood–Magnuson Amendment to the Magnuson Fishery Conservation and Management Act of 1978 (Pub. L. 94–285, 16 USC § 181, as amended); Pelly Amendment to the Fishermen's Protective Act of 1967 (22 USC § 1976).

cation, as the states concerned had a legal right under the ICRW to object to the cessation, which was then not formally binding upon them. The result has been an increase in so-called 'scientific whaling' under permits granted nationally, as permitted in the ICRW. Such national sanction techniques can only work in certain situations, however, and could backfire. In the USA a group of concerned NGOs, able under US law to institute a class action, brought such an action against the Secretary for Commerce concerning his failure to determine that Japan's continued taking of whales after the IWC's ban undermined the ICRW. The action reached the US Supreme Court, which decided against the NGOs, holding that the Secretary of State had discretion in the matter of such a determination and certification.[49]

Another difficulty arises from the fact that some small cetaceans and dolphins are taken as a so-called 'incidental catch' by tuna fishermen in the Pacific. The mammals become entangled in the nets used in this industry and drown. This 'kill' is not within the scope of the IWC since it is not the result of directed whaling. It is, therefore, left to be resolved by the tuna commissions established by the International Tropical Tuna Convention and International Convention on Conservation of Atlantic Tuna. This has resulted in many cetaceans being listed in the Annex of Highly Migratory Species attached to Article 64 of the UNCLOS 1982, although Article 65 relating to marine mammals requires states to work through 'the *appropriate* international organizations' (emphasis added) and this is otherwise generally thought to be the IWC. The United States has attempted through its Marine Mammal Protection Act to regulate this problem by setting quotas for dolphins etc. caught incidentally; this approach is unpopular with concerned non-governmental bodies, since it licenses the killing; internationally it has caused friction concerning the compatability of import restrictions with the GATT.[50]

(iv) *Self-enforcement.*   Ultimately, in municipal systems, the law

[49] *American Cetacean Society* v. *Baldridge*, 604 F. Supp. 1398 (DDC, 1985); *Baldridge* v. *American Cetacean Society*, 678 F. 2d. 426 (DC Cir., 1985); cert. granted 474 US 1053 (1986); 478 US 221 (USSC, 1986). For a critique see also C. S. Gibson, 'Narrow Grounds for a Complex Decision: The Supreme Court's Review of an Agency's Statutory Construction in *Japan Whaling Association v. American Cetacean Society*', *Ecology Law Quarterly*, 14 (1987), 485–516.

[50] Marine Mammal Protection Act 1972, Public Law 97–58, 97th Congress; HR 4084, 9 Oct. 1981; and Report of the GATT Dispute Settlement Panel on *United States Restrictions on Imports of Tuna*, ILM 30 (1991), 1598.

is largely self-enforcing, and the same applies to international law. It is individuals in the final analysis who take (or do not take) the measures required by regulations, even though in many cases they may be acting on behalf of companies or other industrial enterprises. They have to be convinced that the measures are right and necessary in their own interest, their country's interest, and the wider interests of the international community. This is especially so in environmental matters. Thus, though treaties are weak on adversarial enforcement provisions, they are increasingly strong in requiring education and training and, in the case of developing states, technical assistance for these purposes.

5. *Scientific research*[51]

Conventions never specify that scientific advice *must* be followed; indeed this could be impractical, as the advice is seldom unanimous, and even when it is, is generally given in the form of a range of options—for example, a choice of levels of quota for the taking of fish or whales or rates or amounts of pollutants dumped or discharged—because of the many variables and uncertainties. Scientists can often advise reductions in general terms but cannot be very precise concerning exactly what is necessary to produce a specific result. Thus treaties usually say that regulations and measures should 'take into account' scientific advice, or as the UNCLOS puts it in Article 61(2) on the EEZ: 'The coastal state, taking into account the best scientific *evidence* available to it, shall ensure through proper conservation and management measures that its resources are not endangered by over-exploitation' (emphasis added). The Whaling Convention requires that regulations be based on 'scientific findings'. Thus the advice in all cases can be disregarded or tempered to the extent necessary to secure political agreement on reductions and on the concomitant regulations.

It is obviously important also to specify whose advice is relevant, by what means it should be fed into the regulatory process, and whether at the national, regional, or global level. There are three possibilities: to leave the advice to be solicited by each

[51] For discussion of the role of scientific research in the regulatory process see J. Wettestad and S. Andresen, 'Science and North Sea Policy-Making: Organization and Communication', *International Journal of Estuarine and Coastal Law*, 5 (1990), 111–22.

state from its own national scientists; for the organization or commission concerned to employ in-house scientists of its own; or for an outside scientific body to provide the advice. Examples of the various methods are:

(i) *'National' scientists.* The NAFO, NEAFC, and ICRW have all established Scientific Committees that meet before or during the Commission Meetings. These are composed of scientists who are members of their national delegations. The IWC illustrates that where Commission membership includes developed and developing countries, few of the latter carry scientists on their delegations. The practice of allowing scientific observers from FAO, UNEP, and IUCN to participate as observers to some extent alleviates the problem, but clearly technical assistance and training needs to be enhanced to enable such states to participate effectively in such committees.

(ii) *In-house scientists.* The Fraser River Salmon Convention and the International Pacific Halibut Convention provide examples of this type of research; they employ resident scientists to advise. However, some experts think there is a danger that such scientists may develop an 'ivory tower' mentality, i.e. a narrowly species-specific or organization-specific approach.

(iii) *Outside scientific organizations.* The former NEAFC and ICNAF (before EEZ/EFZ developments) sought advice exclusively from the International Council for Exploration of the Sea (ICES). The NEAFC and NAFO and the EC continue to refer to it for advice, though all three also have scientific committees or advisory bodies of their own. The former NEAFC and ICNAF used ICES through a Liaison Committee, which met separately from both ICES and the fishery commissions, but were not bound to follow its advice. They frequently disregarded it for political reasons when quota cuts were advised, with disastrous results, for North Sea herring stocks in particular. The position is being made ever more complex by demands for fisheries to be managed on a multi-species basis. NGOs originally pressed for this at IWC meetings with the better conservation of whales in mind, but the few remaining whaling states have recently turned this proposal to their advantage. Thus Norway, the USSR, Iceland, and Japan indicated that they may leave the IWC, having entered into a Multi-Species Agreement amongst themselves, under the terms of which they would regulate whales, seals, and fisheries in general as part of one ecological unit.[52] This they have suggested might require the 'culling' of seals and whales, in order to facilitate increases in commercial fish stocks, on which their fishermen are economically dependent. The scientific, economic, and political advice involved in this would be intricate and contentious. The question arises as to whether it is humanly possible with present knowledge and techniques so to regulate and manage ecological systems.

The SCAR (Scientific Committee on Antarctic Research) gives scientific advice on environmental issues in Antarctica, but has been given no formal role within the 1959 Antarctic Treaty so to do. Its role could be much enhanced under the 1991 Environment Protocol to the Antarctic Treaty, concluded after NGO-inspired governmental opposition (led by Australia and France) to the 1988 Wellington Convention on exploitation of Antarctic mineral resources.[53]

6. *Monitoring*

Though monitoring the state of the oceans or air to ascertain whether pollutants are present is another important aspect of enforcement, many treaties, including the ocean dumping, Regional Seas, and UNCLOS conventions, require only that states shall '*endeavour*, as far as practicable, directly or through the competent international organizations, to observe, measure, evaluate and analyse' (some say simply 'monitor') 'by recognized scientific methods, the risks or effects of pollution of the marine environment' (UNCLOS, Article 204, emphasis added). This leaves open many ways of avoiding or reducing to the minimum responsibility for this activity. States need do no more than try; if developing states have limited technical skills and equipment, they need do very little. They do not *have* to act through or co-ordinate the monitoring through any, still less any named, international body, since they can act on their own. Yet monitoring is vital to operating regulatory control of emission standards. A

[52] 'Breakaway Threat as Challenges on Whaling Ban Fail', *The Times*, 7 July 1990, p. 6; no copy of this agreement has ever been made publicly available.

[53] See also L. A. Kimball, *Report on Antarctica* (Washington, DC: World Resources Institute, USA); 'The Convention on Antarctic Conservation', ASOC Information Paper (Washington, DC: Antarctic and Southern Ocean Coalition, 1990–1). Antarctic Environmental Protocol 1991, *ILM* 30 (1991), 1455.

multi-media approach covering land, sea, and atmosphere is in creasingly being sought, for example by the EC. The answer clearly is to improve the technical skills and equipment of developing states through national and international schemes.

D. Theoretical Basis of Regulation: New Concepts?

Modern jurists, in the context of the surge of interest in protecting the environment, have put forward several new concepts and ideas in an effort to provide a firmer basis for the necessary regulation of environmentally damaging state conduct. Some have articulated the doctrine that 'common spaces'[54]—areas beyond national jurisdiction, such as the high seas, outer space, and Antarctica—should be regulated for the benefit of the international community as a whole, either by user states acting as stewards on behalf of that community, or by ensuring that there will be equality of access, not free access, to such spaces and their resources, any necessary regulation of activities being done under the auspices of some internationally constituted body. The legal content of the concept of 'common heritage' is unclear; it therefore has to be established by development of custom or treaty, and, in the writer's view, it is only in relation to the deep sea-bed that any progress has been made in this respect (the Moon Treaty does not establish any relevant machinery). As the United Nations Convention on the Law of the Sea (UNCLOS) is not in force, it cannot yet be said that this attempt has wholly succeeded, except to the extent that it is at least generally accepted that the deep sea-bed cannot now be exclusively appropriated and that some form of international regime must govern its exploitation, since no state has put forward exclusive claims.[55] It must be emphasized that such much-used terms as 'common heritage' and 'common patrimony' (in French, it should be noted, 'patrimoine commune' is the term used for the former also) have no intrinsic legal content.

Natural law theory has been expanded recently to comprehend

[54] J. Kish, *The Law of International Spaces* (Leiden: Sijthoff, 1973); J. I. Charney (ed.), *The New Nationalism and The Use of Common Spaces* (Montclair, NJ: Allanheld, 1982).

[55] It had been signed by 159 states and ratified or acceded to by 47, as at 30 Apr. 1991. Part XI enunciates the common heritage concept.

proposed rights to 'a clean and healthful environment',[56] and proposed inter- and intra-generational rights,[57] the latter embodying the idea that future generations have a vested right to have a 'robust' environment transmitted to them.

To accord rights so to determine regulations now to unborn groups of unknown size and location, even if one accepted the theoretical premises on which this proposal is based, does not help us accurately to determine the content of current regulations. The appointment of an Ombudsman for future generations, who would, on their behalf, influence the scope of current regulations, is surely an impractical suggestion. Virtually the only model that can be invoked is the Supervisory Authority established under the 1974 Nordic Convention.[58] As far as the writer is aware, this model, despite its attractions, not only has not been followed anywhere else in the world but has never been activated in any of the countries concerned.

In relation to pollution prevention and reparation for any pollution damage that may occur, application of new principles is also being suggested. For example, the Organization for Economic Co-operation and Development (OECD) and the European Community—both economic co-operation organizations—have espoused at the regional level the 'polluter pays principle', evolved in national legislation, especially in the United States, as

[56] For a good exposition of this approach see J. Waldron, 'Can Communal Goods be Human Rights?', European Journal of Sociology, 17 (1987).

[57] For a full discussion of this proposal, see E. Brown Weiss, In Fairness to Future Generations: International Law, Common Patrimony, and Intergenerational Equity (Dobbs Ferry, NY: Transnational, 1989); see also Brown Weiss, 'The Planetary Trust: Conservation and Intergenerational Equity', Ecology Law Quarterly, 11 (1984), 495. The arguments for and against such an approach have been well ventilated in an exchange of views among A. D'Amato, E. Brown Weiss, and L. Gundling in 'Agora: What Obligation Does Our Generation Owe to the Next? An Approach to Global Environmental Responsibility', AJIL 84 (1990), 190–212. As Gundling points out (pp. 210–12), much of the argument on which Weiss's proposal is based is at an abstract level. Although the moral point that present generations have some responsibility to consider the options they are leaving open to their descendants is valid, a more programmatic approach is likely to yield more positive results than arguing whether or not a right to be handed on a so-called 'robust' environment can be vested in groups as yet unborn, and whether or not corresponding obligations of a wholly unspecific nature are to be placed on the present generation ad infinitum. As Gundling says, the major problem already confronts us: 'What do we have to do to-day to meet our responsibility to future generations?'

[58] Convention on the Protection of the Marine Environment, 1974, in Lay et al. (eds.), New Directions in the Law of the Sea: Documents, iv. 499; see esp. Art. 4.

a political and economic solution to this problem. It remains, however, at the international level, more of a political and economic principle—providing for equitable allocation of the costs of damage consequent to the risk borne—than a legal one for determining liability, though existing funds for compensation of oil pollution damage financed by levies on industry, such as the US Superfund and the IMO's International Oil Pollution Compensation Fund, provide *ad hoc* examples of practical application of the principle.

The *ad hoc* International North Sea Conferences (INSC) convened by North-West European States at Ministerial level to develop measures to protect the North Sea environment, adopted in the Declaration issued at the end of the Second Conference in 1987[59] the so-called 'precautionary principle'. The content and status of this principle remain unclear,[60] even though it was reformulated and restated at the end of the Third INSC held in 1990. Although considered an important, even a primary, principle in the Federal Republic of Germany, it took some time to appear at the regional level. Some NGOs (such as Greenpeace), which contend, for example, that disposal of radioactive waste etc. in the sea causes harm but find it difficult to prove their case, regard the principle as requiring that no potentially polluting substance should be discharged unless it can be proved by the discharger to be harmless in the marine environment (a shifting of the burden of proof from its previous position on the shoulders of those arguing against such disposal to those who want to dispose of substances into the sea). The actual Declaration is open, however, to much less extensive interpretation. It merely accepted 'the principle of safeguarding the marine ecosystem ... by *reducing* pollution emissions of substances that are persistent, toxic and liable to bioaccumulate at source by use of the *best available technology* and other appropriate measures ... especially when there is reason to assume that certain damage or harmful effects are likely to be caused ... even where there is no scientific evidence to prove a causal link

[59] Second International Conference on the Protection of the North Sea, London, 24–5 Nov. 1987, Ministerial Declaration (issued by the Department of the Environment of the United Kingdom, Apr. 1988).

[60] For a good analysis of the status of this principle see L. Gundling, 'The Status in International Law of the Principle of Precautionary Action', *International Journal of Estuarine and Coastal Law*, 5 (1990), 23–30.

between emissions and effects' ('the principle of precautionary action').[61]

Insofar as international instruments refer to the principle expressly or by implication, they are all in the 'soft law' form— examples are the UNCHE Declaration, the World Charter for Nature, the EC Action Programs, and a Resolution of the Paris Commission on Ocean Dumping.[62] It is important in this debate also to recall the limited definition given to 'pollution' in most conventions, for example in Article 1 of the UNCLOS, which does not cover the mere likelihood of changing or modifying the environment as such but requires evidence of the likelihood of 'deleterious effects'.

Another new approach is that put forward by the International Law Commission in Article 19 of its Draft Articles on State Responsibility,[63] namely that certain international acts should be categorized as 'international crimes'. It suggests in Article 19(2) that 'An internationally wrongful act which results from the breach by a State of an international obligation so essential for the protection of fundamental interests of the international community that its breach is recognized as a crime by that community as a whole, constitutes an international crime'. Article 19(3) adds that, on the basis of the rules of international law in force, 'a serious breach of an international obligation of essential importance for the safeguarding and preservation of the human environment' would include breaches of the rules prohibiting *massive* pollution of the atmosphere or sea (Article 19(3)(d)).

There is not space to analyse this approach fully here. Some of the numerous cogent criticisms have been summarized by Gilbert:[64] none of the relevant international conventions clearly establishes such an obligation; customary law, based on the *Trail Smelter* case provides a very weak basis for alleging general criminal responsibility; and it is difficult to see what such a concept adds to environmental regulation. States cannot be punished in the normal penal sense; therefore, the concept of

---

[61] See INSC Declaration, n. 59 above; and Stairs and Taylor, ch. 4 below.

[62] Gundling, 'Status in International Law', 29–30.

[63] ILC, Draft Articles on State Responsibility: Part 1, *Yearbook of the International Law Commission* (1980); Part 2, *YBILC* 1989), 30.

[64] G. Gilbert, 'The Criminal Responsibility of States', *International and Comparative Law Quarterly*, 39 (1990), 345.

criminal responsibility may heighten the level of moral condemnation but adds little to the sanctions against such conduct except
to stress its effect on the community as a whole and to justify that
community's complaints as such.

It is notable that the USSR was not accused of an international
crime after Chernobyl,[65] nor France and China after their atmospheric nuclear tests.[66] It is true that the OAU has branded the
transport and disposal of hazardous waste in Africa a 'crime',[67]
but the subsequent Basel Convention on this topic does not do
so.[68]

As this chapter has illustrated, ample techniques derived from
traditional sources of international law are available for development of regulations to protect the environment. These techniques
are evolving, in response both to the changed composition of the
international community and to its changing concerns.[69] There is
a rapidly growing number of examples of their usefulness and
application in developing international environmental regulation. This is not to say that the regulations are sufficient or adequate to meet the Stockholm Principles as interpreted by some
scientists or environmental conservation bodies, but that means
exist which can be applied to the task if states are so minded, as the
case studies of the international responses to atmospheric pollution, transboundary movement of hazardous waste, climate
change threats, and conservation of whales readily illustrate.

Conclusion

Views differ as to whether the new regulatory regime for protection of the environment that is undoubtedly emerging is or is not

[65] P. Sands, *Chernobyl: Law and Communication* (Cambridge: Grotius, 1988).

[66] *Nuclear Tests* cases, ICJ Rep., 1974, p. 253.

[67] OAU Bamako Convention on the Ban of the Import into Africa and the
Control of Transboundary Movement and Management of Hazardous Wastes
within Africa 1991, *ILM* 30 (1991), 773; OAU Council of Ministers Resolution on
Dumping of Nuclear and Industrial Waste in Africa, 23 May 1988, OAU Res.
CM/Res. 1153, *ILM* 28 (1989), 567.

[68] Basel Convention on the Control of Transboundary Movements of Hazardous Wastes and Their Disposal, 22 Mar. 1989; *ILM* 28 (1989), 657; Final Act and
Resolutions, ibid. 652–6.

[69] For a thoughtful account of the problems this raises and emerging solutions
see: R. Y. Jennings, 'What is International Law and How Do We Tell It When We
See It?', *Annuaire Suisse de Droit International*, 37 (1981), 61–5.

innovatory, in the sense that a new branch of international law has been established, based on new sources and concepts peculiar to it. An alternative view, preferred by this writer, is that using the existing sources and concepts of international law and the wide range of concerned organizations, an identifiable environment-specific regulatory regime has emerged that can be regarded as 'International Environmental Law'. Those using this term now continuously cite the same instruments, the number of which is increasing all the time, as illustrated in this chapter. Given the diversity of the modern international community of states, increasing use is made of the great variety of international forms and forums that now exist (many, but not all, now environment-specific) for purposes of developing the law. The interests of both developed and developing states have to be accommodated to achieve this; increasing amounts of technical assistance in a variety of forums, will be needed if the stricter regulation required is to be uniformly achieved. International Law has to evolve, and to do so in the environmental sphere its basic norms and principles require constant re-evaluation and flexible application. Declarations, resolutions, guidelines, criteria, codes, recommended practices, standards, etc. are increasingly used and increasingly legally significant as signposts on the way to customs and treaties, albeit, as one writer recently put it, they 'belong to the wide world of international texts the legal status of which is questionable'. As he also remarked, 'international law is not that formal: states may choose the way they want to undertake commitments and what they can do individually, they can do collectively . . . a concerted declaration may entail legal obligations. All depends on the intention of the Parties.'[70]

It is doubtful, in the writer's view, whether adoption of such futurological concepts as inter- or intra-generational rights or environmental crimes or a human right to an environment of quality will enhance the existing methods of developing the necessary regulatory regime, although they clearly play political, publicizing, educative roles in raising public awareness and generating the debate that cranks the existing mechanisms into action. They affect the timing of development rather than its content. There are too many scientific uncertainties, too many

[70] Y. van der Mensbrugghe, 'Legal Status of International North Sea Conference Declarations', *International Journal of Estuarine and Coastal Law*, 5 (1990), 15.

developmental differences, too wide a range of political interests in every state for it to be otherwise. States have the will to protect the environment on their terms and by the methods preferred by them, under which they have some control over the pace of regime change. They are not yet ready to abandon theoretical notions of sovereignty—albeit they are now willing to limit it by the means outlined in this paper—in favour of the amorphous demands of future generations or allegedly vested environmental rights of an indeterminate and limitless character. As one commentator has remarked, what seems to be emerging is a concept of 'reasonable sovereignty'.[71]

International law has provided sufficiently flexible modes of developing environmental law to meet all eventualities, if states have the will to use them to regulate their environmentally harmful activities. The question now is how far further to expand the application of these principles.

The survey of the developments that have occurred and those that are in the process of emerging in relation to the historical theories underpinning the evolution of international law, the manipulation of its traditional sources, the increasing use of treaties and 'soft law', the introduction of new principles, the proliferation of international bodies, within whose forums such developments can be generated, indicates that the sovereignty doctrine is still alive but that, in the case of protection of the environment, it no longer manifests itself in the shape of an albatross; its wings have been clipped by a growing number of widely accepted regulations and regulations in the making based on adaptation of old and new principles that are now widely regarded as being indispensable to preservation of life on our planet. Moreover, the process is continuing; the forums are in active use and environmental law is being added to at a remarkable rate. A creature of a new shape is emerging perhaps best renamed, in the context of these wider environmental developments, as 'responsible' rather than 'reasonable' sovereignty.

---

[71] A. V. Lowe, 'Reflections on the Water: Changing Conceptions of Property Rights in the Law of the Sea', *International Journal of Estuarine and Coastal Law*, 1 (1986), at p. 9.

3

Regime Theory and International Environmental Management

Martin List and Volker Rittberger

IT is the incongruence between the international legal boundaries of the state system and the boundaries of ecological causal networks that constitutes the political problem of international ecological interdependence. Using the language of economics, one might say that the global political space is divided in such a way that ecological externalities are unavoidable once a certain level of human impact on the environment has been reached. This became apparent some time ago in such matters as river pollution that crossed national borders. It later became visible on a regional level in the case of marine or air pollution, and has today reached a global scale in such cases as depletion of the ozone layer and the warming of the atmosphere through the so-called greenhouse effect.

One solution to the externality problems that arise from ecological interdependence might be 'internalization', in other words giving up the existing division of politico-juridical space into over 170 sovereign entities and replacing it by a world state. While this is a conceivable solution in theory, it does not seem to be one in practice. To many observers it is both unfeasible and even undesirable, given the costs involved in bringing about a world state and the risks which the necessary centralization of power might imply. Mankind has thus come to a crossroads. For ecological—as well as for other—reasons, nothing very much short of a *Weltinnenpolitik*,[1] i.e. domestic policy-making for the world, will do. Yet world government seems far away.

[1] The term was coined by Carl Friedrich von Weizsäcker as early as 1963; see Carl Friedrich von Weizsäcker, *Wege in der Gefahr. Eine Studie über Wirtschaft, Gesellschaft und Kriegsverhütung* (Munich: Deutscher Taschenbuchverlag, 1979), 243 ff.

It is here that international regimes become important. At the minimum, regimes can be understood as a form of collective action by states, based on shared priciples, norms, rules, and decision-making procedures which constrain the behaviour of individual states in specific issue areas. The demand for international regimes arises from tasks thrust upon states and non-state actors when they have to cope with interdependence and the problems and conflicts that arise from it. These occurred initially mainly in international economic relations but are increasingly evident in international (or rather transnational) ecological relations. Both policy areas show certain analytic similarities and, indeed, are intimately related.[2] It is, after all, the consequences of human economic activity and the way it is organized from the local level to the global that lie at the heart of environmental problems, again from the local level to the global. The similarity between international economic and international ecological relations lies in the fact that both economic and ecological sensitivity or even vulnerability cut across state borders and give rise to problems (and conflicts) of interdependence. Both types of interdependence rest not so much on relations between states as centres of formal authority over specified territories and over their populations, but on relations between these populations themselves or between organizations formed by and among some of their members. They concern matters of 'low politics', as opposed to such 'high political' matters as security relations that formerly dominated the international agenda.

Interdependence theory, the intellectual reaction in the discipline of International Relations to the emerging new realities of economic interdependence in the early 1970s, had several interesting points to make about situations of interdependence.[3] In policy areas characterized by complex interdependence, the crucial relations would no longer be those between states alone (international relations), but between societal forces as well (transnational relations). States would therefore hardly act as unitary actors, and the complexities of foreign policy-making would play a larger role. Finally, military power would largely be

---

[2] The UN has recognized this fact by convening the UNCED 1992 to deal precisely with problems at the interface of these two policy areas.

[3] See Robert O. Keohane and Joseph S. Nye, *Power and Interdependence. World Politics in Transition* (Boston: Little, Brown, 1977); and their later article, 'Power and Interdependence Revisited', *International Organization*, 41 (1987), 725–53.

inoperative in these areas, and therefore the distribution of power as conventionally operationalized would be a less accurate guide to political outcomes. These claims of interdependence theory appear readily transferable from economic to ecological interdependence and almost seem to have become common wisdom today. Other elements of the theory, however, have proved less accurate, in particular the prediction that interdependence would lead to the diminishing importance of states as institutional centres of supreme collective co-ordination and control. Contrary to this prediction, states have proved resilient against the supposedly undermining effects of economic interdependence (as well as, incidentally, against economic dependence), and have thus also made their way back on to the agenda of social science analysis, which is now busy with 'bringing the state back in'.[4]

In the discipline of International Relations, this means that the interesting question is not what is going to replace the state but rather how states can collectively manage global and regional interdependence. The argument here is that the formation of international regimes, the collective response of two or more states to a collectively problematic situation in the form of institutionalized co-operation, is one way to do so. In what follows we shall try to show what regime analysis has to contribute to studying the management of the international environment. For lack of space, we shall not dwell on identifying international environmental regimes descriptively. Instead, we shall deal with the explanation of the formation of international environmental regimes, on the one hand, and with their consequences, on the other, drawing on examples from our own and our colleagues' research wherever this seems useful and possible.

Before doing so, however, we should like to make one further point concerning regimes as forms of the collective management of problems and conflicts. All of the examples of environmental problems referred to above have one common feature. At the core there is the impact of human action on the natural environment, of which human beings are themselves a part. This impact is based on physical causal mechanisms and does not *per se* constitute a political (nor an international political) problem, even if the

---

[4] See Peter B. Evans, Dietrich Rueschemeyer, and Theda Skocpol (eds.), *Bringing the State Back In* (Cambridge: Cambridge UP, 1985).

underlying human behaviour is a social activity (such as production). To the extent, however, that human beings are affected, either because they are part of the ecological system in question or because they are concerned about its state, the ecological problem is given its social meaning.[5] Dealing with this problem, then, is not merely a technical question, although most ecological problems are 'highly technical' in the sense of involving intricate causal networks. Rather, the actors involved will hold incompatible positions concerning goals or values to be pursued or concerning the means of achieving these goals. In other words, conflicts will arise concerning the question of whether there is an ecological problem and, if so, what kind of collective action is required. It is here, in the process of articulating and mediating diverging goals and interests, that the ecological problem gains its political dimension, i.e. that *ecology* becomes *political ecology*. It becomes *international* political ecology when there is divergence between the goals and interests pursued by actors belonging to, or representing, different states.

It is important to make the distinction between the ecological problem as such—understood as a difference between what is and what ought to be—and the social conflicts it may give rise to. Unless one does so, it is easy to commit a kind of system-theoretic or functionalist fallacy that consists in the transition from the talk about 'the solution of ecological problems' to functionalist formulations like 'the political system must adapt to the new challenges of ecological problems'. This, however, is not a description of a solution, but merely a reformulation of the task, and since it leaves out all social conflicts and does not specify any processes of how to handle them, it is neither of much analytical nor practical value. A more pertinent social scientific analysis, while not denying that ecological problems are at the root of international environmental issues, would have to take a closer look at the conflicts arising from, or linked to, ecological problems and at how they are dealt with. This is where regime analysis offers a useful contribution by looking at the way in which conflicts can be managed under the guidance of jointly agreed prin-

[5] Global warming will affect all humans through physical changes in their environment, i.e. because they are part of the global biosphere and hence causally affected by environmental changes. Extinction of species does not affect humans directly (unless it is human self-extinction), but rather because they care for biodiversity. They may do so for various reasons, ethical, aesthetic, or utilitarian.

ciples and norms and through the application of accepted procedures.

A. International Regimes—Definition and Identification

In a larger research project on 'International Regimes in East–West Relations' we have deliberately chosen the perspective of analysing international regimes as a way in which states collectively manage conflicts in various issue areas, four of which concern international environmental problems and will serve as examples later.[6] Our conceptualization of international regimes follows Stephen Krasner's definition but sharpens it somewhat by adding a further behavioural component to the four normative-institutional elements proposed by him.[7] Thus, we would keep principles, norms, rules, and procedures as the four constitutive elements of a regime, but we argue that the identification of a regime requires the observation of norm- and rule-guided behaviour, i.e. some minimal effectiveness which can be measured by the degree of rule-compliance. This also implies that a regime can only be said to exist if a certain density of rules and

[6] Manfred Efinger, Volker Rittberger, and Michael Zürn, *Internationale Regime in den Ost-West-Beziehungen* (Frankfurt: Haag & Herchen, 1988); and Volker Rittberger (ed.), *International Regimes in East–West Politics* (London: Pinter, 1990). The environmental issue areas studied in the framework of our project are protecting the marine environment of the Baltic Sea (see Martin List, 'Cleaning up the Baltic', in Rittberger (ed.), *International Regimes*, 90–116); protecting the marine environment of the North Sea (see Martin List, *Umweltschutz in zwei Meeren. Vergleich der internationalen Zusammenarbeit zum Schutz der Meeresumwelt in Nord- und Ostsee* (Munich: Tuduv, 1991)); controlling long-range transboundary air pollution in Europe (see Gudrun Schwarzer, 'Weiträumige grenzüberschreitende Luftverschmutzung. Konfliktanalyse eines internationalen Umweltproblems', Tübinger Arbeitspapiere zur internationalen Politik und Friedensforschung Nr. 15 (University of Tübingen, 1990)); and the protection and conservation of whales. In addition, H. Breitmeier allowed us to draw on his work on global climate protection (see Helmut Breitmeier, 'Der Schutz der Erdatmosphäre als Problemfeld der Internationalen Beziehungen: Ein Beitrag zum Prozess der Agendabildung der beiden globalen Problemfelder "Zerstörung der Ozonschicht" und "Anthropogener globaler Klimawandel"', MS, Tübingen, 1990).

[7] Krasner defines regimes 'as sets of implicit or explicit principles, norms, rules, and decision-making procedures around which actors' expectations converge in a given area of international relations' (p. 2) in Krasner, 'Structural Causes and Regime Consequences: Regimes as Intervening Variables', in Stephen D. Krasner (ed.), *International Regimes* (London: Cornell UP, 1983), 1–21.

durability of norm- and rule-guided behaviour can be ascertained.

Emphasizing this behavioural component of a regime serves to clarify the difference between a treaty and a regime. Whereas a treaty is a legal instrument stipulating rights and obligations, a regime is a social institution wherein stable patterns of behaviour result from compliance with certain norms and rules, whether these are laid down in a legally binding instrument or not. Moreover, regimes are different from organizations. It is only organizations to which activities and a legal personality can be attributed. International organizations and regimes intersect where the former provide for the 'procedures' of the latter.[8] Note, finally, that regimes are created for *specific issue areas*, which are in turn part of larger, *theoretically determined policy areas*. For example our concern in this chapter is with the policy area of international environmental protection, which breaks down into the issue areas of, for example, 'protecting the marine environment of the Baltic Sea', 'controlling long-range transboundary air pollution in Europe', or 'preserving biodiversity'. The elements of this definition may serve to identify international regimes, the first task of any regime analysis. However, we shall not go into the details of this process of identification, which is basically an interpretative task of structured description.[9] Instead, we shall next address the theoretically more demanding question of explaining regime formation.

B. Explaining Regime Formation

Regime formation is the process by which a regime comes about in an issue area where hitherto none has existed. It includes both the initiation of the regime, for example through international negotiations ending up in an international agreement, and its implementation through norm- and rule-guided action by the

---

[8] Elsewhere, we have dealt in more depth with the relation between international organizations and international regimes: see Martin List and Volker Rittberger, 'The Role of Intergovernmental Organizations in the Process of Initiation, Implementation and Evolution of International Environmental Regimes', Paper prepared for the ESF Programme on Environment, Science and Society, Task Force VI meeting at Seville, Spain, 22–3 Feb. 1991, MS, Tübingen, 1991.

[9] The interested reader is referred to the studies mentioned in n. 6 above.

participating states. Within our project we have come to distinguish several approaches to explaining regime formation.

1. *The problem-structural approach*

A problem-structural approach tries to account for the probability
of regime formation by the nature of the issues in question. For
this purpose we have developed a fourfold typology of conflicts
that includes the following types: conflicts about values, conflicts
of interest about relatively assessed goods, conflicts of interest
about absolutely assessed goods, and, finally, conflicts about
means. This typology is based on the distinction between *dissensual* and *consensual* conflicts.[10] Dissensual conflicts exist 'when the
parties differ in norms, values, or beliefs and either the requirements of co-ordination make those differences incompatible or
one side wants the other to accept the values, beliefs . . .'.[11] Therefore, if actors disagree about what is desirable, not just for each of
them individually but for all of them collectively, a dissensual
conflict exists. State actors, however, may not only differ about
what is desirable but also about how to reach agreed or common
goals. Thus, the category of dissensual conflicts can be further
differentiated. Dissensual conflicts include not only value-related
incompatibilities ('conflicts about values') but also dissensus
about means ('conflicts about means').

In consensual conflicts the actors are confronted with a situation of scarcity in which every actor desires the same valued
object but cannot fully be satisfied because there is not enough for
everybody. The category of consensual conflicts can also be
divided into 'conflicts about relatively assessed goods' (for
example, power and prestige) which gain their value only if one
actor has more than others and 'conflicts about absolutely
assessed goods' (for example, clean water, food) which gain their
value independently of the amount other parties have.

We believe that the type of conflict predominant in a certain
issue is one factor explaining the ease or difficulty with which
states develop a collective response to a conflict by forming an

[10] See Vilhelm Aubert, 'Competition and Dissensus: Two Types of Conflict and
of Conflict Resolution', in *Journal of Conflict Resolution*, 7 (1963), 26–42; and Louis
Kriesberg, *Social Conflict* (Englewood Cliffs, NJ: Prentice Hall, 1982).

[11] Kriesberg, *Social Conflict*, 30.

international regime. From the experience we have gained so far and from general information about international environmental policy, it would seem that the four types of conflict are of varying relevance to international environmental protection.

(i) *Conflicts about values.* These would not seem very likely to predominate in the policy area of international environmental protection. The reasons are twofold. On the one hand, while there are some governments which, along with their societies, seem to lay greater emphasis on ecologically sound policies than others, hardly any government could claim that it generally attributes far greater weight to environmental protection as compared, for example, to national economic development. On the other hand, while there clearly are many governments which attach a higher priority to economic development than to ecological conservation, few if any of them would today—at least in public—completely deny the necessity of taking ecological concerns into consideration.

In the beginning of the international environmental policy debate there was a notable gap between the nations of the North and those of the South. The former were arguing for 'limits to growth', although not always drawing harsh consequences for their own societies. The latter claimed a right to economic development unfettered by ecological concerns, following the historic path trodden by the North. This gap seems to have narrowed over recent years, although it has not disappeared completely.[12] While a change in values may have taken place in some of the advanced industrialized countries, this affects parts of the national societies rather than whole nations. Hence, this may be of importance for explanations of foreign environmental policy at the national level, but would not seem to constitute an international conflict about values.

(ii) *Conflicts about relatively assessed goods.* These are, if at all, only of indirect relevance in international environmental policy. This is so because the value that one country or actor attaches to

[12] Quarrels between industrialized and developing countries about the percentage of reduction or the dates for termination of atmospheric emissions that harm the ozone layer might be an example. However, this might be seen as a conflict about absolutely assessed goods (amount of licensed pollution) or even means (towards the shared end of 'closing the ozone hole') rather than one about values, since the developing countries do not deny the necessity of global emission reductions altogether.

having a healthy environment does not depend on whether a neighbouring state, or any other state, has a healthy environment. In other words a healthy environment is not a relatively assessed good. Economic opportunities in international markets, however, are such goods, and to the extent that environmental protection measures would differentially affect these economic opportunities for different countries, an element of conflict about this relatively assessed good may enter the area of international environmental policy-making. In fact, this is quite common, as in, to give just one example, the case of the EC internal quarrels about emission standards for vehicle exhaust fumes. The difficulties which producers of small cars foresaw with strict standards led France, one of the major producers in this category, to oppose such standards. Similar conflicts have recently arisen between Sweden and Finland within the issue area of marine environmental protection in the Baltic on the matter of emission standards for the paper and pulp industry.[13] Our conflict typological hypothesis suggests that wherever this type of conflict prevails among the actors in a given issue area, regime formation is very difficult to achieve, although it can still be achieved if other, more regime-conducive factors impinge on the situation.

Contrary to the classical assumptions of 'Realists', as well as to their latest formalized presentations, we do not think that 'states are obsessed with concern for relative gains' in international environmental matters.[14] Let us be more specific about when and why states do care for relative gains, and when and why they do not. As already noted, states do not tend to regard a healthy environment as such as a relatively assessed good. However, they are more inclined to do so, firstly, where they see parts of the environment in terms of resources, for example when the matter is not biodiversity as such but the exploitation of a concrete fish-stock. But we are then in the policy area of international economy

---

[13] Sweden felt it could cope technologically with strict emission standards which Finland regarded as too strict for her industry. Public clashes ensued between the two neighbours, due, in part, to electoral campaigning considerations of the ruling Swedish Social Democrats who tried to improve their standing on (international) environmental matters. See List, 'Cleaning up the Baltic'.

[14] For the latter see the thought-provoking article by Joseph Grieco, 'Anarchy and the Limits of Cooperation: A Realist Critique of the Newest Liberal Institutionalism', *International Organization*, 42 (1988), 485–507.

rather than in that of environmental protection. Secondly, the costs of environmental policies may be seen in relative terms, both as immediate costs of implementation (for example, installing catalytic cleaners in stacks) and as opportunity costs (for example, market shares lost due to higher prices for environmentally sound end-products). However, concern for these relative gains and losses must not be over-emphasized. For one thing, environmental expenditures hardly reach 'strategically important amounts' and, as has been shown formally by Duncan Snidal, relative gains become less important as the number of actors involved increases.[15] Amongst other factors, this is because there is not one strategic opponent to whom one loses out in multi-member issue areas (as many environmental issue areas are). Thus, while anticipated gains and losses following from proposed environmental policies may be debated and contested, they tend to be 'absolutely assessed' in our terminology, since their value to each actor is not affected by the amount others win or lose. Finally, both ways in which the concern about relative gains enters the policy area of environmental protection originate in the intersection of this policy area with that of international economic policy, an indication that the two are intimately linked and should be dealt with accordingly—both in analysis and in practice.

(iii) *Conflicts about absolutely assessed goods.* Such conflicts can be identified wherever countries hold incompatible positions about the way in which a common environmental resource is to be used. Downstream pollution may serve as an example. While an upstream user may want to utilize the waterflow as an inexpensive way to get rid of its wastes, the downstream user may want to take its drinking water from the same source. For both sides, using the waterflow is an absolutely assessed good. Since using the waterflow in these ways simultaneously tends to be incompatible, conflict ensues. A similar situation prevailed in regional air pollution matters in the 1960s and 1970s when several European countries tried to solve local problems by a high-stack policy that eventually affected other countries. This was the

---

[15] Duncan Snidal, 'International Cooperation among Relative Gain Maximizers', *International Studies Quarterly*, 35 (1991), 387–402. This paper meets the realist challenge posed by Grieco on the same level of formalization and thus constitutes an adequate, if not definitive answer to his argument.

beginning of the issue area of Long-Range Transboundary Air Pollution.[16]

However, this example again demonstrates that the pure case of a conflict about an absolutely assessed good is not to be expected frequently. For, by following their high-stack policy, the countries in question could also save avoidance costs and thus reap a 'windfall' profit compared to those countries which tried to reduce their emissions and in the end had to recover the costs through higher prices of their products. A conflict at the transnational inter-company level and indirectly at the international level about relatively assessed competitive advantages in the market thus lurks in the background. Moreover, both examples show that the relative ease with which regime formation should occur in cases of a conflict about absolutely assessed goods, according to the conflict-typological hypothesis, may be more than outweighed by the asymmetry implicit in the fact that, in both cases, it is one side which affects the environment of the other and not vice versa.[17] One might in these cases be tempted to speak of ecological dependence rather than of interdependence, something which does not come across in the conflict typology alone, but is caught by the situation-structural approach described below.

(iv) *Conflicts about means towards an agreed end.* Such conflicts may arise, provided the necessary threshold of a common goal shared by all participants exists. The case of international cooperation to counteract Baltic marine pollution would seem to come quite close to this description, since the ecological interdependence among the coastal states is high and all of them are considerably affected by the deterioration of the state of the marine environment in that sea area. But again, as the above-mentioned example of the Swedish–Finnish quarrel about industrial emission standards would suggest, pure conflicts about means are also rare. Nevertheless, the conflict-typological hypothesis that conflicts about means lend themselves rather well to collective management by regimes seems to be confirmed.

There is, however, another problem with the conflict typology we have presented. For reasons of parsimony in the explanation

[16] See Schwarzer, 'Weiträumige grenzüberschreitende Luftverschmutzung'.
[17] This asymmetry is taken into account by the game-theoretic modelling of the structure of the situation; see below.

of regime formation, we have restricted ourselves to what may be called an 'objectivistic' approach, i.e. we have tried to assign conflict objects to the various categories of the typology analytically, independent of the perception of the actors. In real life, however, subjective factors such as the perception of actors clearly intervene. This is so, naturally, in the case of conflicts about values, since valuing is, in the end, a subjective state of mind. Perception is, however, also relevant for the distinction between relatively and absolutely assessed goods. In practice, not only may actors change from one way of assessing a good to another, several actors may also assess the same good in different ways. Finally, concerning conflicts about means, the interesting question is: What makes actors agree on a shared goal? Again, perception is involved, and getting the actors to share a common definition of the situation, for example, to accept that in a concrete case political action is required to protect the environment, is certainly one of the crucial steps in international environmental policy.[18] These are undoubtedly interesting questions of practical relevance, but it is also clear that a different, more 'subjectivistic' approach would be needed to get closer to the answers, for example along the lines of psychological and behavioural analysis of negotiations.[19]

The typology of conflicts just presented is but one way to design what we call a problem-structural approach to the analysis of regime formation. The level of application for the conflict typology is the concrete issue area or even the single object of contention (several of which may make up an issue area). Alternative approaches would try to construct typologies at a higher level of abstraction. An early example for such a highly abstract approach is Rosenau's attempt to give a formal characterization of interdependence issues as such. In his view, they have the following features in common. They concern highly complicated, often technical matters; non-state actors are involved; national decision-making on these issues is 'fragmented'; and dealing

---

[18] Convincing the British that North Sea protection may require the end of dumping, one of the bones of contention in that issue area, would be a case in point.

[19] For a recent overview of the still limited results of this kind of research see Arild Underdal, 'Designing Politically Feasible Solutions', Paper prepared for the ESF Programme on Environment, Science and Society, Task Force VI meeting at Seville, 22–3 Feb. 1991, MS, Oslo, 1991.

with these issues is a long-term task.[20] There is nothing wrong with this formal characterization, and it seems highly appropriate for international environmental issues. But it is too general to explain differing results concerning regime formation on different issues within the field of international environmental protection. The same is true for all kinds of substantive policy area typologies. To the extent that they determine their types by substantive criteria, ending up with a typology that includes, for example, the category 'international environmental policy', they can, by their very nature, only serve to explain the differences in the outcome between various policy areas, not within the same policy area.

This then is an advantage of the conflict typology presented above. It is applicable across all issue areas and across all policy areas. On the other hand, we have already seen that even this typology alone does not provide an exhaustive explanation of regime formation. Other factors must be taken into consideration. This may lead either to a mixed typology or, to be more precise, to a classification reflecting differing classes of international environmental issues, or to complementing a clear typology, like our conflict typology, by other explanatory factors, which is what we did in our project.[21]

What has been said so far about the explanation of international environmental regime formation may be summarized as follows. There are several ways to slice the empirical cake with the problem-structural knife. None of them seems superior, *a priori*, but their usefulness depends on the explanatory question one wants to answer (for example, differences of regime formation in the policy area of environmental protection as compared with

[20] See James N. Rosenau, 'Capabilities and Control in an Interdependent World', in James N. Rosenau, *The Study of Global Interdependence. Essays on the Transnationalization of World Affairs* (London: Frances Pinter, 1980), 41 ff.

[21] An example for such a classification can be found in a recent introductory text on international environmental policy by Harald Müller ('Internationale Ressourcen- und Umweltproblematik', in Manfred Knapp and Gert Krell (eds.), *Einführung in die Internationale Politik*₆(Munich and Vienna, 1990), 350–82). He distinguishes between conflicts about divisible goods, conflicts resulting from different levels of the quality of life or quality of the environment, conflicts about transborder pollution, about public goods, and finally about exports of 'ecological damage' (which includes export of wastes and negative ecological impacts of foreign investment). As should be apparent, this is rather a taxonomy of potential environmental issues than a typology based on a uniform criterion, and the categories are not mutually exclusive.

other international policy areas, or differences among various issue areas within the policy area of international environmental protection) and ultimately must prove itself in the analysis of concrete cases. The presumption is, however, that no problem-structural approach will alone be sufficient for the task.

2. *The situation-structural approach*

Whenever the actions or consequences of actions of various actors interfere with each other, a collective situation may be said to exist. The situation-structural approach tries to model the con-stellation of interests pursued by the actors in that situation in game-theoretic terms. If sucessful, this allows the analyst to make predictions about the likely behaviour of rational-egoistic actors in that situation and in this sense to explain it. Out of the theoreti-cally large number of possible two-person/actor games known by game theory, three types of situations have been identified for their different impact on the possibility and likelihood of regulated conflict management. The three types may be called Rambo games, dilemma games, and co-ordination games.

(i) *Rambo games.*   These are characterized by the fact that non-co-operative behaviour is the preferred option for at least one actor irrespective of what the other actor does. The above men-tioned examples of downstream or 'downwind' pollution are cases in point. While regulation of the underlying behaviour may seem very urgent to the 'victim', it is, *ceteris paribus*, unlikely to emerge, since the downstream or downwind polluter has no immediate interest in changing his course of action.

(ii) *Dilemma games.*   In these games, the most prominent example of which is the Prisoner's Dilemma, a rational-egoistic actor has an incentive to defect, even if mutual co-operation is the collectively optimal outcome, and since this holds for all actors involved, the sub-optimal outcome of mutual non-co-operation is the stable outcome. Since repeated playing of this kind of game ('shadow of the future') and mutual trust are factors that help overcome this stalemate, regime formation may prove to be a way out by increasing the opportunities for future co-operation and for trust to develop, especially if further supportive conditions exist. In international environmental policy, however, the dilemma-creating incentive to defect may well not so much impede the setting of international standards as such, but the compliance with accepted standards which is often technically difficult to monitor, especially if the data for the assessment are ultimately provided by the states themselves. Since only a reasonable degree of compliance (effectiveness of rules) would justify talking about a regime according to our strict definition of the term, this is a theoretically as well as practically important point.

(iii) *Co-ordination games.* These are games in which none of the behavioural options is, as such, preferable to one of the actors but harmonization is necessary. The classical example is road traffic, where neither driving on the left side nor driving on the right side is *per se* preferable while, at the same time, it is in the individual interest of each actor that the same side is taken by everyone.

To illustrate how these types of games may be relevant to the analysis of how international environmental conflicts are collectively managed, let us examine the different situation structures in the cases of Baltic and North Sea pollution control. In both cases a collectively sub-optimal outcome—the degradation of the marine environment—has for a long time been stable. In that sense, both cases show the features of a dilemma game, since there is a rational-egoistic interest for private (or even state) actors to defect from rules that have been jointly agreed. In the Baltic, however, at least concerning the state actors, this dilemma is reduced and the situation brought closer to a co-ordination game by the fact that damages resulting from defection—for example, discharge of wastewater effluents that do not correspond to agreed standards—will also affect the coastal waters of the defecting party. In the case of the North Sea, by contrast, Britain is in the 'lucky position' that the prevailing water currents will carry noxious substances away from her coasts, which puts her in a kind of Rambo position *vis-à-vis* the other North Sea states. The results of the most recent International North Sea Conference with the special conditions granted to the UK are quite in line with this situation-structural analysis.[22]

The advantage of this game-theoretic approach is to provide a non-substantive typology of situations which is applicable to various issue areas, and to allow rational-actor explanations of the corresponding outcomes. Its problems lie not so much in the

[22] See List, *Umweltschutz in zwei Meeren*.

fact that real issue areas may contain elements of a dilemma *and* a co-ordination game or a dilemma *and* a Rambo game (as was shown in the examples just referred to), but in the following three points.

1. Since manageable theoretical solutions exist only for two-person/actor games, a strictly game-theoretic analysis makes it necessary to 'condense' the number of actors to two, a simplification which will not always be possible without leaving out important nuances.

2. The assumption of the rational actor is just that, namely that each party is conceived of as one unitary actor. However, this is particularly problematic in policy areas where, as in environmental matters, actors are often internally split (remember Rosenau's 'fragmented decision-making') due to diverging interests at the societal level as well as at the governmental level. The views which an Environmental Protection Agency, on the one hand, and a Ministry of Economics, on the other, are likely to hold will usually differ greatly as far as the requirements and the feasibility of alternative courses of environmental policy are concerned.

3. Finally, a lot of high-quality information about the internal background of the 'rational actors' must be condensed into the bare numbers of preference orderings. This information is difficult to come by in the first place, and it is no longer visible once it has been transformed into the numbers of preference orderings.

One way to attack the problem of how to establish the preference orderings is through a characterization of the *individual situation* of the actors on the basis of objective criteria. Using the three criteria 'extent of damage caused to oneself', 'extent of damage caused to others', and 'extent of damage caused by others', which may be either 'high' or 'low', the following eight individual situations may be derived (Table 1).

As a little reflection shows, participation in international regulation, i.e. in the formation of international regimes, would seem unnecessary to actors who are in situations 1 and 5. This is trivially true in case 1, in which there is no ecological problem, hence no need for environmental action. Situation 5 is the case of ecological self-exploitation without harm to other states. While internal opposition may be formed against this course by environmentalists, it is not (yet) an international problem due to the

TABLE 1. Eight Individual Environmental Situations

Damage done to oneself	Damage by others	Damage done to others	
		low	high
low	low	(1) No damage caused (ecologically ideal)	(2) Damage done only to others (pure externalization)
	high	(3) Victim	(4) Mutual damage
high	low	(5) Only self-caused damage ('hara-kiri')	(6) Self-caused damage and damage done to others ('kamikaze')
	high	(7) Self-caused damage and victim	(8) Mutual and self-caused damage

absence of damage to other states. Over time, however, the situation is likely to change to that of situation 6, with others being affected by the high degree of pollution as well. In fact, this is very much what has happened in the industrialized (and industrializing) world during the last century or so.

Participation in regime formation is unlikely for actors in situation 2, at least *ceteris paribus*, i.e. unless linkage with other issue areas or other factors occurs. This is so because the pure externalizer has no incentive to shoulder the burden of abating pollution which does not negatively affect himself. Participation in regime formation is likely for actors who are in situations 3 and 7. The victims of pollution would be happy if a regime would help improve their lot. However, given the complementary yet opposed interests of 'environmental perpetrators', regime formation will not come about easily (this was the situation of the Scandinavian countries in the issue area of long-range transboundary air pollution in Europe). States who are in situation 6 may want to join a regime because pollution abatement is in their own interest. They might therefore be willing to go ahead anyway, but may reap the additional benefit of 'good inter-

national reputation in compliance' if they carry out their environmental policy within the framework of an international regime.
Finally, participation in regime formation is likely for states in
situations 4 and 8. The existence of mutual damage implies the
existence of concurring complementary interests, that is, there is
room for reciprocity in the collective situation. Situations like
these are most likely to lead to success in regime formation.

The advantage of this approach lies in the fact that the necessary information about the ecological situation is based on objective facts which may be available (even if they are usually somewhat uncertain). Its problems are twofold. In the first place, there
may well be a gap between the objective ecological situation and
its perception by governmental authorities, a gap which will
clearly influence the foreign environmental policy course taken
by that government. Second, no government can act on the basis
of ecological concerns alone, which once more emphasizes the
importance of the domestic context for international environmental policy-making and thus for regime formation. While this
renders analysis of international regime formation more difficult, it is also an important practical point, since it shows that
there is room for 'sub-systemic' pressure by environmental public interest groups to push for stricter regime norms and rules (i.e.
regime evolution) and for improved compliance with them. The
often-emphasized inclusion of this kind of information in explanations of regime formation is thus particularly necessary in the
case of environmental regimes.[23] At the same time it may be very
demanding, too, due to the fact that environmental policy is
intertwined with many other issue areas of domestic policy.
International co-operation among analysts may be necessary to
cope with the resulting problems of information gathering.

3. Other factors explaining regime formation

Three further factors or groups of factors contributing to the explanation of regime formation may be briefly discussed here.

(i) *Normative-institutional factors.* The supportive effect of
existing international organizations or norms and rules on the

---

[23] This demand is echoed, for example, in the state-of-the-art report by Stephan
Haggard and Beth A. Simmons, 'Theories of International Regimes', *International
Organization*, 41 (1987), 491–517.

formation of international environmental regimes may carry some explanatory weight. The role played by UNEP in organizing regimes for the protection of the marine environment in several regions is a case in point. The transfer of regulatory models or of ready-made packages of norms and rules, as happened between the world-wide MARPOL agreement and the regional Helsinki Convention underlying the Baltic marine environment regime, is another example. Important as these effects may be, they must be considered supportive conditions rather than as prime causes of regime formation.

(ii) *Epistemic communities.* A similar conclusion can be reached regarding a second factor, namely the existence of shared knowledge, or, in a more sociological vein, of 'epistemic communities' that serve to establish this common knowledge and to spread it in decision-making circles. John G. Ruggie referred to the importance of shared knowledge as a basis for regime formation in one of the earliest contributions to regime analysis.[24] More recently Peter M. Haas has emphasized the role played by the epistemic community of marine scientists and administrators in the formation of the Mediterranean pollution control regime.[25]

Given their technical nature, it is clear that tackling environmental problems will always require a considerable input of (scientific) knowledge. The identification of an ecological problem presupposes such consensual knowledge. In its absence, there may not be a uniform definition of the situation by all actors and some may therefore doubt the very necessity to take political action. Shared knowledge is therefore a necessary condition of regime formation, and transnational scientific contacts may help bring this about. This, arguably, is what has happened in the case of the Mediterranean, and in the case of counteracting ozone-layer depletion.[26] Morever, 'ecological learning' is not only a pre-

---

[24] See John G. Ruggie, 'International Responses to Technology: Concepts and Trends', *International Organization*, 29 (1975), 557–83.

[25] Peter M. Haas, 'Do Regimes Matter? Epistemic Communities and Mediterranean Pollution Control', *International Organization*, 43 (1989), 377–403; and his *Saving the Mediterranean: The Politics of International Environmental Cooperation* (New York: Columbia UP, 1990).

[26] For an analysis of the process of international agenda-setting in the latter case see Breitmeier, 'Der Schutz der Erdatmosphäre'.

condition of environmental regime formation.[27] It also counts among its consequences as well, since improved scientific data collection is usually one of the points most easily agreed to by participating actors.[28]

However, useful as the establishment of an international epistemic community may be (especially if it is accompanied by international scientific development aid, as was the case in the Mediterranean regime formation) it is not a sufficient cause for regime formation, and scientific 'politicking' (a battle of experts as substitute for environmental policy action) may even be used to delay regime creation.

(iii) *Systemic factors.* These include features of the international system in general or of the aggregate group of potential regime participants. Two in particular require consideration: the power structure and the density of transactions.

The *power structure* has so far not played a major role in the explanation of international environmental regime formation. The reasons are twofold. First, military power, quite in line with the basic ideas of interdependence theory, is of little avail ('dysfunctional') in the policy area of environmental protection. Economic power is more ambivalent. The closure of large markets to products which do not meet a prescribed environmental standard may exert pressure to adopt this standard internationally. However, as the diverging US and European standards concerning automobile exhaust fumes would suggest, a dual standard approach may be a more likely reaction of both industry and the governments concerned. Furthermore, economic considerations often cause countries not to go along with proposed international standards. To the extent that these countries are among the major polluters, they gain a *de facto* veto power against successful international environmental policy-making. The contribution even of economic power (short of the co-financing of foreign environmental investments, something that so far has been more

[27] By using this term, deliberate allusion is made to the term 'nuclear learning' used by Joseph Nye in dealing with cognitive pre-conditions of the formation of security regimes. See Joseph S. Nye, 'Nuclear Learning and U.S.–Soviet Security Regimes', *International Organization*, 41 (1987), 371–402.

[28] The proliferation of international scientific and technological committees and working groups as part of the procedural side of environmental regimes is an indicator of this phenomenon. The output of these bodies has aptly been referred to as 'negotiated science', since most often participants are not only scientists but national civil servants as well.

discussed than practised) to international environmental regime formation is therefore limited. Second, power resources specific to the issue area in the field of international environmental policy are practically absent, if one disregards cases of ecological dependence—recall the case of downstream pollution (although this explains non-formation of regimes rather than formation).

The *density of transactions* among the actors concerned is a second systemic factor which impinges on regime formation in two different ways. First, it may improve the prospects for regime formation either through the trust-building effect of co-operation in other issue areas or through the possibility of establishing linkages. Second, if transactions imply traffic and traffic implies pollution, the former may literally contribute to regime demand by creating ecological problems. Sea traffic in the Baltic would be an example, as would road traffic across the European Alpine states.

4. *Summary*

What follows from the above discussion of environmental regime formation? First, among the problem-structural approaches, our conflict typology distinguishes itself both by its consistency and by its applicability across all issue areas. But even if the identification of conflict types in concrete cases was more easy than it actually is, this typology alone would not suffice to explain regime formation—nor would any other purely problem-structural approach.

Second, the situation-structural analysis is promising in principle but difficult in practice. Directing attention to the 'structure of the situation' is useful, since this gives a formal, non-substantive description of collective situations and thus increases comparability across various issue areas. It also identifies the transformation of the situation, or the making of linkages, as necessary pre-conditions for regime formation. And it raises the question about the relation between problem-structural and situation-structural explanations, especially which of them prevails if they diverge. On the other hand, game-theoretic modelling relies on restrictive assumptions which, among other things, give too little weight to the analysis of the domestic politics of international environmental policy. While it is relatively easy to come up with a list of factors which may determine national foreign environmental policy choices, it is difficult to check them cross-nationally either because they are idiosyncratic in nature (such as geographical site) or because information is not readily available. The latter problem might be tackled through international co-operation among analysts.

Third, supportive or impeding conditions of regime formation for the management of the international environment can be found among normative-institutional factors, in the form of epistemic communities, and among the systemic factors of power structure and density of transaction.

Finally, subjective factors such as negotiating skills and 'perception management' are certainly among the practically important factors, since they lend themselves to artful manipulation. Precisely for this reason, however, political science research finds it difficult to deal with them systematically.

C. The Consequences of International Environmental Regimes

Among the consequences of a regime, one may distinguish those within the issue area and those reaching beyond it. Within the issue area the most interesting consequence of international environmental regimes is precisely the extent to which the intended goal is attained, i.e. the conservation and protection of the ecological systems concerned. Giving an answer to the corresponding policy analysis question, 'Do international environmental regimes matter ecologically?', may seem a simple task, but in fact it is not, even if one narrows the question to the success of a concrete regime and postpones a comparative answer about regimes in general. The example of the Baltic marine environment protection regime may serve to show why this is so.

Many people, including coast-dwellers, TV-watchers, environmental activists, and even some of the experts (these groups are not meant to be mutually exclusive), might say: 'This regime has not succeeded because the marine environment of the Baltic Sea has not improved.' They point to algae blooms and other symptoms of ecological stress, and in this sense they are right. Others would mention partial improvements such as reduced levels of

DDT and PCB measured in the Baltic area, and they are right, too. This shows two things. First, any such assesssment is based on information plus evaluation. The former would ideally be of a scientific type and is hard (and time-consuming) to come by. Since even at this stage evaluative judgements must be made, consensus is unlikely to emerge.[29] Second, the very process of assessment and the ensuing process of national governmental and intergovernmental opinion formation is demonstrably part of international environmental policy and politics.

To the extent that the activities under the regime contribute to the production of the cognitive input into this process—which is the case for the Baltic Sea regime—they already have consequences, irrespective of their positive ecological impact. The 'objective' assessment of the latter is very much an interdisciplinary task, and the study of international regimes, especially in the field of environmental protection, depends here entirely on the comparison of assessments made by others and cannot itself contribute to them.

Making assessments of the assessment mechanism, on the other hand, would seem to lie more within the range of social scientific policy analysis. A comparative analysis of verification and monitoring procedures of existing regimes might be a feasible task.[30] This could in turn lead to both theoretically interesting propositions about the conditions for procedurally effective regimes and practically important information. However, all (or most) of this is still work to be done.

Given this situation, it is nevertheless worth emphasizing that the production of knowledge otherwise not available seems to be one of the major positive consequences of international environmental regimes so far.[31] In addition, as the Baltic Sea regime also shows, further measures of potentially beneficial impact on the environment have been taken by international consent. Recep-

[29] In fact, in a recent Assessment of the State of the Marine Environment of the Baltic Sea (published as No. 35 in the Baltic Sea Environment Proceedings series, Helsinki, 1990), the summary of findings is mixed: improvement in details is accompanied by a deterioration in the overall state of the marine environment.

[30] A first step towards such a meta-assessment which, however, remains on the level of textual analysis of international treaties, has been made by Wolfgang Fischer, Die Verifikation internationaler Abkommen über Umwelt- und Ressourcenschutz (Jülich: Forschungszentrum Jülich, 1990).

[31] The functioning of the monitoring programmeme (EMEP) in the context of the European air pollution regime is another case in point.

tion facilities for oily wastes have been installed in harbours; safety of sea traffic has been improved; and target values for emission reductions from land-based sources have been agreed upon. The latter, in particular, holds also for the case of transboundary air pollution under the regime of the 1979 Geneva Convention and its additional protocols. All this points to the limits of what can be expected in a world of formally independent states ('sovereign polluters') which are reluctantly driven to co-operate by the dictates of ecological interdependence. More should probably not be expected as long as ecological concerns are not attributed a higher salience by larger parts of more national populations, including the ruling élites.

If we finally consider the consequences of environmental regimes *beyond the issue area*, one of the most interesting consequences concerns the demonstration effect of regimes upon the management of similar environmental problems. Although still largely limited to the regional level, a process of learning from regulative models can indeed be identified and is promoted by contacts between the relevant international bodies (for example, between the Helsinki Commission active within the Baltic Sea regime and UNEP).

More far-reaching and, admittedly, more speculative is the long-term effect that proliferation of regional and even global environmental regimes might have on the nature of the international system. Can we observe the beginning of, to borrow a metaphor from chemistry, a change in the aggregate state of the international system, leaving its components—the individual states as centres of authority over national territories and populations—intact and yet improving the management of relations between this highly complex social system and the ecological systems with which it is so intensively and precariously intertwined? One may hope that this is so, but much will depend upon changes at lower levels. Ecological policy, like charity, begins at home, but, unlike the latter, stopping there is often immediately self-defeating.

Taking a broader view, the spread of international environmental regimes, slow and intermittent as it may be, is part of a broader process of change in international relations. States are switching from the predominant reliance on self-help strategies to the management of interdependence through increased mutual and self-control. While less than world government, the political problems of ecological interdependence (together with economic and security interdependence) are leading to the introduction of novel elements of *governance* into the international system. Only by virtue of this governance, i.e. through the acceptance of non-discriminatory norms and rules that limit their autonomy, can states persist and their populations survive and flourish. Neither international ('world') government nor international anarchy are the poles towards which the collective management of international environmental problems and conflicts will direct itself. Rather, it is a changing mix of unregulated and regulated conflict management which, eventually, will give rise to 'regulated anarchy' and establish co-operation and conflict management on a case-by-case (or issue-by-issue) basis.

We have seen hopeful beginnings of this process at the regional level. Unfortunately, however, the negative impact of human activities is no longer only a regional problem but in some cases has reached a global scale. Global environmental regimes will probably be even more difficult to form, if only for the sheer technical difficulty of negotiating with more than 170 participants. What is more, these 170 or more states form a heterogeneous group, particularly in terms of economic development. North–South issues are thus going to arise frequently in global environmental policy, and will render it more complicated than regional intra-OECD or even intra-'Northern' issues. However, judging from the experience of regional environmental protection regimes, compromises between North and South are possible. Regime theory is one effort which seeks to help explain why and how environmental compromises and institution-building may come about, or are even likely to happen.

4

Non-Governmental Organizations and the Legal Protection of the Oceans: A Case Study

Kevin Stairs and Peter Taylor

IN this chapter we address the topic of NGO lobbying and international law-making, primarily through a study of the case of waste disposal at sea. We shall tackle this by looking at:

- what is broadly encompassed by the term NGO, and in what ways NGOs are involved in the international Conventions dealing with ocean disposal of wastes;
- why there is a need for NGO participation in international law making;
- examples of how NGOs and particularly Greenpeace have lobbied and/or participated in the processes of such Conventions;
- the increasing acceptance and recognition of the role of NGOs, in particular with reference to the growing shift to a 'precautionary approach' with emphasis on clean production technologies which obviate the need for dumping of wastes.

We shall first need to review the current status of international law relating to ocean dumping, and we shall conclude with a view on whether the marine environment can be adequately protected by international conventions.

NGOs represent a diverse spectrum of interests, and in the case of marine issues, the interests cover a wide variety of ocean uses and activities. Some organizations have memberships of several hundred thousands in various countries and millions worldwide: others simply include a few corporate bodies in an association which represents their interests. The latter, for example, may be concerned with the development of ports and harbours, with offshore oil and gas exploitation, with exploitation of commercial (or recreational) fisheries, with estuarian research, with deep-sea submersibles, with shipwrecks, and so on. More often than not, however, the term NGO, as it pertains to ocean activities, is used to refer to environmental and other citizen organizations who are voicing and advancing concerns that deal with protection, conservation, and/or wise use of the oceans. In this latter group, Greenpeace has been particularly active, and in some cases is the only environmental group actively participating in the development of policy. Both the authors of this paper have extensive experience as representatives of Greenpeace on science and policy issues at international conventions.

Broadly defined, lobbying encompasses education, information dissemination, research, and advocacy which is used to influence decision-makers—including not only members of parliaments but also agency officials, international delegation members, and industry representatives. That is a very broad definition, but our experience suggests that in Western Europe and in working with officials of international agencies more generally, lobbying is not restricted to legislators or members of parliament.

A. The Need for NGO Participation in International Law-Making

The task of drawing up and ratifying international treaties falls, of course, to sovereign states, acting through structured intergovernmental meetings often described as 'conventions', or through general or specialized international organizations such as the United Nations or the International Maritime Organization. NGOs, and, indeed, various other intergovernmental organizations not directly concerned with marine pollution or dumping of wastes, are consulted in the process. In theory, the sovereign states are gathering views from interested parties and then acting to balance those interests for the common good.

In practice, of course, governments have proven unreliable in representing what we might call 'environmental' goods, when faced with short-term economic costs, such as potential restrictions on industrial activities, or added costs to those activities in order to safeguard the environment. Thus, environmental groups have had to develop efficient lobbying tactics in order to pressure governments toward environmentally sound policies, and indeed, as we shall see, NGOs have further had to play a research and educational role as crucial areas of science and information exchange and accessibility have been conveniently neglected by governments when it has been obvious that such information would cause public concern.

The current impetus of NGO involvement on marine issues is doubtless due to the mounting evidence of severe environmental degradation. On the level of public perception, the seas are 'at risk', some even regarded as 'near death'. Much of this perceived state is due to the degraded waters of the North Sea, where there have been several highly publicized issues: the deaths of seals from virus disease; the disappearance of cetaceans such as dolphins; widespread increases in fish diseases; catastrophic plankton blooms; and drastic cuts in fisheries quotas.

The waters of the North Sea are bounded by industrialized states which have aware, literate populations, free and active press and media, independent universities, highly developed environmental organizations with their own research and media capabilities, and, of course, populations where living standards are such that people can afford to care about the 'quality' of the environment. We shall see that this arguably 'ethnocentric', northern-industrial viewpoint has important implications in the debate on 'global' standards and regulations.

It should be clear from the recent history of largely unpredicted decline in environmental quality, that past intergovernmental controls have been ineffective. Environmental groups have been warning of such consequences since the early 1970s when many of the key international conventions were formulated. At that time, a philosophy of 'dilute and disperse' was being pursued within a scientific paradigm of predictive modelling and an economic ethic of 'acceptable' damage or trade-off in relation to largely material benefits. It was always assumed that any 'mistakes' would be remedied, first by monitoring, then by establishing the cause, and finally by turning off the offending 'tap'. Concerns voiced by environmental groups were regarded as 'fringe' and their representatives as 'doomsters'.

The 1980s saw radical changes in the standing of protagonists in these debates. As the environmental chickens came home to roost, not only have the populace turned away from the perceived industrial-scientific conspiracy, but governments too have distanced themselves from the industrial interests and sought a middle road. In this new political environment, the former pressure groups have found themselves increasingly requested not only to take part in the formation of policy, but also to help with scientific research, analysis, and data collection. By the close of the 1980s, environmental groups such as Greenpeace (and their land-oriented equivalents such as Friends of the Earth, World Wildlife Fund, The Sierra Club, etc.), had grown into million-dollar, sophisticated multinational operations capable of research, political lobbying, effective media communication, and, in the case of Greenpeace, active policing on behalf of the environment.

In summary, it had ceased to be possible to dismiss environmental lobbying as the voice of purists who believe that nothing should be put into the oceans and that industrial society should be shut down or phased out—although, naturally, many politicians have tried to resuscitate the image in attempts to pre-empt a rational argument that they were rapidly losing. It is still the case, however, that environmental groups are seen as representing anti-industrial or economic interests, as if there were an inevitable conflict between the two. Partly for this reason, industrial lobby groups have also sought and won representation in the bodies responsible for policy and law formulation in relation to ocean protection. For example, at the London Convention (on protection of the oceans against pollution from dumping of wastes from ships), not only are the port and harbour associations represented (dredgers), but also the chemical manufacturers and an association of oil companies.

We shall argue that the 1990s will demonstrate that NGOs have further important roles to play in positively influencing developments in ways constructive to economies and industry generally; that NGOs may be better suited to finding innovative ways forward in this regard.

In the following section we shall examine the institutional, legal, and political realities of international regulation of maritime waste disposal, with particular reference to the contributions and limitations of NGO input.

B. Current Status of International Law Relating to Ocean Disposal of Wastes

We must first make a distinction between two sources of maritime waste disposal: land-based (discharges from pipelines and diffuse sources such as river input, and atmospheric deposition); and dumping from ships or marine platforms. There are no global conventions relating to the former, other than a set of international guidelines (Montreal Guidelines, 1985), and regulation is based upon regional conventions. In fact, land-based sources account for 90 per cent of anthropogenic inputs to the marine environment.

There is a global treaty relating to ocean dumping known as the London Dumping Convention (LDC). We shall use examples from this one global convention to illustrate general points of NGO participation, and briefly review other conventions. Greenpeace has been active in all regional as well as global conventions.

The traditional categories of substances subject to ocean dumping regulations include: industrial wastes; radioactive wastes (which are actually also industrial wastes); sewage sludge; dredge material; inert material (rubble, quarry wastes, fly ash, etc.). The dumping of all these substances poses threats to the marine environment and human health.

At the global level of regulation there is the London Dumping Convention. Other bodies regulating dumping at the regional level also exist, including, for example, the Oslo Convention for the North Sea and North-East Atlantic, and the Helsinki Convention for the Baltic. In addition to these 'legal' entities, the North Sea Conference of Ministers also sets general policy directions and carries out major reviews which influence the Conventions.

Although Greenpeace and other NGOs have been active in lobbying in all the regional conventions, it is only in the LDC that they have had 'observer' status for any length of time (active participation since the beginning of the 1980s), and this status has only recently been granted to Greenpeace at meetings of the regional Oslo, Paris, and Helsinki conventions.

As a consequence of this long-standing involvement, and as a result of fighting the highly political issue of radioactive waste dumping in the early 1980s, Greenpeace has gained some knowledge of the internal dynamic of the Contracting Parties to this convention.

Although Greenpeace has observer status with UNEP (through Greenpeace observer status with the UN Economic and Social Council, ECOSOC), and UNEP has an important role as the parent body of many other regional conventions, access to subsidiary committees and working groups, where in many cases most decisions are made, is in practice sporadic and conferred on an *ad hoc* basis.

1. *The structure of the Conventions*

To some extent, all the Conventions in this area are similarly structured, whether global or regional in scope. The Convention has a treaty document (with or without protocols) which has been ratified by Contracting Parties. The articles of the Convention define the activities to be controlled as well as the area, and Annexes list substances or wastes which must be regulated or prohibited. An annual Consultative Meeting allows all Contracting Parties to consider each other's activities as reported to the Convention.

In the case of the LDC, for example, the contracting parties retain national sovereignty in that they have their own licensing or permit procedures, but these follow guidelines with regard to monitoring and environmental impact assessment. The annual dumping programmes are communicated to the LDC together with the results of the monitoring or other analyses. There are certain general prohibitions—for example, blacklisted substances such as the heavy metals cadmium and mercury, halogenated hydrocarbons, oil, and high-level radioactive wastes. There are further substances which can be dumped but which require special care, such as low-level radioactive waste and certain other metals such as lead, and there are also exceptions to the blacklist when such substances exist in 'trace' quantities only.

Thus, it is left to the contracting parties to interpret the convention, to harmonize their national legislation, and to report their activities. The Convention lacks adequate enforcement mechanisms in that (*a*) there is no procedure for censure or penalty, (*b*) there is no surveillance or policing of the activities of member states, and (*c*) although provision for setting up a liability regime exists, none so far has been promulgated. Indeed, it has been our experience that there is a marked reluctance at the diplomatic level to make any judgement that would involve the naming of an offending state, even where that offence might be deeply felt. Only in the nuclear dumping controversy were these 'diplomatic' conventions within the Convention broken down.

Of course, political pressure within a state may make it unlikely a party would be able to flout the Convention, and this might even be expressed in provisions of national law requiring adherence to the Convention. However, in relation to any resolution passed, even with the required two-thirds majority of states, there is always the key let-out clause which is that no resolution is binding on a non-concurring party! When the majority of parties voted in 1983 to suspend the dumping of low-level radioactive waste (another departure from the diplomatic convention, where consensus is preferred to a majority vote), the UK government declared it was not bound by the decision—in the event a trade union boycott, citing the defence of the Convention, prevented the government carrying out the operation.

In some of the regional conventions, such as the Oslo Convention (dealing with the North-East Atlantic), there has evolved a Prior Notification Procedure whereby potential dumpers must inform their neighbours of intended operations beforehand and, should there be objections, enter into bilateral agreements to resolve differences. Within such regional Conventions, however, neighbours tend to know each other rather well, and economic and environmental values do not differ greatly—with the possible exception of Britain versus the continent of Europe!

When such issues are transferred to the global scale where whole continents may border an ocean, such factors do not operate: there may be huge differences in the state of development of the economy, value systems, scientific abilities or infrastructure, democratic decision-making, and secrecy. As a result, within the LDC, there are major issues of countries failing to make full reports, which might mean anything from a country not dumping, dumping but not recording or monitoring, dumping illegally, or dumping entirely properly but not bothering to inform the Convention. In fact, one of the ironies of the past decade has been that the much-maligned 'dirty man of Europe', the UK, a major and unrepentant user of the marine environment as a receptacle for its wastes, has been by far the most detailed and explicit in its reporting and analysis.

Thus, detailed though a Convention may be in terms of what is allowed, not allowed, and recommended, the only effective forces for compliance at present are reasoned argument and the embarrassment factor. It should be immediately apparent that with regard to the latter, at least, NGOs play a vital role. First, in observing the Consultative meetings—which, being closed to the press, would go unreported (what government would choose to report criticism of its actions?). Second, in then lobbying for change within the political institutions of that country, or, indeed, of neighbouring countries. It can sometimes happen, for example, that a country will take a certain position in advance of the meeting—such as stating that it would support a no-dumping policy—and yet its delegates do not follow through (either because the government has another non-public agenda, or, as is also rather common, the delegates themselves are subverting their own government's public commitment). We shall explore the last inference when we look more closely at the dynamic of 'precaution' versus prediction.

One final aspect of structure which is important in this latter regard relates to the ongoing need not only to evaluate reporting, but also to amend the Convention in the light of the evolution of scientific knowledge. Thus, all Conventions set up scientific working groups. Usually there will be one major gathering of scientific experts each year, and several working groups spawned by that, which may also hold *ad hoc* Meetings. In the LDC, for example, there is a large Scientific Group on Dumping (SGD), where government scientists meet annually. Expert groups have been established on radioactive dumping, review of the Annexes, legal aspects, and future development of the Convention. In all of these, NGOs such as Greenpeace have not only been allowed to attend, but, in more recent years, invited to contribute their specialist skills.

These *ad hoc* groups of experts have assumed greater significance in the past few years as a result of the rising controversies over the degradation of the marine environment and what should be done to change things. For example, at one level or another, the following issues have all been assigned to the scientists to deal with:

- the interpretation of monitoring results (to distinguish anthropogenic change from natural changes in whatever index is measured—usually populations of marine organisms);
- the definition of 'significant' harm to human health or marine ecosystems;
- the assessment of comparative risks of different dumping options, including land v. ocean;
- the development of holistic frameworks which address all environmental media (air, soil, water, etc.) and all substances (for example, radionuclides and toxic chemicals, natural and man-made substances).

It should be immediately apparent that these issues contain much more than simple scientific 'fact'. They involve not only scientific data, but also strategies for the collection and interpretation of data (readily affected by 'interests'), and judgement which involves social, political, and economic values, when such terms as 'significant' damage are defined.

Unfortunately, few of the government-appointed scientists, in our experience, have been aware that value-free science was long ago discredited, and they still have a self-image of 'scientific judgements', which they make, and 'political' decisions, which others make (be they parliaments, the consultative meeting of the Convention, or even environmental groups). They have doubtless been encouraged in this regard by articles in the Convention that require any changes to the Annexes to be made 'on scientific criteria' alone, thus implying that social, political, and economic judgements are somehow not involved.

Consequently, there has been much heated dispute as these 'expert groups' have been pressured into admitting 'critical' experts. They have subsequently come to acknowledge the value of such input, although there has been some backlash as the 'old guard' have tried to reassert dominance with accusations that the debate has now degenerated because 'policy' has been brought into the science. As someone once remarked in mid-debate: 'it seems if I agree with you it is science, if I disagree with you it is policy!'

The results of these more arcane deliberations of the scientific groups are obviously important. In the case of the LDC, such expert groups have not only been redrafting the Convention to respond to the global crisis but have been contributing on a wider scale to a range of adjacent intergovernmental bodies: UNEP, the UN Group of Experts on Scientific Aspects of Marine Pollution (GESAMP), the International Council for the Exploration of the Sea (ICES), the International Commission on Radiological Protection, and the International Atomic Energy Agency.

There are only so many 'leading experts' with suitable international status and experience, and there is much cross-representation. Thus, when it comes to major changes and differences in policy (evaluation of scientific information and development of strategies for change), we have noticed a distinct tendency for this overlap to operate as a closed-rank where scientists of particular policy orientation are chosen for crucial working groups and committees. Individual personalities can thus wield enormous influence—indeed, there have on occasion been embarrassing 'coups' where chairmen have had to be removed when their bias and overbearing nature became rather too obvious.

In some key 'expert groups' and commissions, other UN bodies appear well represented, for example, The World Health Organization (WHO), The Food and Agriculture Organization (FAO), and UNESCO. However, another well-known dynamic operates: experts in the field are always deferred to and carry considerable weight, such that these other organizations are seldom in a position to review or challenge the conclusions of marine scientists. The presence of such agencies thus appears to lend weight, authority, and objectivity, but more often than not merely acts to legitimize the views of a small handful of experts.

Within these expert groups (and often within the Convention itself) a further but less well appreciated aspect of structure becomes of great importance: linguistic competence. There is a premium on being a native English speaker, first because at any meeting it is the dominant language of science and a major lingua franca of diplomacy, and secondly because at the smaller meetings, financial limitations may mean that there is no simultaneous translation. In any case, the Convention secretariat work in English, and they are not necessarily neutral on key issues (for example, the LDC/IMO secretariat organize regional seminars on dumping regulation at which the usual 'assimilative capacity' adherents propound principles of impact assessment, monitoring strategies, etc. which belong to the 'old school' of thought, and may also bring either themselves or colleagues useful contracts).

In Convention language, one word placed differently in a strategic sentence can have enormous implications, but these may only be immediately apparent to the native English speakers, and more especially to an English-speaking Chair. That Chair is also unlikely to be neutral. Indeed, the English-speaking experts of the USA, Ireland, and the UK have been, without exception, philosophically adherents to the old paradigm of prediction rather than precaution, whereas the lead in the new paradigm has been taken by Germans and Scandinavians, often supported by Spanish speakers. Attempts to involve the 'non-aligned' would usually turn to a Canadian or Australian Chair, but not necessarily with much success in countering the inherent linguistic bias.

Having attempted to lay out the structure of the LDC, at least, we can turn more specifically to the major conflict in the structure of prevailing scientific and policy concepts in what is becoming a period of great change.

2. Precaution and prediction: the paradigm shift

It has been forcefully argued, particularly by the Scandinavians, that the only sure way of protecting the oceans from pollution resulting from dumping of wastes is not to dump at all. With regard to the LDC, they argue that this is the ultimate aim of the Convention. Some regional conventions already reflect this: the Helsinki Convention on the Baltic Sea expressly prohibits all dumping.

However, there is no consensus that not dumping is the only way to achieve the aims of the LDC, which are to prevent pollution. It has been argued, largely by the scientific advisers, that dumping is not necessarily 'pollution', which by definition involves some observable 'harm' to the marine environment. Indeed, every convention starts out by defining pollution as harm, implying that some level of damage must be observed. As the marine environment is in constant fluctuation with regard to the populations of all classes of organisms, and as it is largely population changes that qualify as 'significant harm', pollution is not so readily differentiated from natural fluctuations.

Within this definition, the practice of 'dilute and disperse' developed as a way of reducing toxicity to levels that were either 'harmless' or, if some harm was unavoidable, that could be regarded as 'acceptable' because they were either insignificant in overall impact, or worthwhile as a trade-off in relation to the benefits of the activity that produced the waste.

It can be appreciated that scientists have played a key role in defining the impact of dumping programmes and hence the acceptability of these. A whole range of scientific techniques have been developed to predict consequences in the marine environment, culminating in sophisticated and expensive computer modelling of the fate of contaminants.

Unfortunately, because of the complexity of such analyses, the scientists tended to be left to promulgate standards of acceptable damage or insignificant risk, as if these were not in themselves policy issues involving political, social, and economic judgement. Even international bodies such as WHO, ICRP, and IAEA were not immune from this error, and it is even the case that in certain crucial areas, such as radioactive waste, the same scientists were key players in the standard-setting on international bodies such as IAEA or ICRP (International Commission on Radiological Protection), in the Conventions such as LDC, and at home in their national organizations involved in licensing and monitoring individual operations.

There has, of course, been a world-wide shift in perception relating to pollution and dumping activities, such that public pressure has meant politicians have moved toward the 'precautionary' approach exemplified by Helsinki—better not to dump at all. This has often been fiercely resisted by the scientific groups within the Conventions, with initially only a minority of dissenters, mostly Scandinavian or those from NGOs such as Greenpeace. The rationale put forward has been that if waste is produced and disposed to other media, the harm may be greater (for example, landfill dangers to drinking water) and, ultimately, the substances may even return unregulated to the oceans via rivers.

It has been further argued that the LDC should not be promulgating standards born of the mistakes of a grossly polluted northern industrial environment (for example, the North Sea) and of countries rich enough to invest in safer alternatives on land—standards which could not realistically be held to apply over much of the newly industrializing Third World.

Despite many requests to do so, the presenters of these arguments have failed to provide adequate in-depth comparative assessments of risks across different media (with the possible exception of dredge spoil), and of cleaner production or non-waste options, nor have they provided evidence of Third World needs with respect to their development. In fact, a perusal of the protocols to the more recently ratified regional Conventions shows a Third World striving for the zero-options of no-dumping across the board: the South Pacific has banned nuclear and industrial wastes, for example, and meetings of the Organization of African Unity to develop comprehensive control of toxic wastes in their region resulted in the 1991 Bamako Convention banning dumping of imported waste on both land and sea.

Such resistance to change and adherence to the old paradigm of prediction, and to practices of dilute and disperse, has led the LDC to be viewed rather as a 'dumpers' club', such that more environmentally minded Third World states have felt it was hardly worthwhile to attend.

Over the decades of operation, the 'club' may have come to represent the interests not just of the industries in developed states, but of the marine science community that has blossomed with the demand for monitoring and modelling of the effects of dumping. It is largely forgotten, given the 'objective', almost priestly, standing they enjoy, that scientists are a lobby group in their own right. This is because almost all scientists involved in the development of the 'prediction' and 'acceptable damage' policy are based in marine science laboratories; and these laboratories rely heavily upon government funding and contracts to finance ship-time, monitoring and research programmes (university departments are no less free). Therefore, any shift away from dumping toward either land-based alternatives, or waste-prevention technology, means less sites to be monitored, less predictive modelling, and hence ultimately fewer contracts and a reduction in status, if not in jobs themselves.

Thus, it is our perception that the strongest defenders in the pro-dumping lobby have been not government regulators or industrialists intent on cheap options, but marine scientists with a lifelong record of involvement in dumping programmes. These scientists have used the aura of scientific complexity and 'objective' decision-making to further their own 'interests'. This may go some way to explain the apparent paradox that many of the delegations that argue so doggedly for keeping dumping options open have national policies that have for quite some time prohibited ocean dumping (for example, the USA and Canada).

C. The Role of NGOs' Scientific Representation

Given the dynamic detailed above, the NGOs have played a crucial role in fielding 'critical' scientists as advocates within the LDC, and also funding independent research in the universities to assess the performance of government programmes. This role has taken two forms. First, remaining within the old paradigm, the impact assessments have been reviewed and criticized in the light of current scientific knowledge. This may take the form of reviewing case histories that governments have a vested interest in ignoring or painting in a more positive light than is justified, or it may focus upon the uncertainties that are given inadequate representation in models of future impact. Secondly, the new paradigm of 'precaution' has been developed. This begins by acknowledging the limits of scientific prediction, and then focuses upon technological solutions to low-waste scenarios that do not lead to disposal in (any) environmental media.

Greenpeace, for example, first fielded expert scientists in the special group set up to examine the scientific aspects of the radioactive waste dumping controversy following the vote for a moratorium. These experts played a key role in highlighting uncertainties in the model of projected impacts, as well as making clear the consequences of past dumping (including making public hitherto undisclosed dumping programmes such as that of the state of South Korea). The political consequence of these disclosures was a vote to continue the moratorium.

With regard to 'precautionary action', the pace had been set politically by the Conference of North Sea Ministers in 1987, and Greenpeace has lobbied to extend the principle to the international conventions. The North Sea Declaration was not, however, simply a swing of public opinion—it was marked by several respected scientists from North Sea states disavowing their past commitment to 'assimilative capacity' arguments and acknowledging the 'new humility' needed in the face of environmental complexity and obvious evidence of unpredicted degradation.

These scientists did not receive the same support from other states in the LDC that they received from Scandinavia and Northern Europe, and indeed were constantly accused of bringing 'policy' into the science when they sought change within the convention. This can be comprehended both as a defence of vested interests, i.e. an unwillingness to see the point, and also, perhaps equally, as a manifestation of a lingering belief that any change must be supported by positive evidence of cause and effect. The burden of proof in almost all conventions has lain with those who would be cautious! This largely results from the requirement for pollution to be identified in terms of harm, and the origin of that harm pinpointed as a particular substance.

The 'new humility', however, was based upon equally, perhaps more advanced, scientific grounds: that simple cause and effect, as could be identified in laboratory studies with single pollutants, was seldom operative in natural ecosystems, where synergism and multi-factorial causes were likely; that 'proof' could seldom advance beyond a correlation in a complex system not amenable to manipulation to isolate cause and effect; and that the complexities of marine food chains, interactions, and even the place of humans in the web of life was such that no modelling process was likely to generate the required degree of accuracy.

These changes, largely of evaluation, in relation to scientific data, were doubtless prompted by experiences in the North Sea, where unpredicted and as yet not fully explainable catastrophes occurred: algal blooms destroying millions of pounds' worth of fish-farms; viral epidemics killing 40 per cent of seal stocks; high incidence of fish diseases; starvation of seabirds as fish stocks dwindled. It had proved impossible to isolate causes, or even to agree as to whether natural events such as temperature fluctuations, viral mutations, or fecundity cycles were to blame, or whether other anthropogenic causes such as overfishing might be implicated.

There were, in the background, growing suspicions of the role of low-level contaminants which had been assumed by the 'old school' to have no significance in pollution: PCBs, other chlorinated hydrocarbons used as pesticides, dioxins from bleaching processes, heavy metals, etc. In the case of PCBs, there was mounting evidence that low levels could impair the immune system in mammals.

The leading scientists in the vanguard of the 'precautionary approach', in particular German marine biologists, began to argue that it was valid and necessary to take action in advance of conclusive scientific proof that would connect observed degradation with particular substances or sources of pollution, and that, indeed, waiting for such proof could render the situation irreversible. The parallel phenomenon of the disappearing ozone layer, caused by an entirely unpredicted 'contaminant' effect, was providing strong support for this argument.

In the transfer of this new philosophy to the global LDC, the scientific group was the source of the main opposition, and Greenpeace was to play an important role in aiding the German originators. These scientists, often limited to one individual, were at a serious disadvantage linguistically. We observed several incidents where a biased Chair deliberately misunderstood or failed to respond adequately to points made. In these cases, where Greenpeace always comes at the end of the 'pecking-order' for interventions, we were able to pick up these points again, either to clarify or to reassert.

In one case, a single word in a sentence caused debate to be prolonged for six hours—with the chairman on the verge of throwing Greenpeace out of the meeting! The issue was whether the new draft protocols for the Convention could provide for prohibition to be justified by the uncertainty of effects. The debate hung on the apparently innocuous scientific proviso that dumping could be prohibited 'unless uncertainties could be allowed for in the analysis'. This would have meant that anyone opposing a dumping programme would have to show that the uncertainties had not been sufficiently allowed for. The burden of proof rests with the opponent of dumping, and it is all but impossible to prove a point which is not only a value judgement, but by its nature involves uncertainties which may not be precisely defined and weighed. The alternative wording (put forward by Greenpeace) allowed prohibition where there was 'significant uncertainty'. Acceptance of many of the compromise wordings put forward would have left the Germans agreeing that uncertainties could only be legitimate grounds for prohibition after an exhaustive assessment, involving models which would include safety margins and probability assessment designed to deal with uncertainty, whereas what they sought was grounds for prohibition even without an assessment in order to act quickly in situations where data were scarce and waiting for them might prove disastrous. In the event, the offending 'in the analysis' was removed and the LDC had its first legal formula for prohibition which did not require scientific proof of harm.

This ruling was then to be immediately tested in a practical case and a perfect example of NGO intervention. The NGO observing on behalf of the chemical industry, CEFIC, had for years been amassing documentation apparently showing that organosilicon was harmless and should not be classified in the Annexes as a blacklisted substance, being a persistent synthetic. There was no evidence of toxicity in the marine environment. Documentation almost a metre high on the desk was cited as CEFIC requested the substance be delisted. There was a mood of concurrence in the hall, in particular because it was a general axiom that substances which were unlikely to be dumped should not be singled out on the blacklist.

Greenpeace, however, became suspicious at the amount of time and effort being devoted by CEFIC to a substance for which no dumping permits were being sought, and which according to their spokesperson was manufactured in insignificant quantities. Careful questioning of the CEFIC representative in a tea-break turned up the facts that organosilicons were prime candidates to replace PCBs as insulators and di-electric fluids in capacitors, and there was a brake on their manufacture as long as they were identified in the LDC Annexes. Environmentally, Greenpeace was quick to see the significance for uncontrolled future dumping from the millions of tonnes that would be manufactured and used throughout the world.

This was to prove a test case for the principle that 'precaution' was required whenever an unnatural substance that was persistent (non-degradable) and capable of widespread dispersal was under consideration. The fact that there was no evidence of toxicity could not be adequate grounds—such evidence could only come after dispersal if effects were 'ecosystem' based, as happened with the release of CFCs into the atmosphere (CFCs were among the least toxic of all chemicals to living organisms). Green-peace disclosed the facts about the prospective use of organo-silicons (none of the other scientists had been aware of this), and argued passionately for the ban to stay in place. A vote was forced, with the old 'axis' of Britain, the USA, and Japan leading the opposition, and the Danes, Germans, Spanish, and Pacific islands in support. The vote went in favour of precaution, and several of the 'axis' delegates bitterly complained that 'science' was being 'ignored'!

D. The Dilemma of Ineffective Prohibition v. Effective Permissions

One final argument connected with the clash of paradigms out-lined above finds champions on both sides of the fence. Pro-ponents of 'permit-oriented' regimes (called 'permissive' by their environmental critics) have argued that because such systems make rational use of science and allow each state to make its own judgements with respect to social, political, and economic factors, they therefore command international respect. A global treaty that operated a system of prohibitions that was clearly related to non-scientific (i.e. political) factors would not com-mand universal respect and might simply be ignored: states would simply not bother to report, or might dispense with scientific assessments altogether, and the oceans could be at greater risk.

The environmental NGOs have been suspicious of this argu-ment, there being no evidence as to which states might 'not respect' the convention. Indeed, one of the paradoxes of the LDC has been the advocacy of science-based 'permit' systems by non-dumping states such as the USA (which phased out radwaste dumping in the 1970s, and industrial wastes bar dredge spoil and sewage in the 1980s), Canada, and France. These states had all made policy decisions against ocean dumping even within the permit system. The suspicion has been that the USA, UK, France, and Japan were anxious to keep the ocean option open for their future problematic accumulations of bulky radioactive wastes fol-lowing decommissioning of nuclear stations and submarines. Alternatively, these states contain the largest contingents of marine scientists capable of acting as a lobby for their own interests in predictive modelling.

Greenpeace itself always believed that the only safe protection for the oceans lay with policy shifts toward outright banning of all waste dumping. Its scientific advisers did not necessarily agree. Simple banning could lead to uncontrolled waste dumping on land, with the toxic substances ultimately finding their way to the sea, as well as illegal dumping where land-based alternatives were either not developed or politically or economically difficult. Of course, the only real answer is to reduce or eliminate toxic waste at source, but how is this to be furthered? One way would be to tie the waste producer into a system of Waste Prevention Audits as a prerequisite of permit application.

Greenpeace was actually allocated the task of drafting such an improvement to the LDC—this was accepted by the LDC working group on revisions to the Convention, although in the final analysis, Greenpeace decided that even an improved permit procedure would not be adequate protection. It was apparent that as the procedures were tightened, there were moves afoot to make them less than mandatory. There therefore followed an intense lobbying campaign aimed at a phase-out of industrial waste dumping in all states with Greenpeace offices (virtually all the main OECD countries have Greenpeace offices, with a combined campaign budget of $30 million, then greater than UNEP's).

In the event, the 13th meeting of the LDC (October 1990) voted to phase out industrial dumping. This follows a similar move by the regional Oslo Convention to which the UK, France, and Ireland belong, three countries consistently blocking moves toward precautionary action. The LDC vote saw the UK, USA, and France isolated with Japan, with no evidence of newly industrializing states (such as Brazil) supporting them. However, many crucial newly industrializing regions are under-represented: Indonesia and other major South-East Asian states, and most of the Arab states, for example.

It is only a matter of time before the prohibition also extends to sewage dumping, and the newly evolving tighter permit procedures apply only to dredge-spoil. The 1989 decision of the Oslo Commission to phase out industrial waste dumping in the Convention waters (the North Sea and North-East Atlantic) was an important step in this respect. The Third North Sea Ministers Conference in the Hague, held in March 1990, confirmed the 1987 London Declaration agreement to phase out industrial waste dumping and further agreed to phase out sewage sludge dumping.

E. The Methods of Influence: Lobbying and Participation

The involvement of Greenpeace and other environmental groups as observers at the LDC consists of much more than simply observing and making public the workings of the Convention, or, more specifically, the actions of national delegates at meetings of the Contracting Parties. Effective participation has evolved such that NGOs now contribute intellectually to the process of law-making and regulation.

1. *Participation and contribution of Greenpeace*

We can summarize some of the methods of participation:

1. Detailed critical review of scientific justifications for dumping, followed by questioning and debate on the floor of the Convention.

2. Linguistic aid to non-English speakers within the debating process. Here it may be helpful that the NGO is not bound by the diplomatic codes that restrict other delegates from being as forthright in their argument as they might otherwise be.

3. Scientific and technical advice to 'friendly' states willing to take the floor on key issues, including drafting of resolutions.

4. Willingness to publicize incidents (and name the countries involved) where regulations have been broken, there being a reluctance on the part of other states to draw attention to events in offending countries if they themselves do not report them. An example of this occurred in 1988 when Greenpeace was aware that the Portuguese authorities had licensed the scuttling of a fire-damaged ship containing hundreds of imported cars, which contained many listed substances such as lead, plastics, etc. The Portuguese delegation did not report this to the LDC, and although Greenpeace had circulated information, no other state brought the matter to the floor—which Greenpeace then did, the outcome of which was a decision to salvage the vessel.

5. The carrying out of primary scientific work, such as monitoring, and incorporating the results in the process of scientific appraisal.

In addition, on highly controversial matters (which may in the end be put to a vote) a long build-up process of argument, assessment through working groups, etc. generally takes place over a period of several years. Greenpeace has developed an extensive and very effective lobby system which is deployed during this process. Its teams at a Convention may consist of experienced political lobbyists whose sole task is to liaise with embassies, ministries, the press, and the delegates, so that, for example, 'friendly' delegations are kept well-briefed and primed to actually take their seats for crucial votes (some of the poorer states may only have a token presence in the form of an embassy official, in which case they may rely entirely on Greenpeace briefings). There have been times when certain delegates failed to arrive, leading to telexes and phone calls to the distant state and minister concerned to precipitate a hunt at the embassy, with the hapless official being dispatched forthwith to the IMO building in Lambeth. Where the reverse happens, and powerful states such as the USA and Japan exert political (and perhaps economic) pressure on smaller states, such as Pacific island nations, Greenpeace has made high-profile visits by ship to these areas to gather public support. In this lobbying process, Greenpeace has recognized the value of even just one 'friendly' small state if that state's representative is both scientifically trained, well-informed, and co-operative, for that person not only has an automatic right of access to committees and working groups from which NGOs are often excluded, but also, in the one-country, one-vote system, has the same formal power as any other state, however large its delegation. Such contacts are assiduously maintained—for example, the state of Nauru consistently sends a highly effective Professor of Marine Science from a Californian university to represent it at all meetings. Finally, within the process of consultative meetings, there are often several parallel working groups, and attendance at these tests any delegation's representation-in-depth—consequently, NGOs need to field sizeable delegations of competent people, something only Greenpeace has attempted. When crucial issues are on the agenda, the US and Japanese delegations might be 10–15 strong, whereas most other states might not be able to afford more than 2–3, and simply finding competent people has limited Greenpeace to 5–6. Attendant accommodation (at London hotels) and travel costs can be high.

Within the 'unfriendly' states, Greenpeace, of course, is involved in much activity at national office level: commissioned research reports, position papers, evidence to government advisory committees, parliamentary inquiries and hearings, etc. (As far as we know, only the USA holds public hearings on its proposed 'position' on key issues in advance of the LDC.)

2. *The increased acceptance and recognition of the important role of NGOs*

Although the level and degree of NGO participation in the international decision-making process is not as great as it could be if all relevant forums were open, the situation is rapidly improving. The major reason for the improvements is the growing recognition of the contributions which NGOs can make to the task of arriving at adequate solutions.

The Brundtland Commission, which had a mandate to propose long-term environmental strategies for achieving sustainable development to the year 2000 and beyond, recognized the important role of NGOs generally. *Our Common Future* states:

Reversing unsustainable development policies at the national and international level will require immense efforts to inform the public and secure its support. The scientific community, private and community groups, and NGOs can play a central role in this . . . NGOs and citizens groups pioneered in the creation of public awareness and political pressure that stimulated governments to act . . . These groups have also played an indispensable role since the Stockholm Conference in identifying risks, in assessing environmental impacts, and designing and implementing measures to deal with them, and in maintaining the high degree of public and political interest required as a basis for action . . . Several international NGOs have produced significant reports on the status of and prospects for the global environment and natural resource base . . . Many international bodies and coalitions of NGOs are now in place and active. They play an important part in ensuring that national NGOs and scientific bodies have access to the support they require . . . In many countries, governments need to recognize and extend NGOs' right to know, and have access to information on the environment and natural resources; their right to be consulted and to participate in decision making on activities likely to have a significant effect on the environment; and their right to legal remedies and redress when their health or environment has been or may be seriously affected.

These are strong and compelling messages coming not from activists, as would have been the case twenty years ago, but rather from the mainly governmental officials comprising the Commission.

As these forums continue to open up and indeed to rely upon the skills of NGOs, particularly where the states of the Third World are concerned (where there is a distrust of the motives of the powerful industrial states of the northern hemisphere), there will be challenges for the NGOs as well as for the conventions and commissions that include them—both will have to improve upon the present situation. We can highlight some of the areas where improvement on both sides is required.

3. *Improving NGO participation*

Although many conventions and international decision-making bodies permit NGO access as observers, some still do not. Only in 1990 for example, was Greenpeace given observer status with the Oslo and Paris Commissions. Access should be provided throughout the negotiation and decision-making process in these bodies. The LDC is an example where NGOs do have such access although the NGOs do not have voting rights. Such access to the meetings, including subsidiary working groups and committees, is vital if NGOs are to contribute effectively.

This latter point raises awkward problems when NGOs are present but are either denied access to drafting groups or committees, or their arguments are not represented in the record of the meeting (all of which have happened in the LDC). Should they protest, or walk out, running risks of being labelled irresponsible and undiplomatic, or stay in and thereby confer legitimacy on decisions they disagree with? Greenpeace has taken the risks and on key occasions protested, walked out, and incurred the wrath of the Chair. Other NGOs have had rather more supine policies: they may attend but say very little, put only limited resources into research and review, and agree to be co-opted on working groups when they can actually have no real influence.

Greenpeace has in one case been able to obtain representation by one of its national staff on the delegation of a contracting party (New Zealand). We feel this should be encouraged, as many states use 'private-sector' advisers from industry and academia. There is still much secrecy with regard to environmental decision-making. Few states follow the US example and open up their delegation's position on issues for public debate. In the future, there will be a need to examine key background material as part of the licensing process: waste audits, impact assessments, companies' monitoring results or discharge analyses, some of which may be covered by 'commercial confidentiality'.

An issue raised by the Brundtland Report concerns the need to recognize and extend individual and NGO rights to legal remedies and redress when health or environment has been or may be seriously affected. Thus when individual rights, including the right to a healthy environment, are encroached upon, NGOs representing the environmental interests should be granted standing to bring lawsuits on behalf of the environment and public health. NGOs must be given access to the courts. However, welcome as this would be, we are not aware that even contracting parties have effective rights under the present international regimes—legal working groups within the LDC are still grappling with the problems of third-party risks and compensation.

Finally, it is the opinion of the independent adviser in this joint authorship that NGOs need to take great care over their own internal dynamic with respect to motivation and policy. As NGOs grow to multinational million-dollar operations and are dependent upon public funding and media coverage of issues, certain inflexibilities and 'hidden agendas' can develop. For example, Greenpeace evolved a policy of world-wide prohibition of sewage dumping very largely based upon the agenda of its North Sea campaigners. The transference of this policy to, for example, coastal Malaysia via the LDC, without adequate research, could lead to environmental losses rather than gains— there, sewage is largely uncontaminated by industry, and coastal discharges threaten human health and wildlife: sea dumping could be justified if the costs of land treatment were unrealistic.

On this issue, ethnocentrism, and campaign simplicity, led to an uncompromising stand.

4. *The benefits to international law of NGO participation*

From the foregoing, we can summarize the benefits, as seen from the perspective of an active NGO such as Greenpeace, of NGO participation for the broader process of legal development and implementation as represented in international conventions.

Legitimacy of governmental decision-making is enhanced by NGO participation. Regardless of the governmental structure, sooner or later elected or appointed government officials must recognize that decisions which affect the lives of their citizens should allow for NGO participation. An essential component of fair process is the opportunity for persons with an interest which will be affected by a proposed government action to present their views to the decision-maker in a meaningful way *before* a decision is made. When such participation is lacking, and conclusions are made in isolation, they are more likely to be ignored or resisted.

NGO participation improves the quality of decisions. No matter how qualified the policy-maker and staff may be, their range of expertise and experience, and innovative capacities, are necessarily limited. NGO participation brings to the decision-making process facts, information, ideas, judgements, and perspectives which might otherwise be unavailable, and thus improves the quality of the final product. This is particularly true due to the commitment and concentration of NGOs on certain issues, resulting in some situations where the NGO possesses the most expertise on a given issue.

NGO participation helps balance access to decision-makers. Some interests inevitably will have access to decision-makers regardless of the formal opportunities for public participation. Policymakers formulating offshore oil and gas policies in the North Sea, for example, would naturally seek information from oil companies, for example, about proven or estimated reserves. At the same time, however, it is important that NGOs have a fair opportunity to present their information, ideas, and judgements in a way that ensures a fair and complete exploration of all the issues.

NGO participation fosters public education. Almost all NGOs

regard education of their members, constituents, and the public at large as an important priority. Many attempt to educate the public through the media, by publishing books, information brochures, and papers, and holding press conferences on marine issues. By involving NGOs in the decision-making process, their access to facts and opinions is increased. Some decision-makers, unfortunately, appear to favour restricting information, on the grounds that the less NGOs and the public know, the less 'damage' or interference they can cause. This mentality is counterproductive and does not represent a democratic process. Fortunately this view is not pervasive. Indeed, the trend is in favour of increasing access for NGOs, as the opening of the Helsinki, Oslo, and Paris Commissions indicates.

NGOs have many strengths that can benefit decision-makers. Among these are flexibility, imagination, resiliency, lack of bureaucracy, specialized expertise, and independence. Regarding independence, it is very important in addressing marine issues to include input from groups whose only concern is to provide adequate solutions to sources of environmental damage and who are not driven by business interests, election campaigning interests, or other objectives which are opportunistic rather than objective and sincere. These qualities enable NGOs to understand and respond quickly to new problems. Another strength is popular support. NGOs derive their support from people, for example the over four million official members of Greenpeace, who have recognized the necessity of organizing to solve problems. The influence of NGOs lies in their ability to mobilize public opinion and persuade decision-makers. If they lose touch with the public, or with the facts, they soon fail. Currently NGO support from the public is at an all-time high and still growing.

These strengths have made NGOs working on marine issues respected and influential in many nations and on the international scene, and have resulted in remarkable accomplishments over the past fifteen years. Their influence on decisions involving whales and other endangered species, in forums like the International Whaling Commission, or their efforts to promote conservation principles for Antarctica, are just two important positive examples. In the 1990 Third North Sea Ministers Conference in the Hague, Greenpeace published and distributed the most comprehensive analysis of the implementation (or lack of) of the Second North Sea Conference London Declaration. The work was commissioned from independent law and policy experts in each of the North Sea states. In addition, comprehensive reports on improving the implementation of the commitments through the application of clean production methods were commissioned from independent sources. These documents helped provide the basis for subsequent decisions by the Ministers and continue to contribute directly to national environmental policy.

F. Implications of the Shift from Prediction to Precaution as a Means of Avoiding Pollution

We have noted earlier that a paradigm shift is noticeable: indeed the rate at which international conventions and other forums have been adopting the 'principle of precautionary action' has increased markedly. The principle was first adopted at the North Sea Ministers Conference, followed by the UNEP Governing Council, the Paris Commission and implicitly the Oslo Commission, the Barcelona Convention for the Mediterranean, the Nordic Council Parliamentarians Conference, the Nordic Council, and the UN ECE region Bergen Conference, among others.

As we have noted, this principle is founded on a policy of precautionary and preventive action. It has arisen from the realization that the old permissive approach based on the assumed assimilative capacity of the environment has failed. Even the most sophisticated environmental impact assessment models cannot cope with the diversity of chemical compounds, diversity of biological species, and complexity of the ecosystem. Thus any impact model results are inherently limited by substantial uncertainty. The recognition of the limitations of science and impact methodology, coupled with the realization that we must stop using the environment as a large-scale experiment, given the potential for irreversible damage, has led to the new environmental paradigm.

The precautionary action approach thus calls for the prohibition of the release of substances which may cause damage to the environment even if insufficient or inadequate scientific proof exists regarding a causal link. It entails that the environment and human health be given the benefit of the doubt, rather than the polluter. As might be expected, a major shift such as this will have profound implications for conventions, the legal language of which relates to observable damage and justifiable grounds for believing harm will result from disposal. The burden of proof has hitherto lain with those who would limit dumping, but must now be reversed.

It has been argued that the new approach is well intentioned but has little to no means of implementation. This argument is largely put forward by those with past experience of regulation focused upon the marine environment rather than on the technologies that threaten it. Clean production methodology is one obvious means of implementing this new policy direction and is increasingly being recognized as such.

Clean production is an approach whereby the entire life cycle of a product is analysed for the application of the substitution of raw materials, alternative products, alternative processes, and alternative clean production technology. It is based on the fundamental tenet that no toxic waste should be produced, other waste minimized, and that the product itself should not present an environmental problem during or at the end of its life. Unlike Best Available Technology, hitherto related to end-of-pipe solutions to discharges, clean production is not limited to technological fixes (but includes them), nor does it entail end-of-pipe measures which fail to address the problem adequately, at its source.

This is not a futuristic concept but rather a currently available approach. For example, the US Office of Technology Assessment asserted, in a 1986 report entitled 'Serious Reduction of Hazardous Waste', that a 50 per cent reduction in hazardous waste was achievable in five years using measures available in 1986. Clean production centres and experts exist. However, there is a need to increase the clean production infrastructure at the international and national level, in particular in order to administer clean production audits and draft phase-out plans based on those audits for substances, processes, and wastes which pose a threat to the environment. In this way, the research and development into additionally needed clean production methods can be effectively and rationally driven.

However, it is not yet clear how such a 'forcing' mechanism can be created within international law. The problems are great. First, there needs to be effective exchange of information, even though some areas have obvious commercial value. Secondly, some changes will involve new capital investments which may not be affordable by poorer states, especially those just at the end of a capital investment cycle (a parallel is the Chinese production of refrigerators using outdated but cheap production methods and CFC coolant). Finally, given the lack of political will in all but the most advanced industrial states (Sweden, Denmark, Germany), there needs to be an incentive, or a coercive legal mechanism, to force change.

Greenpeace had tackled these issues during the 1990 meetings of the LDC, proposing a system of waste disposal permits that required a Waste Prevention Audit to be carried out, notified to regional centres, and approved by neighbouring states, before the permit procedure could go forward to risk assessment stages. The system advocated regional centres of expertise to provide for review of the audits, and the effective creation of a new technocracy in clean production to replace the old technocracy of monitoring and prediction.

However, this system was predicated on a permit procedure for industrial wastes, and when the decision was taken to phase out all such dumping, there was obviously no immediate need to develop such procedures. They could be relevant in relation to dredge-spoils and sewage, requiring the applicant to make such source reductions as are feasible (the applicant in these cases seldom being the source of the contaminant)—indeed, Greenpeace would have secured the incorporation of such a clause in the LDC had it not been obstructed by a Chair who also represented the largest dredging operation in the world, an incident that caused our first walk-out!

There is therefore an urgent need for all international conventions on protection of the oceans, atmospheres, terrestrial waters, etc., to examine means of 'forcing' technological change. Obviously, one way is for NGOs to mobilize public pressure to introduce such restrictive prohibitions on toxic substances that industry is forced to find methods of clean production. It would be regrettable if such a course were necessary (and such a strategy failed in California in the referenda system), because it would tend to alienate the scientists, regulators, and industry—which is perhaps why the Californian propositions failed to reach the statute books.

Clean production need not alienate the scientific establishment, nor disadvantage industry—but given the dynamic of the ocean protective interests, including the vested interests in predictive modelling, there are at present few champions outside of the NGOs.

G. The Future of Marine Environmental Protection

Ocean dumping, although a serious environmentally destructive practice, is not the main threat to the marine environment. Roughly 10 per cent of marine pollution derives from ocean dumping. Roughly another 10 per cent derives from operational discharges from shipping and offshore activities, leaving the overwhelming balance, about 80 per cent of marine pollution inputs, coming from land-based sources. While there are global conventions concerning dumping (the LDC) and for operational discharges from shipping (MARPOL), both administered under the International Maritime Organization (IMO), there are no global conventions or mechanisms in force to systematically address land-based sources, the main threat to the marine environment.

In 1990 the LDC held the first meeting of its Long-Term Strategy Steering Committee, to which NGOs had access. A central issue discussed was the need for a global convention or mechanism for the protection of the marine environment from all sources of pollution including land-based sources. Part of this discussion focused on the possible expansion of the LDC to cover land-based sources of marine pollution.

The LDC urged that UNCED 1992 consider a comprehensive approach to marine protection, but this was not among the highest priorities for the conference. A comprehensive convention dealing with all sources of marine pollution is needed. Such a Convention must include, if it is to be effective, the following policy foundation:

1. Full endorsement and adoption of the preventive, precautionary action approach implemented through clean production methods and a commitment to zero discharges of toxic

substances and of substances which might have toxic potential—effectively all persistent synthetic substances.

2. Pursuant thereto, a shift in the burden of proof whereby the potential polluter must demonstrate that the proposed activity is not likely to pose a threat to, or to damage, the marine environment.

3. Full freedom of access to information and access to decision-making, including the decision-making and advisory bodies of the convention.

4. Concrete plans based on clean production audits (waste production and toxic use audits and clean production application audits) for the mandatory phase-out of wasteful and potentially harmful products, waste, and processes while phasing in the alternative clean production method.

5. A liability regime whereby the generator of hazardous waste is held absolutely, as well as jointly and severally, liable for any damage caused. In addition, NGOs should be granted express standing to bring lawsuits on behalf of the environment.

6. An effective enforcement regime.

In order to firmly establish the precautionary action approach and clean production as the accepted policy, and to develop the international marine environment regulatory framework in this direction in order to solve current problems, a shift in attitude by certain states will be necessary. This is shown by the fact that the USA and the UK blocked otherwise accepted environmental measures in the Bergen Conference (a follow-up to the Brundtland Commission, and ECE region preparatory conference for the UNCED 1992) held in May 1990. In addition, the USA, the UK, Ireland, and a few others have consistently blocked efforts to phase out ocean dumping of industrial wastes in the LDC, even though they are obliged to phase out the practice pursuant to other legal obligations. There is also a general intransigence and reluctance to change the status quo inherent in government bureaucracy which perpetuates environmentally destructive practices and continues to favour control rather than preventive approaches. There is the further dimension that the international objectives of the USA, the UK, and some other states are based upon a competitive philosophy. In other words, these countries pursue their own interests in a highly confrontational and self-serving manner, at the expense of the environment and indeed of developing countries, rather than working in co-operation with other states for the common good. This mentality is particularly alarming since these are the very countries which have caused major pollution problems whilst reaping the economic 'benefits'. Promotion of, and co-operation in, the exchange of expertise, experience, information, and financial as well as other resources, at the global level, especially in relation to implementing clean production methods, must become a priority. Finally, the general diplomatic codes whereby one country will not interfere with, censure, or even publicize the offending activities of another state (in the LDC no state even names the states who have not provided reports on their dumping activities) must be replaced by a new code whereby diplomacy serves the environment first and national sensitivities last.

Conclusions

The question of whether international law can safeguard the oceans remains open. It will certainly depend upon the continued action of NGOs, but also upon the will of governments not to limit themselves to the minimum required under the law, but to actively further the protection of the environment, and indeed to compete with each other in initiatives in response to the challenges of clean production technology.

Governments, and more particularly intergovernmental scientific bodies, must come to recognize the limits of science, to eschew the arrogance of the past where science was assumed capable of predicting and modelling the infinite complexity of the marine environment, and to find a new humility, an inbuilt precaution, such that, in the words of one of Germany's leading protagonists of the new paradigm, Dr Klaus Sperling, 'all releases of unnatural substances, or natural substances in unnaturally large quantities, are to be avoided so far as is ecologically sensible'. If this can be achieved then the oceans and the lifeforms within, and ultimately mankind itself, will be protected from death by misadventure and ignorance at the least, and certainly from the arrogance and complacency that have ruled in the past.

5

Negotiating More Effective International Environmental Agreements

Lawrence Susskind and Connie Ozawa

TWENTY years after the first UN-sponsored Conference on the Human Environment in Stockholm, the list of environmental problems requiring attention is longer than ever: climate change, ozone depletion, transboundary air pollution, deforestation, soil loss, desertification and drought, conservation of biological diversity, protection of the oceans and seas, protection of fresh water resources, traffic in toxic and dangerous products and wastes, etc. While action by individual countries is necessary to combat these problems, collective efforts are also required.[1]

Most of these environmental problems transcend national borders and require resources and technologies that many countries do not have. Moreover, solutions to these problems may well demand that some countries accept constraints on development that are not in their short-term interest. Without the pressure of collective commitments (and a willingness to share short-term costs) few countries will take unilateral action; nor would these steps be sufficient to reduce the pace of global change to a level the biosphere can accommodate.

Several relatively recent efforts to promote collective action

---

[1] While UNCED 1992 marks an important watershed, much of the most significant normative development and implementation will remain to be pursued in the following years. The Conference was not intended to go beyond such matters as: (1) the signing of conventions negotiated prior to June 1992; (2) the drafting of an 'Earth Charter' setting out basic principles for the conduct of all peoples and nations; (3) Agenda 21 spelling out a work programme for implementing the principles in the Earth Charter; (4) measures for financing the actions provided for in Agenda 21; (5) measures to ensure that all countries, particularly developing countries, have access to the technologies they need to help implement Agenda 21; and (6) measures for strengthening existing institutions and enhancing the environmental capacities of development agencies and organizations.

against transboundary pollution have been successful. The ecology of the Mediterranean Sea, for example, might have suffered
irrevocable damage had sea-bordering nations not convened in
Barcelona in 1975 to launch a concerted effort to end pollution.[2]
Likewise, the Montreal Protocol encouraged many nations to ban
the use of substances that deplete the stratospheric ozone layer.[3]

Negotiations leading to such international environmental
agreements are both complex and time-consuming. They are
usually preceded by extensive scientific fact-finding. Various
strategies for responding to the problem must then be debated.
Any solution is constrained by the costs of deploying new technologies and by concerns about the fair allocation of those costs.
Environmental negotiations are also confounded by long-standing political rivalries. Discussions about the best ways of monitoring and enforcing treaties often fall victim to these rivalries and
to concerns about maintaining sovereignty.

While the existing treaty-making process has produced dozens
of multilateral environmental agreements over the past four
decades, most of these are limited in scope,[4] and few have actually reduced pollution levels, corrected the misuse of critical
natural resources, or substantially modified the patterns of development that would otherwise have occurred.[5] At best, they
have prompted some countries to forestall actions that would
have accelerated the process of environmental deterioration.

A great deal of effort has been invested in 'getting written
agreements'. Far too little attention has been paid to guaran-
teeing that real environmental improvements are made. Very few
agreements have actually prevented development practices that
undermine sustainability. Few, if any, agreements have led to
major reforms within each country that would guarantee
implementation of these environmental treaties. This chapter
discusses what we believe are the deficiencies of the existing

[2] Peter Haas, *Saving the Mediterranean: The Politics of International Environmental
Cooperation* (New York: Columbia UP, 1990).

[3] Chris Granda, 'The Montreal Protocol on Substances that Deplete the Ozone
Layer', in Lawrence Susskind, Esther Siskind, and J. William Breslin (eds.), *Nine
Case Studies in International Environmental Negotiation* (Cambridge, Mass.: Program
on Negotiation at Harvard Law School, 1990).

[4] Lynton K. Caldwell, 'Beyond Environmental Diplomacy: The Changing Institutional Structure of International Cooperation', in John E. Carroll (ed.), *International Environmental Diplomacy* (Cambridge: Cambridge UP, 1988), 13–28.

[5] John Carroll, 'Conclusions', in *International Environmental Diplomacy*, 275–79.

approach to environmental treaty-making; presents several proposals for improving the process of environmental diplomacy; and suggests the kinds of reforms needed to ensure implementation of more effective international agreements.[6]

A. The Convention–Protocol Approach

The usual approach to international treaty-making begins with several years of multilateral negotiations aimed at getting a group of nations to acknowledge the need for action. These discussions typically culminate in the signing of a treaty or 'convention', offering a general policy framework or a set of goals. Governed as to form and interpretation by the Vienna Convention on the Law of Treaties, conventions usually include a definition of terms, a description of the geographic scope of the agreement, a general commitment to co-operate, and an outline of the work that needs to be done at future meetings. The standard provisions of most conventions describe the frequency and structure of future meetings to review new information, reassess the problem, and re-evaluate earlier agreements. They often establish a secretariat to convene future meetings, and spell out procedures for adopting more detailed protocols. Sometimes a convention describes how terms of the agreement will (or will not) be enforced. Before entering into force, conventions must be ratified by a specified number of states; additional or amending protocols often require ratification by a specified majority (usually two-thirds) of the parties to the principal instrument.

Once a convention is signed, the countries involved begin negotiations on one or more protocols—discrete actions directed at achieving concrete objectives (or technical standards) consistent with the convention. Not all the signatories to the conventions necessarily participate in the development of follow-up protocols. While the convention phase of treaty negotiations focuses on developing a general statement of the problem and a possible solution, protocols typically deal with the details of implementation.

---

[6] This paper summarizes a much more extensive presentation that will appear in Lawrence Susskind, *Environmental Diplomacy: Negotiating More Effective International Agreements* (New York: Oxford UP, forthcoming).

Since the Stockholm Conference, the convention–protocol approach has been used to produce treaties dealing with a range of regional and global concerns, including the Convention for the Protection of the Mediterranean Sea Against Pollution (the Barcelona Convention, 1976), the Vienna Convention for the Protection of the Ozone Layer (1985), and the Basel Convention on the Control of Transboundary Movements of Hazardous Wastes and Their Disposal (1989).

The Barcelona Convention provides an illustration. It established an agreement among sixteen countries on what has become known as the Mediterranean Action Plan.[7] The Convention was followed quickly by the acceptance of two protocols— one concerning the Prevention of Pollution of the Mediterranean Sea by Dumping from Ships and Aircraft (the 'Dumping Protocol') and another concerning Cooperation in Combating Pollution of the Mediterranean Sea by Oil and Other Harmful Substances in Cases of Emergency (the 'Emergency Protocol'). Both agreements became effective in 1978.

The Barcelona Convention committed the signatories to act both independently and collaboratively to protect and improve the quality of the Mediterranean, to formalize this commitment in future legal agreements, and to support scientific research and monitoring. The Dumping Protocol prohibited the release of certain chemical substances, and required permits for the dumping of less hazardous substances. The Emergency Protocol called for the timely notification in case of oil spills, co-operation during oil spill clean-ups, and the establishment of a centre in Malta to provide technical training and to facilitate the transfer of information regarding new technologies.

The momentum created by the Barcelona Convention provided the necessary impetus for the adoption in 1980 of a third protocol (the 'Land-Based Sources Protocol') regulating a range of agricultural, industrial, and urban-generated effluents.

While the Barcelona Convention set broad goals for protecting the Mediterranean, the protocols addressed specific sources of pollution and set forth plans for remedial action.

---

[7] For a complete account, see Haas, *Saving the Mediterranean*, 97.

1. *Strengths of the convention–protocol approach*

As demonstrated by the treaties described above, the convention–protocol approach has produced agreements directed at improving regional and global environmental quality. Environmental agreements have been signed covering issues as diverse as oil pollution, species protection, and air quality management.[8]

The convention–protocol approach encourages a step-by-step process that allows countries to 'sign on' at the outset even if there is no agreement on the specific actions that ought to be taken. For example, the Barcelona Convention established procedures for monitoring various sources of pollution in the Mediterranean without ordering specific pollution controls or reduction levels. Most countries could agree that further documentation of pollution levels was desirable. However, commitments to specific targets would have been difficult for some countries because of domestic opposition to the short-term economic consequences. Nevertheless, the signing of conventions creates momentum and encourages a commitment to continued scientific enquiry. Groups within each country concerned about environmental protection can point to the signing of a convention as proof that further action is needed. In some cases, the accumulation of scientific evidence will reduce political resistance to remedial action. In other cases, the force of world opinion may create sufficient pressure to induce reluctant countries to sign follow-up protocols. And sometimes, with the mere passage of time, domestic opposition may weaken, making it easier for the leaders in each country to build support for the specific actions outlined in follow-up protocols.

2. *Weaknesses of the convention–protocol approach*

A major shortcoming of the convention–protocol approach is that it encourages a process that is often long and drawn out. The 1973 Convention on International Trade in Endangered Species of Wild Flora and Fauna (CITES) was not signed until ten years after the International Union for the Conservation of Nature and Natural Resources (IUCN) first called attention to the need for an

[8] A brief history of these agreements can be found in Lynton K. Caldwell, *International Environmental Policy: Emergence and Dimensions*, 2nd edn. (Durham, NC: Duke UP, 1990).

international effort to regulate the export, transit, and importation of endangered animal and plant species and their products. During that decade, many traded animal and plant species disappeared.

While the signing of a convention may create momentum that propels subsequent action, the two-step process can also backfire. The signing of a convention can 'take the heat off' political leaders, allowing symbolic but empty promises to substitute for real improvements. Nations and leaders that have absolutely no commitment to improving environmental quality can sign a convention and claim credit for 'doing something' when, in fact, there will be no improvement.

Often the dynamics of the convention–protocol approach yield 'lowest common denominator' agreements designed to appeal to the largest possible number of signatory states. The Basel Convention, for example, incorporates vague language and avoids the politically difficult task of defining key terms. While this made it possible for reluctant countries to sign, it probably undermined the chances of successful implementation. For instance, the agreement calls for the disposal of hazardous waste in an 'environmentally sound manner'. It does not, however, define this phrase. The standard of environmental soundness is left entirely up to each country to define. In a 1989 meeting of CITES, the group agreed to recategorize the African elephant, shifting it to a list requiring more stringent protection. The proposal was met with resistance from certain ivory-trading nations, and was accepted only after a provision was added allowing individual countries to petition for a 'downlisting' of the African elephant from threatened to endangered. The criteria allowing such downlisting for particular countries were not specified in the regulations, and might ultimately thwart the primary intention of the treaty.

Most international environmental treaties impose the same requirements on all signatories. Indeed, that is why the 'lowest common denominator' solution is often the only viable option. The Basel Convention regulates the movement of hazardous wastes between signatory countries, but allows for bilateral agreements between signatory countries and non-signatory countries. This explicitly contradicts an earlier provision of the agreement that states that signatory countries cannot ship hazardous wastes to non-signatory countries. The provision allowing bilateral agreements can certainly be interpreted as a compromise of the overall agreement—however, its inclusion was politically necessary to hold the agreement together.

The Vienna Convention provides another example of the compromise that often occurs. Because one of the major coalitions threatened to withdraw support for any agreement that included CFC production limits, the 1985 Convention called only for monitoring and research; firm limits were not set until 1987 and 1990.

Obviously all treaty negotiations require a give-and-take among the countries involved. In the case of environmental agreements, however, merely satisfying the demands of the interested states is not enough. The dynamics of the natural systems involved must be respected, and impose a constraint upon possible political compromise.

Another key problem is that agreements produced by the convention–protocol approach sometimes reflect an outright neglect of available scientific and technical information, or incorporate requirements that are technically unfeasible or illogical. In negotiating a pollution control strategy for the Mediterranean, for example, political considerations overshadowed the technical wisdom of including the Black Sea states of Bulgaria and Romania.[9] At the point at which a convention is negotiated, agreements are sometimes made that could not bear close technical scrutiny. Unfortunately, when it comes time to work out specific protocols, the terms of the convention may actually obstruct the conclusion of technically appropriate agreements.

Some observers have noted that the US's support for regulating CFCs was first constrained by Dupont Chemical Corporation, the major domestic CFC producer, but was later actively facilitated by Dupont's development of CFC substitutes. During Convention negotiations, countries will cite scientific evidence that justifies the general policies that they prefer. Since the implications of these policies need not be confronted at that point in time, counter-productive policies, which frequently constrain subsequent protocol design, may be adopted. This is a very real danger of the two-step drafting process.

Finally, negotiations in the typical convention–protocol process are often dominated by the most powerful states. The final

---

[9] Haas, *Saving the Mediterranean*, 99.

'deal' leading to the Montreal Protocol was negotiated primarily between the United States and the European Economic Community, the two largest consumers and producers of CFCs. African states have called the Basel Convention a 'sell-out' by the Third World signatories, because of the inability of the weaker states to win inclusion of provisions which shift the liability of hazardous waste disposal from recipient states to the generating or exporting states.[10] The *ad hoc* nature of the convention–protocol system is partly to blame. In the absence of a formal negotiation system defining the rights of each country to help set the agenda for negotiations and outlining the obligations of the secretariat to achieve a certain minimum threshold of support from all nations before environmental treaties can be considered legitimate, the most powerful states can, in effect, write the rules, dominate the dissemination of technical information, and control the negotiation process.

B. Why Does the Existing Approach Fall Short?

In our view, the *ad hoc* convention–protocol approach as currently practised fails to come to grips with certain negotiation problems. It is also somewhat ill-suited to the unique attributes of environmental problems. Finally, it does not fully address the fundamental realities of international relations, and is deficient as a result.

1. *Negotiation problems*

First, the convention–protocol approach actually encourages the 'hard bargaining' tendencies of many countries. It does little to discourage countries from misrepresenting their needs. It is not designed to encourage countries to separate the tasks of creating options for mutual gain from the task of securing agreement. There is insufficient focus on building informal agreements and coalitions prior to formal meetings.[11] Each of these problems

[10] For the attitude of many African states, compare the 1991 Bamako Convention.

[11] For a discussion of the ways in which the pre-negotiation stage of a multilateral negotiation might work, see Lawrence Susskind and Jeffrey Cruikshank, *Breaking the Impasse: Consensual Approaches to Resolving Public Disputes* (New York: Basic Books, 1987), 136–85.

contributes to the inefficiency of the process and accounts, in part, for the difficulties of achieving the desired results.

Countries often misrepresent or exaggerate their needs as part of their bargaining strategy. This tactic may be useful in 'one-shot', single-issue negotiations. However, in circumstances where effective problem-solving and long-term working relationships are crucial, the parties involved are better off if they only make statements that prove to be accurate. This leads to more effective solutions and makes implementation of agreements easier. In addition, when negotiators are in the business of trading concessions (rather than engaging in genuine problem-solving), they must keep checking back with their leadership at home. An inordinate amount of time is wasted performing the 'concessionary dance'. When negotiations involve many issues and many parties who will have to deal with each other on a continuing basis, it makes more sense to share candid accounts of each side's interests and to avoid positional bargaining.[12]

When negotiations are conducted without clear separation between the steps of creating or identifying policy options for specific issues and choosing among different options, negotiators usually hesitate to fully explore the alternatives. They presume that a willingness to explore an option will be misconstrued as a commitment to that option. The failure to distinguish 'inventing' from 'committing' inhibits creative problem-solving (which usually requires some playing of the 'what if' game). All too often, negotiations become a test of will. The parties lock into a battle over a small number of options without the benefit of creative brainstorming that might have yielded additional alternatives responsive to the benefit of all sides.

The two-stage structure of the convention–protocol approach makes no distinction between the tasks of inventing and committing, although it could. At the convention-drafting stage, the goal is typically to keep discussions at a very general level so that all countries will at least agree that some (unspecified) action is needed to solve a problem. At the protocol-drafting stage, the goal is usually to find a formula that everyone can accept. Such formulas usually contain a great many exceptions, underscoring

---

[12] These points are made quite convincingly in Roger Fisher and William Ury, *Getting to Yes: Negotiating Agreements Without Giving In* (Boston: Houghton Mifflin, 1981).

the fact that in practice no major country can be forced to sign or ratify. Convention writing and protocol writing are usually treated as zero-sum games. By the time countries come together to negotiate treaty language, they have usually 'locked in' to certain fixed positions. Little if any creative problem-solving is possible. When agreements do emerge, they are usually the result of compromise by the most powerful parties rather than the result of a creative resolution of differences.

In the examples cited earlier, the agenda for each negotiation was set through informal communications between the secretariat or lead organization and a few dominant nations. For example, in the meetings of the International Whaling Commission, the agenda was rigidly controlled by the whaling nations for many years.[13] In negotiations in which each nation knows its own interest, the agendas should be crafted to ensure that the issues of greatest concern to all affected states are included. If important issues are omitted, some nations will have no incentive to participate, or they may feel compelled to sabotage the negotiations or subsequent implementation of agreements. A more flexible and inclusive approach to agenda-setting for treaty negotiation is needed. Unfortunately, the narrowing of negotiations that occurs when specific protocols are negotiated one at a time and the general formula is already set by the signed convention pushes environmental treaty negotiations in exactly the wrong direction.

The convention–protocol approach to international environmental negotiations as presently practised also fails to take full account of the special qualities of environmental problems. Many negotiations tend to focus only on allocation of losses incurred through environmental regulations. They do not deal with the gains resulting from wiser resource management and the ways they might be shared. Indeed, most environmental treaties aim to curtail pollution or to regulate the use of common resources by *restricting* the activities of participating countries. The economic losses suggested by these new rules provide solid excuses for many nations to refuse to join these negotiations. Ways of sharing the economic benefits of environmental protection and

[13] Bruce Stedman, 'The International Whaling Commission and Negotiation for a Moratorium on Whaling', in Susskind, Siskind and Breslin (eds.), *Nine Case Studies in International Environmental Negotiation*.

preservation are rarely offered as a compelling rationale for participation, although the gains rather than the losses ought to be the main focus.

2. Special features of environmental issues

Environmental issues almost invariably involve a degree of scientific uncertainty that complicates decision-making. Our understanding of the natural world is incomplete. Forecasting tools provide only crude approximations based on unverifiable assumptions. Disagreement among technical experts on complex environmental issues is pervasive. If one country thinks it will be disadvantaged by a particular policy proposal, it can easily locate sympathetic experts to raise doubts about the adequacy of the scientific evidence put forward by others. If a country wants to delay implementation of costly pollution abatement measures, it is not hard to argue that further study would be desirable before long-term commitments are made.

Many environmental issues also hinge on the problem of how best to manage a common resource, or its converse, how to penalize 'free riders'. If the benefits of regulated development or pollution control are diffuse, and accrue to all nations irrespective of their behaviour, some nations will feel little or no incentive to accept any restrictions. These we call 'free riders'. For example, the Montreal Protocol as initially adopted in 1987 contained only limited provisions to encourage large developing states such as China and India to participate, and might have left them tempted to abstain, since reductions in the use and production of CFCs by other nations (especially bigger users) would in any event slow down the rate of ozone depletion.[14] The tragedy, of course, is that if most countries adopted this rationale, they would not take the actions needed to curb ozone depletion. The need to solve the 'free rider' problem and motivate collective action was recognized in the 1990 London Amendments to the Protocol. Following the 1990 meeting, China and India both announced their intention to join the regime in the future, although the prospect of their further delay signalled their intention to use this bargaining chip on other issues.

[14] Granda, 'The Montreal Protocol on Substances that Deplete the Ozone Layer'.

Environmental negotiations, up to now, have been conducted largely in isolation from negotiations on other international issues such as debt, trade, or security. Negotiations sponsored solely by UNEP cannot speak to linkages between environmentally related actions and other important economic and security-related considerations. Some developing nations have expressed a desire to make these linkages, [15] especially in relation to climate change. For nations facing dire poverty, malnutrition, foreign debts, and rampant illiteracy, the long-term and uncertain consequences of environmental deterioration do not carry a sense of urgency. In such instances, linking development opportunities and environmental considerations may provide the needed incentive for co-operation. From a negotiation perspective, the linking of issues can increase the potential for mutual gains. Since the goal of a well-structured negotiation is not to encourage compromise but to find ways of ensuring that all parties will be better off if they co-operate, linkage may be crucial.

3. *Deficiencies of past convention–protocol practice*

The convention–protocol approach as currently practised fails to respond to two fundamental questions that arise in other types of international negotiations: monitoring and enforcement provisions, and the role of non-governmental interests in the negotiations.

Most environmental agreements worked out through international negotiations include only weak monitoring and enforcement provisions. For example, the International Convention for the Regulation of Whaling (one of the longer-lasting international environmental treaties) established the International Whaling Commission to oversee the provisions of the treaty, but failed to give it any enforcement powers. [16] Monitoring and enforcement are difficult because they conflict with the prerogatives of national sovereignty. Yet, without effective monitoring and enforcement, real implementation of any agreement is highly unlikely. *Ad hoc* negotiations sponsored by a less-than-powerful agency of the United Nations will never be able to overcome the

---

[15] *Environmental Problems: A Global Security Threat*, Report of the Twenty-Fourth United Nations of the Next Decade Conference, Stanley Foundation, 1989.
[16] Stedman, 'The International Whaling Commission'.

resistance to instituting a comprehensive multilateral system for ensuring compliance.

Confusion over the role of non-governmental interests (NGOs, corporations, scientific organizations, etc.) threatens to undermine future environmental treaties, just as it threatens the stability of other negotiated regimes.[17] As non-governmental interests grow increasingly active in negotiations over international environmental issues, their assistance in gathering technical information, devising technologically feasible policies, and mobilizing necessary public support will become critical. Moreover, their ability to undermine the implementation of agreements of which they are not a part will be enhanced. Without a clear redefinition of their role, many agreements (even if signed by substantial numbers of countries) will fail.

There are several devices that can be used to bolster traditional treaty-making. For instance, some treaties include Annexes, or appendices, setting forth procedures for revising a treaty as new information becomes available. These can make it possible to avoid a new round of ratification every time the terms of a treaty need to be fine-tuned in light of new developments. Also, signatories can take exception to certain items in one or another Annex while still signing the general treaty. Finally, interlocking 'framework' conventions have also been suggested as means for ensuring that protocol negotiations are not postponed indefinitely. Ratification of one or more protocols can be required as the price of membership in a framework convention.[18]

In addition to formal treaties, the enunciation of general principles, the adoption of internationally recognized guidelines, and the increasing reliance on standard-setting by international technical bodies have all been used to push countries to accept environmental obligations they would not otherwise accept.[19] The Stockholm principles, and others like the World Conservation Strategy and the World Charter for Nature, for example, have

[17] See the chapters by Stairs and Taylor and Bramble and Porter in this volume.

[18] For detailed discussion see Patricia Birnie's chapter in this volume.

[19] These are nicely described in Peter Thacher's 'International Agreements, and Cooperation in Environmental Conservation and Resource Management', prepared for the Workshop on Managing the Global Commons: Decision Making and Conflict Resolution in Response to Climate Change, 1 Aug. 1989, World Resources Institute, Washington, DC, pp. 9–12. See also his chapter in this volume.

been adopted by the UN General Assembly and thus elevated to a quasi-legal status. Non-binding guidelines or 'recommended practices' endorsed by international bodies have provided non-governmental organizations with the basis of legitimacy necessary to press for modifications in national policy. Highly specialized agencies have, in some instances, been empowered to set and revise standards without governmental ratification. While these non-treaty approaches may help to speed up international efforts, they are not a substitute for formal agreements. We think the treaty-making process can be and ought to be strengthened.

C. Recommendations for Enhancing the Effectiveness of International Environmental Negotiations[20]

Given the difficulties of negotiating international environmental agreements using the existing convention–protocol approach, we propose nine possible improvements. Our measure of success is not how many agreements are signed or how many countries ratify each agreement. Rather, it is the speed and effectiveness with which the nations of the world produce tangible environmental improvements.

1. *Decentralized alliances to encourage action*

Non-traditional clusters of countries should be empowered to caucus well ahead of formal negotiations. There are many 'small bargains' and working alliances that can be made before formal global negotiations begin. For example, the USA, Russia, China, and the EC might meet to review a possible strategy for reducing the emission of so-called greenhouse gases. As the chief emitting countries, their views on the desirability of various control strategies will obviously carry substantial weight. Therefore, preliminary meetings among these nations to consider the advan-

[20] These recommendations are contained in the Salzburg Initiative, an action agenda prepared in 1990 by an international team of more than 100 diplomats, environmentalists, negotiation specialists, and international relations experts. The Initiative was prepared with support from the Dana Greeley Foundation in the United States and the Salzburg Seminar in Salzburg, Austria.

tages and disadvantages of possible courses of action could be quite influential. By including China in this group, the usual North–South split might be avoided. Along similar lines, all the Atlantic coastal nations or all the Pacific Rim countries might meet to consider policy options regarding ocean protection if such a treaty were being contemplated. Non-traditional clusters of countries should be encouraged to meet in exploratory problem-solving sessions. This could avoid the formation of traditional blocking coalitions and possibly develop more positive interactions between developed and developing nations. The primary objective of these sessions should be to encourage a clearer understanding of the needs on all sides before any country is required to take a formal position on specific policies.

New forums in which to convene clusters of countries with shared concerns to do preparatory work on environmental issues are essential. Moreover, maintaining flexibility—even after formal negotiations are under way—is vitally important. This will be difficult to achieve in many cases, since traditional meetings of the representatives of sovereign states are often politically choreographed so far ahead of time that they provide little or no opportunity for the spontaneous inventing of options. Bringing together non-traditional clusters of countries in advance of such meetings might encourage more flexibility. Institutional catalysts willing to host such meetings should not have to depend on the UN system for approval or support. While this recommendation flies in the face of tradition, it does not require major institutional changes. Informal alliance building, joint fact-finding, and creative brainstorming for new policy options by countries with shared environmental concerns or circumstances should be encouraged.

2. Pre-negotiation assistance to individual countries

Many countries find it difficult to prepare for and participate in international negotiations. What time and money they do spend is devoted to hammering out internal agreements. Very little attention is devoted to researching how other countries view the particular problem. Very little information sharing occurs.

Some countries do not have the legal and scientific resources to ensure that their delegations are adequately briefed, particularly on the scientific and technical aspects of environmental policy questions. They could benefit enormously from off-the-record, informal briefings by expert advisers of their own choosing. Conceivably, panels could be assembled to provide seminars-on-demand for any country interested. It is important to provide access to this kind of advice before countries lock into specific positions in the form of draft treaty language. By that time, countries are usually too worried about 'outsiders' knowing what their official positions are, or what their negotiating strategies are likely to be.

It may be that the United Nations Development Programme (UNDP) is best situated to underwrite pre-negotiation assistance ahead of scheduled conferences. Because UNDP has financial support to offer, especially for development efforts that are clearly environmentally sustainable, most countries are likely to take its offer of assistance seriously. To the extent that countries are seeking briefings focused primarily on scientific issues, UNEP might also play a role. Perhaps regional conference secretariats should be named several years before all planned conferences. Such secretariats could assume responsibility for matching up experts, NGOs, or international scientific organizations with countries that request assistance. The existing treaty-making process assumes that each country can do whatever is necessary to build its own negotiating competence. Experience shows, however, that this assumption is incorrect. Providing pre-negotiation assistance to nations that lack the scientific and technical resources of more developed nations is both the 'right thing' to do, and should also save considerable time and money when the full-scale negotiations begin.

3. *New approaches to treaty drafting*

While it is preferable to begin formal negotiation with a single text in hand—especially one that focuses on a relatively small number of points on which disagreements have been bracketed—it may be a mistake to move too quickly to actual treaty language. Instead, conference leaders should encourage pre-conference working groups to prepare multiple proposals that do not represent official commitments of any kind. The widest array of interests should be reflected in developing these early conceptual options. By relying on cross-cutting clusters of countries (including non-governmental interests) to prepare multiple proposals, official national position-taking can be avoided for as long as possible. It is conceivable the UNEP could designate ambassadors-at-large to convene cross-cutting working groups. Formal ground rules regarding the negotiation of future environmental treaties should discourage all countries from announcing positions on specific policy proposals.

After gathering numerous preliminary proposals, the conference secretariat can produce a single text on which to focus formal negotiation.

4. *An expanded role for non-governmental interests*

There are a number of reasons for expanding the role of non-governmental interests in the process of international environmental negotiation. Most important is the fact that international agreements must be implemented by individual countries, and unless there is a constituency in each country that is willing to push for treaty implementation, the results will be minimal. Non-governmental interests help to set the political agenda in many countries. They provide continuity even when the formal political leadership fluctuates.

Key groups left out of the negotiation process may seek to block ratification and impede implementation of agreements that do not respond to their concerns. Thus, within countries, it makes sense to pull together the institutional players needed to achieve a national consensus. These new 'civil society structures' may take different forms in different parts of the world. Regional round tables, such as those organized by the Canadian government, provide one helpful model.[21] Other possible structures include official national advisory boards appointed by the government or unofficial consensus-building coalitions of non-governmental interests.

New ways must be found to ensure that international agreements reflect the concerns of non-governmental interests in each country. This means that the delegations from each country

---

[21] *British Columbia Round Table on the Environment and the Economy* (1990). The Round Table is made up of British Columbians drawn from all walks of life and with strikingly different perspectives.

ought to include a broad cross-section of interests; pre-negotiation ought to involve more than just governmental representatives; and non-governmental interests need to be given an opportunity to review and comment on draft agreements before their respective national governments sign them.

Non-governmental interests also have an important role to play in post-negotiation monitoring. An 'International League of NGOs', for example, might organize monitoring efforts along the same lines as Amnesty International does. It could sponsor and instruct monitoring groups within every country. An environmental version of the Red Cross (i.e. the 'Green Cross') might play a fact-finding role when ecological disasters occur. There are numerous roles for non-governmental interests to play at the subnational, national, and international levels. Implementation of negotiated agreements will depend on the support of these groups.

The involvement of non-governmental interests both within and apart from official delegations can also help overcome traditional sovereignty concerns. Environmental stewardship or similar concepts that call for world-wide and multigenerational concerns that transcend national sovereignty are more likely to be supported by non-governmental interests than by political officials who fear any encroachment on the prerogatives of nationhood.

An approach to treaty negotiation that hangs on the single thread of formal, nation-to-nation interaction will not be as strong as a more elaborate set of interactions that weave together governmental and non-governmental interests.

5. *Recategorization of countries for purposes of prescribing action*

To avoid the push for lowest-common-denominator solutions, it makes sense to think about categorizing countries in ways that lead to variable policy prescriptions that take account of the different circumstances in each part of the world. For instance, countries could be categorized by the extent to which they cause an environmental problem or by the extent to which they have the resources to respond—for example, the 30 per cent sulphur dioxide reduction 'club' under the Geneva Convention on Transboundary Air Pollution. Different standards of responsibility or performance could then be specified for each category. So, for example, countries that produce the most carbon dioxide would be expected to make the greatest percentage reductions. On the other hand, countries that make the greatest percentage reductions relative to GNP per capita might be entitled to the most substantial incentive payments. The prospects for treaty implementation are greater if each country feels it is being treated fairly. Fairness is more likely to be perceived where countries are not all expected to meet exactly the same requirements.

6. *Reinforcement of the proper connection between science and politics*

The integrity of scientific analysis is undermined when technical studies are used primarily to justify politically expedient views. Data must be generated that are credible to all parties regardless of their political biases or priorities. Credible data are more likely to be generated by international collaborations than by national institutes. All nations should commit themselves to strengthening the network of international scientific institutions.

Many diplomats and politicians have the mistaken notion that once the scientific and technical community has defined a problem, the views of experts ought to give way to the political judgement of elected officials. In fact, ongoing scientific involvement is essential. Although elected officials must bear the final responsibility for resolving whatever contradictory claims remain, wise decisions and successful implementation are more likely to result from the continued interplay of scientific and political perspectives.

Negotiations almost always start before conclusive scientific evidence is at hand. Indeed, environmental problems are rarely fully understood at the time political decisions must be made. Additional research is almost always required. Once a baseline is obtained—a significant challenge in itself—it is usually appropriate to monitor ongoing results to determine whether policies are working as intended, and what adjustments in standards or procedures might be needed. Successful implementation of environmental treaties will depend on constant readjustment of goals and methods. This can only be accomplished if accurate monitoring data are available.

In evaluating the economic implications of various responses to

environmental problems, we must realize that economic effects
are as hard to predict as scientific impacts. Policymakers must
realize that every effort to incorporate hard-to-quantify costs and
benefits will always be surrounded by the uncertainty that
plagues scientific forecasting. The monitoring of both economic
and ecological impacts should be linked to a strategy that allows
for mid-course corrections in policy.

In light of the uncertainties and the difficulties of predicting
the effects of alternative policies, it makes sense to rely more on
contingent agreements. Instead of working to forge consensus on
one 'best estimate' of the future, why not specify alternative
courses of action given various possible 'futures'? Even parties
who disagree on the likelihood of certain events occurring should
be able to agree on what ought to be done if such events do
transpire. Of course, this means that continuous monitoring and
periodic recalibration of standards and responses must be built
into agreements. Continuous monitoring arrangements ought to
be a primary feature of all environmental treaties. The Montreal
Protocol and the London Dumping Convention are examples of
agreements that already incorporate such mechanisms in a
limited way.[22]

7. Encouragement of appropriate issue linkage

More creative linkages that can generate economic incentives for
environmental protection should be sought. While institutional
difficulties may seem insurmountable at first, the advantages of
linking environmental improvements to the provisions of the
General Agreement on Tariffs and Trade (GATT), for example, or
to bilateral foreign aid agreements, ought to be considered. There
are numerous development pathways each country can take.
There is no single best or correct pattern of development, and
alternative pathways will look very different from each national
perspective. By pinpointing these differences, it should be possible to identify mutually advantageous trades.

[22] The Convention on the Prevention of Marine Pollution by Dumping Wastes
and Other Matters was signed in London in 1972. It prohibits the disposal at sea of
high-level radioactive waste. It permits the dumping of low-level nuclear waste
under permit by 'competent national authorities'. The listing of what countries
can and cannot dump into the ocean is reviewed periodically as additional
scientific and technical information becomes available.

For example, one set of countries might be willing to work toward greater energy efficiency (and thereby achieve carbon dioxide reductions) as long as these countries receive, in return, access to energy-efficient technologies on a subsidized basis. The countries providing this incentive might well benefit by creating new markets for their emerging technologies. All such linkages and trades should take account of the fact that each country should be free to follow a development path that it finds suitable. Newly industrializing nations need not duplicate the energy choices or the inefficient patterns of development that other nations chose before them.

8. *Removal of penalties for constructive unilateral action*

It is not just scientific uncertainty that discourages nations from taking action that would protect environmental resources or improve environmental quality. There is a fear that following a common course of action will place a nation at a competitive disadvantage. There is little incentive for a country to take unilateral action voluntarily to improve its environment. Moreover, in the long term, there is a concern that should international agreements be reached later, nations that have already taken action will be penalized by being forced to make still further cuts, ignoring the efforts they have already made.

There are ways in which nations may be encouraged to take unilateral action while international negotiations are still under way. The most straightforward approach would be to forge a preliminary agreement among a core group of nations that establishes a baseline against which future efforts will be measured and credited.

So, for example, 'hold harmless' arrangements could be established as follows: (1) A baseline year would be set, after which any improvements would be counted. Early efforts would be worth more than later ones. Indeed, a modest additional credit might be offered for improvements achieved unilaterally. (2) Difficult questions, such as how credits for reductions achieved prior to the base year will be calculated, or what the method of computing a nation's future obligations will be, would be left to subsequent negotiations. (3) It would be essential to describe precisely the types of improvements or efforts that would be counted.

'Hold harmless' provisions can be negotiated quickly among a coalition of countries that promise they will not support any agreement that does not take account of their provisional accord. This would encourage constructive unilateral action.

9. Educative role for the media to play

The mass media have a dual role to play. They need to report events—such as important meetings, agreements reached, and environmental impacts—as part of their news coverage. They have an even more important role to play as a vehicle for public education.

The mass media must be encouraged to provide additional space and time for coverage of environmental news as environmental diplomacy occupies an increasingly important place in international relations. By their action, or inaction, the mass media legitimize in the public consciousness the positions taken by transnational corporations, non-governmental interests, and governments on specific environmental issues. The media's educative role should include anticipating coming events and problems as well as following through with coverage of the success or failure of various treaties and agreements. If the story ends when the treaty is signed, the media have not done their job.

Journalists, especially those from developing nations, need opportunities to sharpen their understanding of international environmental negotiations. They, as well as the particular organizations for which they work, ought to be honoured for their contributions to public education. A world-wide network of scientific organizations and academic institutions ought to take responsibility for building an environmental data bank that the mass media can tap into electronically.

10. Summary

The nine recommendations described above would lead to a new approach to environmental treaty making. They point to the desirability of abandoning the two-step convention–protocol approach in favour of one extended negotiation process beginning with a more elaborate pre-negotiation phase (highlighted by a great many informal caucuses of non-traditional clusters of countries). Actual negotiations would not focus on vague language as in recent conventions, but instead would emphasize the design of contingent agreements emphasizing the pay-offs or benefits of compliance. Different categories of countries would be expected to meet different targets. There would also be considerable emphasis on the design of post-negotiation or implementation activities. These would be spelled out in comprehensive treaties providing an umbrella for multiple protocols. They would emphasize detailed monitoring and reporting procedures, ground rules for reconvening to consider ongoing adjustments in goals and procedures, and explicit dispute resolution mechanisms. Institutional responsibility for handling all these post-negotiation tasks might be assigned to a rotating secretariat or a treaty monitoring group designated by the signatories.

While many of these items could be addressed under the existing approach to treaty making at the time detailed protocols are negotiated, they tend not to be. Too much time is wasted drafting well-meaning but vague conventions. Protocol negotiations are too narrowly focused, missing opportunities for mutually beneficial trades across issues. The emerging notion of negotiating a convention and multiple protocols at the same time makes a great deal more sense—especially if an adequately supported period of pre-negotiation precedes such comprehensive efforts.

D. The Need for Institutional Reform

The current limited powers of multilateral institutions are insufficient for the task of solving environmental problems that transcend national boundaries. Institutional redesign ought to be near the top of any international environmental agenda.

Some observers have suggested that reforms such as those we have suggested here would require changes in the UN Charter. We disagree. The most important reforms could be accomplished by informally realigning the elements of the United Nations system, and encouraging the signing of memoranda of understanding among the various UN agencies as well as the International Monetary Fund, World Bank, and General Agreement on Tariffs and Trade (GATT).

New arrangements are needed to ensure formal linkages between environmental protection and development planning on a world-wide basis. In this respect, the nations of the world ought to do more to build upon the work of the World Commission on Environment and Development (the Brundtland Commission).[23] Rather than focusing on upgrading UNEP to the status of a 'specialized agency', as some have suggested, UNDP and the other development institutions ought to be given greater responsibility (and thus more accountability) for ensuring sustainable development.

All countries should be encouraged to rely more heavily on the International Court of Justice (ICJ) and to allow it to play a more active role in helping to resolve disputes concerning enforcement of international agreements. There are also a variety of roles that experienced mediators might play in assisting particular environmental negotiations. Perhaps they could be assigned by the President of the ICJ or, as in the past, by the United Nations Secretary-General. Activist secretariats should also assume more responsibility for identifying mediation resources that can be of help in specific situations.

A formal structure—perhaps a clearing-house and training locale as well as financial support—for nations and non-governmental interests that want to build their environmental negotiation skills is needed.

Institutional reforms must be made to support a shift from the existing convention–protocol approach to a more complete and effective negotiation process, one that encourages flexibility, appropriate linkages, and a long-term approach to joint problem-solving. We do not need a new world government, nor a new set of multilateral organizations. We do need to take account of what we have learned since Stockholm about the strengths and weaknesses of the existing approach to environmental treaty making, if we are to achieve more effective resource management and pollution control on a world-wide basis.

[23] World Commission on Environment and Development, *Our Common Future* (New York: Oxford UP, 1987).

6

Climate Change: Problems of Law-Making

Elliot L. Richardson

ENVIRONMENTAL concerns that could appropriately become the subject of multilateral conventions in the immediate future include climate change, biodiversity, sustainable development, forestry, and safety in biotechnology. Of them all, the most widely ramified and economically sensitive is climate change. It is also that in which the UN General Assembly has taken the most detailed interest. Efforts to complete a framework treaty, and to elaborate this in subsequent instruments, have been and will continue to be a central focus of international activity. Many of the issues that will have to be resolved in developing multilateral arrangements to deal with climate change are also basic to the other subjects of potential conventions. Much of what I say here thus applies equally to those other subjects.

A. Dimensions of the Task

The shaping of a framework treaty on climate change poses difficulties more dismaying than those surmounted by the negotiators of any previous multilateral agreement. The most complex and ambitious multilateral agreement thus far attempted is the 1982 UN Convention on the Law of the Sea (UNCLOS), the outcome of a conference which laboured from 1973 to 1982. The Conference was a kind of legislative assembly whose task was to enact rules addressing every human concern with the oceans. At stake was jurisdiction over all oceanic living resources, about a third of the world's oil and gas reserves, and a potential new bonanza in the form of deep-seabed mining. For the major maritime countries, freedom of navigation and overflight was a matter of vital concern. For the coastal states, expanded jurisdiction over economic resources was a comparable interest. Regimes for scientific research, protection of the marine environment, and dispute settlement also had to be developed. Although the artificial notion of 'the sovereign equality of states' nominally imposed a one-nation, one-vote decision-making formula, as a practical matter nothing could be decided except by consensus. In a body of 156 independent delegations, the nurturing of consensus required an immense amount of planning, manoeuvring, compromising, and placating.[1] Like a combination of no-limit poker and three-dimensional chess, it was the most difficult and demanding exercise in which I have ever participated.

The Third United Nations Conference on the Law of the Sea that negotiated the LOS Convention was able to draw on a highly developed body of customary international law that had been evolving since at least the publication in 1609 of Hugo Grotius's *Mare Liberum*. Their most innovative concepts adapted existing legal regimes to technological change (the exclusive economic zone and the continental margin provisions) and the prospect of a new industry (deep-seabed mining). Although substantial interests were at stake, particularly with respect to jurisdiction over hydrocarbons, implementation of the LOS Convention will not in any presently foreseeable circumstance entail massive economic shifts or sacrifices.

The framers of a multilateral treaty on climate change did not start out with the same advantages. Customary international law on the environment is scanty, and the existing multilateral agreements are narrow in scope. They protect humans, animals, fish, plants, insects, and other forms of life from the harms caused by

[1] Developments at the Conference were chronicled in a series of articles by John R. Stevenson and Bernard H. Oxman, *AJIL* 68 (1974), 1; *AJIL* 69 (1975), 1; and *AJIL* 69 (1975), 763; and by Oxman, *AJIL* 71 (1977), 247; *AJIL* 72 (1978), 57; *AJIL* 73 (1979), 1; *AJIL* 74 (1980), 1; *AJIL* 75 (1981), 211; and *AJIL* 76 (1982), 1. For documentation see S. Houston Lay, *et al.* (eds.), *New Directions in the Law of the Sea: Documents*, 11 vols. (Dobbs Ferry, NY: Oceana, 1973–81); and Renate Platzoder (ed.), *Third United Nations Conference on the Law of the Sea: Documents*, 18 vols. (London: Oceana, 1982–   ). See also B. Buzan, 'Negotiating by Consensus: Developments in Techniques at the Third United Nations Conference on the Law of the Sea', *AJIL* 75 (1981), 324; P. Allott, 'Power Sharing in the Law of the Sea', *AJIL* 77 (1983), 1; and H. Caminos and M. R. Molitor, 'Perspectives on the New Law of the Sea: Progressive Development of International Law and the Package Deal', *AJIL* 79 (1985), 871.

toxic, radioactive, or disease-causing substances. These harms are widely recognized. Even in the case of the Montreal Protocol (as amended), the most future-oriented of the agreements thus far negotiated, there was general acceptance both that CFCs caused the ozone hole over the Antarctic and that the destruction of the ozone layer would have serious global consequences. Moreover, none of the existing environmental agreements confers on an international institution the power to set binding standards, issue and enforce regulations, or prescribe sanctions. Few provide for dispute settlement.[2]

By contrast, the damage that may eventually result from the accumulation of greenhouse gases cannot be seen or felt; the activities that are believed to be causing it are for the most part unrestricted. But the most striking distinction between climate change and other environmental concerns is that the actuality of global warming is not only distant in time but fraught with uncertainty as to its probable extent and consequences.

The negotiating process is further complicated by the enormous and astonishing variety of the activities that generate greenhouse gases: wood fires, dairy farming, rice growing, power generation, air travel, grass burning, automobile travel, and many others. Conducted on a vast scale, these activities are important in one way or another to every human being on earth. Large economic dislocations are bound to be set in motion by even the most conservative and non-coercive means of reducing the risk of climate change. It is inevitable, therefore, that industrial countries will resist constraints which impair their competitiveness and that developing countries will resist constraints which impair their growth.

By comparison with the limited harms addressed by existing environmental agreements, the devastation that could result from substantial global warming would far exceed the harm caused by any previous human action (except perhaps population growth). Moreover, the accumulation of greenhouse gases is irreversible. Notwithstanding uncertainty, this is a powerful reason for taking preventive action now. But if the long-term

[2] For an illuminating analysis of existing agreements, see Peter H. Sand, 'International Cooperation: The Environmental Experience', in Jessica Tuchman Mathews (ed.), *Preserving the Global Environment: The Challenge of Shared Leadership* (New York: W. W. Norton, 1991), 236–79.

threat of climate change is enormous, so will be the short-term cost of averting it.

Although some of the actions demanded by a serious effort to curb the build-up of greenhouse gases will be painful, many, including energy conservation, will at the same time yield other benefits. Climate change aside, we should be taking steps to make more efficient use of the power generated by coal-fired plants. The 1990–1 Gulf crisis should have given new impetus to developing new energy sources and phasing out gas-guzzling automobiles. Other useful purposes will be served by checking deforestation and promoting reforestation, recycling more paper, cutting down on packaging material, lowering taxes on conservation land, and using more fuel-efficient stoves. Although largely instigated by health worries, a ban on CFCs will also eliminate a source of greenhouse gases (provided the use of harmful substitutes is not thereby encouraged). Meanwhile, the prevention of global warming needs to be seen as part of a broader atmospheric protection effort that includes reducing smog, curbing acid rain, and stopping other toxic emissions.

The fact that there are many good reasons to protect the atmosphere is no guarantee that enough will be done. Nor is the necessity for a network of multilateral arrangements diminished because it is in every nation's—or most nations'—interest to combat climate change. The results of independent national action are bound to be highly uneven. From the standpoint of impact as well as of equity, there is no alternative to broad-based multilateral co-operation.

B. Approaches to a Treaty

Three quite different forms for a treaty on climate change might in principle appear open to consideration. It could comprise one part of the charter for a global environmental protection agency with standard-setting, regulatory, and enforcement powers. It could be part of a comprehensive code of generalized obligations to do the right thing by the environment. Or it could offer an array of procedural devices designed to stimulate action rather than prescribe it. Although the Law of the Sea Conference pioneered negotiating procedures that will serve the environment no less well than they served the oceans, it would not make sense to try to incorporate into a treaty on climate change detailed prescriptive language like that embodied in the Law of the Sea Convention. Besides, the Law of the Sea negotiations began twenty years ago, and the resulting Convention has not yet entered into force.[3] If it is important to prevent climate change, it is important to begin now.

The first of the three approaches would require delegating to a multilateral organization the power to override national environmental policies or practices. Significantly, not even the limited environmental agreements now in effect confer such authority. It is scarcely conceivable, therefore, that a consensus on the composition, decision-making, and regulatory powers of a global EPA could emerge in the early phases of the process of building an effective climate change regime. The effort to create such a consensus would in any case be bound to take a long time. An additional consideration, sufficient in itself to disqualify this approach, is its administrative unwieldiness. The attempt to impose uniform environmental prohibitions, constraints, controls, and standards on over 170 sovereign states would inevitably provoke resistance and resentment in most of them. To overcome these reactions, the global EPA would have no alternative but to deploy a legion of inspectors and enforcers. This, rather than increasing compliance, could well have the opposite effect.

The second approach—a comprehensive code of obligations— would avoid these pitfalls. This approach also has some positive attributes. It would, for one thing, be a useful means of building a broad base of international acceptance of some important objectives. Within member states it would serve as a vehicle for mobilizing domestic support for urgently needed environmental reforms. As a self-contained instrument, however, a comprehensive code of obligations would have serious limitations. Not being declaratory of well-established customary law, it would take a long time to bring state practice into conformity with its precepts. Its necessarily vague and general language would be subject to highly variable interpretations. This same vagueness could also be said to rationalize resistance to higher standards.

---

[3] The Convention provides that it shall enter into force 12 months after the deposit of the sixtieth instrument of ratification or accession. By 30 Apr. 1991 only 47 states had deposited such instruments, almost all of them developing nations.

Standing by itself, a code of obligations lacks a viable means of making something happen.

The third approach comes from the opposite direction. Making things happen is its primary goal. For this purpose it can draw on an array of devices that includes data collection, technical assistance, monitoring, reporting, and standard setting. It can also establish procedures for facilitating the adoption of supplementary agreements or protocols. Separately negotiated, these would deal with concrete problems whenever it became propitious to do so. Meanwhile, a permanent organization would operate a procedural machinery. As previously noted, this approach aims at stimulating action rather than prescribing it. Its weakness is that, until the protocols begin to be adopted, it lacks any substantive content to which its machinery can be hooked up. But there is no reason why a code of obligations cannot be linked to procedures and no reason why action-oriented mechanisms cannot be used to promote the fulfilment of obligations. The obvious solution is to merge the second and third approaches. The qualities of each can thereby be made to offset the defects of the other.

The process of evaluating alternative approaches to the framework treaty has not been free of difficulty. It was apparent that UNCED 1992 would not itself be a suitable forum for a negotiation of this kind, and that a consensus in favour of some version or variant of the three possible approaches was needed before the delegates arrived in Rio de Janeiro. The UN General Assembly asked UNEP and WMO to lay the groundwork for the negotiations on a basis taking into account the work of the Intergovernmental Panel on Climate Change. An Intergovernmental Negotiating Committee began a series of regular meetings in February 1991, with the ultimate task of producing a working draft for the 1992 UNCED. The Preparatory Committee for the 1992 Conference as a whole, chaired by Ambassador Tommy T. B. Koh, was also in close touch with this process.

As to the important question of how the negotiators should resolve their differences, experience strongly favours use of the 'single negotiating text' expedient so successfully employed by the Law of the Sea Conference. As a practical matter, moreover, whatever voting procedure may formally be prescribed, they are likely also to want to depend, as did the Law of the Sea negotiators, on a determined effort to achieve consensus.

Although the rules of procedure of the Law of the Sea Conference contemplated decision-making by a two-thirds affirmative vote, it was not until the last week of the Conference, nine years after it began, that any votes were taken.

C. Essential Elements of a Treaty

To improve the chances of building a consensus around a framework treaty combining substantive and procedural elements, it should be stressed throughout the negotiations that its adoption will constitute only the first stage in a continuing process. As time goes on, the gradual addition of supplementary protocols will supply the concreteness and specificity lacking in the general obligations. In due course either the basic treaty, the protocols, or both can be augmented by provisions for international dispute settlement, private rights of action in domestic courts, and even, perhaps, penalties for violations.

In addition, it is important that the framework treaty contain a provision obligating member states to observe generally accepted international environmental rules, regulations, and standards adopted through the competent international organization(s). Similar provisions are an important feature of the LOS Convention. Standards such as those established by International Maritime Organization conventions or contained in the regulations adopted pursuant to the London Dumping Convention are 'generally accepted'; states that are party to the LOS Convention are thus obligated to observe these standards even though they are not parties to the conventions from which the standards derive.

In short, a framework treaty on climate change should contain three essential elements. The first is a statement of goals, principles, and general obligations. If this statement is reasonably comprehensive and comprehensible, the effort to achieve substantive consensus can rest there: since the statement will, in any case, constitute only the first step in the process of elaborating progressively more concrete substantive agreements, its gaps, ambiguities, and inconsistencies will not be fatal; they can be dealt with later when and as the necessary consensus develops. The second is language establishing the procedures for negotiation and adoption of supplementary protocols. The third is specific provision for a series of auxiliary measures designed to encourage the voluntary adoption of national commitments, permit the monitoring of compliance with those commitments, and mobilize domestic and international public opinion.

. To give effect to this framework, the treaty should also entrust to a permanent multilateral body such functions as data collection, laying the groundwork for supplementary protocols, administering the auxiliary measures, providing technical assistance to member states, and monitoring national performance. It should also create a special fund for the support of these activities. If it were decided to make the body a specialized UN agency, its charter should provide for funding by financial assessment of member states. In any case, it would need to have some kind of an executive council, whose size, composition, and voting procedures would have to be thrashed out.

It is not obvious what kind of an organization would best fill the bill. Some of us think it should be a beefed-up UNEP. Others believe that an entity patterned on the GATT or the IMF would be more suitable. Proponents of the GATT model point to the success with which the GATT deals case by case with the application of general principles.[4] The problem with applying this approach to the environmental context, at least at the outset, is that the obligations undertaken by the parties to a framework treaty are likely to be so general or so closely linked to a best-efforts pledge as to be for all practical purposes unenforceable. If there is nothing to comply with, compliance cannot be required. UNEP, on the other hand, is already there. It has a benign and positive image. It is not threatening. With expanded staff and an increased budget it could take on additional functions such as those mentioned below. On the face of it, there is no reason why UNEP should not have this expanded role, and good reasons why it should.

As non-coercive measures give way to universal norms like those elaborated in the Law of the Sea Convention, the need for dispute settlement procedures will increase. Meanwhile, to the extent that non-coercive measures harden into law it will

---

[4] See e.g. Abram Chayes and Antonia Chayes, 'Adjustment and Compliance Processes in International Regulatory Regimes', in Mathews (ed.), *Preserving the Global Environment*, 280–308.

become important to make available some form of impartial review of the fairness of the particular outcomes thereby induced. A possible solution would be the creation of an international non-governmental commission of highly respected individuals representing expertise in environmental matters as well as business, economic, and political experience. Governments or groups that felt unfairly criticized would be invited to call upon this body to assess the situation and reach a balanced judgement about it. The result would not be binding, but it could be influential. If it turned out that the services of the commission were in substantial demand, it could be enlarged and form panels of its members to address particular situations. Concurrently, individual countries might form similar commissions of their own.

D. Role of a Multilateral Environmental Agency

Assuming that the multilateral body has a clearly defined mandate and the powers and resources needed to carry it out, it may not make a crucial difference whether an old agency is given new duties or a new one is brought into existence. For purposes of the discussion to follow, I shall use the term 'multilateral environmental agency' as embracing both. Several of the functions that a multilateral environmental agency (MEA) should be directed to perform have already been mentioned. Since the MEA will not have a regulatory role backed up by enforcement powers, it will have to make the most of a number of devices that do not depend on the coercive force of official sanctions. This need not mean, however, that the MEA is powerless. Recent experience has shown that non-coercive devices like the auxiliary measures touched on above can be effective in promoting the observance of international norms. This is already happening in the human rights arena, where non-governmental organizations that investigate and publicize violations of the norms of international human rights help to mobilize international opprobrium against offending governments. The very process of implementing a framework treaty on climate change will create awareness that governments have no more right to mistreat their environments than their people.

The MEA should have a role in many if not most of the mechanisms utilized to carry out the purposes of the framework treaty. In roughly ascending order of intrusiveness, these mechanisms include the following:

- The definition of targets, which would be set voluntarily on a country-by-country basis.
- The adoption, also country by country, of strategies for reaching these targets.
- Periodic progress reports to the MEA.
- Monitoring of national performance by international observer teams recruited and trained by the MEA.
- Verification of nationally declared greenhouse gas emissions by remote sensing systems.
- Publication by the MEA of reports assessing national performance.
- Technical assistance to developing countries to enable them to deal with the problems thus identified.
- Promulgation by the MEA of recommendations differentiated, *inter alia*, by measurable stages of economic development.
- Procedures for dispute resolution ranging from conciliation through mediation to binding arbitration.
- The opportunity for private parties to seek injunctive monetary relief for non-compliance with generally accepted standards in the administrative and civil courts of member states.[5]

The skilful use of these devices would create substantial incentives for member states to improve their environmental performance. Non-governmental organizations would be watching, exhorting, and pushing.[6] Domestic awareness of the national effort would be heightened by the international attention it attracted. Media coverage would be correspondingly intensified. The attention thereby focused on the government's response would generate pressure to raise its level. It is arguable, indeed, that the self-reinforcing process thus set in motion could become a formidable substitute for official action—more effective than regulation and far less expensive than its enforcement. If this

---

[5] Cf. Article 235(2) of the LOS Convention. The availability of such recourse would radically diminish if not obviate state responsibility issues of the kind presented by the US–Canada *Trail Smelter* arbitration (1938 and 1941), *Reports of International Arbitral Awards*, iii. 1905.

[6] Cf. the chapters by Bramble and Porter and Stairs and Taylor in this volume.

happens, what has generally been called 'soft law' will become progressively harder.

There are limits, of course, to how much can be accomplished within and across national boundaries by the externally applied pressure of voluntary organizations. Such 'non-coercive' pressure is not likely to be successful, indeed, unless it serves an identifiable domestic interest as well as a global one—energy conservation or improved forest management, for instance. Increasing acceptance by developing countries of the concept of 'sustainable growth' is undoubtedly contributing more to environmental protection than years of negotiations could accomplish. Where, however, a country is asked to do more or give up more than its self-interest would warrant, it must be offered positive incentives to sacrifice for the larger good.

In the case of the Law of the Sea, such incentives were created by wrapping a wide array of interests into a comprehensive 'package deal'. It was recognized early on that only a minority of countries would benefit directly from freedom of navigation and overflight, marine scientific research, the exploration of oil and gas, or deep-seabed mining. If, however, these minority interests could be linked in a single treaty to provisions enabling the majority to share in the proceeds of economic activities conducted outside the limits of national jurisdiction, all countries would then have an incentive to join in the resulting treaty. Except for the producers and operators of climate-control technology, however, few will profit from restrictions on the build-up of greenhouse gases. Other economic incentives must, therefore, be found.

One step in this direction already being taken is the attachment by multilateral lending institutions of loan conditions requiring the recognition of environmental concerns in various ways. Economic assistance programmes are beginning to provide support for reforestation and better forest management. Debt-for-nature swaps are increasingly well accepted. The International Chamber of Commerce has endorsed environmental auditing for business corporations, and this could be made subject to public review by the MEA or, as Maurice Strong has suggested, by the UN Trusteeship Council. It is important, moreover, to focus attention on the sustainability of growth by incorporating into national income accounts quantitative measure of the status of natural resources like forests and wet-lands.

For developing countries there will also have to be a link between their fulfilment of national targets and compensation for the economic losses thereby induced. In this regard, it is encouraging that the World Bank is prepared to commit substantial resources to the Global Environmental Facility.[7] Assistance in obtaining environmental technology and in building national capacities for environmental research and teaching is also essential.

E. Co-ordination of Research

There is a need, finally, for the best possible international co-ordination of research on the extent, causes, and consequences of climate change. The co-ordination process should ensure wide-spread participation by developing countries and embrace the allocation of roles among regions and organizations, the transition between research and operations, the involvement of industry, and the continuing development of environmental indicators.

The co-ordination of research on climate change, particularly to the extent that it seeks to involve developing countries, can also be an important contributor to the negotiating process. To a degree that has no counterpart in any previous multilateral negotiation, the potential for agreement on actions to curb global warming rests on acceptance of the findings of scientific research. Most of this research will have to be done by the nationals of developed countries. It is to be expected, therefore, that developing countries may on occasion tend to be suspicious of assertions of scientific authority that also happen to serve developed-country interests. To minimize this possibility, it is important that all countries, large and small, developing and developed, be kept as fully in touch as possible with the emergence of scientific knowledge about climate change. Like the atmosphere itself, science transcends national boundaries. So also must the sharing of its discoveries.

[7] See generally Ken Piddington's chapter in this volume.

There is a need as well for the application of science and technology to the development of better alternatives to climate-affecting practices and the design of more efficient regulatory techniques. The present level of co-ordination among the existing international environmental programmes and organizations is not adequate to the purpose of systematically addressing these and other global environmental issues. In the case of climate change, the framework treaty should require the MEA to assemble and disseminate scientific information and to co-operate with the WMO in supporting activities designed to improve the collection and analysis of such information.

Conclusion

Although the atmosphere is the universal sustainer of life on earth, no such universality can be found in the diverse national interests affected by every proposal to protect this global common. To have a chance of wide acceptance, therefore, a framework treaty on climate change must be capable of adaptation to the varying situations of individual countries. This, indeed, is the rationale for most of the mechanisms enumerated above, starting with the setting of national targets.

Rather than wait for universal consensus, groups of countries with analogous interests and capabilities may wish to pursue agreements among themselves. The framework treaty should be able to accommodate such small-scale agreements. For example, a group of developed nations might agree among themselves both to undertake significant anti-greenhouse actions and to couple these initiatives with assistance to developing countries in acquiring the relevant technologies. Such an agreement, linked to the framework treaty, would help to encourage earlier and more positive action than would otherwise occur. In short, the framework treaty should be just that—a framework.

To re-emphasize a point made earlier, the negotiation of a framework treaty on climate change must be understood and accepted as the first step in a continuing process. Negotiations within and among many groups and on many levels will have to go forward long after the framework treaty itself has entered into force. Sustaining this process will require strong leadership, sound strategic judgement, and tactical skill. Never easy to come by, these qualities will be in increasing demand as the world community comes to grips with the pervasive concerns that transcend the capacity of any single nation.

PART II. Institutions

7

The Role of the United Nations

Peter S. Thacher

THE purpose of the United Nations is often thought of solely in terms of its opening statement; 'WE THE PEOPLES OF THE UNITED NATIONS DETERMINED: To save succeeding generations from the scourge of war, which twice in our lifetime has brought untold sorrow to mankind.' The UN was also created to be 'a centre for harmonizing the actions of nations' in solving international problems and creating the economic, social, cultural, and humanitarian conditions for a peaceful world.[1] This objective has been largely thwarted by East–West competition during the Cold War and North–South tensions accompanying the end of the colonial era. With notable exceptions, the general efforts to improve human well-being in the social and economic spheres—through various 'development decades'—took second priority to short-term political considerations. But sometimes unifying themes overrode East–West, North–South divisions, realistic goals were set, resources mobilized, and results produced that showed the value of multilateral approaches to common problems: smallpox was eradicated, a World Weather Watch established, material care was delivered to children and refugees in distress, and— even in the face of resistance by sovereign states and political discord—great progress was made towards a central goal of the UN Charter, the advancement of human rights.

Ever since the 1972 UN Conference on the Human Environment in Stockholm, the emergence of environment as a unifying

The author has drawn on material he assembled for discussion at the US Ford Foundation in July 1990 on 'Global Environmental Change and the Evolution of the UN System' and on a paper commissioned by WFUNA, 'Institutional Options for Management of the Global Environment', as well as on information available to him as a consultant to the World Resources Institute. The views in this paper are, of course, only his own.

[1] Article 1 of the UN Charter.

theme has encouraged international co-operation 'to preserve and enhance the environment for present and future generations'. Now, as the centrifugal forces of the Cold War are ebbing, new environmental issues come to the fore that pose global risks to national and human security in forms not foreseen when the UN was created. These include stratospheric ozone depletion, climate change, loss of biological diversity, and a host of other 'global changes' in which human activities are recognized to be a driving force.

This chapter reviews the role of the UN system in helping governments deal with environmental issues that are too large to be handled by any state, or even by any limited group of states. The challenge was posed by the World Commission on Environment and Development (WCED, also known as the Brundtland Commission) whose report, *Our Common Future*, was presented to the General Assembly in 1987.[2] The problem was seen by the Commission in these terms:

Until recently, the planet was a large world in which human activities and their effects were neatly compartmentalized within nations, within sectors (energy, agriculture, trade), and within broad areas of concern (environmental, economic, social). These compartments have begun to dissolve. This applies in particular to the various global 'crises' that have seized public concern, particularly over the past decade. These are not separate crises: an environmental crisis, a development crisis, an energy crisis. They are all one.[3]

To remind us of the dimensions of current change, with which future institutions must cope, the Commission cautioned:

Our human world of 5 billion must make room in a finite environment for another human world. The population could stabilize at between 8 billion and 14 billion sometime next century . . . More than 90 per cent of the increase will occur in the poorest countries, and 90 per cent of that growth in already bursting cities. Economic activity has multiplied to create a $13 trillion world economy, and this could grow five- or tenfold in the coming half-century. Industrial production has grown more than fiftyfold over the past century, four-fifths of this growth since 1950. Such figures reflect and presage profound impacts upon the biosphere, as the world invests in houses, transport, farms, and industries. Much of the

[2] World Commission on Environment and Development, *Our Common Future* (Oxford: Oxford UP, 1987).
[3] Ibid. 4.

economic growth pulls raw material from forests, soils, seas, and waterways.[4]

Noting the fragmented nature of most of the institutions facing the challenges of growth in an interdependent world, the Commission called for change at both national and international levels 'to give the central economic and sectoral ministries the responsibility for the quality of those parts of the human environment affected by their decisions, and to give the environmental agencies more power to cope with the effects of unsustainable development'. In the Commission's view:

The same need for change holds for international agencies concerned with development lending, trade regulation, agricultural development, and so on . . . The ability to anticipate and prevent environmental damage requires that the ecological dimensions of policy be considered at the same time as the economic, trade, energy, agricultural, and other dimensions. They should be considered on the same agendas and in the same national and international institutions.[5]

In light of this and other studies, the General Assembly adopted, as 'the aspirational goal for the world community', the 'achievement of sustainable development on the basis of prudent management of available global resources and environmental capacities and the rehabilitation of the environment previously subjected to degradation and misuse'.[6] This chapter suggests that the linkage between global environmental problems and national development efforts—in both of which the UN system plays a central role—calls for stronger connections between *policies* set in the UN General Assembly and other intergovernmental bodies, and the financial and other *resources* needed to give effect to these policies.

Many other changes since 1945 must also be borne in mind, but are not directly addressed, among them the declining power of states as commanding actors on the international stage, the emergence of a global economy and open flows of information through which non-governmental entities gain influence, and awareness that 'security' requires more than military means for its protection. The time is opportune to strengthen the capacity of

---

[4] Ibid.   [5] Ibid. 10.
[6] GA Res. 42/186 of 11 Dec. 1987 on the Environmental Perspective to the Year 2000 and Beyond, operative para. 4.

the UN system to help nations deal with environmental challenges whose global scope we are just beginning to appreciate, and to tackle underlying causes of international tensions, rather than trying to keep the peace after tensions have already reached dangerous levels.

A. The Institutional Outcomes of the Stockholm Conference: Form Follows Function

Two decades ago governments met at Stockholm to set up a new UN Environment Programme to 'protect and enhance the quality of the human environment for present and future generations'—an issue that was both pressing as well as susceptible of international agreement, even in the midst of East–West tensions and North–South divisions. Before considering new environmental institutions, they agreed that nothing new should be set up until it was clear what needed to be done, and that existing institutions couldn't do it; that environmental issues demanded more 'networking' and co-ordination than any new 'super agency'; that evolving knowledge called for flexibility; that co-ordination was needed, with a clear separation between policy responsibilities and operational functions, and that regional capabilities should be strong. The UN should be the 'principal centre for international environmental co-operation', and environmental activities 'should strengthen and reinforce the entire United Nations system', while recognizing the great diversity of conditions between nations.[7]

The 1972 Stockholm 'Action Plan' consisted of 109 approved recommendations that had been dealt with sectorally, by subject area,[8] and redistributed into three functional components:

[7] These criteria were spelt out in the principal document on which governments based their decisions on institutional issues in 1972; Stockholm Conference document, 'International Organizational Implications of Action Proposals', A/CONF.48/11, 10 Jan. 1972.

[8] Governments at the Stockholm Conference adopted 109 recommendations in five subject areas—human settlements, natural resource management, pollutants of broad international significance, educational–informational–social and cultural aspects, and environment and development. The institutional implications from these recommendations were considered in a sixth subject area, 'international organizational implications of action proposals'. Additionally, the Conference approved the Stockholm Declaration on the Human Environment.

- the global environmental *assessment* program ('Earthwatch'),
- environmental *management* activities, and
- *supporting measures.*[9]

The meanings of these three programme functions were approved in the Stockholm Action Plan for the Human Environment, described in light of recent experience in Annex A to this chapter. Based on these functions and the earlier criteria, recommendations for institutional changes were endorsed in Stockholm and approved by the Assembly and four new mechanisms were established:[10]

- a *Governing Council* of 58 states elected by the Assembly,
- an environment *Secretariat* headed by an *Executive Director* elected by the Assembly,
- an *Environment Fund* to provide additional financing on a voluntary basis, and
- an *Environment Co-ordination Board* for the UN system.

To each of these the Assembly assigned specific responsibilities which are summarized in Annex B below.

While a detailed review of performance of the above mandates is beyond the scope of this paper, it is widely acknowledged that the international *assessment* functions under UNEP's 'Earthwatch' monitoring, research, and information-exchange activities have been well discharged by the UN system together with international scientific and other organizations, with the result that governments have been alerted to environmental threats deserving attention: impure drinking water, forest dieback and deforestation, loss of arable soil and spreading deserts, disappearing habitat and species loss, toxic wastes, marine pollution, stratospheric ozone depletion, climate warming—the list is far from complete.

But when the time came to take *management* action at the national level to correct problems, restore the productivity of natural systems, or reduce international threats, the results were less impressive. While UNEP has helped governments reached agreements on 'Action Plans'—such as to stop desertification—

[9] The 'Framework for environmental action', on which this was based, is described in the Report of the Conference, UN doc. A/CONF.48/14/Rev.1, 1973, ch. 3.

[10] GA Res. 2997 (XXVII), 'Institutional and Financial Arrangements for International Environmental Cooperation', 15 Dec. 1972.

and treaties—to curtail trade in endangered species, protect whales, wetlands, stratospheric ozone, etc.—the effectiveness of these agreements has been curtailed by lack of political will or inadequate resources.

The relationship between environment and development relates directly to the Stockholm *management* function, forms the central theme of UNCED 1992 and follow-up activities, and goes to the heart of the future role of the UN system.[11] It is therefore useful to review how these twin themes became so prominent.

B. From Environment Issues To 'Sustainable Development'

The linked issues of environment and development were put on the UN agenda by the 'Founex Report' early in 1971, which concluded that environmental problems result not only from the development process itself, but also from lack of development. Gradually environment and development are seen as linked, reinforcing issues, rather than in conflict; poverty leads to environmental degradation and calls for economic improvement to stop this harm, while economic growth at the expense of environmental values cannot long be sustained.[12]

UNEP's role since Stockholm in building awareness of this relationship between environment and development issues was buttressed by several principles in the Stockholm Declaration that were a forerunner of the current concept of 'sustainable development': 'The capacity of the earth to produce vital renewable resources must be maintained and, wherever practicable, restored' (Principle 3); 'non-renewable resources . . . must be employed in such a way as to guard against the danger of their future exhaustion . . . '(Principle 5); 'The environmental policies of all States should enhance and not adversely affect the present or future development potential of developing countries . . .' (Principle 11).

---

[11] The UN General Assembly decided in Dec. 1990 that UNCED would be convened at the level of head of state or government.

[12] *Development and Environment: The Founex Report: In Defense of the Earth*, The Basic Texts on Environment (UNEP Executive Series 1, Nairobi, 1981), also published in *International Conciliation*, 586 (1972). This was issued after a June 1971 seminar organized by the secretariat then preparing the Stockholm Conference.

By the mid-1970s, further efforts to define the environment–development relationship advanced the concept of satisfying human 'basic needs' without, however, transgressing 'outer limits' set by the capacities of natural systems to provide these needs.[13] The 1976 World Employment Conference endorsed this approach when it recognized food, shelter, clothing, and essential services such as safe drinking water, sanitation, transport, health, and education as basic human needs.[14] Unfortunately, the 'basic needs' approach was seen as an attempt to divert attention away from the 'New International Economic Order', then being promoted by 'Third World' leaders at the UN, and it was not endorsed in UN policy directives for the Third Development Decade of the 1980s.

Gradually, environmental destruction came to be seen as resulting from *over*-development as well as from *under*-development, especially by wasteful consumption in some industrialized countries. Throughout this period new terms came to the fore like 'eco-development' and 'sustainable development'.[15] A major contribution that illustrates growing NGO influence at the international level was the 'World Conservation Strategy' prepared by the International Union for the Conservation of Nature (IUCN) with support from the World Wildlife Fund (WWF) and UNEP and endorsed by governments at the UN General Assembly in 1980. This high-level policy statement was one of the first to stress sustainability, especially of natural life-support systems in the context of supporting human needs. (Although National Conservation Strategies have been drawn up in a number of industrialized countries, international attention has hitherto focused mainly on trying to address the problem of sustainability in developing countries, without tackling overconsumption in others.)

In its 1987 report the WCED (The Brundtland Commission)

---

[13] The reports of this meeting, a UNEP/UNCTAD symposium in Cocoyoc, Mexico, are also found in the document cited in n. 8 above.

[14] The case for a basic needs approach was put forward in John and Magda McHale, *Basic Human Needs* (New Brunswick, NJ: Transaction Books for UNEP, 1978), and in Paul Streeten, *First Things First* (Oxford: Oxford UP, 1981).

[15] See esp. Mostafa K. Tolba, *Development Without Destruction: Evolving Environmental Perceptions* (Dublin: Tycooly, 1982) and Tolba, *Sustainable Development: Constraints and Opportunities* (London: Butterworths, 1987). For a brief summary of these trends, see Peter Bartelmus, *Environment and Development* (London: Allen & Unwin, 1986).

concluded: 'Humanity has the ability to make development sustainable—to ensure that it meets the needs of the present without compromising the ability of future generations to meet their own needs.' But even this innocuous generalization met resistance by those who feared a new form of 'conditionality' was taking shape, and when the subject came up in UNEP's Governing Council it had to be defined and put to the vote:

Sustainable development is development that meets the needs of the present without compromising the ability of future generations to meet their own needs and does not imply in any way encroachment upon national sovereignty.[16]

None the less, the general goal of sustainable development is clearly before the international community, and the question becomes whether or not sufficient resources can be brought to bear at the national level to support actions needed to achieve it.

C. Environment In Development

One of UNEP's most important accomplishments has been to stimulate awareness of the key role played by development funding, and the need to incorporate environmental considerations in development planning. A 1979 survey of nine international financing agencies revealed 'a general absence (with the partial exception of the World Bank) of systematic attention to environmental impacts of all stages of project conception, design, and execution'.[17]

At a time when the level of ODA in 1976 had reached $27 billion, the environmental significance of these funds was already clear:[18]

[16] Annex II to UNEP GC decision 15/2, May 1989. The sensitivity of sovereign states in relation to the need for freely exchanged environmental information and steps to guard against extraterritorial environmental impacts has been clear since the negotiation of the 1972 Stockholm Declaration of Principles.

[17] Preface by Barbara Ward (Lady Jackson) to Robert E. Stein and Brian Johnson, *Banking on the Biosphere? A study of Environmental Procedures and Practices of Nine Multilateral Development Agencies* (Toronto: Lexington Books, 1979), a work supported by UNEP and the Canadian International Development Agency (CIDA)).

[18] As used here, 'ODA' refers to financial flows to developing countries and multilateral institutions provided by official agencies which have as their main objective the promotion of economic development and welfare of developing

The environmental impact of the $27 billion is indeed much larger than the sum implies. It is larger because the bulk of these funds are matched by counterpart financing by the recipient country. It is larger still because a considerable slice of this money is spent on technical assistance, on planning, on training, and on research. So the multiplier is not only quantitative but qualitative: the programmes financed by development aid agencies will influence the thinking and shape the skills and capacities of people whose decisions will be affecting the environment decades from now.[19]

UNEP's initial effort to introduce environmental considerations into the work of development organizations like UNDP and the World Bank relied on existing mechanisms for inter-agency consultation and co-ordination, chiefly the Administrative Committee on Co-ordination (ACC) chaired by the UN Secretary-General. But largely as a result of the above 1979 study and other reports commissioned by UNEP, a Declaration of Environmental Policies and Procedures Related to Economic Development was drawn up and signed in 1980 by eight multilateral development funding agencies, and a new inter-agency mechanism was created, CIDIE—the Committee of International Development Institutions on the Environment.[20]

By this declaration these institutions declared their intention to:

- affirm their commitment to the Stockholm principles and recommendations;
- ensure that all programmes and projects comply;

---

countries *and* are concessional in character with a grant element of at least 25%. Ordinary lending by the World Bank, except by its 'soft-loan' affiliate, IDA, do not qualify as ODA. For a complete review of related terms, see OECD Development Assistance Committee, *Twenty-Five Years of Development Cooperation* (Paris: OECD, 1985), 171–5) and more recent reports to the UN General Assembly on 'Operational Activities of the UN System'.

[19] *Banking on the Biosphere?*, ch. 1.

[20] CIDIE was formed to help assure implementation of the 'Declaration of Environmental Policies and Procedures Relating to Economic Development' signed at UN Headquarters in Feb. 1980 by the Chief Executive Officers of UNDP, UNEP, the World Bank, the Organization of American States, the Asian Development Bank, the Inter-American Development Bank, the Commission of the European Communities, and the Arab Bank for Economic Development in Africa. These were soon joined by the African Development Bank and the European Investment Bank and later by the International Fund for Agricultural Development, the Nordic Investment Bank, the Central American Bank for Economic Integration, the Caribbean Development Bank, and FAO.

- negotiate with all to ensure 'integration of appropriate environmental measures in the design and implementation of economic development activities';
- provide assistance to develop indigenous capacity;
- sympathetically consider proposals to enhance the environment and natural resources;
- support research and studies on new methodologies for environmental protection;
- support training; and
- disseminate information for guidance on the environmental dimension of economic development activities.

CIDIE's role is to review periodically its members' progress in carrying out the policy laid down in the Declaration, and to encourage further efforts to improve procedures and practices towards this end. Although full membership in CIDIE is open only to international financing agencies, observers from bilateral agencies as well as from NGOs are welcomed. Annual reports by each of the CIDIE members show growing attention to and funding for environmental works as a part of economic development encouraged by these agencies. According to its 1989 annual report, UNDP was then supporting 402 projects targeting specific environmental problems; these projects were valued at $300 million, with an additional $100 million financed from complementary non-core resources devoted to promoting sustainable development through non-governmental and grass-roots organizations.

It was never intended that the Environment Fund, which started at an average of about $20 million per year, would support the full costs of the activities it launched. Rather, it was to be a 'catalytic and co-ordination' fund based on the principle that each operating element of the UN system had its own environmental responsibilities, and that modest additional funding should be available to help them better discharge these responsibilities in a co-ordinated manner.

Under these circumstances, as Specialized Agencies undertake new tasks with initial outside support from UNEP, they are forced either to increase their budget to maintain a new activity, or sacrifice some ongoing activities. This is never easy, and it is to the credit of the UN system that so many sectoral agencies and programmes—in health, agriculture, atomic energy, etc.—

were induced to launch new environmental activities by such relatively minor contributions.

Another reflection of this effect and the limited size of the Environment Fund has been the creation of new trust funds under various regional and global environmental agreements since Stockholm, such as the Convention on International Trade in Endangered Species (CITES) and other global conventions, as well as the 1976 Barcelona Treaty and seven other regional seas programmes for which UNEP retains administrative responsibilities. Some of these, like the Kuwait Fund, were quickly funded by contracting parties, although most were not so easy.

Trust funds under international treaties will continue to be a convenient way to mobilize additional resources for particular environmental agreements, but will not reduce the need for additional funds for the purposes identified above; the demand for such additional funds will continue to grow as the requests for technical assistance for strengthening human and institutional capabilities are outpaced by requests for large capital investments in sustainable growth.[21]

D. International Assistance and the Environment

Under present conditions of indebtedness and lack of public and private capital investment flows into developing countries, the limited amount of ODA funds available and other constraints make it unlikely that the stimulation of economic growth and the provision of food, jobs, and other basic needs will keep pace with increasing demands arising from demographic growth alone. Hence it is not reasonable to expect developing countries to address long-term environmental issues with funds needed for immediate development requirements, nor to bear the cost of reducing their contributions to global risks, especially when most of these risks are attributable to past actions of affluent industrialized countries.

[21] A promising example of how additional resources can be mobilized by international organizations is the new 'Environmental Program for the Mediterranean' (EPM) sponsored by the World Bank and the European Investment Bank. Based on UNEP's earlier work, they see this as 'an important instrument for mobilizing the financial resources required to implement the broad range of actions needed to tackle the Mediterranean region's environmental challenges'.

Whereas until recent years Official Development Assistance (ODA) accounted for only 30 per cent of the international transfers of resources to developing countries—laying the basis, as it were, for far larger sums in the form of private loans and investments in the future development of these countries—today ODA has assumed a role of critical importance. Total ODA has grown from $22 billion in 1972 to over $50 billion in 1989, and because of the decline of private flows it now occupies a far larger portion of the total flow (from 27 per cent in 1981 to 48 per cent in 1989).[22] A declining share of ODA is now flowing through the UN system, a problem first highlighted in the UN Joint Inspection Unit report of 1985 entitled 'Some Reflections on Reform of the United Nations', better known as the 'Bertrand Report'.[23] Reduced Cold War needs for military base rights and political favours may permit a resumption of ODA flows through multilateral channels where the criteria for their use are more pertinent to 'development', as defined in the UN system, as well as to the environment. But whether or not the planet is committed to unacceptable rates of warming or other calamitous trends, it is clear that international assistance flows are not keeping pace with growing needs triggered by demographic increases, shrinking natural resources, indebtedness, and a host of other factors affecting poorer countries.

E. Issues of 'Additionality'

1. *Assistance for participation in international environment programmes*

Thanks in large part to a US proposal made during preparations for the 1972 Stockholm Conference, governments agreed that:

financing will be required to support whatever organization is to be established within the system to deal with environmental affairs; to support the cost of new or expanded international programmes; and to provide

---

[22] These figures are taken from the June 1989 OECD report on 'Financial Resources for Developing Countries: 1988 and Recent Trends', and the 1990 'Development Cooperation' Report by the OECD Development Assistance Committee.

[23] This is the statistical data in the report by the Director-General for Development and International Economic Cooperation reviewing 'Operational Activities of the UN system for the Year 1987', UN document A/44/324/Add.1, 7 July 1989. The 'Bertrand Report' was published in 1985 as UN document JIU/REP/85/9.

additional assistance to developing countries in meeting activities designed to protect and improve the environment.[24]

To finance UNEP's 'new or expanded international programmes' and provide additional assistance to help developing countries take part, a new Environment Fund was set up.[25] Since the term 'additionality' has grown in scope and purpose and importance, it is useful to clarify what was meant. Recognizing that 'efforts to improve the global environment cannot go forward without the means to act' the new fund was proposed by President Nixon to:

help stimulate international co-operation on environmental problems by supporting a centralized co-ordination point for UN activities in this field. It would also help to bring new resources to bear on the increasing number of world-wide problems through activities such as monitoring and cleanup of the oceans and atmosphere.[26]

By the Assembly's decision these funds were to finance international programmes and activities of an explicitly environmental nature, including what was needed to enable developing countries to participate in agreed international programmes of environmental activities—such as monitoring, research, assessment work under UNEP's 'Earthwatch' programme—as well as to take part in the processes of negotiating, administering, and implementing environmental agreements.[27] As noted earlier, voluntary trust funds have also been set up under international agreements to meet similar needs and to relieve the burden on UNEP's 'catalytic' funds (which, unlike chemical compounds, rarely emerge from the process unscathed).

The UN General Assembly itself also sets up voluntary funds to support participation by developing countries in environmental negotiations, such as the negotiations about climate currently

---

[24] Report of the Stockholm Conference, UN doc. A/CONF.48/14/Rev.1, 1973.
[25] GA Res. 2997; see above.
[26] President Nixon's Message to Congress on the Environment, 8 Feb. 1972; text in Appendix E, Third Annual Report of the Council on Environmental Quality, 1972. The US pledged a matching 40% towards a $100 million fund for the first five years.
[27] See the Assessment Section in Annex A, and Section 3 in Annex B.

under way.[28] The principle behind additionality for these purposes is not seriously questioned by anyone; the main differences concern the amounts.

2. *Assistance for national development*

A different need for larger 'additional assistance' emerged during preparations for Stockholm and was reflected in the principles agreed by governments in the 1972 Stockholm Declaration, though not in the approved 'Action Plan':

> Resources should be made available to preserve and improve the environment, taking into account the circumstances and particular requirements of developing countries and any costs which may emanate from their incorporating environmental safeguards into their development planning and the need for making available to them, upon their request, additional international technical and financial assistance for this purpose.[29]

When the Assembly set up the UN Environment Programme in 1972, this question of additional assistance to incorporate environmental safeguards in national development could not be solved and was put aside for further study.[30]

Part of the problem was that much larger amounts are needed to help developing countries meet the 'additional' costs of incorporating environmental dimensions into their national development than were envisaged for the Environment Fund. But more than amounts were involved. A key issue has always been whether a country needing external assistance should sort out its own priorities and make such sacrifices as are necessary to accommodate environmental needs within the total resources available—domestic and international—or whether national development planning can proceed without this concern for the environment on the assumption that environmental needs will be covered by outside funding additional to existing ODA flows.[31]

---

[28] A special voluntary fund was established by the Assembly to support participation of developing countries in the work of the Intergovernmental Negotiating Committee for a Framework Convention on Climate Change; GA Res. 45/212, 21 Dec. 1990.

[29] Principle 12 of the Stockholm Declaration.

[30] See Section 3 in Annex B.

[31] At the international level, such extra costs are generally absorbed by the international organizations who provide assistance, whether it is in the form of grants or concessional or officially backed commercial loans.

This national dimension of 'additionality' gets mixed with other questions about 'foreign aid', especially in parliamentary bodies where ODA funds are appropriated, but these are seldom debated openly within the UN system.[32] Indeed, the whole issue of 'foreign aid'—the springboard for ODA appropriations from parliamentary bodies—is poisoned by images of corruption and capital flight, mismanagement, neo-colonialism, and environmental destruction; and since no one is satisfied that foreign aid can accomplish worthwhile results, the availability of ODA is increasingly at risk, the more so as Cold War rationales disappear.

In any case, given the lack of movement since 1972 and growing imbalances between international development needs and ODA flows, it is hardly surprising that 'additionality' has become a key issue in high-level pronouncements at meetings of developing countries, as in Brasilia in early 1989:

International financing agencies should, through specific institutional facilities, ensure availability of sufficient additional resources, on concessional terms, to fund environmental protection projects in developing countries. In the allocation of resources for that purpose, no conditions should be imposed that would, in effect, result in a reduction of resources available for environmental protection.[33]

3. The new, global dimension of 'additionality'

In addition to these long-standing calls for additional assistance to support national development needs, mounting concern about global warming and other 'global change' issues led to calls by 'donor' countries for increased international funding. In June 1988 a 'World Atmosphere Fund' was proposed, to be financed in part by a levy on fossil fuel consumption by industrialized countries, to mobilize resources for an 'Action Plan for Protection of the Atmosphere', together with a separate Trust Fund 'to provide adequate incentives to enable developing countries to manage their tropical forest resources sustainably'.[34] More than

[32] Bilateral agencies prefer to exchange views on these subjects among themselves in OECD/DAC.

[33] The Declaration of Brasilia, adopted by the Sixth Ministerial Meeting on the Environment in Latin America and the Caribbean, Brasilia, Mar. 1989.

[34] Statement adopted at the Conference on The Changing Atmosphere: Implications for Global Security, Toronto, 27–30 June 1988.

twenty government leaders agreed in The Hague in March 1989 on the proposition that 'most of the emissions that affect the atmosphere at present originate in the industrialized nations' and that these nations 'have special obligations to assist developing countries'.[35]

An April 1989 Norwegian White Paper set a policy for Norway to stabilize CO_2 emissions by the year 2000 and start reducing total emissions of all greenhouse gases, and proposed that the industrialized countries allocate 0.1 per cent of GDP to an International Fund for the Atmosphere to help finance transitory measures in developing countries and reforestation projects. This proposal called for funding in addition to the 1.1 per cent of GDP Norway already gives in ODA (compared to an OECD average of 0.34 per cent).[36] In September 1989 the Government of Japan announced it would provide about $2.25 billion of ODA for environmental purposes in the next three years.[37]

At a November 1989 Ministerial meeting in the Netherlands, countries agreed that:

Many countries, especially developing countries, will require assistance in identifying the causes of anthropogenic climate change, in establishing its extent and effect and also in responding to it. . . . Industrialized countries will take steps to facilitate the transfer to developing countries of technologies to limit the global climate change through financial assistance and other mechanisms to overcome the incremental costs of acquiring and using these technologies. . . .[38]

Although virtually all these proposals were advanced—as in 1971—by traditional 'donor' countries rather than by developing countries, some of the major industrialized countries have not yet

---

[35] The Declaration of The Hague was signed on 11 Mar. 1989, by 24 Prime Ministers or Ministers; 11 of these were heads of government or cabinet officers of OECD member states.

[36] From the Benjamin Franklin Lecture by Prime Minister Brundtland, Washington, DC, 2 May 1989.

[37] Announced at the Tokyo Conference on the Global Environment and Human Response Toward Sustainable Development.

[38] Para. 13 of the Noordwijk Declaration adopted 7 Nov. 1989. This meeting also adopted a 'provisional' target figure for 'world net forest growth' of 12 million hectares a year in the beginning of the next century to increase CO_2 sinks and agreed that 'developing countries will need to be assisted financially and technically' towards this and similar goals. It urged industrialized countries 'to use financial and other means to assist developing countries in phasing out their

accepted new funding in principle. Nevertheless, two important practical steps have been taken that can be seen, with care, as possible precedents for more general application in the 1990s.

(i) *The Montreal Fund.* Barely visible in 1972, the threat posed by CFCs to stratospheric ozone has come into focus largely as a result of UNEP's successful assessment activities, notably the international assessment work that revealed the threat and identified the steps necessary to reduce that threat, as well as the costs. Agreement on a new fund to reduce this global risk was reached in London in June 1990 when contracting parties agreed to accelerate the phase-out of CFCs and other harmful compounds and to set up a fund of at least $160 million over three years to help developing countries switch to less harmful compounds. The precedent is very narrow; the scientific case is beyond any serious question; CFCs really do strip stratospheric ozone and boost incoming harmful radiation—nobody argues otherwise and industry no longer objects; the costs of reducing CFC production and use can be quantified and compared to quantifiable benefits; a strong case can be made that tropical countries are especially dependent on cheap CFCs, such as for refrigeration (chiefly to reduce food spoilage and protect medical supplies), yet lack the means to adapt to CFC substitutes.[39] So as to avoid creating new mechanisms, the World Bank has been asked to administer and manage this fund.

(ii) *The Global Environmental Facility (GEF).* In 1989 France proposed at the World Bank that a new special facility be set up alongside, but separate from, the Bank's 'soft-loan' affiliate (the International Development Association), with a target of $1–1.5 billion for concessional aid devoted to preservation of natural resources, protection of atmosphere, energy efficiency, and other activities supportive of sustainable development. As agreed in a 1990 meeting in Paris involving 25 developed and developing countries and the World Bank, UNDP, and UNEP, GEF is a 'pilot program to obtain practical experience in pro-

---

production and consumption' of CFCs controlled under the Montreal Protocol, and adopted a series of recommendations specifically addressing funding needs related to this issue.

[39] The cost of changing all the valves and compressors in refrigeration units to handle compounds with different physical and chemical characteristics is a more significant obstacle for many developing countries than the higher price of importing 'safe' CFC substitutes.

moting and adopting environmentally sound technologies and in strengthening country-specific policy and institutional frameworks to support prudent environmental management'.[40] It was conceived as also providing operational information relevant in formulating other global conventions and financing arrangements at UNCED and beyond. GEF has four objectives: (1) to support energy conservation, the use of energy sources which will not contribute to global warming, forestry management, and reforestation to absorb carbon dioxide, in order to limit the increase in greenhouse gas emissions; (2) to preserve areas of rich ecological diversity; (3) to protect international waters, where transboundary pollution has had damaging effects on water purity and the marine environment; and (4) to arrest the destruction of the ozone layer, by helping countries make the transition from the production and use of CFCs, halons, and other gases to less damaging substitutes.[41]

What these two developments show is that the 'global' dimension has led donor governments to set up new funds to cover the extra costs of specific actions developing countries could take in a common effort to reduce global risks when the costs of these actions cannot be portrayed as costs that ought to be covered as part of their national development efforts. The case is clear—and well presented in World Bank discussion papers on GEF—that developing countries need additional help as an incentive to join a common effort to reduce global risk.

Many are worried that huge sums may be required for switching to less carbon-rich fossil fuels so as to get more useful energy for less CO_2 (though the estimated costs are small when compared to projected GDP, at least for those countries with large GDPs). Deeper questions arise as costs are estimated for other actions to reduce climate-warming risks. Some assert that the costs of energy-efficiency and conservation measures are marginal for industrialized as well as some developing countries, and may even offer real savings. Costs for planting and maintaining trees to lock up carbon in the developing and industrialized world may be high but there will be associated gains, although

---

[40] See World Bank/UNDP/UNEP Press Release issued at the conclusion of the 27–8 Nov. 1990 meeting.
[41] Ibid. and working papers for the Paris meeting; see also *The World Bank and the Environment*, First Annual Report, Fiscal 1990, a World Bank publication.

the absence of any market-place makes it difficult to quantify the benefits: fuelwood plantations to meet energy needs, watershed management for agriculture, protecting important habitats for genetic diversity, etc. It could also be argued that while additional technical assistance funds should be provided, the extra capital costs ought to be met within the context of national development needs. Meanwhile, the report of the Intergovernmental Panel on Climate Change concluded that the information available to make sound policy analyses is 'inadequate' in part because of 'uncertainty with respect to the costs, effects on economic growth, and other economic and social implications of specific response options or groups of options'.[42]

A thorough airing of these issues is essential to facilitate broad agreement on specific terms under which 'additionality' would be provided and the mechanisms for its administration.

4. *New approaches to funding*

Present international developments give hope for harnessing savings from reduced military budgets for more constructive purposes, and a number of proposals on this are outstanding. But new demands for capital investment to combat desertification, protect stratospheric ozone, and slow climate warming, not to mention mounting pressures in all countries to improve national infrastructure and economic conditions, already seem likely to capture all or most of the savings from reduced budgets for military arms. Even if a 'peace dividend' were realized, it seems unlikely that significant portions would soon be applied abroad. Thus, despite new and more hopeful conditions in a post-Cold War era, the WCED concluded that the additional resources for the transition to sustainable development will not be easy to come by if the international organizations through which they flow have to continue to rely solely on traditional sources of financing: assessed contributions from governments, voluntary contributions by governments, and funds borrowed in capital markets by the World Bank and other international financial institutions.[43]

This conclusion led the Brundtland Commission to favour con-

---

[42] *Intergovernmental Panel on Climate Change, First Assessment Report*, vol. i, Overview, sect. 3(b), Aug. 1990.
[43] *Our Common Future*, 340–1.

sidering 'new approaches as well as new sources of revenue for financing international action in support of sustainable development'. Even if such proposals might not have appeared politically realistic in 1987, 'the need to support sustainable development will become so imperative that political realism will come to require it'.

With support from UNDP and others, the study called for by WCED was undertaken by the World Resources Institute in Washington and is presented in its report, *Natural Endowments: Financing Resource Conservation for Development*.[44] This report recommends four options that might be usefully developed further:

- creating an *International Environmental Facility* (IEF) to identify urgently needed and appropriately designed conservation programmes and to organize support for their preparation, implementation, and expansion;
- mobilizing the private sector through the establishment of pilot investment programmes, called *'Ecovests'*, to help in the leverage of private capital for ecologically beneficial projects;
- linking international debt relief and conservation initiatives through expanded use of the *debt-for-nature concept*;
- taxing emissions of carbon dioxide, chlorofluorocarbons, and other greenhouse gases, with the revenues going in part to a *Global Environmental Trust Fund*.

F. Linking Policy with the Necessary Resources

As 'the only intergovernmental organization with universal membership', WCED felt the UN should 'clearly be the locus for new institutional initiatives of a global character' to be redirected towards sustainable development. But they pointed to the lack of adequate resources as a problem:

Although the funds flowing to developing countries through UN programmes represent a relatively small portion of total official development assistance (ODA) flows, the UN can and should be a source of significant leadership in the transition to sustainable development and in support of developing countries in effecting this transition. Under existing conditions the UN system's influence is often fragmented and

[44] This report of the UNDP/WRI International Conservation Financing Project was published in 1989 and is available in French and Spanish language editions from WRI.

less effective than it might be because of the independent character of the specialized agencies and endemic weaknesses of co-ordination. However, recent moves towards organizational reform and greater economy and efficiency could improve the capacity of the UN to provide this leadership, and should include sustainable development as an important criterion. [45]

Assuming that the preparations for UNCED facilitate agreement on certain aspects of 'additionality' and that governments also agree on the need for some sort of high-level policy mechanism to steer the UN system and other organizations in carrying out the actions called for, the need then arises to link whatever *policy* mechanisms may be agreed for environment-and-development issues with the *funding* mechanisms necessary to give practical effect to agreed policies.

The more one looks at environment and development issues, the more striking is the growing imbalance between the resources available to the *environmental* organizations, with UNEP disbursing about $30–50 million annually, and those available to development organizations, where, for example, UNDP currently administers some $500 million in projects aimed at *environmental* objectives, and far larger sums are routinely handled by the World Bank and its regional affiliates. [46] Perhaps new arrangements between existing institutions might be considered to ensure consistency between policies formulated and applied within the environmental community in the UN system on the one hand, and the use of resources available to the various development organizations on the other.

But, as noted by WCED, this is inherently difficult at the national level because of weak co-ordination in most governments between the central ministries that decide on the use of national resources to achieve economic and other development objectives, and those parts of government responsible for protecting natural resources and environmental well-being. Correspondingly, at the international level, few governments are

---

[45] *Our Common Future*, 317.

[46] World Bank Support for the Environment is well documented in recent Annual Reports of the World Bank and Progress Reports by its Development Committee. Additionally, a Japanese grant of $16.6 million in 1989 enabled the Bank to set up a Technical Assistance Grant Program for the Environment which provides grant funds to IDA and Bank projects and programmes. See also Ken Piddington's chapter in this volume.

capable of supporting consistent policies and priorities in the different international bodies on which they sit. To this day there is no UN system-wide policy on pesticide use, largely because of the unresolvable differences at the national level between health and agricultural ministries.

While various UN system organizations can cope with co-ordination problems despite the absence of governmental policy or direction, and have mechanisms for this, chiefly the Administrative Committee on Co-ordination (ACC), there is no standing intergovernmental body with a clear mandate, or even access to the information necessary, to set policy and oversee environment-and-development activities of the UN system as a whole.[47] Until such time as governments rearrange domestic structures and responsibilities along lines suggested by WCED, it seems likely that 'policy' pronouncements in the central organs of the UN system will be voiced by representatives of ministries that lack the resources needed to give them effect, or, to put it differently, without significant resources at its disposal, there is a limit to the level of policy that can be usefully voiced in the UN system.[48]

Even if better co-ordination at the national level were achieved, complex issues would remain. For example, if high-level policies were to be broadly set under one-country, one-vote patterns prevailing in the UN General Assembly, it would be desirable to ensure that they would be taken into account by those who provide resources in the 'development community'—including both bilateral and multilateral ODA. One approach would be to give policy pronouncements at the UN more authority in the Bretton Woods organizations where very large resources are available. But this highlights the different ways in which decisions are reached. Given the need for a dramatic increase in international funds, it would not seem useful to jeopardize the ability of Bretton Woods institutions to raise large funds on commercial markets by subordinating Bank decisions to the UN General

---

[47] Long-standing efforts to revitalize the Economic and Social Council continue with much likelihood of success; as a practical matter, government representatives at UNCED and its Preparatory Committee perform some of these functions on an *ad hoc* basis.

[48] This may explain the appeal of GATT as a venue for negotiations pertaining to sustainable development, as well as its negotiating procedures, though the lack of success in the Uruguay Round of trade talks weakens the case.

Assembly; i.e., by shifting decisions from weighted-vote procedures that favour governments who back the World Bank with
hard credit, to one-state, one-vote procedures in the UN General
Assembly that favour the recipients.[49]

While co-ordination without clear policy guidance from
governments is not a particularly difficult problem for institutions within the UN system proper—led by the UN Development
Programme (UNDP) and related executing agencies—it is difficult to visualize 'Bretton Woods' institutions being guided by
policies laid down outside their own governing bodies. Bretton
Woods institutions may attend ACC meetings chaired by the UN
Secretary-General, but they are reserved and are usually referred
to as members of the UN 'family', rather than of the 'system'.

As the UN Conference on Environment *and Development*,
UNCED 1992 entails a commitment to addressing difficult issues
going beyond the problem of coping with international environmental issues. These include 'additionality' to support environmental activities as a part of national development, as well as to
encourage countries to reduce global environmental threats and
improve global security. UNCED offers a possible foundation for
a new level of international development co-operation centred in
the UN system, wherein 'top down' flows of significant capital
may be mobilized from outside the UN system and merged with
'bottom up' technical assistance in which the UN system can
draw on extensive experience, technical competence, and strong
strength in the field (where NGOs will have new opportunities to
become active partners).

But this calls for discussing difficult questions that have been
swept under the rug for many decades; issues that lay at the heart
of the division between those kinds of policies and actions that
are decided in one-country, one-vote bodies where, up to now,
talk is easy and performance weak, and those where decisions are
taken by weighted voting, and where significant international
financing is available. The gap between the UN system and larger
sources of private financial support for sustainable development
is even more difficult to bridge.

[49] The Montreal Protocol Fund arrangements, however, show that 'additional'
funds can be established under treaty agreements negotiated under a subsidiary
body of the Assembly, and employ an existing Bretton Woods institution for their
administration.

The UN system is uniquely qualified to help governments assess and reduce global environmental risks and seek economic and social development on a sustainable basis—the best long-term hope of protecting the environment. UNCED and its preparatory process have begun to demonstrate new ways of setting policy and mobilizing resources, accompanied by new relationships between governments and the UN system they created as well as other bodies, including non-governmental organizations, whose increasing role and influence is obvious. On the eve of the 50th anniversary of the UN itself, the opportunity exists to set the goal of 'sustainable development' for the sake of international security based *not* on 'foreign aid' but on international economic co-operation for the common good. The UN could then become a real 'centre for harmonizing the actions of nations'.

Annex A. Stockholm Program Functions

This section discusses the relationship between the three 'Stockholm Action Plan' functions—assessment, management, and supporting activities—in the light of recent experience:

1. *Assessment* functions; improving understanding to provide a rational basis for environmental management, or—as currently expressed—management for sustainable development. Assessment activities like research and monitoring of environmental parameters, and evaluation of resulting data, are normally carried out by national institutions working together in co-operative international programmes to improve the quality, compatibility, and relevance of their results. Many such collaborative programmes are developed by UNEP in close co-operation with other components of the UN system and other international organizations outside the UN system, both intergovernmental and non-governmental, such as the International Council of Scientific Unions, and the International Union for the Conservation of Nature (IUCN), each in their respective areas of responsibility and competence. An example of the close working relationships that now exist is seen the collaboration between two intergovernmental organizations, WMO and UNEP, with ICSU in preparing the Second World Climate Conference in late 1990.

Many such assessment programmes draw on well-established customs for communication and exchanging information; international scientific activities in the Antarctic started in the last century, and co-operative investigations in the fields of meteorology and health were well advanced long before the UN came into being. The success of the International Geophysical Year (IGY) in 1957–8 inspired many similar programmes in different fields, such as the International Biological Program, subsequently converted into a regular, funded activity at UNESCO—the Man and Biosphere Program (MAB)—and there were many other experiences on which to draw.

Thus, it was not surprising in 1972 that governments emphasized *assessment* functions when they illustrated the uses to which the new Environment Fund should be put, in Resolution 2997, by citing the following examples of 'programmes of general interest' for which the Environment Fund was created: 'regional and global monitoring, assessment and data-collecting systems, including, as appropriate, costs for national counterparts; the improvement of environmental quality management; environmental research; information exchange and dissemination; public education and training; assistance for national, regional and global environmental institutions; the promotion of environmental research and studies for the development of industrial and other technologies best suited to a policy of economic growth compatible with adequate environmental safeguards; and such other programmes as the Governing Council may decide upon.' In the implementation of such programmes, 'due account should be taken of the special needs of the developing countries'.

Many of these programmes have since proven their worth in terms of providing reliable data on global problems ranging from measuring changes in mass balance of glaciers as an indicator of climate change, or methyl mercury levels in regional fisheries, or pesticide levels in human tissue; they are now ready for expansion and strengthening. There is widespread agreement on the need for major reinforcement of UNEP's capacity to take the lead in providing 'early warning' of major environmental risks, assessing these risks, and helping states to develop cooperative measures to reduce them or mitigate the consequences (such as through better contingency planning), or adapt to unavoidable changes.

To cope with scientific uncertainty about likely changes, and basic cause-and-effect relationships, continuing processes of assessment have increasingly relied on international groups of experts; like the UN Scientific Group of Experts on the Effects of Atomic Radiation (UNSCEAR) set up by the Assembly some thirty years ago. Another group well known in environmental circles is GESAMP, the Group of Experts on Scientific Effects of Marine Pollution, whose third decadal review has just been published. Experts in GESAMP, unlike those in UNSCEAR, are appointed by international organizations rather than by states; in order to provide assessment information they need to improve the effectiveness of the UN system in dealing with related matters.

GESAMP assessments have gained increasing credibility, in part because its expert members—many of whom come from government institutions—are expressly working in an expert, non-instructed status.

Over time, monitoring and other assessment functions have significantly improved human understanding of processes and trends of change, and with time the direction of these efforts has shifted towards providing the kinds of data useful for economic planning and decision-making in the 'development' context, as well as for measuring performance, such as under treaty agreements, and helping governments to develop national means by which to achieve agreed goals. With the 1992 scheduling of UNCED, this latter requirement for information takes on a new imperative, and a number of moves are under way in the international development community to identify precise requirements for data and assessment.

2. *Management* functions. While assessment activities rely on past experience with international co-operative programmes, there was less experience in international 'management' action on which to draw in 1972, and, in any case, as the Assembly recognized in Resolution 2997, 'the responsibility for action to protect and enhance the environment rests primarily with governments and, in the first instance, can be exercised more effectively at the national and regional levels'. With this in mind, the Assembly specifically called on governments to entrust 'appropriate national institutions with the task of co-ordinating both national and international environmental action'.

Management activity at the international level calls for new policies, practices, agreements—including, but not limited to formal treaties—that make a difference by encouraging changes in state practice and, ultimately, human behaviour. A variety of tasks are performed by international organizations ranging from facilitating processes by which states negotiate agreements and administer them, to designing and implementing the programmes, projects, and activities required to give effect to them.

Parallel to the treaty route to effective international action are such processes as the negotiation of agreed 'guidelines' or 'recommended practices' that are endorsed at the international level in declarations and other forms.[50] Although not binding, these add pressures to modify national practice on environmental matters, particularly when poor performance or non-compliance is brought to public attention by NGOs and

[50] See e.g. the 1981 'Geneva Guidelines on Off-Shore Mining' and the 1985 'Montreal Guidelines for the Protection of the Marine Environment against Pollution from Land-Based Sources' that states and international organizations are encouraged to take into account when developing international agreements in this field. The UNEP series on 'Environmental Law—Guidelines and Principles' also includes agreed guidelines on 'Weather Modification', 'Banned and Severely Restricted Chemicals', and 'Environmental Impact Assessment'.

the media. The kind of information useful for this purpose needs to be carefully selected, reliable means set up to generate it in a timely fashion, and accessibility assured.

Establishing agreed criteria as a basis for standard-setting represents another aspect of increasing reliance on 'soft law' and other forms of agreement that lack the formal characteristics—and some of the drawbacks—associated with the treaty route to international law. A number of new techniques have evolved allowing the process of ratification to be bypassed by formally delegating powers for amendment of standards to a competent international technical body. Highly technical Specialized Agencies like ICAO (International Civil Aviation Organization), ITU (International Telecommunications Union), WMO, and IMO have placed international standards in 'technical annexes' or 'regulations' that are periodically revised by intergovernmental expert groups without having to go through the ratification process each time. Here again, one wants to facilitate the routine assembly of information appropriate to these reviews and ensure proper 'transparency'.

3. *Support* functions can be thought of in terms of strengthening human, institutional, and other resources to ensure that *all* key actors— including developing countries—have the means to contribute to agreed actions and share in the benefits. They also include specific efforts targeted at education and improving public awareness. Supporting measures required for actions in the *assessment* and *management* components that were identified in the Stockholm Conference documentation included education, training, public information, organization of national and international activities, financing, and technical co-operation.

Many of these activities are a part of the normal 'technical assistance' programmes in which the UN system has extensive experience. Currently, however, better appreciation of actions needed at local levels to reduce global change risks—such as the depletion of stratospheric ozone by CFCs—now allow the identification of the capital investments as well as the technical assistance required. Under present conditions of indebtedness and lack of capital flows into developing countries, the need for greater international financing is clear if preventive action is to be taken to reduce risks from future actions in the developing world. The current operation by the World Bank, UNDP, and UNEP of the 'Global Environmental Facility' partially addresses this problem, as well as the need to mobilize additional resources to meet related costs for technical assistance and other supporting measures.

Annex B. 1972 Institutional Responsibilities

The functions assigned by the General Assembly in Resolution 2997 (XXVII) may be summarized as follows:

1. to the Governing Council:

- to promote international co-operation ... and to recommend ... policies to this end;
- to provide general policy guidance for direction and co-ordination of environmental programmes within the UN system;
- to receive and review periodic reports on programme implementation within the UN system;
- to review the world environmental situation and ensure that emerging problems are adequately considered;
- to promote contributions by scientific and other professional communities to knowledge, and to programme formulation and execution;
- to review the impact of environmental policies on developing countries, and their costs, and ensure compatibility with national development plans and priorities;
- to review and approve the uses of the Environment Fund as well as formulate procedures for its operation.

Also, the Council was to report annually through ECOSOC with particular attention 'to questions of co-ordination and to the relationship of environmental policies and programmes within the UN system to overall economic and social policies and priorities'.

2. To the Executive Director of the small secretariat serving as 'a focal point for environmental action and co-ordination in the UN system':

- to provide substantive support to the Council;
- to co-ordinate environment programmes in the UN system, and review and assess their effectiveness (and to chair the Environment Co-ordination Board: see below);
- to advise intergovernmental bodies of the UN system on environmental programmes;
- to secure co-operation from scientific and other professional communities worldwide;
- to provide advisory services for promotion of international co-operation;
- to submit proposals to the Council on medium- and long-range planning for UN programmes;
- to bring any matter to the attention of the Council;
- to administer the Environment Fund (and keep the problem of additional financial resources for developing-country needs under review);
- to report on environmental matters to the Council;
- to perform such other functions as entrusted by the Council.

In order to strengthen the Executive Director's co-ordination role (despite opposition by the UN and agencies concerned), the Assembly decided he would be *elected* by the Assembly on the *nomination* of the UN Secretary-General.

3. The Environment Fund was established 'to enable the Governing Council . . . to fulfil its policy-guidance role for the direction and co-ordination of environmental activities'. While the costs of servicing the Council and of providing the small secretariat were to be covered by the UN regular budget, operational programme costs and programme support and administrative costs of the Environment Fund would be covered by the Environment Fund, which the Assembly mandated to 'finance wholly or partly the cost of the new environmental initiatives undertaken within the UN system', including those envisaged in the Stockholm Action Plan, with particular attention to 'integrated projects'.

Given the need 'to ensure that the development priorities of developing countries shall not be adversely affected', the Assembly asked the Executive Director to keep under continuing review the problem of measures 'to provide additional financial resources on terms compatible with the economic situation of the recipient developing country'. The Fund was expressly to be used to support co-ordination inside and outside the UN system.

4. 'In order to provide for the most efficient co-ordination of United Nations environmental programmes' an Environment Co-ordination Board (ECB) was established within the framework of the Administrative Committee on Co-ordination (ACC) but under the chairmanship of the Executive Director (which was the chief reason for having him elected by governments, rather than appointed by the Secretary-General). All organizations and regional economic commissions of the UN system were 'invited'—the Assembly could do no more—to co-operate, as were other organizations and governments. The ECB was asked to report annually to the Governing Council.

8

The Role of the World Bank

Kenneth Piddington

Two aspects of the present moment in history are of special significance to the topic of this chapter. From the development perspective, we take the population–poverty–environment nexus which generates a great deal of pessimism about the prospects for the future. From the experience of wealthy countries, we have the concept of pollution on a global scale, or to be more precise, the fact that certain features of the planet's ecosystem have been, or are likely to be, modified as a result of human activity— typically through a discharge of substances to the atmosphere, although some forms of water pollution are beginning to be global in their impact.

The notion of sustainable development gained currency in the late 1980s as the philosopher's stone which would enable practitioners of development economics to resolve the first of these dilemmas. The second set of issues, in particular the destruction of the ozone layer and the likelihood of a 'greenhouse effect', raised a new issue in international economics, namely how should the world community deal with global externalities. In the public mind, growing concern about climate change and other possible outcomes, such as changes in sea level and increased skin cancer, elevated the issue of sustainability and caused it to become more than a criterion for national development. By 1990 it had become part of a planetary agenda. Endless publications and special

This chapter is a revised version of a lecture originally delivered at Exeter College, Oxford, in June 1990. The material has been updated by the author to take account of developments in the World Bank up to the time that he left his post as Director in the Environment Department in May 1991 to become Special Adviser to the Bank's team preparing the 1992 World Development Report. For a comprehensive account of the Bank's activities since the establishment of the Environment Department in 1987, see *The World Bank and the Environment*, an annual report series introduced in 1990.

supplements appeared with the fragile Earth seen from space as the cover picture. A new political literacy on the environment was created, with rapid electoral repercussions in some countries.

It is important when considering the role of the development institutions to note that while industrial countries were to display a more vigorous form of 'green politics' over this period, there was nevertheless a world-wide progression in the acceptance (and acceptability) of environment as a serious factor in economic planning and administrative practice. So the developing countries which borrow from the World Bank have been part of the overall trend, although they may have moved more slowly (at least to begin with) and they do have a different agenda. They are for the most part now positively interested in the goal of sustainability and how it is to be achieved, and they are increasingly part of the debate (and sometimes part of the action) on the issues which are regional or global in their scope. This has been reflected, for example, in the discussions about preventing damage to the ozone layer, and in the new series of international negotiations relating to climate change.

I will discuss the role of the World Bank against this background. I will attempt to deal with the views of those outside the Bank, as well as the reality as it appears to those of us who form the environmental community inside the institution. Since this book is concerned with the international politics of the environment, I will not canvass the work programmes, budgets, and 'strategic planning' which represent the institutional response to the introduction of a new topic. Neither will I cover the legal aspects, which tend to increase in importance as the new policies become operational and which are clearly influenced by the strong political currents which tend to characterize all environmental initiatives.[1] My aim is to focus instead on some of the administrative principles that have been applied in the Bank, because I believe that they are potentially of general interest and may prove to be transferable (at least in part) to other institutions. It should be noted therefore that we are dealing with the real-life experience of introducing an environmental dimension into the work of a large entity where the staff are predominantly econo-

---

[1] See I. F. I. Shihata, *The World Bank in a Changing World* (Boston, Mass.: Martinus Nijhoff, 1991), esp. ch. 4, for an exhaustive presentation of the legal perspective on the Bank's environmental work.

mists or financial experts by training and where the central mission of the institution is the management of resource transfers to promote development. I also want to demonstrate that these principles, and in particular the strategy of 'internalization', have a bearing on the political judgement which is made on the Bank's 'performance' by outsiders (even if they are close enough to look over the wall every day).

A. What is the World Bank?

The International Bank for Reconstruction and Development was a judicious choice of title in the mid-1940s. It looked ahead to the task of post-war recovery, mainly in Europe. It was the Yin to the Yang of the other institution set up at Bretton Woods, the International Monetary Fund. By committing its allotment of capital, each member government became a shareholder, and the institution was then able to operate in the world's financial markets with an optimum credit rating. It could borrow at the most favourable rates and on-lend to its less secure shareholders, who thus enjoyed the benefits of mutual security in terms of financial flows and interest rates.

You hardly hear the long title these days, although it applies in every sense to the Bank's current operations in Eastern Europe. It is interesting in this context to note that the new European Bank for Reconstruction and Development echoes the Bretton Woods formula in its own acronym EBRD, and in the full version of its title. For the purpose of this discussion, however, the important fact to note is that with the end of colonialism in the 1950s and 1960s, the World Bank's effort became almost entirely directed to the developing world. It moved to become a development institution, it recruited a staff who could analyse the problems faced by developing countries, and, most important, those countries became shareholders in their own right with representation on the Bank's governing body, the Executive Board.

The focus of its activities is the country lending programme. The bulk of the professional staff are working in country departments, they have an intimate knowledge of the politics, economics, and social situation in the countries they are dealing with, and they may spend several weeks each year out of Washington in the capital of the borrower, or in the field. In order to prepare the forward lending programme they are in dialogue at a very senior level with the governing élite; they will also have a range of other contacts in the country, including bilateral donors, NGOs, and other multilateral agencies such as UNDP.

If you believe that historical process is driven as much by the accident of networks as by the carriage (or rather miscarriage) of grand design, then it will be apparent that the World Bank is in a unique position. It certainly has some influence on the global network of decision-makers. Its staff are in varying degree driven by a set of principles, some of which relate to sound financial practice and prudent economic management, and some of which derive from principles of equity among people and equality among nations (which can both be seen as a function of sharing the fruits of development). Despite the emphasis placed by the Bank on the free operation of the market, it is also noteworthy that the majority of its professional staff possess a clear grasp of the ethical dimension of good government—a factor which I have always seen as central to the proper execution of environmental policies.

These are all relevant factors for the environmental administrator as he or she prepares to plough a furrow inside the institution. The receptivity of the culture inside the Bank will determine how to approach the task, as well as its ultimate success. Let me describe the sequence of events so far.

B. Recent History

Early April 1987—the Brundtland Report[2] has not yet been published, although many are aware of its message; the World Bank is coming up to a painful process of restructuring and the Development Committee is considering a major document on the environmental agenda for the Bank.[3] A month later, Mr Conable,

---

[2] *Our Common Future* (Oxford: Oxford UP, 1987). This report was prepared by the World Commission on Environment and Development, commonly referred to as the 'Brundtland Commission', during the period immediately preceding the decision to restructure the World Bank.

[3] The Development Committee paper was prepared by Jeremy Warford, one of the leading architects of the Bank's environmental strategy, and was subsequently published under the title *Environment, Growth and Development* (World Bank, 1987). For the address by President Conable to the World Resources Institute, Washington DC, in May 1987, see *The Conable Years at the World Bank* (World Bank, 1991), 21-9.

still a relatively new President, was to spell out this agenda in a public address to the World Resources Institute in Washington. His message related to environment and the need for the Bank to give it 'special emphasis'. The Bank must assist its borrowers to achieve sustainable development, and this will be done by integrating environmental considerations into the mainstream of the Bank's country programmes. Mr Conable acknowledged that failure to do this had in the past led to errors in project implementation; it was his aim to preside over a reform of the institution's approach.

This led to the establishment of the Environment Department in mid-1987, as part of a wider process of reorganization instituted by Mr Conable when he took office. The Department was placed in the policy and research complex of the Bank, which does not have direct responsibility for the lending programme but which acts as monitor and mentor to the 'regions', the four vice-presidencies which do handle operations. The regions are Latin America, Asia, Africa (south of the Sahara), and 'the rest'—Europe, the Middle East, and North Africa, or EMENA as it is called in the acronymic idiom of the Bank. In each of these 'regions' a small environmental unit was set up in the Technical Department, and this turned out to be vital element in the overall design, as we shall see.

By 1988, when I arrived in Washington, the bureaucratic foundations were therefore in place and a great deal of work was under way, partly as a follow-up to the programme which Mr Conable had launched. 'Environmental Issues Papers' for each borrower were being prepared throughout the Bank as a starting point; in several countries in Africa these were to lead quite rapidly to the formulation of environmental action plans.[4] These plans rested on a clear political commitment by the country in question to give priority to key environmental problems. They were similar in concept to the National Conservation Strategies

---

[4] e.g. Mauritius, Madagascar, and Lesotho, which pioneered the National Environmental Action Plan approach. A second group of countries in Africa (Rwanda, Ghana, Burkina Faso, and the Seychelles) has now completed the formulation of such Plans, and implementation will follow once they are approved. A further ten countries in Africa are now embarked upon the process, so this formula has become the dominant framework for the Bank's environmental activities in African countries. See *The World Bank and the Environment—A Progress Report* (World Bank, 1991), 29 ff.

which IUCN had helped to draw up in a number of countries, with the important distinction that the National Environmental Action Plans (which became the standard terminology for the Bank's initiatives) led directly to investment decisions, and also acted as a trigger for the necessary financial flows from the Bank and other sources.

There was, however, another script about the Bank, which received considerable exposure in Washington and elsewhere during the late 1980s. I will try to present it objectively, because I respect the motives and endeavours of the individuals in the NGO movement who gave it currency.[5] They were undoubtedly instrumental in bringing about the changes that were initiated in 1987, and they keep in close touch with Third World NGOs through their institutional networks, which means that they do offer an important perspective on the impact of Bank-funded projects.

The script, in briefest compass, runs along these lines: 'The World Bank is preoccupied with the process of pushing large sums of money through the lending pipeline, it likes big projects and quick-disbursing loans. That is how staff get promotion and they do not want to pay more than lip-service to the environment because this may slow down the lending process and change the type of project. In energy, for example, the Bank should be lending for conservation programmes and efficient end-use rather than building large hydro dams, or worse—thermal power stations. The massive destruction of tropical forests has come about with the collusion of the Bank because of its preoccupation with production forestry. Social impacts of project and policy lending have been ignored; the Bank deals with governments who do not care about indigenous minorities and the poorer classes/tribes and do not therefore even respect their basic human rights.'

[5] The literature produced by the NGOs is extensive, and in most cases represents a special genre which is directed to certain 'campaign objectives' (political, fund-raising, or transnational 'bans' on certain activities, such as dam-building or timber production in the moist tropics). The objectives may or may not be explicit, but in practically all cases they generate both a selectivity of material and the use of linguistic and other forms of imprecision. See e.g. Bruce Rich, 'The Emperor's New Clothes: The World Bank and Environmental Reform', *World Policy Journal*, 10 (1990), 305–30; and Stephan Schwartzman, *Bankrolling Disasters: International Development Banks and the Global Environment* (San Francisco: Sierra Club, 1986).

The script often includes reference to the Bank's lack of accountability, the problems for NGOs in Washington and elsewhere in obtaining the information they need, and a closed decision-making process which offers no window for public involvement. There are variations which move on through the increasing burden of debt in Latin America and in other areas of the Third World, and sometimes end up with a conspiracy theory in which the Bank (and the IMF) are the tools of world capitalism—as in the Marxist version extant in Berlin when our joint Annual Meeting was held there in September 1988. Since late 1989 or so, not much has been heard of this particular theme. Overall, however, the NGO critique as set out above does represent one yardstick against which to measure the Bank's progress.

Another yardstick can be derived from the administrative goals which were promoted by my Department and adopted by the Bank. These can be summed up in one word—integration. In other words, we need to judge the extent to which environment has now been integrated as part of normal work across the entire Bank structure, and the degree to which environmental factors now have a real bearing on internal decision-making and on the policy dialogue with the borrowing countries. Here the dilemma clearly is that the more successful the policy, the less there is that can be separately identified as the Bank's 'environmental programme'. We must therefore look for the indicators that will show whether shifts are taking place, with what speed and with what practical effect.

C. Not a Facelift . . .

Before accepting this assignment, I made it clear that if the Bank's aim was to have a green frontage, behind which the mode would be 'business as usual', the work would need to be done by a 'façadiste', not an environmental administrator such as myself. The architect of this genre, it is true, works with great elegance to produce the illusion from the outside that the spirit and style of the façade pervades the structure within. The environmental administrator, on the other hand, has a role more akin to that of the plumber or electrician, crawling around the innards of the system to see which pipe is connected where, or how some re-wiring might redirect total energy flow.

As we go about the work, what we are really looking for are the command systems in the institution. Unless we can connect with those, we know that environment will be marginalized and will not be seen as central to the purpose and ethic of the organiz-ation. This is the shared experience of those who in recent decades have been asked to 'run' environment in corporations, in governments (local, regional, or national) and, increasingly, in international organizations.

President Conable's strong personal commitment, the political interest of our shareholders as reflected in the Executive Board, the new funding initiative which the Bank took in 1990 and which led to the creation of the 'Global Environment Facility' in 1991—all these factors ensured that there was nothing marginal about the environment in the World Bank's policy process. This in turn created sensitivity among colleagues about what should be covered in country programmes, and also meant that by early 1990 the environmental community in the Bank had to deal with a sharp increase in requests for urgent professional advice. Nothing is more welcome, or more demanding, than success in such a tangible form—it triggered the need for an upgrading of Bank in-house resources in many areas of environmental exper-tise. These increases were (intentionally) concentrated in the Re-gional Environment Divisions, which grew approximately four-fold between 1988 and 1991.[6]

By early 1991, when it was announced that Mr Conable would step down and that a prominent merchant banker, Mr Lewis Preston, would replace him as President on 1 September, it was apparent that the changes introduced in the Bank's structure and in its way of doing business were in effect irreversible. Mr Con-able's last few months in office were marked by the adoption of a new policy on tropical forests which removed any ambiguity about the priority to be given to conservation values in future

[6] The level of staff effort in World Bank units is notoriously difficult to calculate, given the extensive use of consultant services. The First *Annual Report on the Environment* in 1990 gave a total of 30 professional staff and 15 consultants in the regions, with 24 professionals and 8 consultants in the Environment De-partment.

Bank activities in this sector. It stated, for example, that no Bank funding would in future be made available for commercial logging in the remnant tropical forests.[7]

A first principle of environmental administration is to give priority to the establishment of a standard procedure for environmental assessment and to ensure that this is a much more open process than the decision-making sequence followed by most 'closed-circuit' institutions. In practice, this meant that environmental assessment in the Bank would need to bring in the legitimate interest of various groups at the local level. Colleagues therefore worked out how state-of-the-art practice on environmental assessment could be applied to the subtleties of the Bank's relationship with its clients, who as already mentioned are also its shareholders. The Operational Directive on this subject was adopted in October 1989 and there has now been sufficient experience to assess some of the initial results and fine-tune the detailed procedures.

The Directive linked the normal components of an environmental assessment procedure to the project cycle of the Bank. For example, it required a preliminary screening to be carried out as soon as a possible project was identified. It would be rated according to potential environmental impact. Thus, a Category A project would require a full Environmental Assessment (EA), whereas a Category B project might only require limited analysis of specific impacts. A Category C project would be unlikely to have significant environmental impacts and an EA would not therefore be required. A fourth category (D) was assigned to environmental projects, for which separate EAs would not be required—on the grounds that the environment was the major focus of project preparation.[8]

Even though very few projects have yet gone through the full cycle since the Directive was introduced, it is clear that some aspects will prove to be of special importance. One is the fact that

---

[7] For a full discussion of the policy shift in this area, see World Bank, *Annual Report on the Environment*, 1991.

[8] During 1991 the Environmental Assessment Sourcebook was published in three volumes to provide detailed guidelines on the application of the Directive. (World Bank Technical Paper No. 139—see in particular vol. i, ch. 1, for a full discussion of the Bank's procedures, and Fig. 1.1 for a representation of the concordance with the project cycle.) Category D was eliminated in the review of the Directive in 1991.

the assessment (both the documentation and the process) is the responsibility of the borrower, not of the Bank. It is therefore the borrowing government which is asked 'to take fully into account' the views of affected people and local NGOs during the assessment process, which means in effect that it must happen early in the project cycle. The Bank has made it clear that this will be one of the elements to be tested by staff at the appraisal stage, which is the final review of the project by the Bank prior to presentation to the Board.

Linked to this issue is the major boost which the assessment work has given to a more open flow of information about the Bank's activities. Once the forward pipeline has been screened for environmental sensitivity, the results are published in a quarterly supplement to the Monthly Operational Summary, which is the main document through which the Bank conveys information about its future activities to interested parties. I have yet to hear any evaluation by NGOs of the value to them of this (by historical standards) dramatic increase in the Bank's release of information.

1. *Environment and economics*

The aspect of environmental administration which was bound to be given special prominence in the Bank is the need to establish maximum convergence between environmental goals and economic policy. This is a fertile area which has been pursued for many years by Bank economists, and where progress was made well before the reforms of 1987. In the field of energy, for example, the Bank has pressed public utilities (usually monopolies) to reflect true marginal costs in their pricing structure. This can probably do more than any other single measure to promote efficiency at the point of end-use, as well as conservation.

The removal of other distortions—such as agricultural subsidies, fiscal incentives for land clearance, low stumpage fees—has been shown in the literature to have considerable (favourable) impact on the environment. Since the Bank has a comparative advantage in linking economic policy choices with desired environmental outcomes at the country level, this will remain a focal point in our approach.

The issues here are very important. If you start from the dictum 'environment is long-run economics', it would follow that by applying appropriate valuation techniques all environmental problems could be resolved, at least in theory, by the standard tools of economic policy. In practice, however, climate systems and the habitat of endangered species do not readily fit into any workable system of economic valuation—and this is largely because there are too many unknown factors and long-run uncertainties.

Environmental economics still has a pivotal role; linked to an effective process of environmental assessment and to the key points in the decision-making sequence, it can in my view be the decisive element in the Bank's overall approach.[9] Let us now look at one of the possible obstacles to this happy scenario for progress.

2. Market interventions . . .

It is common knowledge that some forms of environmental protection require intervention, either through regulation or through fiscal and other incentives. The 'environment' can in this context be seen as a public good, although in many cases, such as the crumbling built heritage of Oxford or the magnificent natural heritage of New Zealand, the public purse cannot stretch to maintain the asset in perpetuity. One has to be selective, and probably one has to involve the private sector.

We can nevertheless expect the policy framework to include the core functions of environmental management within the public sector. Even where economic devices, such as tradable permits, are used to control pollution, there has to be some public interest agency to act as referee, and also to monitor the discharge levels to air and water. Laws and regulations require a further order of administrative firepower, particularly when parties have to be taken to court in order to demonstrate the credibility of the regulatory provisions.

All this is familiar background in most OECD countries. The situation is different in the developing world, and the Bank encounters two orders of difficulty. The first is the deliberate move we have made in the opposite direction, namely to support

---

[9] The fact that the Bank's 'flagship' publication, the World Development Report, is in 1992 devoted to 'Environment and Development' is likely to entrench this pivotal role of environmental economics as a standard feature of future work by Bank economists.

deregulation as part of the strategy to speed economic reforms in our borrowing countries. The second, not wholly unrelated to the first, is the absence in those countries of the institutional framework and technical skills which are needed. Other gaps may include baseline data and other information systems, and various types of hardware and other paraphernalia familiar to environmental ministries in industrial countries.

It is becoming apparent that support for new institutional capacity in developing countries may be the most useful form of assistance from the Bank or any other aid agency in the years ahead. Let it be clear, however, that there is no magic formula which will produce effective institutions in Country A, Country B, and Country Y within a given period. Each case is *sui generis*: we can outline the principles which should apply, we can suggest the process that should be followed, but we cannot impose some standard exogenous design.

Neither can we assume that the human resources will be immediately available. There is great variation in the situation of individual borrowers. Some of the larger countries have considerable resources already—I understand the EPA in China has 20,000 staff. At the other end of the scale, I prepared advice for the government in an island nation which was based on the imminent return of one highly competent individual. Most smaller developing countries are in fact likely to have other priorities for the use of their qualified people.

3. *He kokonga whare e kitea—he kokonga ngakau kore e kitea*

There are variations of this Maori proverb in many cultures, but apparently not in English. It says that you can always see the corner of a house, but when attitudes and feelings reach a turning-point, nothing is visible. Here I come to a question to which I do not have the answer, namely whether the NGO movement in the industrial countries is now likely to enter a different phase in its impressive international campaign to bring about improved respect for the environment.

The shortage of skilled resources dramatizes the issue. For example, one can guess that what has happened in industrial countries will be replicated in developing countries and in Eastern Europe. This is that qualified people who have found an outlet for their environmental commitment through NGO activities will be attracted in growing numbers into government administration. There are already some significant examples of this, for example in France, where the Minister was formerly an NGO activist, and in Brazil, where both the Minister and his senior official under the Collor administration are household names in the NGO movement world-wide.

For that movement, there may therefore be a strategic watershed ahead, perhaps in the aftermath of UNCED 1992. I am not suggesting that NGOs should abandon their vigilant watch over national governments and international agencies, including the World Bank Group. But I expect that activism will find diminishing returns from these campaigns, at the very time when more rewarding opportunities are opening up to work with the many governments which are displaying a verdant tinge, or at least are claiming that they are prepared to give weight to certain environmental objectives.

It is logical and resource-efficient, therefore, to see the coalescence of public sector and NGO interests as a feature of the next stage of integrating environment and development. There may be perceived gains and losses on both sides, the transition may at times be difficult for either party, but there may be no other way in which the tasks we are facing can be accomplished on a global scale.

In order to reinforce the point that free-ranging NGOs will still be needed, let me point to the work needed in industrial countries to bring about a conscientious response at government level to the interrelated problems of over-consumption and waste. It may appear that this has nothing to do with the World Bank, but as we engage the global agenda referred to at the outset, we will find increasingly that the obstacles to progress are not in the South but in the North.

All lobbyists and activists have to make finely tuned decisions about the marginal return to be derived from the expenditure of additional energy. My hypothesis, again subjective, is that the main strategic objectives for the NGOs in pressing for reform at the World Bank have been fulfilled. As already noted, the changes which have taken place are irreversible. True, there is a great deal of further work to be done, but it needs to be approached in partnership. This will involve all development institutions, governments, and NGOs—both in the North and in the South. Hitherto, habits of closed government and the lack of democratic process have certainly impeded such a partnership in some countries. With the changes that are now afoot throughout the world, there is a real prospect that the climate will become markedly more conducive to this partnership. Should this be the pattern of the 1990s, the prospects of achieving sustainable threads in the fabric of development must surely be improved.

D. How Does the Ledger Stand?

Reference has already been made to the problem of measuring the Bank's performance, a problem that will become more rather than less difficult if the environmental function becomes truly integrated in all the activities of the World Bank Group.[10] Nevertheless, there are some useful indices of both inputs and outputs which can be derived from the 'dedicated' environmental components of the Bank's work, such as the free-standing environmental projects or trends in staffing the environmental units. Some illustrative examples may be quoted.

(i) *Environmental lending.* In fiscal 1991, the annual volume of lending for environmental projects had grown to $1.6 billion, approximately 7 per cent of total Bank funding. (The 1991 Annual Report on the Environment states that projects are deemed to be 'primarily' environmental 'if either the costs of environmental protection measures or the environmental benefits accruing from the project exceed 50 per cent of total costs or benefits'.)[11]

(ii) *Special financing mechanisms.* The growing interest of donor governments in making funds available for specific aspects of environmental work led to a rapid growth in the number of targeted funds, some of which were managed exclusively within

[10] The World Bank Group is the term that covers the four closely associated institutions which operate under the Bank's management structure. These are the International Bank for Reconstruction and Development (IBRD), International Development Association (IDA), International Finance Corporation (IFC), and the Multilateral Investment Guarantee Agency (MIGA).

[11] See also the 1990 *Annual Report on the Environment*, ch. 4, for a detailed description of primarily environmental projects, such as the $117 million loan to support the first three years of Brazil's national environment programme and the $18 million Environment Management Project in Poland. In the 1991 *Annual Report on the Environment*, see p. 35 (Mauritius) and p. 43 (Philippines).

the Bank, while others were operated jointly with agencies such as UNEP and UNDP. An example of the latter is the Interim Multilateral Fund established under the Montreal Protocol, which is designed to assist developing countries meet any additional costs they incur by eliminating the use of substances damaging to the ozone layer. Over the initial three-year period, this Fund could account for up to $240 million of grant funding for eligible activities. A similar principle lay behind the Global Environment Facility (GEF), launched in 1991 as a three-year pilot programme to enable actions to be funded in areas where no international agreement had yet been negotiated, such as the limitation of greenhouse gas emissions. GEF funds available for transfer during the pilot phase could rise to $1.5 billion. Again, the operation is jointly managed by the Bank with UNEP and UNDP. [12] Although these resources do not fall within the criteria for development assistance, they should be seen as additional funds for developing countries to use when they embark on actions which help to protect the global environment.

(iii) *Staff resources.*   The annual report for 1991 gives a Bank-wide total of about 270 staff years devoted to environment, or approximately 7 per cent of total Bank effort. This is projected to increase to an average level of 314 staff years over the period 1992-4. These trends should be set alongside the extensive training programmes which have been put in place for 'regular' Bank staff as well as the efforts directed towards officials in borrowing countries, mainly under the aegis of the Bank's Economic Development Institute (EDI).

Conclusion

The above sketch of the Bank's recent history reveals a sizeable redirection of effort and a process which has in effect reached beyond the Bank's façade. Indeed, no institution is completely static. Larger institutions are more likely to appear inert than smaller, less structured groups. But even the most conservative

---

[12] For a full description of both the Interim Multilateral Fund and the Global Environment Facility, as well as the technical assistance funds managed within the Bank for environmental purposes, see Shihata, *The World Bank in a Changing World*, ch. 4.

juggernaut will be discovered on closer inspection to be seething with microbial life. The energy in this process will, however, be largely absorbed inside the Kafkaesque corridors, and the outsider may see no external evidence of change in direction.

In the case of the World Bank, which has its quota of corridors, the environmental mission has been as externally directed as any of its major initiatives. As the momentum increases, and as the flow of resources builds up, this means that there will be mutations inside the Bank as well as outside. The process is under way, but the philosophic problem remains. Once an object is moving, it is not possible at a given point in time to have an accurate picture of its position, because it has already changed. It is difficult to present in a freeze frame an assessment of the movement within the Bank, but I would rather face that problem than have to leave unchallenged the mythology of inertia inside or outside the institution.

9

The European Community and International Environmental Policy

Nigel Haigh

'WITHIN their respective spheres of competence, the Community and the Member States shall co-operate with third countries and with the relevant international organizations . . .'[1]

A. The Ambiguous Character of the European Community

One of the marks of nation statehood is the ability to enter into agreements with other nation states. This ability is shared by the European Community (EC) even though it is not itself a nation state but a 'community' established originally between six, and now twelve, nations each of which continues to express its own sovereignty by pursuing its own foreign relations. It is therefore hardly surprising that when the EC and its Member States negotiate with other countries there is some ambiguity about their relative roles.

The tasks, powers, and institutions of the EC are set out with a fair degree of clarity in the Treaty of Rome which created the EC in 1957. By establishing a common market the founding fathers sought to achieve closer relations between the Member States. Although there are many who would like to see the EC evolving into a kind of United States of Europe, it is easy to demonstrate that it has not yet achieved the quality of nation statehood. For a start it has no head of state, nor a constitution adapted for dealing with all eventualities, nor even the power to raise taxes directly from citizens. All these are characteristics normally regarded as

[1] Article 130R (5) of the Title of the Treaty of Rome concerning environmental policy.

essentials of nation statehood. On the other hand, the EC is more than an international organization established between nations to pursue some prescribed activity without fundamentally ceding any of their sovereign powers. What distinguishes the EC is its possession of institutions able to adopt legislation which directly binds the Member States without further review or ratification by national institutions. In the environmental field the extent of the legislation is such that it is now impossible to understand the policies of any EC Member State without understanding EC policy. Member States are no longer entirely free to pursue their own policies, either at home and abroad.

The EC legislature is composed of the Commission acting together with the Council (composed of national Ministers). The Commission proposes the legislation and the Council adopts it after receiving an opinion from a Parliament directly elected by the citizens of the Member States. The European Court of Justice has the power to find against a Member State that fails to apply EC legislation correctly, and the Commission does not hesitate to bring cases before the Court. The powers of the EC to legislate are certainly confined to subjects prescribed by the Treaty of Rome, but a generous interpretation has often been given to the Treaty, and the EC was able to adopt an environmental policy in 1972 despite the absence of express powers. Such powers were not introduced until the Treaty was amended in 1987 by the Single European Act.

The influence of the EC on its Member States has increased rapidly at some times, less so at others, and in certain fields there has sometimes been near-immobility. In December 1990 an intergovernmental conference began work on a revision of the Treaty for the purposes of monetary union and political union, which could substantially extend the EC's powers. One of the tasks of the conference is to give greater precision to these concepts. As the powers of the EC increase, and its internal policies more deeply influence the Member States, so the EC is strengthened in its ability to act in its own right on the international stage. This will apply in the environmental field as it will in others, but since the result is a diminution in the ability of the Member States to act on their own, the path is unlikely to be smooth. This evolution of the EC coincides with the emergence of the environment as a major new subject of international affairs. The EC has already played an important role on the world stage in the protection of the ozone layer and is beginning to do so with global warming. But as the policy responses to global warming may have profound effects on many aspects of national life, the exact role of the EC will not be decided easily.

B. Is European Community Policy Foreign Policy?

If the role of the EC relative to its Member States in external affairs is one ambiguity, another one has also to be confronted. Is EC internal environmental policy to be regarded as international on the grounds that it involves relations between several nation states, or does the title of this chapter confine discussion to the EC's external relations?

To regard internal EC policy as within the scope of this book, as the editors have wanted, is a perfectly tenable view, even if by accepting it one compounds a confusion that commonly surrounds the EC. It is as well to get to the bottom of this confusion since it is particularly important in the environmental area, where responsibility for implementing policy—and thereby helping to make it—frequently rests with local authorities or other sub-national bodies who would not normally expect to be involved in foreign affairs, but who increasingly find themselves having to come to terms with EC affairs.

One of the reasons why the EC is so difficult to understand is that it does not fit the simple model of public policy, which is commonly divided into home and foreign affairs. EC policy-making shares so many of the characteristics of foreign policy-making that it is easy to think of it as such. For a start, it involves other countries and is usually made abroad. Despite the growing role of the European Parliament, EC policy is prepared largely in secret following the traditions of diplomacy, and legislation is adopted by a Council of Ministers behind closed doors. The process is thus much more like treaty-making than the open process of adopting national legislation which is the hallmark of parliamentary democracies. It is still possible for EC legislation to differ in significant respects from the proposal originally published by the Commission without outsiders knowing who was responsible for the changes or why. But EC legislation once adopted is quite unlike a Treaty and can have the same force as national legislation. One form of EC legislation—the Regulation—is directly applicable by national courts just as if it were national legislation. Another form—the Directive—binds national governments as to the ends to be achieved and can also be applied by national courts in some circumstances.[2] Both these forms affect internal affairs without further review or ratification by national parliaments. If a Member State fails to fulfil the obligation set out in an EC Directive, the Commission can bring an action before the Court and so draw attention to the failure. All Member States effectively now have two legislatures, and the higher legislature (EC) can influence internal decisions just as does the lower (national) legislature.

The implications of this point are best illustrated with an example. Duich Moss is a peat bog on Islay, one of the Western Isles of Scotland. Islay is the seat of a distillery producing a single malt whisky that is renowned for a flavour imparted to the malted barley by the burning of peat. A few years ago the distillery wished to expand its production and applied for planning permission involving a new site for digging peat, and an access road. The planning application was opposed by the Nature Conservancy Council (NCC), the UK Government's official adviser on nature conservation matters, and by a private body, the Royal Society for the Protection of Birds (RSPB). In winter, 4–5 per cent of the entire world population of the Greenland White-Fronted Goose is to be found feeding at Duich Moss.

This is a typical case of a conflict arising between two interest groups, the resolution of which it is one purpose of home policy to provide for. In this case, national rules exist and are administered locally, unless exceptional circumstances suggest that the central government should intervene. Under the town and country planning laws, permission to develop land is granted or withheld by the local authority, after certain matters have been taken into account, and after interested parties have had a chance to make representations. In this case, the authority decided in favour of the distillery. In the ordinary course of events that would have been the end of the matter, but the RSPB, having lost

[2] The European Court has developed the doctrine of 'direct effect' whereby national courts can apply a Directive, in the absence of national implementing legislation, if its requirements are sufficiently clear.

the battle under the rules of home policy, proceeded to play an EC card. They complained to the EC Commission in Brussels that the United Kingdom was in breach of the EC Directive on the conservation of wild birds, which requires Member States *inter alia* to classify special protection areas for the conservation of named species of bird. The RSPB argued that under any reasonable criteria, Duich Moss should have been classified as a 'special protection area' and that had it been so classified the outcome of the planning application would have been different.

Complaints to the Commission from individuals, local authorities, and interest groups, are a growing feature of the implementation of EC legislation. The Commission has been encouraging this as one way of keeping itself informed. The Commission registers these complaints and, since it has no inspectorate of its own, it usually writes to the Member State asking for an explanation. In this case, however, the Commission official decided to go and see for himself. As a matter of courtesy, the Foreign Office was informed of his intended visit and was thereby thrown into a state of mild panic. Nothing like this had ever happened before in the EC. Did the official have the right to come? Was his visit desirable? Could he be stopped if he insisted on coming? One can imagine the questions being asked. There was no doubt that the official could visit Islay as a holiday-maker to watch birds, but he was intending to come as a representative of the EC institution that is the guardian of the Treaty, in order to investigate a complaint, by a private body, against a Member State for failure to fulfil an obligation under the Treaty. The Treaty gives no guidance whatever on the right to visit.

In the event, the British Government put a motor-car at the disposal of the official and had him accompanied to Islay. He wrote a report which, according to press leaks, recommended that infringement proceedings be started against the UK in the European Court. But as so often happens, the matter was settled before it reached the Court. The UK Government's Scottish Office persuaded the distillery to think again. The distillery decided that another source of peat was suitable. The digging of Duich Moss did not proceed.

So here we have a local dispute decided first one way and then another. Originally it was an aspect of home affairs, but by the time it was finished it had become something different. But it certainly was not foreign affairs in the traditional sense of the relations between two or more sovereign states, and one would have to look hard to find an international treaty governing relations between two nation states which allowed an official of one to travel to another so as to overturn a locally made decision.

Of course the outcome was not just of local interest, since not only did it involve a site of importance for a significant proportion of the world population of a protected species but it also had implications for other Member States when dealing with the birds Directive. British home policy in this case can be criticized, not just for a failure to identify a site as required by the Directive, but also for leaving to a local authority a decision that was really beyond it. In this case EC intervention has shown up a national error of judgement. An alternative view is that the local authority should itself have recognized the significance of the nature conservation aspect and of the EC Directive without central government involvement.

This story illustrates how EC policy is becoming so intertwined with home policy that it is not always possible to understand home policy without taking account of EC policy. Although EC policy has the attributes of foreign policy during its formulation, it then becomes integrated with home policy in its implementation. This originality was recognized by the European Court as long ago as 1964 when it described the EC Community as establishing 'a new legal order of international law'.[3]

One can say that for those subjects where there is a corpus of EC law, the EC is best understood as a federal system with more than one legislature, but where the higher level of government is not itself a nation state. This is a reversal of the situation with existing federations with which we are familiar—the USA and Germany, for example—in which the higher level is a nation state and lower-level bodies are not.

C. Origins of the European Community's Environmental Policy

Although the Treaty took effect in 1957, it was not until 1972 that the Heads of State and Government decided that the EC should

[3] *Van Gend en Loos* v. *Netherlands Fiscal Administration*, Case 26/62 ECR [1963] 1.

adopt an environmental policy and called upon the Commission to draft a programme of action. The Treaty, being a creation of the 1950s, did not refer to protection of the environment. It was developments in the Member States, and in other international forums, such as the 1972 UN Conference on the Human Environment at Stockholm (UNCHE), that created the pressure for the EC to move in this direction. It was entire coincidence that Britain, Ireland, and Denmark joined the EC in the very year that it adopted the first action programme on the environment.

It was not until 1987, when the Single European Act amended the Treaty of Rome, that environment policy was explicitly provided for. Until then environmental legislation was adopted under a rather generous interpretation of the Treaty that attracted criticism despite some endorsement by the European Court.[4]

The first action programme on the environment covered the period from 1973 to 1976, and we are now more than two-thirds of the way through the fourth action programme. These programmes have two main purposes. They suggest specific proposals for legislation that the Commission intends to put forward over the next few years, and they provide an occasion to discuss some broad ideas in environmental policy and to suggest new directions for the future. The first programme was needed to chart a wholly new course and was a long and comprehensive document. It started with a general statement of the objectives and principles of EC environmental policy, and went on to spell out action that the Commission would propose.

The international dimension of environmental policy was recognized from the beginning, and no less than four of the eleven principles relate to international relations. They can be paraphrased as follows:

- Activities carried out in one country should not cause deterioration of the environment in another.
- The effects of environmental policy in the Member States must take account of the interests of the developing countries.
- The EC and the Member States should act together in international organizations and in promoting international and world-wide environmental policy.
- In each category of pollution it is necessary to establish the

[4] House of Lords' Select Committee on the European Communities, *Approximation of Laws under Article 100 of the EEC Treaty*, 22nd Report, Session 1977–8.

level of action (local, regional, national, EC, international) best suited to the type of pollution and to the geographical zone to be protected.

The Single European Act gave legal force to several of the eleven principles and added the most important new principle that 'environmental protection requirements shall be a component of the Community's other policies'. Concerning co-operation with other countries on environmental matters, the Single European Act used the words quoted at the head of this chapter. Before discussing what this means in practice, we must briefly look at the EC's internal environmental policy.

D. The European Community's Internal Environmental Policy

The EC has now adopted over 280 items of environmental legislation. Many of these are of a narrow technical character with little policy content, but several are important by any standard and some, such as that dealing with acid rain, for a time entered the realm of 'high politics'. They have all been described elsewhere and only a few are touched on here.[5]

Given that EC environmental policy began without a clear legal base in a Treaty that was primarily concerned with the creation of a common market, it is no surprise to find that much environmental legislation is concerned with setting standards for products in trade, or with avoiding distortions to competition in industrial activities. If it could be shown that standards set in just one country were affecting the common market then there was a justification for EC involvement. The role of environmental policy then was to ensure that the common standard was a high standard. But even from the beginning the EC concerned itself with matters that hardly touched the common market, such as standards for bathing waters or bird protection. Protection of birds is a subject that obviously cannot be handled at national level alone since birds fly across frontiers, but the justification for EC as opposed to national standards for bathing water is harder to find. The EC never confined itself to the two classic justifica-

[5] See Nigel Haigh, *EEC Environmental Policy and Britain*, 2nd edn. (London: Longman, 1990).

tions for international environmental policy, first, that some issues (air pollution, sea pollution, transfrontier rivers) are not confined by national frontiers and may indeed be global in character and, second, that international trade is impeded by differing standards.

The adoption of any item of EC legislation is a process of accommodation between a number of countries. Sometimes, such as with standards for drinking water, each individual Member State will be concerned largely with the effects on its own internal procedures and with the cost, since what other Member States do will have little or no impact on the environment of others. With other Directives, environmental effects between countries have been at the heart of the discussions. An obvious case is the so-called Seveso Directive, named after the suburb of Milan where a major accident at a chemical plant spread dioxin across the countryside. Under pressure from the European Parliament, who suspected that the Swiss company had located its plant in Italy because of laxer standards, the Commission proposed a Directive. Provisions of the Directive that was finally adopted require the production of a safety report, an 'on-site' emergency plan, an 'off-site' emergency plan, and that the local population be informed of the correct behaviour to adopt in the event of an accident.

The proposal as put forward by the Commission had no transfrontier provisions, but the Benelux countries pressed for a requirement that a Member State give all appropriate information to other Member States who might be affected by an accident. Member States would also have had the right to consult on the necessary measures. This was resisted by the French government. Although the proposed Directive specifically excluded nuclear power stations, France feared that it would set a precedent which might then be used by other Member States to comment on the siting of French nuclear power stations. This dispute held up adoption of the Directive for eighteen months and in the end a compromise was achieved under which information is to be made available between Member States only 'within the framework of their bilateral relations'. This means that the Commission does not have the same right to insist on implementation as it would have had otherwise, and means that other Member States have no rights at all.

Another important Directive, known as the 'sixth amendment', requires the manufacturer of any new chemical to supply a file with the results of tests for effects on man and the environment to an authority. The authority can call for extra information and if not satisfied can prevent marketing of the chemical. The file is also sent to the Commission, which passes it to the authorities in all Member States. Any one of these authorities can ask for further information. Unless objections are raised within 45 days, the manufacturer has assured access to the whole EC market. The Directive simultaneously seeks to prevent environmental problems arising and serves the purpose of a common market in chemicals. Its successful operation depends very much on collaboration and mutual trust between the authorities in different countries.

The 'sixth amendment' was adopted in 1979 with support from the chemical industry in Europe, which is surprising given that the industry was not then known for welcoming environmental legislation. One explanation for this is that comparable Regulations were being developed in the USA by the Environmental Protection Agency under the Toxic Substances Control Act. The European chemical industry feared that impediments could be put in the way of exports to the USA, and believed that comparable rules in Europe could be used as pressure on the US authorities. They felt that the US might be deterred by denial of access to the whole EC market—which is considerably larger than the US market—in a way in which they would not be deterred by lack of access to, say, the French or German markets alone. In the event, no trade war across the Atlantic has developed, and the hope remains that ultimately the procedures that enable a new chemical to be sold in the US market will be recognized in Europe and vice versa.

The best-known item of EC pollution legislation dealing with a transboundary issue is the Directive that seeks to tackle the issue of acid rain. Known as the large combustion plant Directive, it limits emissions of sulphur dioxide and nitrogen oxides from such plants. The issue of acid rain reached the political agenda in Sweden in the late 1960s, and in 1972 Sweden managed to make it an international issue at the UN conference on the environment held in Stockholm that year. Pressure from Sweden and the other Nordic countries eventually led to the Geneva Convention on long-range transboundary air pollution being adopted in 1979 under the auspices of the UN Economic Commission for Europe. This UN grouping includes not only countries from Western and Eastern Europe, but also the USA and Canada. Largely because of opposition from the USA, West Germany, and the UK, the Convention did not include any firm targets for reduction in emissions.

The key date for acid rain policy in Europe is 1982 when the German government changed its position from passive resistance to enthusiastic support for a policy of significant reduction in emissions. It then persuaded the Commission to propose a Directive similar to German legislation. After a long struggle, a Directive was agreed that set emission standards for new plant and required each Member State to reduce emissions from existing plant by certain percentages in three stages. The Commission had originally proposed that each Member State should reduce emissions by 60 per cent by the year 1995 compared to a 1980 baseline. The economic, geographical, and fuel supply circumstances were so different that a uniform reduction proved unacceptable to several countries. As a result a compromise was eventually achieved with different countries having quite different reductions that nevertheless should result in a 58 per cent reduction in overall EC sulphur dioxide emissions by the year 2003—a slippage of two percentage points and eight years from the Commission's original proposal. This differentiated reduction may yet prove a better model for the global warming issue across the world than the uniform reductions agreed for ozone-depleting substances.

E. The European Community's External Environmental Policy: Conventions

The development of the EC's external powers—that is to say, its ability to deal with other countries much as does a nation state—has come about largely as a result of decisions of the European Court of Justice. The development of these powers has been analysed extensively, but only rarely have their practical implications in the environmental field been discussed, very probably because they are well known only to those few officials involved.

A rare glimpse of problems that have arisen is that given by André Nollkaemper, based on interviews conducted during a course of probation in the Ministry of Foreign Affairs in the Netherlands.[6] This account draws heavily on Nollkaemper's description. Needless to say, not all the problems that have arisen have been resolved, a major one being implicit in the quotation at the head of this chapter.

Before the judgment of the European Court in the *AETR* case of 1971, it was possible to argue that the Community was only competent to conclude international conventions when this was expressly provided for in the Treaty.[7] Even this assumed that other countries were prepared to deal with the EC, and not all were. In the *AETR* case, and on a number of occasions since, the Court decided that competence for external affairs can also be implied by the Treaty as well as by the acts of the institutions performed under the Treaty. Of paramount importance is the link between internal and external powers. In the *AETR* case the Court held that whenever the EC has promulgated internal rules in a certain field, i.e. has taken measures binding on the Member States, then the powers to act externally in that field are created. Moreover, under certain conditions, these powers will be of an exclusive nature: as soon as the EC comes into possession of these powers, the Member States will have lost them. Needless to say, one of the most important—and complex—questions that arises concerns the conditions under which powers become exclusive.

A most important consequence is that the EC's external powers expand without the express approval of the Member States simply in the course of developing the EC's internal policies. An extra constraint has therefore been added to EC internal policy-making, since the Member States should now always consider whether the adoption of some desirable item of EC legislation might not result in the undesirable (to them) loss of external competence.

Only rarely is this soul-searching made public, but this happened in Britain during the negotiations that led to Directive

---

[6] A. Nollkaemper, 'The European Community and International Environmental Co-operation: Legal Aspects of External Community Powers', *Legal Issues of European Co-operation*, 2 (1987), 55–91.

[7] *Commission v. Council (AETR)*, Case 22/70, [1971] ECR 263.

80/51 on aircraft noise. In a debate in the House of Commons, concern was expressed that adoption of the Directive might lead to an extension of Community competence into the field of aviation generally and not just aircraft noise.[8] Some felt that the Commission might want to represent the Member States at international meetings, such as those of the International Civil Aviation Organisation (ICAO). However, any fears in the minds of the UK Government on that occasion seem to have been overcome, since the Minister, Norman Tebbit, expressed himself satisfied that 'the extension of the Community's authority which the Directive will produce is justified by the extra powers that it will bring to enable us to limit the noise of aircraft from other Member States'. These words suggest a balancing of the risks and advantages. The reason for resisting EC competence in this area was given by the Minister. He explained that 'political issues were rarely raised in ICAO' and 'the power blocs are little in evidence'. The implication was that if the EC began to act as a bloc this would encourage other countries to do likewise. The UK Government must have felt confident that other Member States would think in the same way, and it is interesting to note that although three years later the Commission asked for observer status at ICAO, this was refused by the Member States. Another example is the refusal by the Council to adopt a Directive on the dumping of wastes at sea, which the Commission had put forward at least partly in order to be able to accede to international dumping conventions (the Oslo and London Conventions). Some Member States believe that accession by the EC will lead to a duplication of activities while adding nothing to environmental protection.

Where the EC has exclusive competence for all the subject-matter of a Convention, it is possible for the EC to become a party to it without the Member States also being parties. This has happened in some fields, such as trade in commodities, but it has not yet happened in the environmental field. Conventions to which some or all of the Member States have become parties as well as the EC are known as 'mixed agreements'. A recent example of the consequences of this arose with the Montreal Protocol to the Vienna Convention for the Protection of the Ozone Layer. At the meeting in London in June 1990 at which amendments to the

[8] House of Commons, *Official Report* (19 June 1979), cols. 1251–83.

Protocol were agreed, the EC had competence for negotiating the percentage reductions in the quantity of ozone-depleting substances that could be produced, because of the existence of an EC Regulation covering this. However, the EC had no competence for the decision to establish a fund to assist Third World countries to obtain the more expensive alternative substances and technologies, and on this point the Member States acted on their own.

Where, under a mixed agreement, the EC has competence, the Commission will negotiate on behalf of the EC in accordance with a mandate given unanimously by the Council, i.e. by the Member States. Sometimes this is set in advance, but sometimes instructions are given *sur place*. Where there is no unanimity among the Member States problems arise. In 1985 at a meeting in Buenos Aires of the parties of the Washington Convention on trade in endangered species (CITES), unanimity could not be found so that all ten Member States abstained, leading to a substantial loss of influence.[9] In the same year at a meeting of the parties of the Bonn Convention on the conservation of migratory species of wild animals, agreement could not always be reached on matters where the EC had competence, and it was accepted that Member States could not act independently. However, where the EC did not have exclusive competence it was decided that Member States could act independently. This means that individual Member States can advance different arguments and may even vote against each other, though this of course results in a breach of the principle of EC solidarity.

Yet another example of the problems of mixed agreements arose with the Paris Convention for the prevention of marine pollution from land-based sources. In 1982 the EC Commission had taken the view that nothing prevented Member States adopting more stringent standards under the Paris Convention than

[9] The Commission wanted abstention by the Member States in the absence of a common EC position being agreed. This was because, in its view, the issues under consideration (bullfrogs and hooded seals) were already within exclusive EC competence since CITES was a common commercial policy matter. Hence the Member States were not entitled to act unilaterally in an external context with respect to them. The Member States, or at least six of them, took a different view, arguing that, as the species were not already within the CITES Appendices or the EC CITES Regulation Annexes, they were not within EC competence and hence Member States were entitled, in the absence of an EC common position being established in accordance with Article 5 of the Treaty, to take whatever action they individually deemed best.

comparable EC standards, but since 1984 this has been disputed. Disagreements arose relating to standards for mercury, cadmium, and PCBs, and the EC Commission even succeeded in preventing the adoption of proposals for PCBs on the grounds of the EC's exclusive competence. Needless to say, these disputes between the EC Commission and the Member States as to their relative powers are particularly irritating to non-Member States and may well be incomprehensible to them. They can paralyse the work under the convention. In the case of this Convention (following the accession of Spain and Portugal to the EC), the only non-Member States are Sweden and Norway. Sweden followed this episode by tabling a list of questions relating to the powers of the EC.

The EC is now a party to a large number of conventions covering a wide range of environmental concerns. It is seeking to be a party to more. The broad interest of the Commission, with the support of the European Parliament, is to enhance the position of the EC in the world. The extension by the Court of the EC's external powers has allowed this, but without recognition of the EC by other countries as an appropriate party to Conventions this would have counted for nothing. As recently as the early 1980s, during the negotiations of the Vienna Convention on the ozone layer, the USA was querying the basis on which the EC could participate. Eventually, with the support of the Soviet Union, and despite resistance from the Commission, the US insisted on a clause in the Convention relating to the conditions under which the EC could be a party. Before that, in the 1970s, EC participation in the Helsinki Convention on the Protection of the Marine Environment of the Baltic Sea Area was refused by the other parties, led by the Soviet Union.

The position with respect to third countries now seems to be that the principle of participation by a 'regional economic integration organization' is accepted but the conditions, including voting procedures in the subsequent implementation of the Convention, still have to be negotiated each time. The precedent set in the Barcelona Convention (see below) is that when the EC is given voting powers and votes in the place of the Member States, it has as many votes as the number of participating Member States. However, in the Baltic Fisheries Convention, which is not a 'mixed agreement', the EC only has one vote, although two

Member States have a coastline on the Baltic. The more the EC acquires exclusive competence and the more it appears to third countries as if it is acting as a nation state itself, the greater will be the pressure for it to be accorded only one vote.

F. The Participation Clause

The evolution of the 'participation clause' in various conventions has been described by Kiss and Brusasco-MacKenzie.[10] The first environmental convention to which the EC became a party (in 1975) was the Paris Convention for the prevention of marine pollution from land-based sources. This took place apparently without difficulty, perhaps because a majority of the parties were EC Member States. Next was the Barcelona Convention of 1976 for the protection of the Mediterranean Sea against pollution, where Member States were in a minority among the contracting parties. This Convention includes Article 24, which mentions the European Economic Community by name and provides for it to sign as well as any other 'similar regional economic grouping at least one member of which is a coastal State of the Mediterranean Sea area and which exercises competence in fields covered by this Convention'. This created the theoretical possibility that other groupings such as the Arab League or the Organisation of African Unity could sign if, and to the extent that, sovereignty over the subject matter of the Convention had been transferred to them.

The 1979 Geneva Convention on Long-Range Transboundary Air Pollution, drafted under the auspices of the United Nations' Economic Commission for Europe (ECE), does not name the EC but foresaw participation by 'regional economic integration organizations' constituted by sovereign member states of the ECE having competence to negotiate, conclude, and apply international agreements. This formulation was accepted by the countries of Eastern Europe who did not at that time recognize the EC.

The EC has now clearly established itself as an actor on the international stage in environmental as well as in other affairs.

[10] A. Kiss and M. Brusasco-MacKenzie, 'Les Relations Extérieures des Communautés Européennes en Matière du Protection de l'Environnement', *Annuaire Français de Droit International*, 35 (1989), 702–10.

Although the Commission is anxious to expand this role, we have seen that there have been subjects such as aircraft noise and dumping at sea where the Member States have, for certain reasons, prevented the EC adopting the role that it has acquired for other subjects. Even where the EC has become a party to international conventions the problems of competence arise. The extent of EC competence depends on internal EC rules, and because these may not be coterminous with those in a convention—and the provisions of a subsequent protocol to the convention may not be knowable in advance—the Member States are likely to retain some competence. The division of competences can be very confusing for third countries and can make negotiations difficult or, in the extreme, even block them.

This complicated process has given the EC greater power in the world, but that by itself cannot be a justification. EC involvement on the international stage must be justified in the end by the extra contribution that the EC can make to solutions to international problems. It must add something to what the Member States acting independently could themselves have done. Fortunately there is an example in the environmental field.

G. The Ozone Layer: The Montreal Protocol

The hypothesis that certain gases called chlorofluorocarbons (CFCs) would deplete the stratospheric ozone layer was first advanced by scientists in 1974. Any decrease in the ozone layer allows more ultraviolet radiation to reach the earth's surface and so increases the risk of skin cancers. The response to this hypothesis differed in different countries in the 1970s. The USA banned the use of CFCs in aerosol cans for non-essential uses, but did not regulate other uses, for example as solvents, refrigerants, and in blowing foam. Canada, Norway, and Sweden followed the US example. The EC took a different course, and in 1978 the Council adopted a Resolution calling for a limitation on CFC production. Then in 1980 it adopted a Decision that placed a production capacity limit on two types of CFC. While the US action resulted in a significant reduction in production, the EC action had little immediate effect as EC production capacity was higher than actual production.

In 1977 the United Nations Environment Programme (UNEP) began a review of scientific aspects and in 1981 initiated negotiations for a global convention. The Council of the EC authorized the Commission to participate on behalf of the EC in these negotiations, and in 1985 many countries, among them several EC Member States, as well as the EC Commission signed the Vienna Convention for the Protection of the Ozone Layer. It is what is sometimes called a framework convention since it covers such matters as co-operation on monitoring and research but does not itself place any obligation on the parties to take any specific measures to protect the ozone layer. These were to be laid down in separate protocols.

During the negotiations a dispute broke out between two groups of countries—the EC and what was called the Toronto Group (Canada, USA, Finland, Norway, and Sweden). Each group proposed that the first protocol to cover CFCs should embody the policies already adopted in their own group of countries. The Toronto Group's proposal was for a world-wide extension of a ban on uses of CFCs as aerosol propellants but involved no limit on other uses of CFCs. The EC, not surprisingly in view of the approach it had already adopted, proposed a production capacity limit. The Toronto Group advanced their proposal on the grounds that it was the quickest way of obtaining an immediate reduction in CFC releases. The EC maintained that an aerosol ban did nothing to prevent releases from growing non-aerosol uses and that, since it is the total amount of CFCs released that affects the ozone layer, the only effective action was to limit total production. As a result of this dispute, no protocol was adopted in 1985, and negotiations did not start again until 1986.

Before the new negotiations started the United States government changed its position. It dropped its proposed aerosol ban and proposed instead a freeze on CFC production by all countries followed by a series of reductions leading to a production ban. Effectively the USA had conceded the merit of the EC production limit approach, though reformulated and extended in a much more stringent form. Arguably the log jam was broken when, first, US environmental organizations, and then industry, abandoned the US Government's original negotiating position and embraced the EC approach. While the EC's 1980 Decision was originally largely symbolic, it had defined an intellectually defensible approach which ultimately became incorporated into the Montreal Protocol.

Following the US proposal, the EC in March 1987 agreed negotiating guidelines for the Commission which included a freeze at 1986 levels on entry into force of the Protocol followed by a 20 per cent reduction four years later. This was not achieved without considerable initial resistance from some Member States, including the UK, under the influence of their industries. In subsequent negotiations the EC agreed to a further cut amounting to a 50 per cent reduction by the turn of the century. This was embodied in the Montreal Protocol in September 1987, which came into force on 1 January 1989. The EC and most Member States ratified it simultaneously.

No sooner was the Protocol agreed than a consensus developed that the recently discovered hole in the ozone layer was caused by CFCs and it became evident that the reductions in the Protocol were not enough. Fortunately the Protocol included a review mechanism, and in June 1990 an amendment required additional reductions. In December 1990 the EC went further than the Protocol requires by agreeing to phase out CFCs by 1997.

The US deserves the credit for creating the pressure in 1986 and 1987 for significant reductions in CFC production, and US negotiators did not always conceal their irritation with the EC for what they saw as foot-dragging and the complications that it introduced.[11] It is therefore worth speculating on what might have occurred had the EC not been involved. Presumably a protocol along the lines of the Toronto Group's proposal would have been adopted in 1985, and several EC Member States would no doubt have become parties. This would have been a less satisfactory protocol, which would have needed complete revision after confirmation of the ozone hole discovery, and several important countries might well have stayed outside, at least initially. The lack of solidarity would have weakened the whole effort. In the event, the EC not only ensured that the Protocol had a better form but also delivered intact a bloc of twelve industrialized countries central to any successful global action since between them they produced more CFCs than the USA or Japan or the USSR. The result was an ideal situation whereby several

[11] R. E. Benedick, 'US Environmental Policy—Relevance to Europe', *International Environmental Affairs*, 1. 2 (Spring 1989).

countries contributed solutions to a global issue and learned from one another during the process.

H. Global Warming

The Vienna Convention with its associated Montreal Protocol was the first convention to deal with the global atmosphere and is therefore inevitably seen as a precedent for a possible convention on global warming. The idea of a freeze followed by percentage cuts applied equally to all countries is firmly before us. In preparation for the Second World Climate Conference held in November 1990, the EC Council—at a meeting exceptionally composed of both environment and energy Ministers—agreed that the EC collectively should stabilize carbon dioxide (CO_2) emissions by the year 2000 at 1990 levels. No legally binding instrument was adopted, but this 'political' decision enabled the EC Commissioner, Carlo Ripa di Meana, to make a bid for leadership. The Ministerial Declaration made at the end of the Conference welcomed 'the decisions and commitments undertaken by the European Community with its Member States' as well as those of a number of other countries to stabilize their emissions of CO_2. The United States was not one of these, so it cannot be a foregone conclusion that this commitment will necessarily form part of a convention if the world's largest emitter of CO_2 is to be a party to it.

The EC's political decision was made possible by some Member States—and most notably Germany—having already agreed to cut their emissions significantly. This, combined with estimates of what might happen in other countries that had set themselves no targets, and in the United Kingdom that had adopted a target of stabilization by 2005, made stabilization by 2000 for the EC as a whole a realistic possibility in the view of the Council. To translate this hope into more of a reality, the Commission could now propose a Directive allocating different targets to different countries on the model of the sulphur dioxide reductions set out in the large combustion plant Directive. Without some greater definition, it is not at all clear what the overall EC commitment to stabilize actually means in practice to those Member States who have not yet adopted national targets.

Should a Directive along these lines be agreed, it would give the EC the necessary competence to become a party to a convention that involved stabilization by the year 2000, or any subsequent date. But it cannot be assumed that the Council will agree such a Directive. We have already seen how the Council has on occasion not provided the Commission with a mandate to negotiate on its behalf on some subjects, and some Member States might not want to lose the power to negotiate on their own behalf on a subject that has such profound implications for national policies as does energy consumption. In this respect the Montreal Protocol does not provide a perfect analogy. CFCs are a traded product, and for that reason the EC is almost bound to be involved in its regulation. The Member States by agreeing to the Montreal Protocol transferred competence to the EC for all further control over the quantity of CFC production, but since CFC production will now cease in a few years the loss of competence will soon be of theoretical interest only. Carbon dioxide, by contrast, is not a manufactured and traded product but is the by-product of innumerable activities which will have to be controlled or influenced if agreed targets are to be achieved. Whole areas of national life, including the pattern of industrial development and electricity generation, not to mention personal mobility, will be affected forever by any target. Whereas individual countries may be willing to agree an initial target, they may well be apprehensive about the loss of influence over selecting subsequent and more stringent targets. One possibility which would enable the EC to be a party to a convention is for the EC to agree a Directive that sets an overall EC target of stabilization by the year 2000 but instead of allocating individual differentiated targets for each Member State requires each of them to produce an overall strategy for controlling CO_2 emissions, involving detailed plans for all of the major sources of CO_2 and the practical steps for achieving these plans. The overall EC target would provide the pressure on the Member States to make their own contribution. If the aggregate of the national strategies is such that stabilization by the EC would not be achieved, then pressure can be brought on those Member States who are not contributing enough.

The lesson of the Montreal Protocol can be applied here in reverse. Once the EC has adopted a policy as a result of a process of negotiation between twelve countries, it becomes difficult to shift. This happened with CFCs, and fortunately the policy the EC adopted in 1980 provided the model for aspects of the Protocol. But if it had been an inadequate policy it would not necessarily have been taken up in the Protocol. Similarly, if the EC adopts a detailed carbon dioxide policy on its own, which is not adapted to other countries, it may make it difficult for the EC and its Member States to play a constructive role in the negotiations on a global warming convention. Flexibility will therefore be needed.

The EC's competence in international environmental policy is suddenly being put to the test. Collectively the EC has already played a role and is exerting pressure, on the USA in particular, in a way that individually the Member States would not have been able to do. But it needs practical action on the part of the individual Member States if a reality is to be made of any target, be it stabilization or reduction. Practical action could require flexibility that can be lost when power is lost. One can anticipate that the allocation of responsibility between the EC and its Member States as negotiations proceed over the years will require a consensus that may not be achieved without some struggle. The stakes are high and are worth the struggle. Other countries may sometimes have to show patience as they watch.

PART III. Power and Conflicts of Interest

10

Global Warming and International Action: An Economic Perspective

Wilfred Beckerman

As is widely known, there is a possibility that serious climate change, including a significant rise in average global temperatures, will result from excessive emissions of greenhouse gases (GHGs) in the course of innumerable human activities. These emissions constitute what economists call 'externalities', reflecting the fact that they are, in a sense, unintended 'external' effects of the activities in question, including effects on future generations. But without going into semantic issues of whether or not the effects are 'intended', the key point is that the agents responsible for the activities have no pecuniary incentive to take them into account in deciding on the scale or character of these activities. Other people are affected—for example, by noise or smoke—but the agents responsible for generating the effects do not incur the costs of doing so. This will usually be the case when there are no property rights in the medium affected (for example, clean air or water), so that the agent generating the externality— such as a firm polluting the air—has no need to purchase the rights in question. For example, property rights in clean air or quiet or clean water and so on are usually either non-existent or vague or unenforceable for one reason or another. In the case of GHGs, the people who may be most harmed are future generations, to whom it is obviously not easy to give any rights that can be enforced today (though I am working on it).

But from the point of view of its implications for international negotiations, the main economic characteristic of the excessive emissions of GHGs is that they represent a particular class of

I am indebted to discussions with too many people to be able to enumerate them all here, even just those who have not been responsible for my errors.

externality, often known as 'the tragedy of the commons'. This refers to situations in which nobody can be excluded from the use of an asset—such as common grazing land, or fishing grounds, or the atmosphere—either on account of the technical characteristics of the asset (for example, radio broadcasts, or light from light-houses) or the legal arrangements, but where, nevertheless, one person's use of the asset reduces the amount available to other potential users (unlike radio broadcasts or the light from light-houses). In such a situation unrestricted use of the asset can easily lead to over-use, so that only if some voluntary or enforce-able exclusion mechanism is introduced can the supply be matched to the demand.

It is now feared that the environment—including the atmo-sphere—is approaching its capacity limit. That is to say, all nations have a right to pollute the atmosphere as much as they like but its absorptive capacity is no longer believed to be inex-haustible in certain important respects. In particular, it is feared that the concentration of 'greenhouse gases' (GHGs) in the atmo-sphere, which, other things being equal, would have an effect on global climate, is being raised by anthropogenic activity to a level at which the effect on global climate will be significant and, in some people's opinion, highly damaging to life on this planet. At the same time it is neither rational nor effective for any one country to act alone to reduce GHG emissions, for reasons which are discussed more fully in the final section of this chapter, so it is not surprising that there is a widespread clamour for internation-ally co-ordinated action.

It is sometimes believed that the problem of global warming is one on which scientists, not economists, have an exclusive right to pronounce and that the degree to which countries should try to reduce GHG emissions is a matter for scientists to decide. For example, a recent major report on numerous aspects of global warming has twenty contributors, almost all of them scientists of one kind or another, and not one economist among them. This report deplored the fact that the Response Strategies Working Group (of the UN Intergovernmental Panel on Climate Change) 'did not even come down on the side of the freeze in greenhouse-gas emissions, much less the deep cuts the scientists clearly in-dicate will be necessary if any attempt is to be made to slow or arrest the greenhouse effect. The IPCC scientists calculate ''with confidence'' that, to stabilize the carbon dioxide composition of the atmosphere at its present level, cuts in global emissions of that particular greenhouse gas would need to exceed 60 per cent.[1] But, to the economist, the question of how much one should cut GHG emissions now in order to reduce global warming in the future is a matter of the relative costs and benefits of alternative courses of action. And, as shown below, in the light of current information, a cut in CO_2 emissions of this order of magnitude would be much greater than can be justified by the costs of achieving it compared with the damage done by failing to do so.

Of course, scientists have to provide the information about the technical and physical characteristics of global warming. And their contributions to the construction of models to predict long-run changes in the climate constitute an outstanding intellectual achievement. But values have to be attached to the effects and to the costs of reducing GHGs which have then to be incorporated in the economist's paradigm of balancing costs and benefits at the margin. For example, just to put the problem into perspective, if the growth rate of output per head in the world were to be, say, 1.5 per cent per annum over the next century, which is well below the rate achieved in the post-war period,[2] average real incomes per head in 100 years' time would be 4.4 times as high as they are now. If the economic estimates of the reduction in total world output resulting from a doubling of CO_2 concentrations in the atmosphere are to be believed, then, at the outside, real incomes would be reduced by only about 1 or 2 per cent in 100 years' time. In that case, instead of being 4.4 times as rich as today the population in 100 years' time would be about 4.3 times as rich. It is not up to scientists, any more than it is up to economists, to decide that present generations—which include vast numbers of very poor people—should accept heavy costs and economic burdens in order that the population in the year 2090 should be 4.4 times as rich as they are now rather than only 4.3 times as rich. How

[1] Jeremy Leggett (ed.), *Global Warming: The Greenpeace Report* (Oxford: Oxford UP, 1990), 5.

[2] Over the whole period 1950 to 1985, the average compound rate of world output has been 4.0% and the rate of growth of output per head has been 2.1% (estimates from UN *Statistical Yearbooks*, 1965, 1971, 1978, and 1985/6). Insofar as the rate of growth of world population is slowing down considerably whereas the rate of spread of education, which is the mainspring of technical progress, is increasing, the postulated increase of only 1.5% p.a. over the next century is a very conservative figure.

much resources society should devote today to curbing GHGs is not a matter that can be decided purely on scientific grounds.

Apart from its externality aspect, global warming has other important economic characteristics. These include the time dimension and the associated problem of the appropriate discount rate to use, the uncertainties involved and the theory of decision-making under uncertainty, and, most importantly from the point of view of this volume, the international aspect, given that global warming, by definition, would affect all nations and is a phenomenon to which all nations contribute.

It would be impossible in a chapter of this length to give more than the flavour of the first two of these aspects of the problem, and I shall concentrate here on issues that have a bearing on the scope for international agreement. But this requires setting the stage on which the international actors ought to be playing their parts. There are two aspects to this. First, how will the costs and benefits of international action to curtail GHGs be distributed between nations? Secondly, since, as will be argued below, the distribution of the costs and benefits is such that reaching international agreement will be uniquely difficult, it is important to get some idea of how far the game is worth the candle—or in other words, how catastrophic would it really be for the world as a whole if no effective international agreement was reached? The next section, therefore, attempts to give some broad-brush idea of the overall costs and benefits of action to curtail GHG emissions.

A. Global Warming in Perspective

In the first place, it should be appreciated that GHGs are not produced only by human activities. Indeed, the anthropogenic contribution is relatively very small. Burning of fossil fuels emits about 5 billion tons of carbon per annum, which is small compared to the natural exchange between the atmosphere and the Earth's surface (including the oceans) of about 200 billion tons per annum.[3] Much carbon is emitted by vegetation, such as rotting and decaying trees, but it would be difficult to impose a carbon tax on nature. After all, records from air bubbles trapped in ice cores revealed in the Vostock ice core experiment show enor-

[3] B. J. Mason, 'The Greenhouse Effect', *Contemporary Physics*, 30. 6 (1989), 417–32.

mous variations over the last 150,000 years in CO_2 concentrations, long before humans were having any impact.

There are, of course, great uncertainties about the scientific characteristics of global warming and the greenhouse effect in general. At the same time there is enormous and legitimate public concern about the environment, and it is desirable that policy priorities genuinely reflect the relative importance of alternative environmental problems. For the current near-hysteria about global warming greatly exceeds the concern being expressed about twenty years ago—sometimes by the same scientists—over the impending ice age.[4] As a result, there are pressures on governments to allocate resources in a way that probably does not reflect what the relative preferences of a well-informed society would be as between the effects of climate change on very distant, and no doubt much richer, future generations, and other urgent environmental needs—such as dealing with current local water and air pollution that severely affects the lives of current generations in many parts of the world—or numerous other current concerns, such as housing, health, and hospitals, education, research and training, industrial investment, transport, population control, crime, drugs, and so on, not to mention social problems such as peace, stability, tolerance, and racial harmony—the absence of which all over the world probably causes far more suffering than would the effects of the sort of climate change predicted over the course of the next century. It is important, therefore, to try to get a rough idea of the costs and benefits of global warming or of policies to attenuate it.

---

[4] Stephen Schneider, the author of a well-known book, *Global Warming*, was the author of a book about the coming ice age, entitled *The Genesis Strategy*, at a time—the late 1960s and early 1970s—when global temperatures seemed to have been following a downward trend for about twenty years and ice age predictions were fashionable amongst many 'concerned scientists'. See references to other assertions about the coming ice age in Lewis Bessemer, 'A Brief History of Climatic Doom', *The Spectator* (3 Mar. 1990). William D. Nordhaus reminds us of a series of studies carried out about twenty years ago, under the auspices of the National Research Council, of the impact of global cooling. As he points out, many of the losses resulting from global cooling, which would be likely gains in the event of global warming, have not been considered at all in the recent major study of global warming consequences by the US Environmental Protection Agency, from which he invites us to draw the conclusion that 'environmental impact studies can find the cloud behind every silver lining'. 'To Slow Or Not To Slow: The Economics of the Greenhouse Effect', draft paper, Feb. 1990, pp. 26–7 n.17.

Even this is an immensely difficult task, since what the economist wants is to sort out the costs and benefits of *different degrees* of
abatement of GHG emissions. In general it is preferable to avoid
all-or-nothing scenarios, since if there is one thing that we learn
from economics it is that optimal policy consists of equating
benefits from different courses of action at the margin. (It is rarely
optimal to go out shopping with the determination to buy only
fruit or only fish or only vegetables, according to which happens
to be cheaper, rather than some combination of them.) Hence,
ideally, one would like to draw up a schedule of costs of different
levels of carbon dioxide emissions and the costs of different
degrees of abatement in order to arrive at the optimum policy.
Unfortunately, most of the estimates that have been made of the
economic effects of global warming relate to specific degrees of
warming or of abatement, at specific dates, although some
attempts have been made, notably by Professor William
Nordhaus of Yale University, to convert such estimates as are
available of the costs and benefits of alternative CO_2 emission
scenarios into schedules of the kind required.[5]

As indicated above, the scientific side of global warming is a
matter of considerable debate and uncertainty. But the general
consensus amongst scientists, such as it is, is that in the absence
of special measures to restrict CO_2 emissions the concentration of
CO_2 in the atmosphere will double some time towards the end of
the next century and this will lead to a rise in average world
temperature of between 1.5°C and 4°C.[6] Most reputable scientists seem to agree that there are still major gaps in their understanding of the global warming phenomenon in general and, in
particular, the relationship between carbon dioxide and global
warming, with corresponding very large differences in the predictions made by alternative climate models.[7] There appear to be

[5] Nordhaus, 'To Slow Or Not To Slow'.
[6] WHO and UNEP, *Scientific Assessment of Climate Change*. The Policymakers'
Summary of the Report of Working Group I to the Intergovernmental Panel on
Climate Change, June 1990 (hereafter: IPCC, *Scientific Assessment*): 'the average
rate of increase of global mean temperature during the next century is estimated to
be about 0.3°C per decade. . . . This will result in a likely increase in global mean
temperature of about . . . 3°C above today's (about 4°C above pre-industrial)
before the end of the next century' (p. 13).
[7] For example, whilst all the main models predict that there will be increased
precipitation as a result of global warming, the estimated increases in precipitation range from +3% to +15%!

three main reasons for these uncertainties. First, modelling the earth's climate is a task of heroic proportions and there are still enormous gaps in the models currently used. Second, contrary to widespread belief, the models that predict increases in world temperature as a result of increased CO_2 concentrations are not confirmed by temperature changes over the past century. And third, there are natural influences on the climate, not all of which are understood, and which include some relatively short-term natural variations such as changes in the angle at which the equatorial plane is inclined to the Earth's orbital plane (about 23 degrees).

In addition, the average effect is not predicted to be uniform. One of the conclusions on which the current models (on which the dire predictions are based) agree is that the rise in temperature will be least near the equator, and greatest as one nears the poles. Since it is hottest in the former regions and coldest in the latter, one might be tempted, as Thomas Schelling points out, to conclude that this would be a desirable outcome.[8] However, some people are hard to please and everybody will have heard predictions of all sorts of alleged likely terrible consequences of a 3° rise in temperature, to which I shall refer in more detail below.

But meanwhile, let us consider another simple fact. At present the world's population is distributed over parts of the globe that differ enormously with respect to their average temperatures. Yet over a very wide range there is no obvious correlation between average temperature and the income level of the countries in question. In other words, without doing any complicated and highly conjectural calculations to predict how a 3° rise in temperature would affect world output in 100 years time, it is perfectly clear that the human race can flourish in a great variety of average temperatures and climates. One does not get the impression that it is some fragile species that can only produce and survive in a museum with a controlled temperature the variation of which is confined to some 3° band.

[8] Thomas C. Schelling, 'Global Environmental Forces', in *Energy: Production, Consumption, and Consequences* (Washington, DC: National Academy Press, 1990), 75–84.

B. Some Economic Magnitudes

However, this chapter is not about the science, and the above points are made not only because they are relevant to the relatively sophisticated issue of the theory of choice under conditions of uncertainty, but because of their much more practical relevance to the problem of achieving international agreement about the sharing out of costs and benefits of reductions in GHGs in a situation in which each country's scientists, as well as economists, will easily be able to challenge the assumptions and estimates made by those of other countries. This is particularly relevant in so far as the models are so far very bad at predicting relatively local effects, and from the point of view of individual countries what matters is not so much whether the world as a whole will get a little warmer or whether there is a slight increase in average rainfall in the world as a whole but whether their particular patch of it gets hotter or not, and by how much, and whether it gets more rain or less rain.

But meanwhile, let us concentrate on the average effect on the world as a whole and adopt, for the sake of argument, the current existing consensus amongst most scientists indicated above, namely that in about a hundred years' time average world temperature will rise by about 3 °C—though there are many eminent scientists who dispute this consensus—and, too, that this will lead to an overall increase in rainfall, though, again, the opposite effect will occur in some large continental regions far removed from seas.

What can be said, in a rough and ready way, about the orders of magnitude of the economic effects that such climate changes would produce? Here, too, once one looks at such estimates as have been made, and before trying to perform a 'Nordhaus' on them to estimate marginal cost and cumulative discounted marginal benefit schedules for different degrees of reduction in greenhouse gas emissions, one sees that the economic impacts hardly justify the alarm and the calls for dramatic action that characterize much public discussion of this issue. In other words, whatever one does with the estimates they are unlikely to demonstrate that the present state of scientific knowledge justifies great trouble and expense to cut CO_2 emissions by very large amounts. The reasons for this quickly become apparent.

It is true that the estimates referred to below are confined to estimates of the effects of the CO_2 concentration doubling, which is not expected to occur until the second half of the next century. And it has been argued, notably by William Cline (to whose estimates for the doubling scenario considerable reference is made below), that one should extend one's time horizon much further. For a distinction needs to be made between the amount of warming that will have occurred by any particular date and the amount of eventual warming that is expected to result from the cumulative emissions and future emission levels by the time that the global climate system has reached equilibrium. Given the time lags in the dynamics of climate change, notably those caused by the inertia introduced into the system as a result of the take-up of CO_2 by the oceans, it is quite possible that, although global temperatures have risen by only 3 °C by the end of the next century, there is a further unavoidable rise of a few more degrees in the pipeline.[9]

Of course, the further one projects into the future the more uncertainty has to be attached to the projections, and Cline's projections, which are, in effect, projections over another century of what are already projections of trends well beyond the predictive power of the models, are open to serious question on this account. Faced with the vast technological changes that have taken place in the last 100 years and the near certainty that these will be totally dwarfed by the changes that will take place over the next century, during which an incomparably greater number of people will be engaged in technological and scientific research all over the world, nobody can suppose that the world of the late twenty-first century will bear much resemblance to the world that we know today and that energy will still be produced on a large scale by dirty and polluting substances such as coal. Furthermore, the need to discount the future implies that the benefits in two centuries' time from abating GHG emissions now would

[9] This point is stressed in the IPCC reports (e.g. IPCC, *Scientific Assessment*, 13–16), in which a distinction is drawn between 'realized' and 'equilibrium' climate change. The relationship between the two is not proportional so that e.g. 'the realised temperature rise at any time is about 50% of the committed temperature rise if the climate sensitivity (the response to a doubling of carbon dioxide) is 4.5C and about 80% if the climate sensitivity is 1.5C ... but it is not certain whether it would take decades or centuries for most of the remaining rise to equilibrium to occur' (box on p. 16).

have to be astronomic to justify significant current sacrifices. Hence, we shall confine ourselves here to such estimates as have been made of the effects of the scenario selected above, featuring a doubling of the concentration of CO_2 and a rise in temperature of 3 °C.

1. *Agriculture*

One of the most important effects of global warming, if any, will be on agriculture. The climate models predict that global warming will cause the interior of continents to be drier, which will have an unfavourable effect on agriculture in many areas. But they also predict favourable effects in other areas, partly on account of longer growing periods in northern areas, partly on account of greater rainfall resulting from generally increased evaporation over land and sea, partly because of the fertilization effect on plants of higher CO_2 concentrations. Experiments at the US Water Conservation Laboratory have shown that, with higher CO_2 concentrations, the same amount of plant growth can be obtained with less water.[10] For the USA alone, estimates by the Environmental Protection Agency show that the net effect on agriculture is uncertain, with the possible range of effects lying between a net gain of $10 billion and a net loss of $10 billion.

Now this may sound like big money to the layman, but of course, by the standards of the American economy, it is negligible—about the size of an average monthly trade deficit in recent years. Agricultural net output constitutes about 3 per cent of total US national product—i.e. about $150 billion out of a national product of about $5.2 trillion. Thus even if one takes the extreme worst-case estimate of a cut in net agricultural output of about $10 billion, this still constitutes only 0.2 per cent of total national product. Even if the estimates are wildly optimistic and the actual effect is to halve US agricultural output, this is still only 1.5 per

[10] See Robert White, 'The Great Climate Debate', *Scientific American*, 263. 1 (July 1990), 23. However, such experiments under somewhat artificial conditions are not a totally reliable guide to the effects of a genuine global rise in CO_2 concentrations, as has been pointed out in a survey of various experiments by William E. Easterling III, Martin Parry, and Pierre Crosson, in 'Adapting Future Agriculture to Changes in Climate', in Norman J. Rosenberg, William E. Easterling III, Pierre R. Crosson, and Joel Darmstadter, *Greenhouse Warming: Abatement and Adaptation* (Washington, DC: Resources for the Future, 1989), 98.

cent of total national product—i.e. less than one year's growth. If US national product per head grows by about 1.5 per cent per annum, in real terms, over the next 100 years, by the year 2090 it would be over four times as large as it is now. In other words, even a cut of 50 per cent in net agricultural output as a result of global warming, which nobody would suggest is likely, would merely mean that the index of *real* national product in the USA in the year 2090, taking 1990 = 100, would be 436 instead of 443.[11] To use a way of looking at it employed by Schelling, it means that the American population will have to wait another year, in 2090, to achieve the living standards that they could otherwise have expected to achieve in that year.[12] I think the American population will find ways of adapting to this disappointment over the course of the years.

Of course, in other countries the effects will be different. In some, notably Canada, the USSR, and China, the net effects will be favourable as the production regions move northwards and growing periods are extended.[13] Nordhaus surveys estimates for other countries and reports: 'Detailed studies for the Netherlands and Australia found that the overall impact of a CO_2 equivalent doubling will be small and probably difficult to detect over a half-century or more. The Coolfont Workshop (in which teams of experts gathered on a very short-term basis) estimated the impact of climate change upon six large regions—the US, Europe, Brazil,

[11] Estimates of an approximately zero net effect on agricultural output were made by the EPA in 1988 (see J. B. Smith and D. A. Tirpak (eds.), *The Potential Effects of Global Climate Change on the United States*, Draft Report to the US Congress (Washington, DC: Environmental Protection Agency, 1988)). These have been confirmed in a more recent and very detailed study, breaking down the USA into a large number of regions and using alternative climate models. See Richard Adams *et al.*, 'Global Climate Change and US Agriculture', *Nature*, 345 (17 May 1990), 219–24. William Cline, however (in 'Economic Stakes of Global Warming in the Very Long Term', draft of Nov. 1991, REV1, p. 2 n. and p. 22), refers to some estimates of much higher agricultural losses. But his own calculations, taking these into account, still suggest a loss of agricultural output of only $150 billion as a result of eventual warming of 10 °C. Since this is not predicted to occur, in his extrapolations, until about 200 years' time, when, assuming the same 1.5% p.a. growth rate, the USA's GNP would amount to just over $100 trillion, the loss of agricultural output would still be only 0.15% of GNP.

[12] See T. C. Schelling, 'Climatic Change: Implications for Welfare and Policy', in *Changing Climate*, Report of the Carbon Dioxide Assessment Committee, Commission on Physical Sciences, Mathematics, and Resources (Washington, DC: National Research Council, National Academy Press, 1983).

[13] See Cline, 'Economic Stakes', 23.

China, Australia, and the USSR. This report found the impact of climate change to be generally favourable.'[14] Thus Nordhaus finds that, for the world as a whole, 'our best guess is that CO_2-induced climate change will produce a combination of gains and losses, with no strong presumption of substantial net economic damages'.[15]

Furthermore, all this leaves out of account (i) the probable—indeed inevitable—contribution that will be made by the continued rapid improvements in agriculture and plant technology as a result of genetic engineering, so that even if, on balance, global warming did raise the real costs of achieving given agricultural output by, say, 10–20 per cent by the middle of the twenty-first century, this is likely to be swamped many times over by continued increases in control over plants, possible production of new proteins, technological progress in water conservation and irrigation, and so on; and (ii) the fact that over the last four decades food production has been rising faster than demand, so that some barely noticeable cut in the rate of growth of agricultural production—if any—does not spell mass starvation.[16] Famines, in recent years, as Amartya Sen has shown, seem to have been more the result of appalling policies, civil strife, and discrimination, than of acute physical food shortages in any given area.[17]

2. *Sea-level rise*

The situation does not change much even if we bring into the picture the other main fairly certain effect of global warming, namely the rise in sea levels. The estimated rise in sea levels has been greatly reduced over recent years. As recently as 1980 it was seriously believed that sea levels might rise as much as 8 metres. In early 1989 the prevailing estimate was down to about 1 metre; in early 1990 it was down to about 65 cm by the end of the next century (as in the IPCC report), and later authoritative estimates

[14] Nordhaus, 'To Slow Or Not To Slow', 27.

[15] W. D. Nordhaus, 'Economic Policy Making in the Face of Global Warming', paper presented to MIT Conference on Energy and the Environment, Mar. 1990, p. 10. Exactly the same conclusion is reached by Cline, 'Economic Stakes', 23.

[16] Easterling *et al.* 'Adapting Future Agriculture', 92.

[17] Amartya Sen, *Poverty and Famines: An Essay on Entitlement and Deprivation* (Oxford: Oxford UP, 1981).

put it as low as about 30 cm by the end of the next century, assuming a 4 °C rise in average temperature by then. [18] (If one were to extrapolate trends in these estimates, they would soon be predicting a fall in the sea level, with consequences for many seaside resorts that might be as serious as a rise!) Although alarmists frequently refer to the impact on sea levels resulting from the disintegration of the West Antarctic Ice Sheet and the melting of sea-ice cover and so on, most glaciologists now discount the possibility of the former, and there is, as yet, 'no evidence that the Arctic sea-ice cover has changed appreciably over the last two or three decades', a conclusion that has received further confirmation in more recent findings. [19]

But suppose sea levels did rise appreciably, what would be the economic consequences? Estimates by the United States Environmental Protection Agency for an even greater rise in sea levels (namely 1 metre) are that the capital cost of protecting US cities by sea walls would be about $100 billion at current prices. Applying a 1.5 per cent per annum compound growth rate to the present US GNP of about $5.2 trillion, would give a GNP by 2090 of $23.0 trillion, so that as a fraction of GNP in the year 2090 the once-for-all capital cost of the sea walls would be about 0.43 per cent! As a fraction of cumulative GNP over the whole of the next 100 years, during which time the work would have to be carried out, the amounts involved are, of course, totally trivial.

What about the rest of the world? Estimates by William Cline, assuming a 1-metre rise in the sea level and that the costs of sea walls for other threatened coastal cities are comparable to those of

[18] See A. Solow and J. Broadus, 'Global Warming: Quo Vadis?', Fletcher Forum (forthcoming), 7; IPCC, Scientific Assessement, 1; Mason, 'The Greenhouse Effect', 431. More recently, research carried out in the Geography Department of the University of Edinburgh shows that much smaller rises in the sea level would be associated with a 3 °C increase in global temperatures (reported in The Times and the Independent, 4 Jan. 1991).

[19] Mason, 'The Greenhouse Effect', 431, and A. S. McClaren, R. G. Barry, and R. H. Bourke, 'Could Arctic Ice Be Thinning?', Nature, 345 (28 June 1990), 762. Even back in 1988—which is a long time ago given the speed of downward revision of predictions in this field—it was thought that 'Changes in the mass balance of antarctic ice will probably have little impact on SLR (sea level rise) in the next few centuries. . . . Indeed, it is possible that an increase of precipitation over Antarctica due to climate change could act to reduce the rate of SLR.' (Cf. Gjerrit Hekstra, 'Sea-Level Rise: Regional Consequences and Responses', in Rosenberg et al., Greenhouse Warming, 54. This publication was a report of a conference in June 1988.)

the USA, arrive at costs of adaptation, plus valuing the land lost in Bangladesh, of about $2 trillion. By the year 2090 world GNP would be about $115 trillion (assuming the US share remains roughly constant at one-fifth of world GNP), so that the once-for-all capital cost of the sea-level rise would still be only about 2 per cent of one year's GNP, so that as a fraction of *cumulative world GNP* over the whole period it would still be negligible.[20] And given that (a) the latest predictions of the rise in the sea level are about half those assumed in these estimates and (b) a given reduction in the estimated sea-level rise implies a more than proportionate reduction in the costs of adaptation or the damage done through land loss,[21] the costs of adaptation and land loss for the world as a whole would be negligible even allowing for a generous margin of error in the above estimates.

Now that may be all very well for the world as a whole, but it is not much consolation for the people of Bangladesh, where 20 per cent of the land could be lost under the sea with a 1-metre sea-level rise. True—leaving aside the falling trend in estimates of sea-level rises—but suppose, purely for the sake of illustrating the logic of the choices to be made, that measures to prevent the climate change and the consequent sea-level rise would cost the world community $20 trillion—i.e. ten times as much as the estimated cost of protection against the rising sea level. It would clearly be in the world's interest—and of the Bangladeshis and everybody else concerned—to make some sort of deal, such as not incurring the $20 trillion costs that would be needed to prevent the sea level from rising and handing over, say, a fifth of the resulting saving—namely $4 trillion—to the people who would suffer from the sea-level rise. The latter then gain—US$4 trillion to carry out work costing only $2 trillion—and the rest of the world is still $16 trillion better off.

In other words, the alternative course of action that is being urged on all sides, namely to prevent the sea level rising *at any cost*, would mean that the world is being asked, in effect, to incur costs of $20 trillion—or whatever the cost would be—to prevent

[20] William R. Cline, *Political Economy of the Greenhouse Effect*, preliminary draft (Washington, DC: Institute for International Economics, Aug. 1989), 18.

[21] Cline, 'Economic Stakes', 26. Of course, as one moves into the even longer term, so that the sea-level rises could be much greater, Cline's point about the non-linearity works in the opposite direction—namely, the cost of adaptation would rise more than proportionately.

the Bangladeshis and others from suffering the effects of the sea-level rise when there would be very much cheaper ways of sparing them from these effects, and possibly of raising their overall income levels substantially, such as helping them move away from the threatened coastal areas, building dikes (after all, half the Dutch population live below the sea level), improving flood control, and, perhaps, allowing more of them to emigrate!

During the last two or three decades flooding, which is often attributed to wider fluctuations in the river levels that have nothing to do with the climate change, has added greatly to the general terrible poverty of Bangladesh, yet the rest of the world has shown no sign of genuine willingness to hand over, in the form of aid, resources commensurate with the task of eradicating that poverty or preventing the existing flooding. So the notion that it should now suddenly be seized by a fit of unprecedented altruism and incur possibly enormous costs to reduce GHG emissions in order to prevent the flooding that would, allegedly, result from global warming, rather than accept the far less costly alternatives of adaptation one way or the other, is absurdly naïve and unrealistic. If the estimates of the costs involved in significant reductions of CO_2 emissions referred to below are anywhere near reality, it is clear that the world and the Bangladeshis would be far better off if adaptive policies were pursued rather than drastic action to prevent the threatened rise in sea levels. Anyway, since far more land is being lost every year as a result of soil erosion than is likely to be lost through climate change, if the world is seriously concerned about the land loss there are policies that could be adopted to reduce it without drastic reductions in world CO_2 emissions.

Finally, perhaps one should be reminded of the fact that since the end of the last Ice Age, about 12,000 years ago, the sea level has risen by about 65 metres. During this time humankind seems to have flourished.

3. *Other effects*

Estimates have been made for other effects of climate change, such as greater need for air conditioning (offsetting less need for space heating), forest loss, and the sheer disutility for some people of living in a warmer climate (but not for all those people who would like to do so but cannot afford to, or who are tied to their present locations by other factors). However, these effects are even more uncertain than those referred to above, and are likely anyway to be less significant.

Of course, the pressure groups or individuals whose *raison d'être* or livelihoods thrive on prophecies of doom will appeal to other ecological scare stories, such as the effect of global warming on the frequency of storms and so on. But, in fact, very few hard results have been produced concerning this effect of global warming, and for a very good reason. On the one hand it is true that in so far as the seas become warmer the area over which hurricanes 'breed' will expand. But, on the other hand, storms are correlated with temperature gradients—i.e. the transition between high and low temperatures—so that in so far as the temperature increase is greatest in high latitudes, where it is generally colder, the world-wide temperature gradient will diminish. To calculate the incidence of storms would, therefore require a far more accurate breakdown by small geographic area of the effects of the climate change than is feasible given current modelling. Storms, like heatwaves or incidence of rainfall, depend very much on more local conditions than can be encompassed in the present state of the art of climate prediction. Hence, it is not surprising that the IPCC scientific working group reported that 'climate models give no consistent indication whether tropical storms will increase or decrease in frequency or intensity as climate changes; neither is there any evidence that this has occurred over the past few decades'.[22]

Hence, it seems impossible to escape the conclusion that even under pessimistic assumptions, the annual cost to the world as a whole of global warming associated with a doubling of CO_2 concentrations is likely to be almost negligible by comparison with the value of world output over the period in question. It is true that an estimate of the annual cost could understate the true total cumulative cost of global warming, though suitable discounting means that this is highly unlikely.

[22] IPCC, *Scientific Assessment*, 18; and W. E. Reifsnyder, 'A Tale of Ten Fallacies: The Sceptical Enquirer's View of the Carbon Dioxide/Climate Controversy', *Agricultural and Forest Meteorology*, 47 (1989), 349–71. Reifsnyder reports specific studies to check for the existence of trends in the variability of climates and of the occurrence of climatic anomalies as well as of their correlation with changes in overall climate states. All these studies, he says, produce negative results.

4. *The optimum level of GHG emissions*

Ideally, however, what is needed is not merely comparative estimates of 'all-or-nothing' choices, since this is anathema to the
economist. What the economist wants is some schedule of the
marginal costs and benefits of different degrees of CO_2 emissions
in order to identify the optimal level of emissions from the point
of view of maximizing society's welfare. This is, of course, an
immensely difficult undertaking. Fortunately, as already indicated, William Nordhaus has undertaken it, and has provided
an ingenious transformation of the snapshot estimates of costs
and benefits of alternative abatement policies into the sort of
marginal cost and benefit schedules referred to above. He has
analysed the results on the basis of alternative assumptions—
including very conservative assumptions—concerning the
appropriate discount rate to use. He also takes as his baseline
snapshot estimate alternative estimates of the damage done in a
future year by a CO_2 doubling. On the basis of a medium damage
assumption and even assuming a very low discount rate, he
arrives at the conclusion that the optimal policy would comprise a
reduction in GHGs of only about 12 per cent, most of which
would be achieved by cutting out CFCs, accompanied by a small
reduction in CO_2 emissions.[23] Although different forestry
policies would also help reduce GHGs emissions, the quantitative contribution that this low-cost method could make is really
very limited.[24]

[23] William Nordhaus, 'Economic Approaches to Greenhouse Warming', paper
presented to the conference on Economic Policy Responses to Global Warming,
Rome, Oct. 1990, p. 28; see also his 'To Slow Or Not To Slow'. A more extensive
discussion of the Nordhaus model is contained in the present writer's chapter on
'Global Warming: A Sceptical Economic Assessment', in D. Helm (ed.), *Economic
Policy Towards the Environment* (Oxford: Blackwell, 1991).

[24] The costs of reducing deforestation are low, and possibly even negative, in so
far as much of it represents a market failure (e.g. subsidies to those who cut down
the trees to cultivate the land, or simple absence of property rights). But even if the
whole of the tropical rainforests were burnt immediately, the concentration of
CO_2 would rise by 5% to 10%, which, on the basis of the usual models, would only
raise temperatures by between 0.25 and 0.5 °C. Secondly, outsiders tend to ignore
the contribution made to local agricultural output by the land released. For
example, in the Cerrado area in Brazil several million hectares of land have now
been put into production, and, in spite of allegations that land reclaimed in this
way is of poor quality, soyabean yields there are almost equal to those of the USA.
See Richardo Radulovich, 'A View on Tropical Deforestation', *Nature*, 346 (19 July
1990), 214.

Since the greater the cut in CO_2 emissions the greater the marginal costs incurred, it follows from the above that if, say, carbon taxes were raised to levels necessary to bring about reductions in GHG emissions of the order of 50 per cent, for which many environmentalists are calling, the net losses to the world as a whole could be very large indeed. For example, it is usually estimated that the carbon taxes needed to reduce CO_2 emissions by 50 per cent will need to stand at a few hundred dollars per ton of carbon, which usually translates into taxes of 400 or 500 per cent on the net price of energy. And estimates along these lines by John Whalley show taxes of this magnitude leading to net economic welfare losses over the period 1990 to 2030 of about $18 trillion, or about 4 per cent of total world output over the same period. For some areas, such as North America, the loss would be far greater, namely about 10 per cent of GNP.[25]

However, the margin of error in estimates of these costs must be substantial. For much will depend on what is done with the revenues and the time period over which the taxes are phased in. As regards the former, it is not simply a matter of the welfare loss of the rise in the tax on energy. Insofar as the object of the operation is not to influence the level of demand in the economy but to change the allocation of resources, the extra revenues ought to be given back in the form of reductions in other taxes of one kind or another. Hence, to estimate the net loss of welfare requires comparative estimates of the 'deadweight' welfare losses incurred by paying higher taxes on energy with the corresponding gains if the resulting tax revenues are used to finance reductions in other taxes. The real economic welfare cost of such a shift in the pattern of taxes and output might well be negligible, and even negative. No firm a priori statement can be made about the welfare cost of a change in the tax when starting from a position which is already sub-optimal on account of the existence of some taxes.

There is a second possible source of welfare loss that has to be taken into account. This is because what is at stake here is not just

[25] J. Whalley and R. Wigle show estimates ranging from $392 to $500 per ton of carbon, depending on different assumptions concerning supply elasticities, in order to reduce emissions by 50% below the 2030 'business as usual' level, in 'The International Incidence of Carbon Taxes', paper presented to the conference on Economic Policy Responses to Global Warming, Rome, Oct. 1990. They estimated world carbon tax revenues to vary between $40 trillion and $50 trillion over the period 1990–2030.

a switch in taxes on final output but the imposition of a tax on a basic input into the productive system, namely energy. As Bruno and Sachs have shown in connection with the effects of the oil shocks, a cut in energy inputs can have a significant effect on total output.[26] In that case the demand impact of the oil price rise could be rightly analysed as if it were a tax imposed on Western oil consumers the proceeds of which accrued to oil producers where there were no offsetting tax reductions. But in the context of a carbon tax, in so far as the counterpart tax reductions were to be on taxes on other factor inputs—such as on labour income, or a payroll tax, or a profits tax—a shrinking of the economy's productive potential resulting from a cut in energy inputs could be offset by the induced increase in labour and capital inputs. Again, it is obvious that the information about the relative supply elasticities that would be needed to make anything like a firm estimate of the net effect on output for the world as a whole is simply not available.

5. *Uncertainties*

Of course, every aspect of the problem that one peers into merely reveals a whole new mass of uncertainties. Before going into the uncertainties arising out of the considerations just discussed, there are great uncertainties in estimating the costs of reducing CO_2 emissions arising out of the variety of estimates of one component of such estimates, namely the sensitivity of response of CO_2 emissions to alternative taxes on carbon, or to some corresponding price mechanism disincentive.[27] In a survey of some of the estimates, Terry Barker points out that estimates for the UK alone of the tax rates needed to achieve the Toronto target of cutting GHG emissions by 20 per cent below 1988 levels by the year 2005 varied from 41 per cent on coal (and less on other fossil fuels) in Scott Barrett, through anything from 123 per cent to 277

[26] Michael Bruno and Jeffrey Sachs, *Economics of Worldwide Stagflation* (Oxford: Blackwell, 1985), esp. chs. 1 and 2.
[27] See widely different estimates of the size of carbon tax needed to produce given reductions in emissions in e.g. Scott Barrett, *Memorandum to the Select Committee on Energy*, (London: HMSO, 1 May 1990), sect. 2.2; Whalley, 'The International Incidence of Carbon Taxes', 5 and *passim*; Congress of the United States, Congressional Budget Office, *Carbon Charges as a Response to Global Warming: The Effects of Taxing Fossil Fuels*; Michael Grubb, *The Greenhouse Effect: Negotiating Targets* (London: The Royal Institute of International Affairs, 1989), sect. 5.1.

per cent on coal (depending on timing assumptions) in Ingham and Ulph, and up to about 600 per cent in Capros *et al.*[28] Depending on the elasticities of response of fossil fuel use to alternative taxes, one would arrive at alternative estimates of the costs to society of this particular method of reducing GHG emissions. These costs are difficult to estimate even without uncertainty as to the elasticities.

One of the reasons for the wide variations in the estimates of the elasticities of energy use with respect to changes in prices resulting from the imposition of taxes is that, as David Newberry points out, much will depend on the relative price changes of individual fossil fuels and also on the range over which the tax changes in question are to be allowed to vary.[29] For example, it may well be that the elasticity of response will vary greatly according to the size of tax change in question. As he points out, 'One suspects that at a sufficiently high price of carbon, other technologies (e.g. hydrogen produced from nuclear fuel) suddenly become attractive, so that the elasticity suddenly becomes very high at some backstop price.'[30]

Whilst it seems fairly clear, therefore, that relatively very high taxes would be needed to effect significant cuts in GHG emissions and the real costs of doing so would also be enormous, the margin of error in the estimates is considerable. Much will depend on the type of measures adopted—for example, quantitative restrictions would be far more costly than some price mechanism policy. The incidence of the tax will also vary enormously according to whether it is imposed on consumption or production of energy. Furthermore, the simplifying assumptions usually made in estimates of the real effects of any reduction in energy inputs, such as the use of constant return to scale, or the use of simple time trends to represent technical progress, could be nowhere near the mark in the real world.[31]

[28] Terry Barker and Richard Lewney, 'A Green Scenario for the UK Economy', in Terry Barker (ed.), *Green Future for Economic Growth* (Cambridge: Cambridge Econometrics, 1991), 15.

[29] David Newberry, 'The International Incidence of Carbon Taxes: A Comment', comment on Whalley, 'The International Incidence of Carbon Taxes', 3. Econometric confirmation of the influence of the cross elasticities is also provided clearly in Barrett, *Memorandum to the Select Committe*.

[30] Newberry, loc. cit.

[31] I am particularly indebted to Dr Terry Barker, of Cambridge Econometrics, for information on this point.

But perhaps the greatest source of uncertainty is the whole area of technological improvements that take the form of energy savings or a switch to forms of fossil fuel use that are less carbon intensive, not to mention the use of renewables (solar power, wind power, and so on). So-called 'no regret policies' would take the form of trying to encourage the greater use of economically viable technological innovations of this kind. Much is known about some of the technological possibilities, but relatively little is known about the economics of introducing them.[32] Whilst many environmentalists proclaim that there is enormous scope for such economically justifiable energy-saving techniques, the question arises why, if that is the case, have they not already been introduced?

There are many perfectly valid answers to this question for there is no doubt that, in addition to the inadequate allowance for the externality effects of energy consumption, the real world is full of market imperfections. These could include (i) simple lack of information—though there is a limit to the amount of information that it is economically worthwhile any agent trying to get; (ii) private discount rates exceeding the social discount rate, so that there may be technologies that would be viable but that do not provide the rapid pay-offs that users might require in this area (a simple case being the very high pay-off required by householders for house insulation—particularly if the owner does not expect to be able to recoup the capital outlay in the subsequent sale price of the house); (iii) liquidity constraints on account of imperfections in the capital market; (iv) principal-agent problems—for example, the people in an organization who are responsible for certain investment decisions are not those who are concerned with economizing in energy operating costs; and, finally (v) a host of government regulations and subsidies that actually reduce energy efficiency.

However, there is, as yet, not much hard evidence about these

[32] A very detailed summary of some of the most important British work in this field is contained in Gerald Leach and Zygfryd Nowak, *Cutting Carbon Dioxide Emissions from Poland and the United Kingdom* (Stockholm: Stockholm Environment Institute, 1990); E. Barbier, J. C. Burgess and D. W. Pearce, 'Slowing Global Warming' (London: London Environmental Economics Centre, Sept. 1990). See also William Fulkerson, Roddie Judkins, and Manoj Sanghvi, 'Energy from Fossil Fuels', *Scientific American*, 263. 3 (Sept. 1990); and Dennis Anderson and Catherine D. Bird, 'The Carbon Accumulation Problem and Technical Progress', draft paper, Oxford, Sept. 1990.

and other possible market imperfections affecting energy use.[33] So the problem is to identify those that have impeded the greater take-up of energy-saving technologies or the shift to less carbon-intensive forms of energy. But it is important to note that the estimates referred to above of the costs of abatement of GHG emissions might be far greater than the real costs that would be incurred through economically viable policies to stimulate energy conservation. It could well be that economically viable policies to accelerate the diffusion of knowledge about existing possibilities and to accelerate their application could lead to some relatively costless, if limited, abatement of CO_2 emissions over the next few years and that, with suitable policies to promote further research and development in this area, as well as to follow up the dissemination and diffusion of energy-saving technologies, other gains could be made in subsequent years.

Nevertheless, the fact that the developing world is so far behind the advanced industrial countries in energy consumption per head suggests that it would need more than the widespread adoption of energy-saving techniques to prevent a significant increase in world-wide energy consumption and CO_2 emissions over the course of the next century. For example, China's carbon emissions already constitute roughly 10 per cent of world total and half of that of the USA. But China's emissions per head are just over one-tenth of those of the USA. Hence, if nobody else increased their carbon emissions at all, and China raised its per capita emissions to half of the US level, total world emissions would rise by about 40 per cent! Clearly, encouraging people in advanced countries to put the lids on their saucepans when cooking or to insulate the lofts of their houses is not likely to make any impact on emissions in a world in which all the developing countries will be increasing their emissions on a massive scale.

6. *Uncertainty and choice*

Given the margin of error in estimates of the damage done by global warming, and of the costs of preventing it, particularly if allowance is made for the relatively unquantifiable scope for technical progress in energy efficiency, one is faced with the ques-

---

[33] See Leach and Nowak, *Cutting Carbon Dioxide Emissions* for an excellent survey of some of the main material available.

tion of the choices to be adopted under conditions of uncertainty. It is sometimes argued that since the climate-change effect of GHG emissions is irreversible in a relevant time period and that it just *might* be catastrophic—all the evidence set out above to the contrary—it is urgent that action be taken without delay. This argument is just as false as is the zero-discount argument discussed in the next section. As Arrow and Fisher put it in 1974: 'Just because an action is irreversible does not mean that it should not be undertaken. Rather, the effect of irreversibility is to reduce the benefits, which are then balanced against costs in the usual way ... Essentially the point is that the expected benefit of an irreversible decision should be adjusted to reflect the loss of options it entails.'[34] If human beings took no action that would have irreversible consequences, the human race would have ceased to exist a long time ago!

Up to a point the response to the possibility of climate change can be analysed in terms of the traditional economic analysis of choice under conditions of uncertainty, the key feature of which is the maximization of the *expected* utility associated with alternative possibilities. A serious outcome with a very low probability could have less weight than a less serious outcome with a high probability.

However, it can be argued that this approach cannot be extended to cover the case of catastrophe, particularly when, in addition, there is no statistical basis for assessing the probabilities to be attached to the outcomes. It is sometimes proposed that '... strong catastrophic risks should, in the limit, not be undertaken at any price' and that risk aversion should justify 'prudence' even if the risks of catastrophe are minimal.[35] Nevertheless, people do not invest time or resources in measures to avoid every minu-

[34] K. J. Arrow and A. C. Fisher, 'Environmental Preservation, Uncertainty and Irreversibility', *Quarterly Journal of Economics*, (1974), 88, 312–19. A very sound outline of some of these issues in relation to environmental disaster in developing countries is contained in Mary B. Anderson, 'Analyzing the Costs and Benefits of Natural Disaster Responses in the Context of Development', Environment Working Paper No. 29 (Washington, DC: World Bank, May 1990).

[35] See e.g. D. Collard, 'Catastrophic Risk: Or the Economics of Being Scared', in D. Collard, D. Pearce, and D. Ulph (eds.), *Economics, Growth and Sustainable Environments* (London: Macmillan, 1988); D. Pearce, A. Markandya, and E. B. Barbier, *Blueprint for a Green Economy* (London: Earthscan, 1989), esp. pp. 16–17. A recent summary discussion of this issue is in D. Pearce and R. Kerry Turner, *Economics of Natural Resources and the Environment* (London: Harvester, 1990), esp. pp. 314–20.

scule risk that they face, even where the consequences of their failing to do so just *might* be catastrophic and would also be irreversible. This is obvious in the way people drive! Or in the degree to which they invest in measures to ensure that, for example, their houses never burn down under any circumstances or they are never hit by an out-of-control drunken driver whilst walking along the pavement minding their own business. When Skylab recently was reported to be out of control and certain to fall to Earth one knew not where, few people, if any, thought it worthwhile sheltering all day in the nearest subway station, although the consequences for them of it falling on their heads would have been very serious indeed and certainly irreversible.

In any case, since it appears that even if nothing is done to reduce GHG emissions the damage by the end of the next century will be far from catastrophic, it is clear that postponing action for a decade or more cannot possibly be the cause of unavoidable catastrophe. The more rational policy in the face of the global warming threat is to avoid embarking on very costly draconian measures to reduce GHG emissions as soon as possible but to invest now in more research into climate change. If it then transpires, for example, that the probability of serious climate change is, indeed, considerable, it would then become worthwhile incurring greater costs to prevent it. At the same time much more research could be undertaken into ways of reducing energy use and GHG emissions per unit of energy use at low cost, through the elimination of market imperfections and the promotion of research into appropriate technologies. This should, of course, be combined with policies of the 'no regret' type that can already be identified.[36] Indeed, the unknown scope for future technological progress in energy conservation constitutes an offsetting argument to the 'risk of catastrophe' argument. In other words, there are favourable uncertainties as well as unfavourable ones. With more evidence and research one may be better placed to take an informed view of the balance of probabilities and the associated costs and benefits.

---

[36] See discussion of this issue in Nordhaus, 'Economic Approaches to Greenhouse Warming', 34 ff.; A. S. Manne and R. R. Richels, 'Buying Greenhouse Insurance', in *Global 2100: The Economic Costs of CO$_2$ Emission Limits* (forthcoming); and Cline, *Political Economy of the Greenhouse Effect*.

7. Discounting the future

In any analysis of the economies of global warming, the crucial role of the time dimension means that estimates of the relative costs and benefits, suitably adjusted for uncertainty where possible, will be very sensitive to the choice of the discount rate. And whilst most economists would probably accept that, for society as a whole, there is no justification for a discount rate that merely reflects 'pure time preference'—i.e. simple impatience, or what Pigou called 'defective telescopic faculty'—discounting the future can still be justified on the grounds of diminishing marginal utility of income. That is to say, it may be accepted that the marginal utility of an extra dollar to a rich person will be less than its value to a poor person. Hence, it may be rational to discount the future on the assumption that economic growth will continue so that future societies will be much richer than those of today.[37]

In addition, one must also take account of the rate of return that can be obtained on investment today. Given that it is positive, if one did not discount the future at all—as some extreme environmentalists seem to advocate—the logical implication would be that all resources ought to be turned over to investment and that consumption levels should be reduced to a bare subsistence level. For if the prospect of an extra dollar of consumption in, say, fifty years' time was regarded today as having the same value now as a dollar of consumption today, then it follows that anything greater than one dollar of consumption in the future, say $1.01, would be valued more highly than $1 today. It follows that if by giving up one dollar of consumption today one could consume a fraction more than one dollar in the future—however small the fraction—one should make the present sacrifice and invest instead. But clearly that sort of rule would justify cutting consumption to the bone today in order to turn over nearly the whole of our resources to investment, since although it might be difficult to find many more investments

---

[37] A good recent survey of this issue in the context of environmental policy is contained in Pearce and Turner, *Economics of Natural Resources and The Environment*, chs. 14 and 15. A more extensive survey of the more philosophical aspects of this issue is contained in R. K. Turner, 'Wetland Conservation: Economics and Ethics', in Collard, Pearce, and Ulph, *Economics, Growth and Sustainable Environments*.

that yielded, say, 10 per cent rates of return per annum, it should not be difficult to find investments that yielded some infinitesimally small rates of return.

Such a Stalinist policy of starving the present in order to turn over everything to investment, which would lead to very high growth rates, is obviously not what society wants, or what even the extreme environmentalists would want if they understood the implications of their views on discounting.[38] Nor is it what poor countries, who are not in a position to make much sacrifice of current living standards in the interests of the future, would want. There are good theoretical and empirical grounds for the view that poorer people will apply much higher discount rates than richer people.[39] Thus, although it may be perfectly true that future generations are not represented in the determination of interest rates and hence the rates of return required on current investment, and might have preferred lower rates of discount than those that operate, this is no justification for the complete absence of any discount rate, even if one did not allow for diminishing marginal utility of income and the fact that future generations will be wealthier than those of today.

Even if the 'low discount rate' school of thought do not go quite so far as to advocate a near-zero rate, it is still inconsistent to apply a relatively low rate—say of the order of 4 per cent—to global warming when the discount rate expected in most parts of the world, and particularly in the developing countries, is at least twice this. Even if the high discount rate were believed to be more appropriate for representing the interests of future generations in current decisions, there is no reason why all the extra investment should go into preventing global warming. It is reported, for example, that the social rate of return to investment in education in poor countries is around 25 per cent for primary education, and 16 per cent for secondary education. It would appear that if, as a

[38] This point is made, albeit more diplomatically, and technically, in A. Markandya and D. Pearce, 'Environmental Considerations and the Choice of the Discount Rate in Developing Countries', Environment Department Working Paper No. 3 (Washington, DC: World Bank, May 1988), para. 3.4, p. 30. The authors also point out that a lower discount rate also implies more investment, which will require more use of natural resources and possibly more pollution.
[39] Some striking evidence for this is given in J. A. Hausman, 'Individual Discount Rates and the Purchase and Utilization of Energy-Using Durables', Bell Journal of Economics, 10 (1979), 33–54.

result of using a lower discount rate than currently employed (for example, in World Bank projects), more investment were to be made in the future welfare of poor countries, reducing world GHG emissions would not come high among the priorities since investment in other forms would produce much greater benefits. Faster economic growth would then increase the world's capacity to switch to less energy-intensive forms of output (as in Japan, France, and increasingly so in other advanced countries) as well as making it better able to afford action to adapt to such climate change as would eventually come about.

C. International Negotiations for Reducing GHG Emissions

All this leads to two apparently conflicting reactions. One is to conclude that international action is essential if anything effective is to be done to slow down global warming. The other is to ask whether the game is worth the candle. This is not simply a matter of the apparent excess of the costs of reducing GHGs significantly relative to the damage done by global warming. It is also a matter of the difficulty of reaching international agreement. Even if all countries gained by measures to reduce global warming significantly, it would be very difficult to reach international agreement for reasons set out more fully below. But given that some countries gain and some lose, and by different amounts, as a result of global warming or of measures to prevent it, the obstacles in the way of arriving at some optimal collective agreement are incomparably greater.

The above estimates suggest that it will only be optimal for the world as a whole to cut GHG emissions by fairly modest amounts and by concentrating the reductions on the cheapest forms—such as the elimination of CFCs, the 'no regret' policies, and a modest, low-cost cut in CO_2 emissions. Beyond that, the net results to the world from more drastic action are likely to be negative, so that the gainers could not compensate the losers and still be better off. And even if the net results from action on the more drastic scale widely suggested—such as cutting CO_2 emissions by about 50 per cent or more—are perceived, rightly or wrongly, to be positive, this would, as argued below, impose such heavy costs on key players in the game that the chances of successful international agreement seem to be negligible.

As some commentators, notably Schelling, Skolnikoff, Cline, Grubb, and Cooper have demonstrated,[40] these difficulties are enormous when one takes account of the divergent interests between countries and between different groups within countries, not to mention the scope for everybody to be able to quote scientific evidence on their side. Given all the uncertainties set out above, particularly those concerning the effects on individual countries or regions, it is difficult to imagine any effective international co-operation to take serious action until some of these uncertainties are resolved.

Nevertheless, it is fairly clear that, taken as a group, the industrialized countries will lose little from global warming, chiefly because agriculture—the sector where, in principle, there would be the biggest effect—is relatively a very small component of their output. The net effect on other sectors, such as transport or construction, of shorter winters, less snow and ice and fog, and so on, is likely to be favourable. Other effects on life in advanced countries are difficult to quantify, but they are likely to be small by comparison with other things. As Schelling puts it: '. . . what we eat and drink and smoke continue to have vastly more effect than climate on our health and comfort. As to comfort . . . it is worth noticing that in North America and in Europe most people go south for vacations both summer and winter and if they move upon retiring tend to go south not north.'[41] The same is probably true of Japan. Hence, the industrialized countries as a whole may not see any clear narrow national interest in adopting expensive measures to reduce CO_2 emissions. Yet these are the countries that can best afford either to take action themselves or to provide some sort of assistance to other countries where action would be more appropriately carried out.

By contrast, most other countries would either suffer from

[40] Cline, *Political Economy of the Greenhouse Effect*, 48 ff.; Schelling, 'Global Environmental Forces'; Grubb, *The Greenhouse Effect*; R. Cooper, 'International Economic Cooperation: Is It Desirable? Is It Likely?', *Bulletin of the American Academy of Arts and Sciences*, 39. 2 (1985); and E. Skolnikoff, 'The Policy Gridlock on Global Warming', *Foreign Policy*, 79 (1990).

[41] T. C. Schelling, 'Economic Responses to Global Warming', paper presented to the conference on Economic Policy Responses to Global Warming, Rome, Oct. 1990, p. 9.

drastic measures to curb CO_2 emissions or are too poor to attach much priority to measures to do so anyway. Significant cuts in CO_2 emissions would involve large reductions in CO_2 intensive fuels, of which coal is the worst, followed by oil. Hence, countries such as China or India that have large coal resources would lose significantly. Furthermore, these happen to be countries that desperately need to raise their current standards of living. As they do so they will increase their energy use. As Michael Grubb points out: '. . . if China and India emitted carbon at the same per capita level as the US, world emission would be nearly trebled'.[42] The prospects of China or India making sacrifices of current standards of living or immediate growth prospects in order to improve the standards of living of the world in 100 years' time are virtually non-existent. They refused to sign the Montreal Protocol on CFCs and, like other developing countries, will no doubt continue to refuse to make the far greater sacrifices that would be required to prevent major increases in their GHG emissions except in return for substantial compensation from the industrialized countries that will no doubt not be forthcoming. And the rest of the world should not expect them to act otherwise.

For most developing countries, where agriculture is more important, the best policy is probably to help them develop and become less dependent on it. For this purpose they would need massive transfers to make it worthwhile for them to follow alternative policies, and this raises enormous political obstacles. In any case, if the advanced countries are prepared to make substantial transfers to the developing countries to enable them to improve their standard of life in 100 years' time, it is most unlikely that they can best do so by investment in GHG abatement rather than by investing directly in economic growth. And faced with this choice there is little doubt that the developing countries would agree.

In fact, if one were selecting optimal policies for raising the standard of living of many developing countries, whilst taking account of the global warming threat, the optimal policy would be to slow down or hold down current rates of population growth. In China and India, two of the countries that matter most

[42] Grubb, *The Greenhouse Effect*, 17. Grubb reports that China envisages expanding its coal consumption fivefold by the year 2020, which would add nearly 50% to current world-wide carbon emissions! (p. 20)

from point of view of future fossil fuel use, reducing or keeping down their rates of growth of population would probably do more to slow down GHG emissions than heroic anti-carbon taxes. The most likely impact of climate change is on agriculture and food production. And in most developing countries the biggest limit on food per head is population growth, so it does not make sense to concentrate on the relatively minor effect on food per head that climate change would produce compared with reducing their population growth, which would also ease their burdens in other ways.

The same applies, in a slightly different way, to East Europe and the former USSR. Many of these countries have been poisoning their drinking water, the air they breathe, and their topsoil, so that their environmental priorities should be to concentrate on immediate threats to health and child development. It is in the interests of the West that these economies emerge from the present crises, making rapid headway towards economic recovery and progress, and restore economic viability. It is not in the West's interest that this be impeded by draconian measures to limit CO_2 emissions or energy consumption in general. The West has little interest, therefore, in encouraging them to give much priority to making current sacrifices in order that the world be fractionally richer in 100 years' time than it will be anyway, which is what the estimates of the damage done by global warming suggest would be the alternative to action to prevent it.

In short, as Schelling puts it, 'virtually all the rest of the world is too desperately in need of economic development to penalise itself with reductions in energy use or with investments in lower carbon emissions for their own sake. I think we cannot expect China, India, the Soviet Union, the countries of Eastern Europe or the rest of the developing world to burden their current economic growth for the sake of a possibly more benign climate 50, 75 or 100 years from now than they should otherwise anticipate. Nor would I urge them to.'[43] At the same time, since some of these countries will become increasingly major contributors to world CO_2 emissions, failure to ensure their co-operation would greatly weaken any collective efforts to stabilize GHG emissions. It is in the poorest countries that carbon emissions are increasing most rapidly, and although they account for only a quarter of the

[43] Schelling, 'Economic Responses to Global Warming', 10.

total at present, they will account for over a half by the middle of the next century.

If, in the interests of agreement, an attempt was made to arrive at some simple, rough-justice formula, such as equiproportionate cuts in GHG emissions, this would encounter objections, such as those raised above (for example, France emits much less CO_2 per head than the USA), as well as being economically inefficient by comparison with a system that allocated emission reductions most where it was least expensive (for example, recent Swedish moves to help Poland reduce its air pollution, which can be donè much more cheaply there than in Sweden, and similar steps taken by what was West Germany). Given the obvious conflict between some sort of rough justice and what would be a more equitable formula, there is little chance of it being agreed internationally. There simply seems to be too great a mismatch between the optimal distribution of abatement among nations and what would be an equitable distribution of the costs of abatement.[44]

One is driven to the conclusion that most of the countries that could afford to do anything about GHG emissions have little incentive to do so and those that may have more incentive to do so from the point of view of the longer-run impact of global warming on their economies cannot afford to do anything about it. Michael Grubb is no doubt correct in concluding, with respect to international quantitative agreements to curtail GHG emissions, that 'The idea that a protocol on limiting carbon emissions will be like the Montreal Protocol writ large is an illusion best dispersed before it leads us irretrievably down a blind alley'.[45]

For most countries the optimal policy will merely be to do

---

[44] Another possible obstacle to international agreements is the scope for dispute over the scientific issue of how to measure each country's emissions of GHGs. This is not simply a matter of monitoring; it is also a problem of what is the conceptually relevant unit given that different GHGs have different effects on global warming over different time periods. Methods have been proposed (notably by the IPCC) to combine different GHGs into some composite index that allows for their different effects, but the scientific uncertainties in the models that have to be used for this purpose leave much scope for dispute that could greatly hamper international agreement, even where the agreements are limited to CO_2 emissions and ignore other GHGs (see discussion of this issue in A. L. Hammond, E. Rodenburg, and W. Moomaw, 'Accountability in the Greenhouse', *Nature*, 347 (25 Oct. 1990), 705–6; same authors, 'Accountability for Global Change: A Comparative Analysis of Greenhouse Gas Emissions', *Environmental Magazine* (Mar. 1991); and D. G. Victor, letter to *Nature*, 347 (Oct. 1990), 431).

[45] Grubb, *The Greenhouse Effect*, 22.

nothing and act as free riders on other countries' abatements, from which they may benefit in more ways than one. For example, the losses incurred by major producers of CO_2 intensive fuels have a corresponding gain in terms of trade for fuel-importing countries, who would find that the ex-tax price of fuel would fall on account of the reduced demand for it.[46] Furthermore, the greater the cut in emissions by other countries, the less incentive there is for any given country to cut its own emissions. For the costs of doing so will be unchanged but, in so far as global warming would become less likely to be serious, the benefits of doing so will be reduced.[47] And some countries might well gain from global warming itself, and so would hope that nobody else does much to stop it.

It might look as if an alternative would be an agreement under which gainers compensate the losers for the losses that they would incur by co-operation. Something along these lines appears to be what is emerging with respect to CFC controls. But the above economic analysis suggests that if significant cuts in CO_2 emissions were to be achieved, there would be some very big losers but not many big gainers, if any. Countries that are major producers of fossil fuels, such as China, India, or oil-producing countries, are likely to be big losers under any policies to significantly reduce CO_2 emissions, so that the amount of compensation required would be enormous, which raises questions not only concerning the feasibility of establishing an acceptable international machinery for handling the real transfers required, but of the rationality of making such payments from the point of view of the donor countries.

For, as pointed out, the industrialized countries do not lose much from global warming but, given the scale of their GHG

[46] Much would depend, however, on cross elasticities of substitution between different fossil fuels. For if the different fuels were taxed according to their relative carbon contents, the negative effect on the demand for oil, say, of the tax on oil, could be more than offset by the positive effect on the demand for oil of the relatively greater rise in the price of coal.

[47] The economics can be translated into an exact counterpart to the 'reaction curve' in a Cournot duopoly situation, in which the more a competitor increases output the less is the optimum output of the given firm. This is because the demand curve for the given firm's output shifts left. See Congressional Budget Office, *Carbon Charges as a Response to Global Warming*, 57; and Mark Pearson and Stephen Smith, *Taxation and Environmental Policy* (London: Institute for Fiscal Studies, Jan. 1990), 9 and 16.

emissions and their consumption of fossil fuels, they would incur heavy costs from significant abatement. It is difficult to imagine that, if there is nothing to be gained from it for the American public, the US Congress will inflict taxes on electors to enable hundreds of billions of dollars to be handed over to the major CO_2 producing developing countries, given its apparent incapacity to raise a relatively small amount of extra taxes in order to curb its own large budget deficit.

Schelling estimates that to have any significant impact on world GHG emissions it would be necessary to impose taxes of about 50 cents per gallon on gasoline, which is far greater than the proposed 12 cents a gallon on gasoline that, in October 1990, led to such Congressional opposition that it brought parts of the US government to a halt. A tax at this level would raise revenues of about \$125 billion, and it is obvious that Congress has great difficulty in raising taxes to reduce budget deficit by a small fraction of this. This figure is very much in line with Nordhaus's estimates that a 50 per cent cut in world emissions would need a tax that would yield revenue in the USA alone of at least \$100 billion.[48] The USA, which is usually very reluctant to hand over relatively trivial sums to the World Bank and other aid agencies, would never agree to handing over this amount, which is about one hundred times the current annual budget of the United Nations, to some international agency to hand out to developing countries for carbon abatement! And there must be great doubts whether any international agreement will get off the ground in the absence of USA support, if not leadership.[49]

More generally, whatever precise compensating mechanism is sought, there would be enormous problems of negotiating the appropriate quotas or taxes and subsidies. In principle the formulas would have to take account of all the variables determining capacity to pay, and dependence on energy use, both overall and by type of energy. Hence, allowance would have to be made for per capita GNP, population density, climate, industry mix, non-fossil fuel resources, existing inherited technology in construction, industry, housing, transport, and so on,

[48] As pointed out in the previous section, the tax revenues resulting from any given carbon tax must not be confused with the *real* economic costs of the tax (usually known as the 'deadweight' loss), which are usually much less. But they may be just as important from the policy point of view.
[49] Grubb, *The Greenhouse Effect*, 32.

not to mention issues such as how far the USA should be penalized for its gasoline-guzzling car population or France rewarded for its shift to relatively less polluting forms of energy production (nuclear fuels).

Econometricians could no doubt produce econometric estimates of how the quota should vary from country to country to take account equitably of these variables, but governments would only be concerned with how hard they were hit. No doubt each country could find scientists to demonstrate that the long-run lifetime climatic effects of their particular energy uses were not as great as others made out, as well as economists who could demonstrate that the economic effects would be whatever their government wanted to show. The economics profession has never failed in this respect in the past and there is no reason to believe it will do so in the future. Furthermore, for any agreement in this area to be useful it must cover a long period of time, so that the formulas would have to allow for projections of future energy use, population dispersion, economic growth rates, and so on. And in so far as richer countries have to hand over something to developing countries to ensure their co-operation, the same sort of variables would have to be taken into account in negotiating criteria for making the transfers.[50]

In addition to all the above difficulties, account must be taken of the extent to which countries can effectively implement any agreements into which they may enter. It is one thing for countries gaily to announce their targets and another for them to set up effective implementation machineries. And, of course, countries differ in their abilities to enforce change either because of weak administrative and fiscal institutions or because of the role of the private sector and other restrictions on the private sector's activities. For example, even if the USA wanted to switch to nuclear energy and, say, imposed differential carbon taxes which

[50] One possible model for arriving at international agreement that has been suggested by Schelling is something on the lines of OEEC Marshall Aid negotiations or NATO cost sharing. But in these cases there were limited numbers of countries, and in the case of the OEEC exercise to share out Marshall Aid, there was a clear positive gain to all the recipients that had to make the share-out. Furthermore, as Schelling points out, even in these relatively favourable circumstances, in the end the beneficiaries failed to reach full agreement and the USA had to decide on the final share-out. In the GHG case there will be far more countries, and many stand to incur heavy costs with little apparent gain to themselves.

would obviously favour nuclear energy, it has no means of ensuring that private energy production would build the nuclear reactors, especially in the national context of other environmental pressure groups hostile to nuclear energy.

Thus, one way or another, the practical problems of reaching any form of international agreement over policies to achieve significant cuts in CO_2 emissions, even with some countries subsidizing others, seem enormous at present. The time taken to reach agreements in other similar areas in which the difficulties and uncertainties have been much smaller make this obvious. It is true that, for example, some steps have been taken—notably in connection with the Mediterranean and oil pollution of the seas—to moderate certain forms of transnational water pollution, and that there has even been quite a lot of progress in reaching international agreement to reduce CFCs. Nevertheless, the failure to achieve more drastic breakthroughs in some cases, even where relatively few countries are involved, such as US–Canadian negotiations over acid rain, does not bode well for the prospect of dealing with the incomparably more difficult case of the reduction in carbon dioxide emissions that would be necessary in order to have any significant impact on global warming.

Hence, there seems to be more chance of success in pursuing discussions of methods of using the price mechanism in such a way as to leave countries the choice of how far they reduce their own GHG emissions or, in effect, compensate other countries to do so, in a situation of appropriate price incentives. Some form of tradable permits would seem to be the most likely approach. But even this system is open to the objection that the poor countries will just cash in their permits so that, in the end, the rich countries will be doing all the abatement and merely handing over aid to the poor countries disguised as payments of GHG emission permits. Also, rich countries could accumulate permits that other countries might be forced to buy back at higher prices at a later date when they had exhausted their own opportunities to reduce GHG emissions cheaply. On the other hand, some system, of leased permits—i.e. countries do not buy outright indefinite rights to emit GHGs and have to renew them from time to time—goes some way towards meeting these objections.[51]

But pending international agreement, however vaguely and

[51] See Grubb, *The Greenhouse Effect*, 33–8.

generally defined, it may still make economic sense for individual countries to pursue 'no regret' policies of the type referred to in the previous section. This would be appropriate in any case and certainly appropriate for those countries who, for one reason or another—such as responding to internal political pressures—feel impelled to do something about global warming even if, for the reasons given earlier, it does not make much sense to cut GHG emissions unilaterally. For such countries, the sort of no regret and research policies mentioned above involve little cost and could provide examples and information that would give the right sort of signals to the rest of the world, rather than providing the rest of the world with incentives to do less than they would otherwise have done to reduce GHG emissions.

Such policies are, therefore, much more likely to be implemented than premature attempts to forge international agreements to cut GHG emissions. Such attempts seem to be doomed to failure. And perhaps this is just as well. If there is no rational basis for inflicting relatively heavy burdens on current generations in order that, in 100 years' time, the average income per head be 4.4 times as high as it is now instead of only 4.3 times as high, it is just as well that the chances of imposing such a burden are slim. Alternatively, in so far as the chances of reaching effective international agreement are negligible, it is just as well that there is no real cause for alarm.

D. Conclusions

The above survey suggests that, according to the latest scientific consensus, such as it is, the damage done by the predicted climate change will be nothing like as great as is widely believed and certainly not the inevitable global catastrophe scenario hawked around by most environmentalist movements, politicians trying to get some mileage out of the environmental bandwagon, or sections of the media that love scare stories of any kind. There is plenty of time to think and to weigh up the costs and benefits of alternative courses of action. At the same time, it is quite likely that the real costs of measures to cut GHGs are not as awesome as they might seem, provided the measures take the form of some price mechanism instrument, such as tradable permits or carbon taxes, and provided allowance is made for the offsetting tax reductions that ought to be made elsewhere in the economy.

However, this would depend on avoiding dislocation costs associated with the rapid introduction of high carbon taxes, or their counterpart in high prices on a very limited volume of tradable permits. Thus it seems difficult to avoid the unexciting conclusion that what is needed, in addition to the obvious research into the relevant science, is further research into measures to activate 'no regret' policies, such as those associated with the removal of existing market imperfections that may hamper the introduction of economically viable technologies that economize in energy or in GHG emissions, as well as, perhaps, some modest carbon taxes or tradable permits scheme that could help stimulate further technological progress in this area. International agreement along these lines would be far more fruitful than attempts to negotiate some share-out of draconian cuts in GHGs, and governments should not let ecological horror stories frighten them into making any moves in that direction.

11

United States Policy Towards the Global Environment

Richard N. Cooper

THE US Administration has come under criticism within many European countries and within the American community of environmentalists for adopting what is considered to be too relaxed a view toward the question of global climate change, more particularly toward the prospect of a substantial warming of the surface of the earth sometime during the next century. While the motives of the administration may not be above reproach, and no doubt they vary considerably among officials, I believe that their relatively cautious attitude toward strong actions in the early 1990s and toward setting emissions targets for carbon dioxide in the near future is entirely warranted. This chapter suggests why. The alternative to stringent targets and strong actions, however, is not no action. There are important steps which can and should be taken, both to gather more information germane to intelligent decisions on the complicated questions at issue, and to attenuate the rate at which greenhouse gases are emitted into the atmosphere, thus providing additional time at relatively low cost. This chapter suggests what such actions toward gathering information, creating new options, and attenuating emissions might be.

The United States has characteristically been cautious about adopting radically new policies, or encouraging other countries to adopt policies, that might alter significantly a set of economic and social arrangements that, for all of their deficiencies, have produced a historically unparalleled level of prosperity and security for the average individual in the United States, Western Europe, and more recently Japan. To put it bluntly, those arrangements have directed an all-but-universal personal vice, greed, into socially constructive channels. Pursuit of personal gain under approximately competitive conditions in a stable social and political system receptive to new technologies has over the decades greatly increased material well-being, reduced the drudgery of labour, increased leisure, lengthened life, increased tolerance of diversity, and created more possibilities for realization of human potential than any other arrangements known. Given that broad record of success, a heavy burden of proof must be met by proposals for radical alterations.

Of course, the arrangements fall far short of many idealizations of human society, and some components of those idealizations might actually bring still greater improvements. Constant discussion and even tentative experimentation with respect to alternative arrangements, or more modest improvements in existing arrangements, should and do occur. In particular, if the collective consequences of gain-motivated individual action result in reduction rather than expansion of human welfare, through what economists call externalities, governmental or international action to redirect individual actions will be in order. That is the claim that is made these days with respect to the consumption of fossil fuels and the pursuit of modern agriculture, two of the activities that have made so much material improvement possible, as well as a host of other economic activities. Concretely, the emission on an unprecedented scale of carbon dioxide, hitherto regarded as a harmless, colourless, and odourless gas, useful to plants, and of methane and certain nitrogen oxides is said to lead eventually to a warming of the atmosphere to a degree that threatens mankind, or substantial portions of it. If this contention is correct, it creates a considerable problem for societies and governments. Not only will a failure to substantially restrain the offending activities be disastrous, but an attempt to do so on the required scale will intrude government heavily into the private decision-making that has proved to be such an important source of progress. That is not something that should be undertaken lightly.

It should be noted at the outset, before getting into a discussion of the scientific basis for concern about greenhouse gas emissions, as they are called, that the United States has not been hostile over the years to concerns about preserving or improving the natural environment, either domestically or internationally. As early as 1872 a vast tract of land (3,468 square miles) was set aside as Yellowstone National Park, so that this unique natural environment could be enjoyed indefinitely. Since then several dozen national parks and recreation areas have been created with an area of 108,000 square miles, or about half the size of France. Strong national legislation to limit air and water pollution was passed in the late 1960s, legislation that had been preceded by action in a number of states.

At the international level, the United States played an active role in sponsoring the Stockholm conference on the environment in 1972, and in leading that conference to establish the United Nations Environment Programme (UNEP). In the mid-1970s the United States worked actively to control pollution by vessels at sea, and passed legislation stiffer than that called for by international agreements.[1] It also promoted actively the OECD international agreement on toxic waste disposal. More recently, the United States took the lead in drawing attention to the possible destruction of stratospheric ozone by man-made CFCs, and when evidence of serious ozone depletion over the Antarctic became known, along with the availability of less damaging substitutes for CFCs, it took the lead through the Montreal Protocol of 1987 in establishing an international programme for the worldwide reduction in the production of CFCs.[2]

A. Scientific Background

The basic science with respect to greenhouse warming is straightforward and uncontroversial. The earth absorbs energy from the sun and re-radiates it to space at a lower frequency. The molecules of certain gases, notably chlorofluorocarbons (CFCs), methane, water vapour, and carbon dioxide absorb energy of the frequency the earth radiates, and in so doing they heat the lower atmosphere to the point at which it can radiate enough energy to equal the incoming radiation. This 'greenhouse effect' makes possible life as we know it, for the earth would otherwise be

---

[1] For details see A. L. Hollick, *US Foreign Policy and the Law of the Sea* (Princeton: Princeton UP, 1981), 367–8.

[2] See Richard Elliot Benedick, 'Protecting the Ozone Layer: New Directions in Diplomacy', in Jessica Tuchman Mathews (ed.), *Preserving the Global Environment* (New York: W. W. Norton, 1991), 112–53; and Benedick, *Ozone Diplomacy* (Cambridge, Mass.: Harvard UP, 1991).

uninhabitably cold. Since the beginning of the industrial revolution, however, people have been cutting trees and burning coal, oil, and natural gas at an ever-greater rate, producing carbon dioxide faster than the earth's natural processes can recapture and sequester it. The result has been an increase in atmospheric concentration of carbon dioxide from about 275 parts per million (ppm) two centuries ago to 350 ppm today, and continuing. The extension of agriculture through cutting trees, which decay into carbon dioxide, cultivating wetland rice, and establishing large herds of cattle, both of which produce methane, has also contributed to greenhouse gas emissions, although the net contribution of the latter two is unclear since many methane-producing swamps have also been cleared and natural herds of ruminants have been depleted.

Increasing the concentrations of greenhouse gases in the atmosphere should be expected, on the basic physics, to increase atmospheric temperature. The controversy begins over estimating the rate at which greenhouse gas concentrations will increase, on the one side, and over the impact that any given increase in concentration will have on surface temperature. The first issue arises because nearly half of the carbon dioxide that has been produced through human activity in the last 200 years, mainly through burning fossil fuels, cannot be accounted for. If the 'sink' that has been absorbing the missing carbon is becoming saturated, a given level of emissions may result in more rapid concentration in the atmosphere in the future; but since we do not know where it is going, it has become conventional to assume that in the future as in the past only half the carbon released finds its way into the atmosphere.

On that assumption, and on plausible projections of fossil fuel use and other relevant human activity during the next century, atmospheric concentrations of carbon dioxide and its equivalent in other gases can be expected to reach twice their 1800 level, i.e. 550 ppm, in the middle of the twenty-first century. What effect is that likely to have on global temperature and on other features of global climate? There is much less agreement on the temperature impact of a doubling of carbon dioxide than there is on the basic science, and still less on the climatic effects of a given temperature change. Current consensus on the former point suggests an increase in average equilibrium temperature of the surface of the earth ranging between 1.5 and 4.5 °C, with 2.5 °C representing a best guess. Average precipitation will rise with increasing temperature, sea levels will probably rise due partly to some melting of glaciers and mainly to thermal expansion of surface water (the consensus range is 29–90 centimetres, 11–35 inches, by 2090), and the temperature increases will be greater toward the earth's poles than at the equator, leading to lower temperature gradients between equator and poles than now exist.

The projected temperature change is wide because many secondary consequences of warming come into play, some of which reinforce it (for example, warming increases the water vapour content of the atmosphere, and that in turn enhances warming) and some of which attenuate it (for example, increased cloud formation at certain altitudes increases reflection of the sun's energy, and thus reduces the amount of energy reaching the earth's surface). Many of these secondary effects have been identified, but their detailed operation and magnitude are poorly understood; yet details are important.

There is another source of uncertainty. The basic analysis relies on equilibrium states. Yet it may take some length of time, called the transient, between the arrival of the stimulus (for example, a doubling of carbon dioxide equivalent) and the attainment of the new equilibrium. The transient in the case of global warming is unknown; it may be as little as a decade, or as long as two centuries. The key variable here is how much heat the oceans absorb, and that in turn depends on how rapidly the oceans churn up their deep, cold waters, about which little is known. If the oceans churn very little (which is possible, because cold water sinks), the relevant transient will be relatively short; but if churning is great, the transient could last for decades running into centuries as the water of the oceans absorbs heat from the surface.

The major analytical tool for studying climate change is the global climate model (GCM), of which five were functioning in 1990. These are large-scale mathematical and numerical models of the world's climate that can simulate climate change for many notional decades on large-scale computers following some autonomous change, such as increased carbon dioxide introduced into the atmosphere. These models are intellectually very exciting, but they remain relatively primitive (a single point of 'observation' on the earth's surface is roughly the size of Colorado, for instance), and there is low agreement among them on crucial details, particularly on the regional effects of increased average surface temperatures. Yet these regional effects are crucial for assessing the impact on society. Also, since the computational time required for each simulation is enormous, less sensitivity analysis to alternative assumptions has been done than would be desirable. In short, our basis for conjecturing future warming of the earth's climate is some basic physics combined with known and forecast increases in emissions. The detailed projections rely on simulations on large-scale numerical models that have been calibrated against reality only roughly, and which have no forecasting history because of their relative newness.

One way to test a model is to forecast a historical period with known exogenous variables (for example, change in carbon dioxide concentration) and compare the results with what actually happened. Such forecasts have not actually been undertaken because of the expense involved, but if performed in 1890 they would probably have predicted a rise in equilibrium average surface temperature of the earth by 1990 in the vicinity of 1.5–2 °C. How does that compare with what actually happened? Unfortunately and perhaps surprisingly, we do not know exactly what happened to average global surface temperature over the past century. The reason is that three-quarters of the earth's surface is water, some of it remote from places of habitation and major trade routes, and our measurements of water temperature a century ago are spotty and inaccurate. None the less, a best guess is that the earth's temperature rose about 0.5 °C. over this period. What interpretation can we put on that increase, assuming it took place? First, it is positive, but substantially below the likely forecast increases. By itself, that suggests either that the forecasts are too high, especially at the high end of the range;[3] or that the transients are quite long, since we are comparing forecasts of *equilibrium* temperature changes with observations (more accur-

---

[3] Indeed, Wigley and Raper suggest that if warming since 1860 is attributed to the enhanced greenhouse effect *alone*, the implied equilibrium temperature increase for the equivalent of doubling carbon dioxide is in the range of 1.2–1.6 °C, considerably lower than the consensus range. But they caution that this strong assumption cannot be made confidently. T. M. L. Wigley and S. C. B. Raper, 'Detection of the Enhanced Greenhouse Effect on Climate', *Proceedings of the Second World Climate Conference* (Cambridge: Cambridge UP, 1991).

ately, estimates) of *actual* temperature changes. Moreover, most of the increase observed over the last century occurred in the first half of that period; average temperatures showed no trend between the 1930s and the 1970s, contrary to the pattern that would be expected on the basis of ever-increasing greenhouse gas emissions. The 1980s, however, were the warmest decade of the century.

Interpretation of such data is complicated by the fact that there are large year-to-year variations in average temperature, much greater than the observed trend; and average temperatures changed over time before mankind arrived on the scene, so the presumption of no temperature change over the century in the absence of greenhouse gas emissions may be erroneous. In particular, if the earth is once again on a natural cooling trend, the estimated rise in temperature from that trend would be higher than 0.5 °C. Moreover, other human activities, such as the emission of sulphur dioxide and other pollutants, may have reduced the incidence of the sun's energy on the surface enough to obscure a stronger effect from greenhouse gas emissions. So the historical results do not strongly support the use of GCMs as forecasting tools, but there are many reasons for regarding that test as inconclusive, and hence they cannot be decisively rejected.

B. Social Impact

The social impact of a global increase in temperature over the next century is similarly uncertain. Temperature increases in the consensus range have been alleged to entail mass dislocation, especially along coastal areas, and mass starvation due to declines in staple food output, which in turn is due to desiccation of the major grain-producing areas.[4] Such outcomes are no doubt possible. But they are far from certain, and indeed are improbable. Carbon dioxide is itself a critical ingredient in photosynthesis, the process whereby plants make food. An increase in atmospheric carbon dioxide, especially if combined with increased precipitation, which is also a likely consequence of surface warming, will

---

[4] See e.g. the TV documentary, 'Race to Save the Planet', 1990.

more likely permit an *increase* in total food production, compared with what would be possible otherwise, especially
when allowance is made for the improvements in plant and
animal strains that we know are possible over a century,
permitting adjustment to the changed circumstances. Of
course, considerable adaptation would be required, and some
of the areas that are highly productive of food today may
become less so with alterations in patterns of temperature and
rainfall. But overall conditions would be more propitious for
food production, unless by bad luck the additional rainfall all
occurred over oceans, and rainfall over agricultural areas actually declined. Moreover, with a reduced temperature gradient
between equator and poles, major storms, hence storm damage, would possibly become less severe, although again patterns would change and some areas not today subject to
major storms might become so. Rising sea levels would require construction of sea walls in inhabited lowland areas, or
would require migration to higher ground. Some uninhabited
lowlands would become inundated, i.e. would revert to salt
marsh or mangrove, both highly productive natural environments.

Human adaptation to gradual climate change over the next
century seems to be possible without undue hardship or excessive cost for those societies sufficiently wealthy to make the
expenditures required for adjustment. Indeed, it is likely to fall
well within the compass of adaptations to many changes, such
as rapid population growth and technical change, that have
taken place over the last century. Very poor societies, however,
might find it impossible to make the required expenditures, for
example on sea walls or water storage facilities, and some
countries might simply have inadequate land to provide for
their populations if significant areas became inundated or desiccated. The result could be mass migration of desperate people
searching for a viable place to live. Moreover, some natural
ecological systems, particularly forests, might not be able to
move on their own rapidly enough to adapt to the changing
temperature and patterns of rainfall, or they might encounter
barriers of inland water or inhospitable soil that prevented further migration. They would not be able to survive without
human assistance.

C. Policy framework

In face of the challenge of greenhouse warming, a number of politicians have called for strong action to reduce greenhouse gas emissions, and some countries have set emission targets which would require substantial changes over the next decade. But what is the basis for a call to strong action now? In part it seems to derive from a philosophical view that 'nature knows best', and therefore that anything that aralters nature substantially should be halted and preferably reversed. This philosophical view finds awkward the position of man in the universe, and in particular whether he is part of 'nature' or not. If not, what is the basis for excluding him but not other species; if so, are not his actions encompassed by the general encomium to nature? Moreover, nature is fundamentally Malthusian, such that (mankind and other creatures protected by mankind partially excepted) individuals of each species multiply to the point at which they run up against the limits imposed by nutrients or predators. All endure a parsimonious, frightened existence, conducive perhaps to perpetuation of the species (although most in the end have failed to survive), but certainly not to realization of the full potential of the individual, as anyone who compares an oak in a mature forest to one on an English country estate can observe. This perspective, in my view, does not provide an adequate foundation for public policy.

What does provide some basis for public policy is the objective of leaving a desirable world to our children and (here) our great-grandchildren. We cannot anticipate their preferences, but we can try to ensure that they have at least as many opportunities and options as we have had. With that in mind, our actions, including those with respect to climate change, should be seen as investments, and should therefore be compared with alternative investments as vehicles for bequeathing a desirable world. These alternative investments include the conventional ones of an enlarged physical capital stock, including infrastructure, but also the intangible ones of more education and advancement of the frontiers of knowledge.

Those late in the next century can plausibly be left to look after the century after that, since if this generation performs adequately they will have both better knowledge and more options for dealing with the problems they and their grandchildren will face.

Actions to mitigate excessive greenhouse warming that are costless should of course be undertaken, since by assumption they do not compete with alternative investments. But most actions have some cost, and some of the actions proposed, such as drastic reduction in consumption of fossil fuels over a relatively short period of time, entail substantial costs in terms of dislocation and forgone income. Incurring those costs will only be worthwhile if they are ultimately recovered in terms of improved welfare—in the case at hand that may involve avoidance of disastrous changes in climate—and if the gain is greater than that on alternative investments.

The strategic alternatives are posed schematically in Figure 1. The horizontal axis measures the passage of time, and the vertical axis measures real income, net of the costs required to generate it. On the basis of past experience and current knowledge we can assume that real income will continue to grow as technology advances and capital is accumulated, as shown in schedule (1). The prospect of adverse climate change that some see in greenhouse warming, however, suggests that simple extrapolation of past practices will not be possible, since climate change in a variety of ways will reduce real income, such as in schedule (2), which as drawn still shows some increase over time; the most dire predictions point to a decline in incomes, leading to a downward-sloping schedule (2) after some point. If schedule (1) is not possible, however, neither is schedule (2) likely, since as climate change becomes evident, societies will take adaptive actions—building sea walls, constructing dams for irrigation of desiccated areas, developing new seeds appropriate to the new climate, and so on. Those actions will be costly, however, so they produce schedule (3), which lies below (1). It will, however, lie above (2), since adaptive actions that do not represent an improvement on (2) will not knowingly be undertaken. Actions taken in the near future to mitigate climate change with the objective of avoiding serious consequences in the more distant future are indicated as schedule (4), which is depicted below (1), (2), and (3) in the near future (reflecting costly actions now that reduce income available for consumption or other investments), but above (2) and (3) in the more distant future, since large-scale climate change will have been avoided.

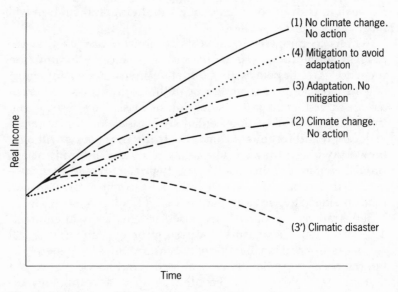

Fig. 1. Greenhouse Warming: Strategic Alternatives

The relevant comparison is between (3), adaptation to climate change as it occurs, something societies will surely do, and (4), actions now to avoid climate change in the future (mitigation, for short). Mixed strategies are of course possible, since many actions are encompassed by each of these broad categories. But for purposes of analysis it is useful to keep them distinct. The investment nature of the issue is clear: compared with adaptation, mitigation involves lower income in the near future and higher income in the more distant future. The appropriate course of action therefore depends on how we value the future with respect to the present, i.e. it depends on the choice of a discount rate to be applied to future as opposed to present income.

D. Choice of a Discount Rate

Some have suggested that the appropriate discount rate is zero, even that it is immoral to treat future generations less generously than present ones. To pose the issue in this way misrepresents the issues. Today's generation has many ways to invest at positive rates of return, and those investments with long maturities will benefit future generations. We would be doing a *disservice* to future generations if we reduced such investments in favour of mitigation actions designed to help future generations, but with a lower rate of return; future generations would actually be worse off if this were to occur. Alternatively, we could increase total investment, adding mitigation actions to other investments that we are already undertaking. Apart from the unlikelihood of that occurring in the presence of costly mitigation actions, there is some question whether it should occur. World wars and severe social disruption aside, each generation for the last 150 years has been considerably better off than its forebears: what is the case for requiring still higher savings today to improve the well-being of future generations who are likely already to be better off (climate change apart) than the current generation? An appropriate minimum standard is to leave a world no worse than ours in terms of income, and with more options for action, and more knowledge about the implications of these options. That standard requires comparing mitigation actions with alternative forms of investment, and choosing investments with the highest returns, appropriately measured.

What discount rate should be applied? Rates of return on private investment in the United States average around 12 per cent, taking one year with another and correcting for inflation. The US government formally requires that public investments exceed an estimated return of 10 per cent in real terms, 7 per cent for investments in energy activities. A recent evaluation of over 1,000 World Bank projects commenced between 1974 and 1987 showed an average real rate of return of 22 per cent at the time of initial evaluation, and 16 per cent at the time of completion.[5] It is well known that the return to investment in intangibles such as education and research typically exceeds returns to physical investment. With returns such as these, it is desirable to require mitigation actions to achieve a real return of at least 10 per cent. This information on rates of return of course applies to the late twentieth century. If returns to normal investments were to fall sharply in the next century, such that the average return over the

---

[5] Gerhard Pohl and Dubravko Mihaljek, *Project Evaluation in Practice* (Washington, DC: The World Bank, Dec. 1989).

next 100 years were below 10 per cent, a lower target return on mitigation actions would be warranted. But there is little historical evidence for substantial long-term declines in the rate of return to new investment, and it is unlikely to occur in the future. Yet at a 10 per cent discount rate, the present value of a dollar fifty years from now is less than 1 per cent, and that of a dollar 100 years from now is less than one-hundredth of one cent. In other words, far distant pay-offs from current investments are worth practically nothing today, unless the pay-offs are very large.

The discount rate criterion of 'at least 10 per cent' may have to be qualified in two respects. The first derives from the fact that gross world product (GWP) can be expected to grow over the next century. To the extent that the costs of global climate change are proportional to GWP, the costs will rise over time. While discounting reduces the present value of more distant costs, the possibility that they may grow over time cuts in the other direction. GWP per capita can be expected to grow at a rate between 1 and 3 per cent a year over the next fifty years, a magnitude that depends partly on advancing technology and partly on the rates at which existing technology is absorbed by economies that are not operating at the frontier of existing technology. If the costs of climate change are proportional to per capita GWP, and if that quantity grows, say, at 2 per cent a year, then the yield criterion for mitigation actions drops to 'at least 8 per cent'.

It should be noted that the costs of global climate change may not be proportional to GWP. As change begins to be evident, societies will take adaptive actions, and it is the costs of future adaptive actions that are in part avoided by mitigation actions now. But the costs of some adaptive actions will not be proportional to GWP. For example, the costs of building sea walls to protect against rising sea levels, if that should occur, may not rise with GWP, even though the flood damage in the absence of sea walls might rise with GWP.

The second qualification concerns the uncertainty which attends predictions about future climate change and the costs associated therewith. Uncertainty is a very big topic, one that is conceptually different from comparing present costs with (known) future benefits, and one that will not be taken up in detail here. However, one aspect of uncertainty deserves mention, because it could influence the choice of a discount rate, especially if the uncertainty cannot be entered directly into the cost–benefit calculation, as it should be.

It is widely taken for granted, at least on big issues, that people dislike uncertainty; they have aversion to risk, and are willing to pay something to reduce risk. This is the attitude that underlies the willingness to take out fire or liability insurance, to pay a certain known cost (the insurance premium) to mitigate the possible costs of uncertain and perhaps even improbable events. The conflagration of one's house is a costly event, but the costs are at least partly offset by a payment by the insurer. The uncertainties associated with mitigating global climate change and its attendant costs are in the current state of knowledge at least as great— probably greater—than the uncertainties associated with other forms of investment that we could undertake today, and on that account, given risk aversion, it will perhaps be concluded that costly mitigation actions should not be undertaken. However, the pay-off from mitigation actions now will be greatest if the magnitude of global climate change and the associated costs turn out to be high, even if that is judged to be a contingency of low probability. Of course, if the costs associated with global change are low, any investment in mitigation actions will have a low return. But such investment may still be worthwhile as insurance against an uncertain but possibly costly contingency.

How do these considerations influence the discount rate? The precise answer is not all straightforward, unless the uncertainty itself is related in a particular way to the passage of time. Roughly speaking, however, one can say that where an uncertain outcome (the future pay-off from mitigation actions) is negatively correlated with our overall economic prospects, and where the uncertainty grows exponentially with time, some deduction from the discount rate used to evaluate mitigation actions is warranted. How much? That depends in detail on the nature of the uncertainty, an issue that needs much greater discussion, and on the degree of our aversion to risk. But presumably it was this sort of consideration that led US policy-makers in 1980 to stipulate a discount rate of only 7 per cent for energy-related projects, three percentage points lower than the general standard for government investments. Serious disturbances in the field of energy, unlike other areas, can lower GNP by a multiple, so some component of the energy investment can be regarded as an insurance premium whose purpose is to attenuate the economic impact of large disturbances in the world oil market. Even with a 5 per cent discount rate, however, allowing for the two adjustments indicated, the present value today of a dollar fifty years from now is less than nine cents, and that of a dollar 100 years from now is less than one cent.

E. International Considerations

Greenhouse warming, like ozone depletion but unlike acid rain, is obviously a global problem, in principle affecting all societies. Similarly, preventive action to be effective must take place on a global scale, although actions by individual countries can serve to mitigate the greenhouse effect. It is true that in the late twentieth century most fossil fuel consumption takes place in the rich countries of Europe, North America, and Japan, plus the formerly centrally planned economies. But even then emissions from deforestation and rice cultivation occur mainly in developing countries. Moreover, on current projections, developing countries as a group will be major consumers of fossil fuel in the twenty-first century, so their co-operation in reducing emissions will eventually be essential—if emissions are to be reduced.

There is increased consciousness among leaders and intellectual élites in developing as well as developed countries about environmental degradation as a result of human activity—not least because some of the large urban areas in developing countries have become so unattractive from an environmental point of view. But while there is increased consciousness of environmental degradation compared with ten to twenty years ago, other issues command much more attention. Leaders in developing countries must deal with the fact that (in general) the 1980s were not a good decade in terms of economic development. Large external debts continue to weigh heavily on many countries. And a number of governments are politically shaky, in part (but only in part) for economic reasons, and some are even embroiled in civil war. These are much more pressing issues than the environment, even than the possibility of dramatic change in the next century.

Developing countries are not likely to constrain their economic

growth, hence their demand for energy, for the sake of environmental improvement. Furthermore, they will argue with some
plausibility that, apart from local air and water pollution, the
contribution to global environmental degradation is made overwhelmingly by the rich countries, with some significant help
from what were the centrally planned economies of the socialist
bloc, which, although smaller in population, use much more
energy and generate much more waste per capita. The position
of the developing world is largely correct with respect to present
and past conditions, and the fact that the relative contributions
can change markedly with successful economic development is
a matter that they are likely to be willing to take into consideration only after that development has actually occurred.

The bottom line is that many developing countries will co-
operate with developed countries in reducing the emission of
greenhouse gases into the atmosphere so long as it does not
require great commitment on their part (for example, in terms of
domestic political conflict) and so long as the developed countries incur the extra costs associated with that co-operation. Indeed, developing countries individually or as a group may
attempt to extract a price from co-operation on environmental
matters beyond the incremental costs of changing their
behaviour, to the extent that they detect that the environment
has become a priority issue for the developed countries. Developing countries have long felt frustrated over lack of adequate
'bargaining leverage' with respect to the rich countries, many of
whom were former colonial powers. This helps to explain the
apparently perverse applause by many oil-importing developing countries in 1974 when OPEC sharply raised the price of
oil, as this gave developing countries as a group important
bargaining leverage. That price increase certainly caught the
attention of the publics as well as the leaders of the developed
countries in a way that no previous issue (except wars for independence) had done, although in the end it proved to be a
weak bargaining weapon, in large part because there was no
way to wield it effectively. Even when the governments of developing countries agree on the desirability of improving the
environment, or restraining its deterioration, their priorities will
be elsewhere, and it would not be surprising to find them trying
to extract some quid pro quo for their environmental co-oper-

ation in some other area in which developed countries can be helpful to them.

For these reasons, the international negotiating environment for mitigation actions is likely to be very complicated, to say the least. One strategy is for the OECD countries to take on the assignment among themselves, in the hope that developing countries will later join the consensus actions after their incomes and their fossil fuel consumption have risen considerably. This strategy does not exclude actions within developing countries, provided the OECD countries are willing to pay for it, for example through World Bank loans that take account of climate change considerations in their design. The problem with this strategy is that there seems to be no right time for a country to graduate from developing to developed status, especially if it is costly, as we have seen in resistance to being graduated from eligibility for highly concessional IDA (international development assistance) loans or from tariff preferences under the Generalized System of Preferences.

Even among developed countries there is likely to be serious debate over how costly actions should be shared among countries. This source of contention is present in the best of circumstances whenever a collective good is involved, since there is no obviously correct principle for burden sharing. Contribution to the problem, ability to pay, and accrual of future benefits all vie for consideration, along with the diverse practical political constraints that countries face. But it is especially a source of contention when ignorance about the nature and distribution of the 'good' in question—in this case, the benefits from mitigation actions—is as great as it is at present.

International co-operation in other fields has progressed most successfully when there was agreement not only on the objective, but also on how best to achieve it. As the prolonged and sometimes acrimonious history leading to international co-operation in containment of contagious diseases—hardly a controversial objective—suggests, absence of scientific consensus on key aspects of how greenhouse gas emissions translate into global temperature changes will make even more difficult agreement on how to share costly action, or indeed on what actions should be taken.[6] Moreover, some countries may be expected to benefit from at least a modest amount of warming (for example, weather might become *less* uncertain in the grain-growing areas of the states of the former Soviet Union), and this possibility may also induce reluctance to contribute to an international effort.

These various considerations will tend to push countries away from mitigation actions towards reliance on adaptation, where the actions are in response to identifiable localized problems (for example, a shore being inundated, or croplands being flooded), and where expenditures are willingly made by the direct beneficiaries. Even foreign aid in this case can be focused on well-defined mitigation of visible hardship, a factor that makes garnering foreign support easier. In short, the demands for international co-operation, while frequently present on a regional basis, will be much less acute with a broad strategy of adaptation than they would be with a major commitment to mitigation.

F. The Risk of Disastrous Outcomes

The relatively low cost of adaptation to climate change, its lower requirements for international co-operation, considerable ignorance about both the total and the distributional impact of global climate change, and a historical record that points to the low rather than the high end of the range of scientific consensus on temperature change during the next century, all suggest the absence of a strong case for major efforts to reduce emissions of greenhouse gases in the near future. However, while the scientific community does not put a high probability on them during the next century, what about the possibility of truly disastrous outcomes? Three are sometimes mentioned: (1) sufficient warming to release the extensive methane contained in the arctic perma-frost, leading to a strong, possibly rapid reinforcement of warming; (2) sufficient warming to break up the Antarctic ice dam and release great volumes of ice into the ocean, raising its

[6] See Richard Cooper, 'International Co-operation in Public Health as a Prologue to Macroeconomic Co-operation', in Richard Cooper *et al.*, *Can Nations Agree? Issues in International Economic Co-operation* (Washington, DC: Brookings Institution, 1989), 178–254.

level several metres rather than half a metre, and rapidly; or (3) glacial melting in Greenland of sufficient volume and character to deflect the warm North Atlantic currents, paradoxically making Europe a much *colder* place. In terms of Figure 1, these or other disastrous outcomes could be depicted as schedule (3'), adaptation to a warming path (2') that is not shown.

These possibilities, however remote, raise the question of risk aversion and how much insurance societies are willing to buy against improbable but highly costly contingencies. There is no doubt that individuals vary greatly in their degree of risk aversion, and that commercial insurance policies do only a modest job of bringing these diverse preferences into harmony. Each society has its own mechanism, through the political process, for deciding and acting on the degree of collective risk aversion. But there is no such mechanism for the world as a whole.

Are there actions that could be taken in the near future, not too costly, that would considerably mitigate greenhouse gas emissions, and that might be taken in the interests of buying insurance against remote but costly contingencies? The answer for the United States turns out to be affirmative, and very likely a similar response applies to other countries as well. A recent study by a panel of the National Academy of Sciences offers rough estimates of the cost per ton of reduced carbon (or equivalent) emissions associated with various actions.[7] Taken together, these suggest that at a modest cost the United States could by 2010 hold its greenhouse gas emissions to approximately the level of 1990 without compromising growth of the economy. These actions rely most heavily on phasing out the production of CFCs, already agreed under the Montreal Protocol (as amended) concerning ozone, and on a concerted programmeme of energy conservation, involving especially improved vehicle efficiency and heating, lighting, and air conditioning of commercial buildings. Indeed, many of these actions offer a yield in excess of 10 per cent, so by that standard would not be costly at all. (See Fig. 2.) Actions such as these, and similar actions by other developed countries, could postpone by some decades the time at which atmospheric carbon dioxide reaches 550 ppm or any higher level, and this would provide more time to gather information on the

[7] National Academy of Sciences, *Policy Implications of Greenhouse Warming* (Evans Report) (Washington, DC: National Academy Press, 1991).

dynamics of climate change and to develop low-cost options for avoiding or countering it.

Conclusions

As noted at the outset, the United States is cautious about embracing bold programmes that involve heavy intrusion into the functioning of an economic and social system that relies predominantly on private initiatives and that on the whole has been highly successful. Obviously the prospect of calamity will induce actions that would not otherwise be taken. A cool assessment of the prospects of global climate change suggests that calamity is not likely within the next century, and therefore that drastic and costly action is not warranted. However, our ignorance of the processes involved in climate change is vast, and certain remote possibilities could indeed be calamitous. An appropriate course of action, therefore, would involve three elements, all in collaboration with other rich countries and with encouragement and help to the poor countries:

1. Launch a strong and comprehensive research programme to reduce substantially our ignorance about the sources and nature of climate change. In particular, this would involve major programmes on deep ocean currents, on cloud formation, and on the destination of the missing carbon. Expanded work on the global climate models is more controversial, since there are grounds for fundamental scepticism about the results of simulations of large, non-linear systems. However, I would favour more resources in this direction, in particular to discover possible unpleasant surprise outcomes.

2. Launch a major programme toward low-cost reduction in greenhouse gas emissions, on the grounds that there are ample other reasons to undertake most of the actions involved (enhancement of energy security, reduction of conventional pollutants, preservation of ozone), and that they would attenuate such global warming as is going to occur.

3. Develop a programme to enlarge options for future generations. This would have several diverse components. First, developed countries should examine systematically the requirements for adaptation to climate change, and position themselves to make the adaptation as smoothly as possible, for example

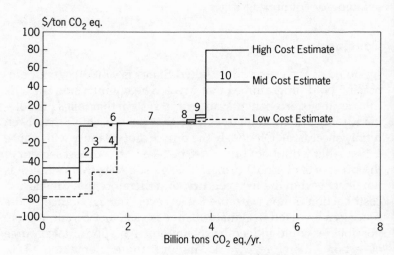

Mitigation Method	Net Implementation Cost[1] $/t.CO_2 equivalent			Max. Potential Emission Red.[2] B.t.CO_2 eq./yr.	Percent Reduction in US Emissions[3]	
	Low	Mid	High		CO_2(%)	CO_2 eq.(%)
1 Resid. and comm. energy efficiency	−78	−62	−47	0.9	18	11
2 Vehicle efficiency (no fleet change)	−75	−40	−2	0.3	6	4
3 Industrial electric efficiency	−51	−25	1	0.5	11	7
4 Transportation system management	−50	−22	5	0.05	1	1
5 Power plant heat rate improvements	−2	0	2	0.05	1	1
6 Landfill gas collection	0.4	1	1	0.2	5	3
7 Halocarbons	0.9	1	3	1.4	29	18
8 Agriculture	1	3	5	0.2	5	3
9 Reforestation	3	7	10	0.2	5	3
10 Electricity supply	5	45	80	1.0	21	13

through enlarging their seed banks and planning ecological migration corridors. They should also contribute to easier adaptation by developing countries by continuing to foster their economic development, since, as noted earlier, wealthy countries will find it easier than poor ones to make any necessary adaptations. Furthermore, development assistance could now be oriented more toward reducing the growth in future requirements for energy, in so far as this can be done without compromising the more important achievement of self-sustaining growth.

Finally, initial inspection suggests that several techniques of 'geo-engineering' might be effective and not too costly to offset the warming effects of higher greenhouse gas concentrations. One approach absorbs carbon from the atmosphere, largely by encouraging plant growth in large parts of the oceans that are currently barren because of inadequate mineral nutrients, especially iron. A second approach reduces the incidence of sunlight on the surface of the earth by propelling particles of dust into the

---

Fig. 2. Low-Mid-High Mitigation Cost Comparison, assuming 100% Implementation for the United States

1 Mitigation options are placed in order of cost-effectiveness based on the average (arithmetic mean) of the costs of each option within that category at a social discount rate of 6%. If the cost provided is a range, the cost range is averaged to determine the options cost. Only a select number of emission reduction methods are included. Those greater than $100/t. CO_2 eq. or whose costs are unknown are not included.

2 Cumulative sector emission reductions are computed by adding the emission reduction from each mitigation option in that sector in billion tons per year. If the emission reduction is a range, the arithmetic mean is used to compute the cumulative emission reduction. To remove double-counting, the energy supply emission reduction potential was reduced by the amount of reduction potentially available for the less expensive efficiency options. For non-CO_2 emission reductions, the equivalent impact of a CO_2 reduction is computed by multiplying the non-CO_2 reduction by the 100-yr. global warming potential factors.

3 Percent reduction is in terms of 1988 US CO_2 emissions, which are assumed to be approximately 4.8 billion t. CO_2 per year. Total US greenhouse gas emissions are, of course, larger than this and include emissions of halocarbons, methane, and nitrous oxide. They are assumed to be approximately 7.9 billion t. CO_2 eq./yr.

Source: National Academy of Sciences, *Policy Implications of Greenhouse Warming, Report of the Mitigation Panel*, 1991, Fig. 11.1.

upper atmosphere. (Space mirrors, by contrast, do not on quick inspection appear to be cost effective.) These and other promising lines of approach should be explored further, both to test their feasibility and cost effectiveness, and to ascertain any undesirable side effects that they may have, with a view to providing possible and relatively quick-acting sources of mitigation if in the future that should prove to be warranted.

12

Non-Governmental Organizations and the Making of US International Environmental Policy

Barbara J. Bramble and Gareth Porter

By the beginning of the 1990s, environmental organizations had become increasingly important actors in global environmental politics. A large number of groups, known by the cumbersome UN-spawned title of non-governmental organizations (NGOs), were now routinely attending and influencing conferences of some of the most powerful institutions in the world. For example, in the summer of 1990, more than 30 NGO leaders, representing 150 groups in 14 countries, stalked the halls where the Economic Summit of the seven leading Western industrial nations (the Group of Seven) took place in Houston, Texas. Press accounts credit the NGOs with keeping the environment on the agenda of the Summit, for the second year running, against the express wishes of the United States Government. A promising initiative emerged, when the Group of Seven heads of state called for an international agreement on forest conservation, although no major commitments were made in the critical area of climate change.[1]

As usual for the last four years, NGOs from around the world then gathered at the site of the annual meeting of the World Bank and International Monetary Fund, to lobby for a series of reforms in structural adjustment policies and development projects. Even the President of the World Bank has credited NGO pressure with spurring needed changes in how the Bank does business. Similarly, coalitions were building through 1990 and 1991 to

---

[1] *Wall Street Journal*, 9 July 1990, R. 19; and series of articles *Houston Post*, 9–12 July 1990.

press for environmental reforms in the latest rounds of negotiations of the General Agreement on Tariffs and Trade (GATT) and
of the North American Free Trade Agreement (NAFTA). A strong
contingent of groups from Europe, Canada, and the US attended
the December 1990 Ministerial Meeting on GATT, which was to
have been the final session of the Uruguay Round negotiations.
The NGOs were seeking to define the conditions under which
trade liberalization should occur. In 1991, under pressure from
environmental groups regarding the NAFTA, the US President
felt compelled to issue an action plan responding to their concerns. This plan included a commitment to conduct an environmental review of the projected consequences of the NAFTA.

The IMF, the GATT, and the Group of Seven are far broader in
scope than the International Whaling Commission and CITES
(the Convention on International Trade in Endangered Species),
which were among the main foci of international environmental
interest in the early 1970s. This broadening of activities was due to
three factors: first, a deepening of the NGOs' understanding of
the nature of environmental degradation and its links to international economic and political forces; second, the development
of strong alliances among NGOs from many nations, North and
South; third, the emergence of a new set of issues during the
1980s that had not been identified or understood during the first
wave of environmental activism of the 1960s and 70s—the destruction of the ozone layer, greenhouse warming, and the loss of
tropical forests. The role of NGOs changed as environmental
issues were increasingly seen as affecting national economic decisions. When activists concentrated primarily on air and water
pollution or wildlife conservation, they dealt with the Environmental Protection Agency or the Department of the Interior,
which were established to deal with these problems; the role of
NGOs was to persuade friends in the agencies to do a better job,
and to help increase their budgets. But this work was on the
periphery of national economic policy. Environmental groups
were tolerated but were shunted off to low ranking officials of
relatively obscure bureaucracies considered irrelevant to the
economic engines of modern industrial society. They were
denied access to decisions being made at the White House,
Treasury, or Commerce Departments. Now NGOs deal with the
central national decision-makers, because sustainable develop-

ment is as much an economic as an environmental goal. NGOs now advocate budget *cuts* as often as increases; evaluate and publicize the social impacts of development strategies; propose alternative accounting systems, pricing schemes, and trade rules.

In 1990, as preparations for UNCED 1992 were gaining momentum, environmental issues had indeed moved into a prominent place in world politics. Many activists expressed the hope that the 1990s would be the Decade of the Environment. Even around the US Congress one could hear the phrase, 'We have ten years to save the world'. Many Members of the Congress who had never been interested before were leaping on the environmental bandwagon with their own pet conservation proposals. But the early 1990s also brought economic and political developments that impacted on the agendas of the environmental NGOs. Economic recessions, cresting in country after country, concentrated public and governmental concern on keeping jobs and paring costs. And for nine months after Iraq's invasion of Kuwait in August 1990, the world's attention was focused on the Middle East. In the United States, every other national priority was temporarily obliterated. However, as the Gulf War faded from memory in the United States, and the Soviet Union collapsed, new opportunities arose to advance global environmental goals.

In this chapter, we analyse some of the ways in which NGOs have attempted to influence international environmental policies, especially those of the United States, by comparing three case studies from the 1980s. We will show how relative success has depended on the differing characteristics of the specific issues, yielding uneven opportunities for political leverage, as well as on NGO strategies and tactics. We will then derive lessons to be learned for future NGO efforts—especially with reference to the UNCED Conference and beyond. To begin with, however, we will outline how US NGOs operate in the international sphere, and the policy situation in the Reagan years which led them to become more deeply involved.

A. US Environmental NGOs and Global Issues

While NGOs are united by certain fundamental values, the universe of US environmental NGOs is highly diverse in terms of size, composition, interests, tactics, capabilities, and often in their positions on issues. Besides the score of well-known national organizations with large memberships and professional staffs of scientists, lawyers, lobbyists (notably, the Sierra Club, National Audubon Society, National Wildlife Federation), there are literally thousands of community groups (most with only volunteer staffs) concerned with chemicals, solid waste, water quality, or wetlands problems in their localities. There are the 'direct action' groups, such as Earth First, who put sand in the fuel tanks of tractors or plug up polluting discharge pipes; and there are policy think tanks like Worldwatch Institute and the World Resources Institute. There are specialist activist groups established to campaign on specific issues (such as the Rainforest Action Network and the Antarctica Project), and others whose one goal is to protect certain key tracts of land, by purchase or arranging donations (for example, The Nature Conservancy). Some groups support scientific research (for example, the New York Zoological Society) and others help establish parks and protected areas around the world (for example, the World Wildlife Fund). Some of these environmental NGOs have allies among other NGOs such as church groups, community development and social action groups, labour organizations, and foreign aid lobbyists.

Among all these organizations in the United States, only a small subset has been involved in global environmental problems, although that number has risen remarkably in the last five years. The most influential of those that follow international issues are of three general types: first the large, general membership organizations, with broad environmental interests but focused primarily on domestic environmental issues; second, organizations whose primary orientation is toward international issues and which are part of a larger international network of affiliated organizations; third, 'think tank' organizations without large membership whose primary influence comes through research, publishing, and/or legal work.

Except for Greenpeace, the major US membership environmental organizations were, for the most part, established earlier in the century or even in the last century: Sierra Club 1892, National Audubon Society 1896, the Wilderness Society 1935, and the National Wildlife Federation (NWF) in 1936. The membership of these groups remained small (a few tens of thousands of members each) until the late 1960s and early 1970s, when all of them multiplied several times over. Most of these groups are organized into state chapters or affiliates, each of which can communicate the concerns of the local citizens directly to their Senators and Congressional representatives. These organizations and their millions of members were thus pivotal in lobbying for the adoption of the major US framework legislation on pollution control and management of public lands (especially clean air and water, toxic and solid waste disposal, forest management, and strip mining control).

In the 1980s, these organizations experienced another surge in membership caused by a general public reaction against the anti-environmental policies of the Reagan Administration. Total membership of the dozen or so major national organizations increased from about 4 million in 1981 to roughly 7 million in 1988.[2] By the beginning of 1990, these organizations had an estimated 11 million members, and their combined revenues totalled more than $300 million.[3] In the 1980s almost all of these groups made a major commitment to work on global issues, as the existence and magnitude of the problems (such as climate change, ozone depletion, and loss of biological diversity) became clear.

The second type of organization dealing with global issues is the international NGO—a network of affiliates that is either regional or global in scope. The fastest growing environmental organization in the US in the 1980s, Greenpeace USA—which was doubling its membership and budget every two or three years, and was adding 50,000 new members each month by 1989[4]—is part of such an international network. From five international affiliates in the late 1970s, Greenpeace International has become a federation of twenty national organizations, all committed to an overarching international programme, with more than 3.3 million members.[5] World Wide Fund for Nature (formerly World Wildlife Fund) has 23 national organizations with a total of 3

[2] Stewart L. Udall, 'Encounter with the Reagan Revolution', *The Amicus Journal*, 10 (1988), 7.

[3] Bill Gifford and the editors, 'Inside the Environmental Groups', *Outside*, Sept. 1990; National Wildlife Federation, *1991 Conservation Directory*, Washington, DC.

[4] Interview with Peter Bahouth, Greenpeace, Washington, DC office, 10 Aug. 1989.

[5] Clark Norton, 'Green Giant', *Washington Post Magazine*, 3 Sept. 1989, p. 26.

million members, while Friends of the Earth (FOE) is a loose coalition of 38 affiliates which has no single source of authority. Reflecting the technological changes broadly influencing the environmental movement, all 38 FOE affiliates were expected to be linked through instant communications via fax, telex, or electronic mail by 1992.[6]

These organizations devoted much of their staff time to international environmental negotiations, attending a wide range of conferences and using their international networks to advantage in their lobbying activities. Greenpeace and FOE have been deeply involved in the Antarctic minerals negotiations, as well as those to strengthen the Montreal Protocol on protecting the ozone layer, the London Dumping Convention on disposal of wastes at sea, the Convention on International Trade in Endangered Species (CITES), and the whaling moratorium put in place by the International Whaling Commission.

The third type of environmental organization with an international orientation typically has a small membership, and derives its influence primarily from scientific-technical or legal expertise. These organizations are relatively new, reflecting the upsurge of interest in the environment during the 1970s and 1980s. The World Resources Institute (WRI), founded in 1982, carries out ambitious programmes of research and publishing on global environmental and resource issues. Both WRI and the Worldwatch Institute (1974) publish annual analyses and data on the state of the world's environment and natural resources. The Natural Resources Defense Council (1970) and the Environmental Defense Fund (1967) employ scientists and lawyers to lobby for changes in US policies and bring lawsuits to court in order to compel administrative organs to implement environmental laws or industrial polluters to obey pollution regulations.[7] NRDC and EDF have also been actively involved in international conferences that involve scientific and technical issues, such as ozone depletion and climate change.

This diversity of organizations with divergent strategies and philosophies, and occasional internecine conflicts, suggests to

[6] Interview with Alex Hittle, Friends of the Earth, Washington, DC office, 11 May 1990.
[7] EDF and NRDC have grown significantly in membership and now have an estimated 150,000 members each.

many observers a lack of cohesion in the environmental community. There is, however, considerable informal consultation
among groups which work on similar issues, and several networks or working groups have been set up for specific campaigns
(such as toxics, acid rain, tropical rainforests, or multilateral development banks). A formal committee, initially called the Group
of Ten but later renamed the Green Group, was established in
1983, made up of the heads of twenty of the major NGOs in the
United States, for planning and co-ordination of major initiatives. It was this committee that agreed to a joint media campaign
on six major environmental issues at the Group of Seven Economic Summit in Houston in 1990.[8] Moreover, there is a basic
agreement among most of the NGOs on the overall goal of these
efforts—to change the current short-sighted and consumption-
driven waste of the earth's natural resources, which is pursued
by most societies in the name of economic growth, into a type of
true 'development' that is environmentally sustainable and
socially equitable.

Nevertheless, there remain divergent perspectives on intermediate objectives, priorities, and tactics among many organizations. For example, while some of the more conservative groups
believe it imperative to set up dialogues with industry, others on
the opposite end of the political spectrum believe their only deal-
ings with major corporations should be through consumer
boycotts. Some groups have formed political action committees
to give direct support to certain candidates for national office, a
strategy rejected by other groups. There are ongoing debates
over such issues as whether there should be a green party in the
United States, and whether imposing air and water pollution
charges, or establishing a market in tradable emissions permits,
would be more effective than the current regulatory system.

In the view of some observers, the big US NGOs are too conservative, too comfortable, too connected to the establishment in
Washington, and co-operating in upholding a hopeless economic
system. Indeed, the major groups have grown and changed from
the days of student activism, and sometimes they take pragmatic

[8] The issues included were global warming, biological diversity, population,
and ocean pollution, Eastern Europe, and global economic bargaining. See
'Summit Environmental Accountability Project: Scorecard Summary', 8 July
1990; 'EnviroSummit Briefing Sheets', July 1990.

positions instead of principled stands on issues. But in most cases this is the result of tactical calculation, not moral capitulation. All of the groups indulge in too much squabbling over media headlines and money; and there are continuous battles between issues staff and the fundraisers in many groups over whether to take corporate donations, or government contracts.

Some of the groups, mostly the smaller or more radical NGOs, are accused of inattention to factual accuracy, or making exaggerated claims, and appealing to the public's emotions. While there are occasional isolated examples of this sort, we have seen little that would indicate there is an effort to 'tamper with the evidence'; in many cases the best weapon the NGOs have, in a lobbying contest with industry, is the credibility of NGO research and data.

There is an important question about who the NGOs actually represent, and how they determine what is in the 'public interest'. Some of the groups (such as NWF and Sierra Club) have active memberships which participate in the policy-making of the organization. Others are in fact directed by the staff; but of course members only continue to belong if they like the direction they see.

The fundamental features of the US NGO environmental movement are that it has a broad political spectrum from right to left wings, including almost everything in between; that it is democratic, in the sense that there is no single leader or 'party line'; and that there are absolutely no right answers to the problems we deal with. Since environmental problems are social problems, the solutions will have to be negotiated in a messy bargaining process, among the groups, the wider public, and with government and industry. Therefore, the diversity of NGOs can be seen as a strength, not a liability, rather like an ecosystem, which is more resilient if it has a wide range of species that can respond to changes in conditions.[9]

In Washington there has long been a tradition of the 'revolving door' in which individuals move easily among government, Congress, business, and lobbying positions. Some view this as a

[9] Gifford and the editors, 'Inside the Environmental Groups', 70. Even the 'Arch-druid' himself, David Brower, former head of the Sierra Club and Friends of the Earth US, agrees that diversity is essential: he supports groups all along the spectrum, even while quarrelling with most of them on ideological grounds.

process of co-option, but in fact it often has positive results. In the environmental field, throughout the 1970s, the expertise of environmental activists flowed into the government, changing the policies of whole departments, and making possible several of the major initiatives of the Carter Administration.[10] During the Reagan years, many experienced and dedicated officials left government and along with some defeated members of Congress joined environmental NGOs. This enhanced the group's ability to understand both government agencies and Capitol Hill. And to complete the circle, prominent activists such as Claudine Schneider, a Republican from Rhode Island, ran for Congress and won.

The risks of the revolving door for environmentalists are that entry into administration or Congress might blunt the ideals of some of the best leaders, or a particular NGO might find it difficult to criticize a former president. But a corollary benefit has also occurred: due to the diversity of views represented in the spectrum of the environmental NGOs, from conservative to radical, different activists can be effective in different roles depending on the direction of the political winds at the time. And if one group's boss enters government, this does not preclude other groups from criticizing his or her decisions.

For this reason, it has been the essence of NGO success in the US political arena to maintain the wide spectrum of the environmental groups, united in the broad goal of a just and sustainable society, and unconnected to a single political party. This has made it impossible to label and dismiss the 'environment' as a single or partisan issue.

As the environmental movement has developed internationally, NGOs have formed alliances across national boundaries, increasingly involving NGO colleagues from the Third World. There are networks and coalitions of hundreds of groups, some of which started or are based in the South, but with members world-wide, such as the Pesticide Action Network (started in Malaysia), Environmental Liaison Center International (based in

[10] e.g. The Council on Environmental Quality (CEQ) regulations on environmental impact assessment; the first serious attempt to stop federal funding of unnecessary big dams; alternative energy and agriculture research and dissemination programmes; and pioneering research on biological diversity and global warming, long before these were commonly understood terms.

Nairobi), Third World Network (offices in Penang and Mon-
tevideo), and World Rainforest Movement (London and
Penang). These have greatly broadened the range of subjects on
the international environmental NGO agenda—from wildlife
conservation and endangered species to rural development and
community decision-making; free trade and patenting of biological materials; technology transformation and curbs on multinational corporations; external debt and terms of trade; structural
adjustment and 'conditionality'. The environmental aspects of all
these topics are central to government negotiations that could
lead to sustainable forms of development. NGOs do not always
agree on these tough issues that are central to North–South co-
operation. But the dialogue and negotiations among NGOs
themselves offer a path for international problem-solving that
may be a good alternative to the often-paralysed intergovernmental forums.

B. The US Political Context: The Reagan Administration, Congress, and the NGOs

In the 1970s, major US environmental organizations were scarcely
involved in international environmental issues.[11] This was primarily because the most visible and immediate problems during
that period (and their members' interests) were domestic in both
cause and effect (air and water pollution, pesticide contamina-
tion, solid waste disposal, coal strip mining). Moreover, the
Nixon and Carter Administrations exercised leadership on a
number of international issues, such as oil spills, ocean dumping,
and protection of marine mammals and other endangered
species.

---

[11] An important exception was a series of legal actions, brought by the Sierra
Club, Natural Resources Defense Council, and others to force US government
agencies to consider the environmental impacts of their actions abroad (such as
financing the infamous Philippine nuclear reactor; constructing a highway
through the Darien Gap from Panama to Columbia; furnishing pesticides banned
in the USA to farmers in developing countries). Most of these cases were settled
when the Carter administration issued Executive Order 12114, 4 Jan. 1979,
governing environmental impact assessment rules for a limited set of overseas
projects. But the legal issue remains alive regarding projects not covered by the
order.

On the whole, the US played a constructive role at the United Nations Conference on the Human Environment in Stockholm in 1972, and provided the largest national voluntary funding for the United Nations Environment Programme during the 1970s. In addition to establishing procedures for preparation of environmental impact statements for major US government actions abroad, the Carter Administration promoted a strong Law of the Sea Treaty and initiated discussions with Canada on the control of acid rain. It even restricted exports of products deemed too hazardous for sale in the United States, [12] and published the path-breaking *Global 2000 Report*, which warned of looming threats to natural resources and the environment if existing patterns of economic activity continued unchanged. Thus, traditional environmental organizations viewed the Nixon and Carter Administrations for the most part as allies to be supported on international issues rather than targets for political pressure or persuasion.

When Ronald Reagan entered the White House in 1981, one of his first actions was to revoke Carter's executive order on the export of hazardous products. [13] The Reagan Administration undertook a number of actions that reversed the trends in US international environmental policy. It rejected the Law of the Sea Treaty; confounded relations with Canada by refusing to acknowledge that acid rain was actually a problem; fought all attempts to restrict exports of pesticides and other hazardous chemicals; put policy toward international trade in endangered species in the hands of free-trade ideologues; tried to eliminate all US funding for UNEP; declared at the 1984 UN Conference on World Population held in Mexico City that rapid population growth was not a factor affecting economic development, and then halted US funding for the United Nations Fund for Population Activities and the International Planned Parenthood Federation; and stood alone among members of the United Nations in voting against the World Charter for Nature in 1984.

The Reagan Administration was also determinedly anti-multilateralist. International development financing institutions which did not allow the United States to discriminate against

---

[12] EO 12264, 15 Jan. 1981.   [13] EO 12290, 17 Feb. 1981.

certain countries (such as Nicaragua) for ideological or strategic reasons were clearly downgraded in Administration policy priorities. During the 1980s, the United States tried to reduce its contributions to the World Bank and other regional banks in favour of targeted assistance by the US Agency for International Development. The United Nations was no longer considered a useful forum for negotiations, and the Reagan Administration fell behind in its dues, cut its voluntary contributions (hitting UNEP particularly hard), dropped out of UNESCO and threatened to withdraw from other UN agencies with strong influence from developing countries.

In the context of this radical shift in policy orientation by the Executive on many global environmental issues (not to mention the assaults on domestic programmes and budgets), US environmental NGOs began to widen the scope of their interests and diversify their political tactics. Whereas the older groups had been narrowly concerned with pollution, wildlife, or open space protection before the 1980s, they realized—as the decade progressed—that individual species or protected areas could not be saved without dealing with the full range of forces that impact on the environment and natural resources: these include the policies of the major engines of global economic development, such as the International Monetary Fund and the World Bank, as well as such delicate matters as domestic land tenure rules in developing countries.[14]

With the Executive in the hands of an administration generally uninterested in environmental problems and unfavourable to NGO views, US environmental NGOs turned to Congress to get things done. The House of Representatives remained in the control of the Democratic Party even in the face of the overwhelming Reagan victory of 1980. This made possible a new role for the Congress, which on occasion could mount an effective opposition, to rescue a programme or agency targeted for oblivion by the Administration, or, more rarely, to promote a new initiative. With NGO prodding, Congress restored at least a small US contribution to UNEP each year, over the strong objections of the White House; Congress forced the Agency for International De-

[14] See David Runnalls, 'The Role of Northern NGOs in Tropical Forestry', Unpublished Paper for ITTO Seminar on Sustainable Utilization and Conservation of Tropical Forest, Yokohama, 12 Nov. 1988.

velopment (AID) to initiate a programme for the conservation of biological diversity, and earmarked funds for exclusive use in environmental programmes when AID proved reluctant to spend the money.[15] Within the Congress, the most powerful levers for international policy change are often not the committees with direct jurisdiction over subject-matter, such as the Senate Committee on Environment and Public Works or the House Committee on Interior and Insular Affairs (which has jurisdiction over national forests), but those which control the funding—the House and Senate Committees on Appropriations. Thus the NGOs had the best chance of making a difference on natural resources problems if they could be connected to US funding, through either bilateral assistance programmes or the multilateral banks.

In the 1980s, US and international environmental NGOs sought to influence US international environmental policies in three ways: by lobbying in Washington for changes in US environmental policies, particularly through the Congress; by lobbying the representatives of other governments or international bodies at international conferences; and by indirect pressures on policy through consumer boycotts aimed at corporate economic actors and public education. The three case studies which follow illustrate the role of NGOs in each of these types of political methods.

C. The Multilateral Development Bank Campaign

Perhaps the most important NGO effort to influence international environmental policy in the 1980s was the campaign to reform the environmental policies of the multilateral development banks (MDBs). It was important both in terms of the major changes it portended in the NGOs' own world view, and in the results it generated.

The multilateral lending organizations play a central role in

[15] Individual Congressmen, especially chairmen of appropriations subcommittees, sometimes put pressure on the Administration without having to pass legislation. For example, an ambitious programme to spray most of Central America with pesticides to control against occasional outbreaks of Mediterranean fruit flies was put on hold when enquiries were made by several Congressmen, including the Chairman of the Subcommittee on Foreign Operations of the House Appropriations Committee.

global development finance and have a powerful impact on both local and global environment: the four biggest development banks existing in the 1980s[16] together lent $32 billion for development projects worth $100 billion in 1989, and the World Bank alone lent a total of just under $21 billion in both 1989 and 1990. But the decision to target the multilateral development banks for a reform campaign did not result solely from the size of their loans. They are even more influential than their loan portfolios would indicate because private investors follow the MDBs' lead in lending decisions; and the banks' priorities have been a central influence on the economic—and environmental—policies of recipient countries.[17]

The NGOs that began to investigate the underlying causes of accelerating degradation of natural resources in developing countries were looking for the engines of destruction, not just the immediate and obvious drivers. External development finance, and the pressure to pay mounting international debts, were among those engines fuelling agricultural expansion on to marginal lands, desertification, deforestation for cattle, timber, export plantations or colonization, and wetlands destruction especially for shrimp ponds in coastal mangroves.[18] Thus, from the beginning, the MDB campaign was conceived as a method of exposing the mistaken priorities of modern development theory, not just to modify specific projects, nor even simply to reform the MDBs themselves. The banks were targeted because they were seen as effective levers for eventually modifying development theory and practice around the world.

The lending decisions of the World Bank and other MDBs are

[16] The MDB Campaign has concentrated on the World Bank, the Inter-American Development Bank, the African Development Bank, and the Asian Development Bank. The USA does not participate directly in the Caribbean Development Bank; and the International Bank for European Reconstruction and Development has not yet been operating long enough for its distinct sphere to have become a campaign focus.

[17] Pat Aufderheide and Bruce Rich, 'Environmental Reform and the Multilateral Banks', *World Policy Journal*, 5 (1988), 303.

[18] Bruce Rich, 'The Multilateral Development Banks, Environmental Policy and the United States', *Ecology Law Quarterly*, 12 (1985), 685–8; M. T. Farvar and J. Milton (eds.), *The Careless Technology* (Garden City, NY: Natural History Press, 1972), a volume of case studies of internationally financed and ecologically destructive development projects; R. Stein and B. Johnson, *Banking on the Biosphere? Environmental Procedures and Practices of Nine Multilateral Development Agencies* (Toronto: Lexington Books, 1979).

shaped in part by institutional bias toward large-scale, capital-intensive, and centralized projects; by the habit of assessing projects on the basis of a quantifiable rate of return; by discounting longer-term social and environmental costs and benefits; by the tendency to be too cosy with client governments at the expense of other social strata in the borrowing countries; and by their lack of accountability to affected people or to taxpayers in the donor countries. But at the core of the problems are the basic belief in export-led economic growth as the only effective method to increase incomes of poor countries, and use of the per capita gross national product (GNP) statistic as an appropriate measure of wealth. The destruction of natural resources is accepted, and actually encouraged, in this world view because a reduction in the stock of resources is not counted in the national income accounts, but the sale of timber or palm oil is.

'Development' projects may fail to increase the welfare of the poor who are dependent upon forest, water, or fisheries resources, and may even further impoverish them by degrading or destroying their resource base. But this is masked by the GNP per capita, which is an *average* measure across all income levels. The World Bank has supported a number of major development projects that have had disastrous environmental and social effects. Most notorious have been rainforest colonization schemes in Brazil (Polonoroeste) and Indonesia (Transmigration), cattle ranching projects in Central and South America and tobacco projects in Africa that have contributed to accelerated deforestation, and a cattle development project in Botswana that has intensified desertification of the savannah.[19] Until its 1987 reorganization, the World Bank had only three environmental specialists to review more than 300 new project proposals each year. The regional banks had only one or two each.

The NGOs' decision to pursue reform of the MDBs was based not only on the fact that the banks have enormous leverage on the development priorities and natural resources decisions of the borrowing countries, but also because the United States govern-

[19] For critical analyses of the environmental impacts of various MBD loans, see Rich, 'The Multilateral Development Banks'; Stephan Schwartzman, *Bankrolling Disasters: International Development Banks and the Global Environment* (San Francisco: Sierra Club, 1986); and the Bank Information Center, *Funding Ecological And Social Destruction: The World Bank and International Monetary Fund* (Washington, DC, 1990).

ment has important leverage on the MDBs, since it is a major
funder. The United States, as the single largest shareholder in the
World Bank, has nearly 17 per cent of the votes on its Executive
Board, giving it a major—though not determinative—influence
over Bank policies. The Bank must seek capital replenishment
(for its 'soft loan window') every three years from principle donor
members, and US funds for that purpose must be allocated by the
appropriations committees of the US Congress. The same applies
with even greater force to the Inter-American Development Bank
(IDB), in which the United States has one-third of the votes on the
Bank's Executive Board. The potential influence that the US Congress could exert was central to the environmental NGOs'
strategy for reshaping the policies of the World Bank and other
MDBs.

In 1983, a coalition of environmental organizations, including
both a traditional large-membership group (National Wildlife
Federation) and newer environmental research and action organizations (NRDC and the Environmental Policy Institute), began a
co-operative campaign to force changes in the way the MDBs
made and implemented their lending decisions. The first stage of
the strategy was to take advantage of the potential for Congressional action to get the United States government to play a lead
role in examining the environmental policies and procedures of
the MDBs.

The NGOs began by persuading the staff and members of
several Congressional Subcommittees, including the all-impor-
tant House and Senate Appropriations Subcommittees on
Foreign Operations, to hold several series of hearings on the
environmental performance of the MDBs during 1983–4.[20] At the

[20] Environmental Impact of Multilateral Development Bank-Funded Projects:
Hearings Before the Subcommittee on International Development Institutions
and Finance of the House Comm. on Banking, Finance and Urban Affairs, 98th-
Cong., 1st Sess. (1983) (hereafter cited as 1983 Environmental Hearings); The
Multilateral Development Banks and Health: Hearing Before the Subcomm. on
International Development Institutions and Finance of the House Comm. on
Banking, Finance and Urban Affairs, 98th Cong., 2nd Sess. (1984) (hereafter cited
as 1984 Health Hearing); Draft Recommendation on the Multilateral Development Banks and the Environment: Hearings Before the Subcommittee on International Development Institutions and Finance of the House Committee on
Banking, Finance and Urban Affairs, 98th Cong., 2nd Sess. (1984) (hereafter cited
as 1984 Draft Environmental Recommendations Hearings); Tropical Forest Development Projects—Status of Environmental and Agricultural Research: Hear-

first session, representatives from EPI and NWF testified in depth on the serious environmental and social impacts of bank projects in the energy and agriculture sectors, while NRDC concentrated on bank staffing and review procedures.[21] Eyewitnesses from the borrowing countries were brought to the United States by the NGOs and invited to testify by the Congress on the impacts of the projects, particularly the Polonoroeste forest development scheme in Amazonia, and the cattle loans in Central America.[22] The House Banking Subcommittee on International Development Institutions forwarded some of the early testimony through the US Treasury Department to the MDBs. Although the initial responses from the MDBs denied any serious problems, a precedent had been established for a practice that quickly became a major source of pressure on the MDBs.[23]

The next step was to work with the staff of the House Banking Subcommittee to draft a set of recommendations regarding new procedures for MDB lending decisions bearing on the environment. The Banking Subcommittee then held hearings for review and commented on the recommendations.[24] After admitting, through a Deputy Assistant Secretary, that it had been unaware of environmental problems in MDB operations, the Treasury Department accepted all but one of nineteen recommendations as the basis for its own environmental policy *vis-à-vis* the MDBs.[25] By January 1985, the Treasury Department was beginning to review critically the environmental implications of MDB loans.

That same month, based on discussions with Brazilian NGOs, the US groups sought to stop an IDB loan to Brazil. The project was to extend the same highway that had been such a destructive force in the World Bank's Polonoroeste development. The Brazilian and US NGOs complained that the safeguards against uncontrolled migration and forest destruction in the IDB loan agreement were even weaker than in the Polonoroeste project.

ing before the Subcommittee on Natural Resources, Agricultural Research and Environment of the House Committee on Science and Technology, 98th Cong., 2nd Sess. (1984) (hereafter cited as 1984 Tropical Development Hearings).
[21] 1983 Environmental Hearings (Statements of Barbara J. Bramble, Brent Blackwelder, and Bruce Rich).
[22] 1984 Tropical Development Hearings (Statements of Jorge Illueca, Jose Lutzenberger, Brent Millikan).
[23] Rich, 'The Multilateral Development Banks', 724–8.
[24] 1984 Draft Environmental Recommendations Hearings.
[25] Ibid. (Statement of James W. Conrow).

NGOs prevailed on the Treasury Department to intervene with the IDB to express serious concern about the proposal. The NGOs were not successful in stopping the project, but the US executive director to the Bank abstained from voting for the loan on environmental grounds, effectively vetoing a significant portion of the funds—the first veto on such grounds in the Bank's history.[26]

During 1985, the NGO campaign group significantly expanded with the addition of the Environmental Defense Fund and the Sierra Club, and the formation of the Rainforest Action Network which promoted the establishment of Rainforest Action Groups associated with college campuses around the country.

One of the key reasons for the progress of the campaign was the personal attention and interest given to these issues by Republican Senator Robert Kasten and Democratic Representative David Obey, both men from the state of Wisconsin and Chairmen of the Senate and House Appropriations Subcommittees on Foreign Operations, respectively. They and their able staff advisers became staunch allies in the effort to reform the MDBs. Kasten had been known for his sceptical attitude toward multilateral assistance generally, while Obey had been supportive of the MDBs. In 1985, Kasten and Obey held hearings on the banks' environmental performance and began sending letters of enquiry to the Secretary of the Treasury about specific loan projects of the banks, which were then sent on to the MDBs for detailed answers.

A key development occurred that year when, at the request of the NGOs, Senator Kasten's staff drafted language to insert into the appropriations bill for foreign aid that required the US executive directors to the MDBs to work for reforms in project design and implementation—such as hiring more environmental specialists, involving indigenous people and local NGOs in the planning and implementation of projects, and financing more environmentally beneficial projects.[27] The US executive director of the World Bank began raising those issues at a meeting of the Board in April 1986, and the United States cast its first clear 'no' vote on environmental grounds two months later, in opposition to a half-billion-dollar power sector loan to Brazil.[28]

[26] Rich, 'The Multilateral Development Banks', 724–8.

[27] Continuing Appropriations Act, 1986, HJ Res. 465, 19 Dec. 1985 (Public Law 99–190).

[28] Aufderheide and Rich, 'Environmental Reform', 308–9; Schwartzman, *Bankrolling Disasters*, 19–20.

In 1987, the NGOs supported the full appropriation for the World Bank, based on the Bank President's recent commitment to reform. But the IDB was still racing forward with such destructive projects as the completion of the BR364 highway in Brazil. The NGOs suggested that the US contribution to the IDB should be cut, and the Appropriations Subcommittee on Foreign Operations slashed it by 75 per cent.[29]

During the period 1984–7 media coverage of the MDB campaign was limited but helpful. Only a few newspaper articles covered it, but they were influential.[30] The CBS magazine show '60 Minutes' broadcast a piece on the disastrous Polonoroeste Project in 1985; and a much more accurate and profound documentary was filmed over several years which covered the MDB campaign and explained the dire consequences of Brazilian and World Bank development policies in the Amazon. This was a series called *The Decade of Destruction*. Parts of it were broadcast around the world in 1984 and 1987 (although not in the US until 1990). The *Decade* series played a part in the MDB campaign, even during filming, as US NGOs used footage from one of the programmes in a 1984 Congressional hearing to show the effects of the Bank-financed Polonoroeste project. The combination of these pieces almost certainly convinced the World Bank (but not the other MDBs) to take the campaign more seriously.

The MDB campaign marked a new phase in NGO international relations. It was clear from the beginning that the only way to convince the Congress to support the need for reform of the MDBs was to bring direct evidence, from the borrowing countries, of the harm that was being caused by the banks' projects. Especially in the House of Representatives, the main supporters of the MDBs were liberal members of Congress, who believed in the development mission preached by the MDBs. Concerns expressed by American environmental NGOs about forest and wildlife destruction in the Third World would have been simply

[29] Statements by Barbara J. Bramble and Stephan Schwartzman before Subcommittee on Foreign Operations of the Committee on Appropriations, 30 July 1987.

[30] 'World Bank Urged to Halt Aid to Brazil for Amazon Development', Erik Eckholm, *New York Times*, 17 Oct. 1984; 'World Lenders Facing Pressure from Ecologists', Philip Shabecoff, *New York Times*, 30 Oct. 1986; 'Rainforest Misuse Prompts Ultimatum', Timothy Aeppel, *Christian Science Monitor*, 14 Aug. 1987; 'Environmental Concerns Derail Brazilian Road Loan', Dianne Dumanoski, *Boston Globe*, 6 Aug. 1987.

dismissed in the face of the imperative of alleviating poverty. Thus the campaign has always stressed the negative economic and social effects of the projects, which are closely linked to the destruction of natural resources. In many cases, local people have been made worse off, not assisted, by the projects, while the soils, forests, and water supplies they need for their future have been degraded.

The US NGOs formed alliances with NGOs in developing countries to provide credible evidence of the real on-the-ground effects of the loans. The local NGOs guided the US activists on which projects were of most concern to them, and provided information about the effects on local people, especially tribal minorities. They also suggested alternative projects that would make sense for long-term development.

In 1985, NWF and EDF staff began collaborating with two Brazilian NGOs who were criticizing MDB loans for Amazonian development: the National Council of Rubber Tappers and the Institute for Amazon Studies. Both were demanding that the Brazilian government support extractive reserves—areas in which forests would be preserved for local people to extract non-timber products, such as rubber and Brazil nuts—as an alternative to government-aided development projects that threatened to destroy tropical forests. They were also concerned about the IDB road-paving loan that would proceed without first demarcating Indian lands or resolving land conflicts between rubber tappers and cattle ranchers, despite loan conditions that were supposed to safeguard the environment.[31]

The two US NGOs invited the rubber tappers' leader Chico Mendes to the United States in 1987 to meet members of Congress and World Bank and IDB staff, and to go to Miami for the annual meeting of the Inter-American Development Bank. There he and the EDF anthropologist Stephan Schwartzman lobbied the executive directors of the IDB on extractive reserves and the road-paving loan. As a result, the World Bank and IDB both formally endorsed the concept of extractive reserves for the first time. Later that year, the road-paving project was suspended, in part because of the pressure from the US Congress, especially Senator Kasten. It was the first suspension of a loan by the IDB on en-

[31] See 'Rise of the Rubber Tappers', Randall Hyman, *International Wildlife* (Sept.–Oct. 1988).

vironmental grounds.[32] Over the next year, the IDB undertook a precedent-setting effort to persuade the Brazilian federal and state governments to negotiate a satisfactory agreement for land and forest protection, with the local rubber tappers and Indians. The loan was not reinstated until the local groups' representatives agreed to the terms.

In May 1987 World Bank President Barber Conable admitted that 'the Bank had been part of the problem in the past', and announced a sweeping change in environmental policy. This was in line with the US legislative mandate, and included building up the Bank's environmental staff to sixty professionals and financing more explicitly environmental programmes.[33]

That speech signalled the beginning of a new stage of the MDB campaign, in which US-based NGOs shifted their emphasis to sectoral lending policies in forestry and energy. NGOs pointed out that few of the World Bank loans to the forestry sector have addressed the source of the problems that are driving tropical deforestation, whereas the largest share went to support the expansion of commercial logging in the tropical forest countries. The Bank resisted shifting its energy lending to energy efficiency or renewable projects, as the Bank's Energy and Industry Department argued that too little was known about global warming.[34] By 1989 it had devoted only 2 per cent of its energy and industry loans to projects with end-use energy efficiency components.[35]

Over the years, similar collaboration to that in Brazil has developed between US-based NGOs and those in other borrowing countries, especially India (to protest against the forcible displacement of hundreds of thousands of people for Bank-financed power plants and dams), and Indonesia (to slow down the Transmigration Project, which aims to colonize the forested outer islands with excess population from crowded Java, causing deforestation of vast areas and subjugation of the

---

[32] Stephan Schwartzman, 'Deforestation and Popular Resistance in Acre: From Local Movement to Global Network', Paper delivered to symposium on The Social Causes of Environmental Destruction in Latin America, Annual Meeting of the American Anthropological Association, Washington, DC, 15–19 Nov. 1989.

[33] Address by Bank President Conable (n. 1 above).

[34] Vicki Monks, 'The Bank Responds to the Challenge of Global Warming', *Annual Meeting News* (Washington, DC) 26 Sept. 1989, pp. 34–5; *Boston Globe*, 21 May 1989.

[35] Bruce Rich, 'The Emperor's New Clothes: The World Bank and Environmental Reform', *World Policy Journal*, 7 (1990), 316.

indigenous inhabitants). More recently, the National Wildlife Federation has worked closely with the indigenous peoples federation of Bolivia (CIDOB) to reform another lowland tropical rainforest settlement project funded by the World Bank.

In addition, a massive number of supporting NGOs have joined the effort from Europe, Canada, Japan, Australia, Latin America, and South and South-East Asia. Virtually all of these groups now have some direct communications across North/ South lines. All are in agreement on the close links among economic and social issues, human rights—especially of tribal minorities—and the more 'traditional' environmental issues of pollution and species loss. This has had a profound effect on many of the Northern NGOs, particularly in the United States, where even the most concerned environmental sympathizers often know very little about other countries. The involvement of environmentalists in human rights issues has led to the possibility of much stronger NGO alliances during the 1990s.

The MDBs are now in the process of implementing the reforms they have promised, and processing new loans under the new rules. They tell us it is still too early to expect results. So it is not yet clear whether profound change is possible in such large institutions.[36]

To some, the reforms already accomplished appear significant. With continued NGO pressure, some of the worst of the recent loan decisions have been modified, and some genuinely positive projects have been funded.[37] The US Agency for International Development regularly conducts an 'early warning' review of projects, which it shares with other governments to assist their voting decisions on loans. The Treasury Department has instituted its own voting guidelines for projects involving tropical forests, wetlands, and arid lands. These were developed in close collaboration with NGOs.

The World Bank has instituted an Operational Directive on environmental impact assessment and a new forest policy. Both responded significantly to NGO concerns from both South and North. All of the MBDs have upgraded their environmental and social science staffs, and their project review procedures.

---

[36] Cf. Ken Piddington's chapter in this volume.
[37] e.g. the $117 million National Environmental Policy loan for Brazil, approved 1990.

In this, the World Bank is the clear leader, and its Environment Department is promoting significant initiatives, such as a pilot programme on river basin management. The IDB has both an advisory staff unit on environmental and social issues *and* a high-level operations management body to review problem projects.

But major work remains to be done. Despite the screening processes, seriously flawed projects are still approved.[38] Instead of the institutions taking on their own responsibility to review projects for social and environmental impacts, NGO resources are stretched extremely thin in trying to check on projects coming through the pipeline. The Bank has established a Global Environmental Facility to make money available, at low interest rates or as grants, to help developing countries cover the costs of projects dealing with global environmental issues such as climate change and biological diversity. While this relatively small, separate fund may support some good projects, it must not be permitted to divert attention from the real priority, which is still to reform the big, normal loans that are the banks' 'business as usual'.

Perhaps the most valuable result of the campaign was the acceptance, at the policy level, of the NGO demand that local communities be consulted in the development process. This has given a new prominence to NGOs, tribal minorities, and other local groups within their own countries, and they are now more able to intervene in many issues of national and international concern. The MDBs are clearly making greater, if sporadic, efforts to involve local people in policy formation and project reviews. If the other MDBs would follow the IDB's lead in pushing for local NGO negotiations with their own governments, much progress could be made in designing less destructive projects.

Most of the bank operations staffs are unfamiliar with how to work with local groups on project reviews and are reluctant to try. The World Bank has put out a manual to assist their staff in

---

[38] See e.g. 'An Environmental and Social Disaster in the Making: The African Development Bank's Coastal Road Project in Côte d'Ivoire', Environmental Defense Fund, 30 Nov. 1990; memorandum, 'The Conservation of Cameroon's Tropical Forests: A Test Case for the Global Environmental Facility and the New Forest Policy', Environmental Defense Fund, 5 Apr. 1991.

identifying ways to involve NGOs and other groups.[39] Despite these efforts, the institutions remain fundamentally unaccountable to the public in both borrowing and donor countries. Most documents are withheld even from the banks' boards of executive directors.[40] Opening the decision-making process remains a vital step if MDBs are to facilitate progress toward sustainable development.

D. NGOS and the Protection of the Ozone Layer

International regulation of the emission of substances that deplete the ozone layer is a more traditionally 'environmental' issue, albeit one with significant economic implications in terms of necessary product and process conversion. The threat posed by stratospheric ozone depletion is so serious that it needed to be confronted for that reason alone, quite apart from any precedent value. Much of the depletion is caused by a narrow range of chemicals found in frequently purchased consumer products, thus opening up the possibility of consumer education and boycotts and other pressure on industry as a strategy for NGOs. The major producers and users of the ozone-destroying chemicals are still the industrialized countries, so many of the costs of necessary changes in law and industrial processes would be incurred in the North, where NGO strength is greatest.

Since the United States would play a pivotal role in the negotiations, for good or ill, NGOs sought to influence US ozone policies both directly and through other states. Most US NGOs did not become actively engaged in the ozone issue before the Montreal Protocol on Substances that Deplete the Ozone Layer was signed

[39] On the other hand, this process can raise its own problems, especially the issue of whether NGOs should accept funds from the banks to serve as consultants. Most Third World groups could not undertake travel to meetings, analytical studies, or monitoring functions for bank projects without being paid for their services, but they would then lose their status as independent critics. Several organizations prefer financial security (and still do serious analytical work), but others would consider them to have been co-opted. After much discussion among many NGOs, a consensus appears to be emerging that here, too, diversity is the key. Some groups will choose to undertake Bank consultancies and some will not. Co-operation can continue, and information can be shared, while different groups take on different functions.

[40] Rich, 'The Emperor's New Clothes', 321–5.

in September 1987.[41] The Montreal Protocol was billed as a compromise that was supposed to reduce CFC production by 50 per cent of 1986 levels by 1999.[42] However, the net reduction in CFC use to be brought about by the agreement fell far short of what was needed even to stabilize the ozone layer. The protocol failed to ban continued use of several ozone-depleting chemicals, or to call for a phase-out of hydrogenated CFCs, which also threaten the ozone layer and were expected to replace CFCs for most uses. Even more important, the agreement failed to specify any method of funding to defray the costs of switching to substitutes for CFCs in the developing countries.[43] China, India, and Brazil all refused to sign it.

Three weeks after the Montreal Protocol was signed, the thirty-three (then existing) affiliates of Friends of the Earth International at their annual meeting passed a resolution making ozone-layer protection their top priority. While recognizing that the agreement would have to be strengthened, they decided to use the Montreal Protocol as an organizing tool to achieve a world-wide ban on CFCs in aerosol sprays and the adoption of substitutes for all uses of CFCs. A co-ordinated global environmental campaign aimed first at industry and then at consumers was launched in late 1987.[44] Each national campaign was geared to the status of its government's ozone policy: in Britain, the Netherlands, West Germany, Belgium, Australia, France, Cyprus, Hong Kong, Malaysia, and other nations where aerosols were still the major use of CFCs, FOE and other groups called on industry to phase out CFCs. When that didn't work they called for consumer boycotts of CFCs. In the Netherlands, after three

[41] The NRDC was the exception to this generalization: at a workshop sponsored by the EPA and UNEP in 1986, NRDC lawyers learned from Du Pont, the world's largest manufacturer of CFCs, that it could create chemical substitutes for CFCs that would not harm the ozone layer, if the incentives were right. So NRCD advanced the first proposal anywhere in the world for a virtually complete phase-out of both CFCs and halons over ten years. David Doniger, 'Politics of the Ozone Layer', *Issues in Science and Technology* (Spring 1988), 89.

[42] Because developing countries were permitted to increase their use of CFCs substantially for the first decade, the net reduction in CFCs to be brought about by the agreement was actually only 35–40%, compared with the 85% generally regarded as necessary to stabilize the level of ozone depletion.

[43] *ILM* (1987), 1550.

[44] This account is based on Elizabeth Cook, 'Global Environmental Advocacy: Citizen Activism in Protecting the Ozone Layer', *Ambio*, 14 (Oct. 1990), 334–8; see also R. Benedick, *Ozone Diplomacy* (Cambridge, Mass.: Harvard UP, 1991).

months of pressure, the aerosols manufacturers agreed with the environment ministry to stop using CFCs by the end of 1989, while in Britain they announced a phase-out just three days before the consumer boycott was to be announced. These campaigns instantly accelerated the timetable for the 50 per cent cut in CFC use and served as the basis for campaigns calling for a complete phase-out and use of safe substitutes for all ozone-destroying chemicals.

In the United States, which had already banned aerosol use of CFCs in the late 1970s, the first target was the food packaging industry. FOE urged customers not to buy products packaged in styrofoam, which is usually manufactured by the injection of CFCs into liquid plastic, in a campaign called the 'Stratospheric Defense Initiative' (SDI) or 'styro-wars'. Under pressure from FOE, McDonald's announced a complete phase-out of CFCs in their packaging in 1987, after which other fast-food chains made similar pledges.

In the spring of 1988, after negotiations with FOE, NRDC, and EDF, the Foodservice and Packaging Institute, the trade association for the industry in the US, agreed to eliminate the use of CFC 11 and 12 in all food packaging by the end of 1988. It agreed as well to set up a working group with the three environmental organizations to encourage safer alternative blowing agents than the compound called HCFC-22 (hydrogenated CFC) which would otherwise immediately replace CFCs 11 and 12. Admittedly, the success in forcing an entire industry to abandon CFC use was a symbolic victory, since it accounted for less than 3 per cent of CFC consumption in the United States.[45] The real value of the 'styro-wars' campaign, however, was in raising public consciousness about the ozone depletion issue as a basis for demands to strengthen the Montreal Protocol.

While educating the public on ozone depletion, NGOs worked at international conferences to ensure that the Montreal Protocol would be amended to phase out CFCs and other ozone-depleting chemicals at the earliest possible time. The World Conference on the Changing Atmosphere in Toronto in June 1988 was a major

---

[45] Foodservice and Packaging Institute, 'Fully Halogenated Chlorofluorocarbon Voluntary Phaseout Program', 12 Apr. 1988; letter to the editor of the *Washington Post* from Liz Cook, Ozone Campaign Director, Friends of the Earth, 13 Dec. 1989.

turning-point in the politics of the ozone layer. The NGOs present at the conference put forward an 'action plan' calling for a CFC phase-out by 1995, and a series of other government actions to halt global warming. The Conference, attended by 300 scientists and policy-makers from 46 countries, recommended the revision of the Montreal Protocol in 1990 to 'ensure nearly complete elimination of the emissions of fully halogenated CFCs by the year 2000'. The Canadian Ambassador to the UN, Stephen Lewis, observed that this recommendation was 'pilfered' from the NGO Action Plan.[46]

NGOs further developed their position on the Protocol at a symposium convened just prior to British Prime Minister Thatcher's Saving the Ozone Conference in London in March 1989. NGOs issued a statement which called, among other things, for a technology transfer fund to help developing countries phase out ozone-depleting chemicals. That statement was then presented at the First Meeting of the Parties to the Montreal Protocol in Helsinki in May 1989 on behalf of 93 NGOs world-wide.[47] The meeting was deadlocked on the issue of a funding mechanism for developing countries, with key donor states, including the USA and Japan, suggesting use of existing bilateral and multilateral arrangements as an alternative to a new fund. The parties could only agree on an open-ended working group to study modalities of financial mechanisms. NGO observers, representing FOE in the United States and the United Kingdom, NRDC, and the European Environmental Bureau, called attention to NGO support for a special international fund and proposed that industrialized countries carry out feasibility studies to determine what developing countries would need to implement the protocol. The Norwegian government asked for a more detailed proposal along these lines.[48]

By the time of the Second Meeting of the Parties in London in June 1990, several industrialized countries were pushing for a phase-out timetable as early as 1997, while the United States and the United Kingdom were resisting any date earlier than 2000. Similarly, a number of countries wanted to impose controls on

[46] Cook, 'Global Environmental Advocacy'; *The Changing Atmosphere: Implications for Global Security, Conference Statement*, Toronto, 27–30 June 1988, p. 3.

[47] Cook, 'Global Environmental Advocacy'.

[48] Liz Cook, 'Report on the First Meetings of the Parties to the Vienna Convention and the Montreal Protocol, Helsinki, Finland, April 26–May 5, 1989', 15–16.

HCFCs (hydrogenated CFCs), which were much less destructive of the ozone layer per unit than CFCs, but were expected to do significant damage if their use grew sufficiently. The central argument was over whether safe alternative technologies would be available for the full range of uses of CFCs and HCFCs.

At the Working Group sessions preceding the London Conference, representatives of Greenpeace and Friends of the Earth sought to influence the position of the USA and the UK, both by lobbying their delegations and by providing information and arguments on alternative technologies to the Australian and Norwegian delegations, who were working for a 1997 phase-out date.

At the time the advocates of a faster timetable failed to budge the USA and the UK from the year 2000 for CFC phase-out. But the successful negotiation in London of a compromise on the funding mechanism to support the incremental costs of CFC substitutes for developing countries brought pledges from the Indian and Chinese observer delegations to recommend to their governments that they join the protocol. Also, the final agreement reached in June 1990 did include a phase-out of both halons and carbon tetrachloride (ozone-depleting chemicals not controlled under the original protocol) by 2000, and methyl chloroform five years later. This was a significant move forward, since as late as January 1990, both the EC and Japan had been unwilling to agree to a phase-out. Hydrogenated CFCs, which are expected to increase rapidly in use in the future, remain uncontrolled.[49]

The ozone protection campaign is an example of a political effort waged by international NGOs using all three major means of influence: national lobbying, international lobbying, and pressure through consumer boycotts. In this case, NGOs took advantage of convergent favourable circumstances: the signing of a major international convention, albeit a relatively weak one; the appearance of new scientific evidence; the link between ozone depletion and commonly used consumer goods; and the relatively small number of major producer countries that were needed to lead the agreement. NGO advocacy of a fund for assisting developing countries with technology conversion, at a moment when government negotiators lacked creative solutions

[49]   In February 1992 the United States announced that it would end production of CFCs in 1995, five years ahead of the previous target. This followed NASA reports of damage to the ozone layer in the Northern hemisphere.

and leadership, enhanced NGO influence on the issue as well. It is impossible to assess how much the achievement of the 1990 London agreement can be attributed to NGOs, but there is certainly enough evidence to suggest that it happened sooner because of the NGO campaign.

E. Deforestation and the International Tropical Timber Organization

The International Tropical Timber Organization (ITTO) was established in l986 as a result of the International Tropical Timber Agreement of l984, which is an international commodity agreement based on the principle of free and unrestricted trade. It has no commodity stabilization arrangements based on buffer stocks. ITTO includes 22 producing states and 24 consuming states, accounting for over 95 per cent of the international trade in tropical timber. Producer countries as a block have equal voting power to the block of consumer countries. ITTO is dominated by Japan, which held 380 out of the 1,000 consuming-country votes when the organization was established, and provides its operating budget.

ITTO is officially committed to promoting the sustainable use of tropical forests and conserving their genetic resources, and has a unique voting scheme that allocates influence among producer states on the basis of both remaining forests and export volume. For that reason, a few NGOs saw ITTO as a worthwhile target for international lobbying, since it might gain enough clout to slow tropical deforestation in regions where forest loss is related to commercial logging (principally in South-East Asia and West Africa). Other NGOs were sceptical, because of ITTO's position as a captive of timber-trading interests on both the producer and consumer sides. Moreover, the overwhelming balance of the international funding that promotes tropical deforestation flows outside the purview of ITTO. Thus it was unclear to many NGOs either what leverage ITTO would really have on forest destruction, or what leverage the NGOs could have on the powers that controlled the institution.

Nevertheless, a growing number of NGOs have joined in the effort to press ITTO to fulfil its purposes. *Ad hoc* coalitions of as many as sixteen environmental NGOs from ten countries have attended its biannual meetings and have been permitted to intervene in the discussions. Northern groups have paid for the fares of Southern NGO representatives to attend ITTO meetings, and strategy sessions are now organized before the official meetings.

Some of the international NGOs that have been actively involved in lobbying ITTO (primarily WWF and FOE) have defined the problem of the tropical timber trade in terms of the need for an alternative model of forest management. They argue that current timber extraction systems use mechanized equipment which is too destructive to be compatible with maintaining the tropical forest ecosystem. They point out that less than one-eighth of one per cent of the tropical forests from which timber is being extracted are managed in a manner that could possibly be sustainable. They favour a phase-out of conventional commercial logging and its replacement by both alternative logging methods and reserves for the extraction of non-timber products.[50] These international NGOs have sought to convince the member delegations to ITTO to approve establishment of codes of conduct for producers and consumers; to fund projects demonstrating alternative methods of forest management; and to adopt an action plan committing the industry to a transition to different ways of managing forests.[51]

There seems to be something of a split among the Southern NGOs, with most activists who come to ITTO from Asia favouring drastic action to halt logging, and those from Latin America favouring a more moderate approach. Many of the Latin groups support ITTO funding for pilot projects to test sustainable logging techniques.[52] Perhaps this stems from the fact that many Latin American environmental groups are used to working on externally funded demonstration projects in co-operation with

[50] See François Nectoux and Nigel Dudley, *A Hard Wood Story: Europe's Involvement in the Tropical Timber Trade* (London: Friends of the Earth, 1987); and James N. Barnes, 'Statement of the Environmental Policy Institute, Friends of the Earth, and the Oceanic Society, to the Enquete-Kommission of the Bundestag Concerning Tropical Forests', 28 June 1989, Bonn. Other groups, notably the World Rainforest Movement, have called for a complete halt to logging in primary forests, since alternative so-called 'sustainable' logging has never been demonstrated.

[51] See World Wildlife Fund International, 'Tropical Forest Conservation and the ITTO: a WWF Position Paper' (Spring 1987).

[52] Interview with Robert Buschbacher, World Wildlife Fund USA, Washington, DC, 12 July 1991.

governments. On the other hand, it may have more to do with their different experiences with deforestation. In Asia, logging is the primary and visible cause of the extraordinary destruction of forests in recent years whereas, up to now, logging in Latin America has usually facilitated entry, with cattle ranching and agriculture the main reasons for forest conversion. When the accessible forests of South-East Asia are felled, the pattern may change and Latin America may become the logging target. NGOs have succeeded in persuading government delegates to allocate ITTO funding to model projects on sustainable forest management in Brazil and Bolivia. But a 1989 NGO proposal to label tropical forest exports according to whether they were produced under 'sustained yield management' has been frustrated by producer members of ITTO, led by Malaysia.

NGOs were instrumental in the negotiation of an agreement with the Malaysian delegation to permit an ITTO-sponsored 'experts' mission' to inquire into the situation in Sarawak, where the rate of logging threatens to eliminate primary forests within a decade, and to deprive tribal minorities of their homelands much sooner.[53] The resulting report regrettably ignored most of the human rights issues posed by the rapid and destructive logging in Sarawak, but it did recommend a significant cutback in the rate of timber removal from the island.[54] In response to US NGO lobbying and Congressional inquiries, the US delegation took a strong stand at the November 1990 ITTO meeting in Yokohama, seeking an ITTO Council resolution that would implement the Sarawak report by establishing a firm timetable and numerical targets for reduction in the allowable timber cut on Sarawak. However, consensus could not be reached, and the US backed down.[55]

[53] Report by Jim Barnes on May 1989 ITTO meeting, 7 Aug. 1989; interview with Jim Barnes, Senior Attorney, Environmental Policy Institute, 23 Mar. 1990.

[54] According to independent calculations, the 'experts mission' significantly misstated the amount of logging that could be sustainably carried out on Sarawak. Thus instead of the 50% cut in logging which they recommended, their underlying research leads to the conclusion that logging should be reduced by 85%. See ITTO (VII)/7, 'The Promotion of Sustainable Forest Management: A Case Study of Sarawak, Malaysia', 7 May 1990; cf. Guillermo Castilleja, 'Reducing the Annual Timber Harvest in Sarawak: How Much?', National Wildlife Federation, 15 Oct. 1990.

[55] Interview with Robert Buschbacher, World Wildlife Fund USA, Washington, DC, 12 July 1991.

Annual efforts by NGOs to promote an action plan with teeth have thus far failed to bear fruit. A 1988 draft action plan which bore the imprint of NGO ideas was watered down before finally being passed. In 1990, the ITTO Council adopted the target of the year 2000, by which time all tropical timber exports should come from sustainably managed forests. But the plan failed to define what that would mean in practice, thus rendering it almost meaningless.[56]

With the exception of the Sarawak report, the US delegation has not taken strong positions on these issues, either for or against, although they profess to be supportive of sustainable forestry. Congress has no definitive role here, since ITTO is not dependent on funding from any source but Japan. Even so, the Congress could force the Administration to press for tougher ITTO rules, a serious code of conduct, and an action plan to reach 'sustainability'; but so far the Congress has not been asked by the NGOs to get involved.

Taking a different tack, some NGOs have threatened or actually carried out boycotts of tropical timber products that are not sustainably produced as a method of pressuring ITTO producers to adopt codes of conduct. In 1987 the Rainforest Action Network and Greenpeace boycotted Burger King, one of the USA's largest fast-food chains, which imported 700,000 steers annually from Costa Rica, where conversion of rainforests to cattle ranching has been rampant since the 1960s.[57] And Friends of the Earth in the UK and the Netherlands have both organized boycotts of tropical timber products to pressure producing states to abandon unsustainable commercial logging. The UK organization drew up a list of products, identifying the species of tropical wood imported to Britain and the brand names of the products made from them; they distributed it to consumers through some 200 local groups and asked 200 retailers to stop selling those products. FOE Netherlands succeeded in getting 60 per cent of the Dutch municipal governments to pass laws banning the use of tropical timber in municipal projects.[58]

But consumer boycotts have also been criticized by other en-

[56] International Tropical Timber Council, 'Criteria and Priority Areas for Programme Development and Project Work: Report of Panel of Experts to Integrate ITTO's Action Plan', 5 Oct. 1990.

[57] World Rainforest Report, Aug./Sept. 1987, No. 10.

[58] Interview with Alex Hittle, 10 Apr. 1990.

vironmentalists who argue that eliminating markets for tropical timber would weaken the incentives for future codes of conduct on sustainable forestry methods, and could actually speed up forest destruction through encouraging conversion of forests to more valuable export crops. In addition, a northern boycott of tropical timber products could put Southern NGOs in danger if they are accused of joining foreign forces to undermine their national economies. It could also destroy the precarious trust among NGOs and governments that is slowly being built up through the MDB campaign. It has been difficult enough to convince borrowing governments that the NGO aim is to change the ill-conceived policies of the banks, and not to deprive poor countries of needed development loans. At a 1989 workshop on the tropical timber trade, several environmental organizations concluded that a boycott of tropical timber products would not promote the preservation of tropical forests.[59]

The imperviousness of ITTO to NGO lobbying so far, in contrast to the relative success of the MDB and ozone campaigns, can be explained in terms of the way the NGOs have conceived of it, as well as the obvious structure of the interests of ITTO members. Because 'sustainability' is part of the charter, NGOs have taken the approach of making low-key presentations to the delegates to convince ITTO to carry out what is seen as a common purpose— rather as NGOs might treat the US Environmental Protection Agency or the International Whaling Commission. But in reality, the objective of ITTO is to promote the timber trade and no decision-maker in it has a primary interest in conservation. The institution seems seriously committed to the wrong direction, and NGOs should probably be confronting it as they do the World Bank or the FAO. In particular, the main interest of producer countries has been to obtain funds for more modern logging equipment and better market access for their timber exports. Japan, the most important consuming state in the organization, is interested primarily in maintaining its timber imports at their present level, while most EC states are interested in maintaining

[59] For a discussion of the issues, see Ken Snyder, 'Boycotts: Assessing the Effectiveness of Boycotts as a Strategy Tool in a Campaign to Save Tropical Forests', Rainforest Alliance Workshop on the US Tropical Timber Trade, 14–15 Apr. 1989, New York City.

a flow of hardwoods to continue their furniture-manufacturing industries.

The United States, which is the world's largest importer of finished tropical hardwood products (and the largest exporter of softwood products), is unwilling to put itself at odds with producing states with whom it has close political-military ties, such as Malaysia and Indonesia. It is also reluctant to be too aggressive regarding primary forests in developing countries while the issue remains unresolved in the United States.

Finding a lever to move ITTO policy is made much more difficult by its character as a trade organization with no public constituency except business organizations. Moreover it has very little public funding and no public accountability. Because it is not dependent on funds from the USA, it is virtually insulated from the kinds of pressures that US NGOs have been able to utilize in relation to the World Bank.

In lieu of major reforms, some NGOs have successfully sought modification or rejection of specific ITTO-funded projects, while promoting others. Other NGOs, having grown increasingly frustrated with the obstacles to changing tropical forest policies through the ITTO, now advocate its abolition if it cannot be restructured to be more effective and accountable to the affected communities.

F. Lessons to be Learned

The results of the three case studies can be distilled into several lessons to guide NGO strategies in the future:

1. *Leverage*

The first lesson is that NGOs must find points of leverage—first, a target institution that has leverage on the problem, and second, leverage that NGOs can bring to bear on the institution.

In the case of the MDBs, while the institutions do not control all or even the greater part of development finance, they are among the most influential leaders in forming and applying development theory and strategy. As a result, the environmental and social policy changes they have adopted under NGO pressure, are beginning to have an impact on some of their borrowers. The leverage of the NGOs is through public pressure on the donor nations. Since there is no forceful constituency of support for the banks, they can threaten MDB funding with little opposition. Specifically, the campaign benefited from the facts that: given the importance of the Congressional power of the purse, the NGOs were advocating *less* funding, not more; alliances were formed with key Congressional committee chairmen who shared the NGOs' immediate objectives if not their goals; the NGOs were able to produce credible information on the social and environmental impacts of MDB loans through alliances with NGOs in borrowing countries.

In the case of ozone, the governments most involved in the Montreal Protocol negotiations were clearly the bodies with competence to eliminate the bulk of CFC use. NGO leverage was through traditional domestic lobbying pressure on each government. It was fairly obvious to all delegations, by the time of the 1990 London negotiations, that ozone depletion was a real crisis that must be dealt with. Most governments were convinced of the need for at least minimal action, and the argument was over speed and funding. The NGO role was thus to support the voices for stricter controls inside the governments—to prove that decisive action would be good politics.

Circumstances that aided the campaign were: the role of consumer goods in the ozone depletion problem; the timing of an NGO call for a complete CFC phase-out coinciding with the emergence of new scientific evidence for serious ozone depletion; the development of alternatives; and the alliances NGOs made with the governments of a few industrialized countries on a faster timetable for a CFC phase-out.

In relation to ITTO, there are two problems: it is not clear what control or influence ITTO can really have over most tropical deforestation; and NGOs have not found a lever to move the ITTO decision-makers. The ITTO lobbying effort illustrates that NGOs have been handcuffed by fundamental disadvantages: the organization is not dependent on financing from donor nations that are publicly accountable; and it is dominated by Japan, which has been firmly committed to the status quo on logging in tropical forests, and which still has a relatively weak domestic NGO community.

2. *Importance of NGO Alliances*

Flexible groupings of NGOs, both domestic and international, were crucial prerequisites for progress in each of these cases. No single organization, no matter how many members in how many countries it represented, could convince authorities that it spoke for a broad range of public opinion. An individual NGO may in fact not represent very many members; but when a large number of groups can reach agreement on an issue, that is something governments are much more likely to take into account. In the past, coalitions among US environmental groups had been put together occasionally on key issues, such as Alaska and clean water in the 1970s, and clean air (especially acid rain) in the 1980s. Although they were effective when they worked, they were difficult to organize and keep together, so they were not a favourite mode of action among most groups. International coalitions scarcely existed before the 1980s, except on such traditional wildlife issues as endangered species and saving marine mammals.

Thus the methods of international co-operation developed in the 1980s to deal with global problems were something new. For the groups working on the MDB campaign, it was a matter of necessity: the NGOs in the North had insufficient credibility, and the NGOs in the South had no access. Since it was clear that neither could succeed without the other, even ideologically opposed organizations were able to co-operate on specific issues.[60] Over time, communications about single projects led to the convening of large conferences of NGOs at the annual meetings of the World Bank and International Monetary Fund, and smaller numbers at the annual meetings of the other MDBs. This made possible the formation of broader alliances of mutual

[60] For example, the International Division of the National Wildlife Federation, one of the most conservative US NGOs in terms of membership, works closely with the National Council of Rubber Tappers, many of whose members are (or have been) avowed Marxists. The key to their co-operation was that these organizations were able to agree on what was wrong with World Bank and Brazilian government policy in Amazonia, and they concentrated on those issues. Moreover, the tappers' proposal for an alternative development strategy and their demand to be consulted in decisions that affected them were eminently sensible and fair. And in any event, by the end of the 1980s, the concepts of 'right' and 'left' were beginning to lose their old meanings.

assistance on domestic conflicts in many countries,[61] and co-operation on a wider range of global issues, from reform of the Tropical Forestry Action Plan[62] to the Climate Action Network, which is seeking (mostly Northern) government action to reduce emissions of greenhouse gases.

As the MDB campaign has evolved, the Third World NGOs are taking more and more responsibility for directing it. For the 1991 World Bank/IMF annual meeting in Bangkok, the Thai NGOs planned a completely different format and agenda for the NGO conference than the previous ones that took place in Washington and Berlin. Tougher issues were taken up, including inter-national debt and trade, and whether the MDBs should be abol-ished. Debate on such subjects can be acrimonious at times, with biases and historical resentments emerging. So far, agreements have been reached when they were needed, such as the NGOs' demands for improvements in the World Bank's forest policy.

In the ozone case, the co-operating NGOs were mostly from the industrialized nations, not the South. This makes sense, in so far as these countries are responsible for the bulk of the problem, although questions of technology transfer or compensation to the South for lost development opportunities may well have been seen in a different light with more participation of Southern NGOs. The ozone alliance was not formal, but NGOs traded information about their respective governments' positions and occasionally visited delegations in multinational groups. Many of the NGOs worked on their domestic governments, not the inter-national negotiations; but again, co-operation was the key to securing simultaneous NGO pressure in all the CFC producer countries.

ITTO is an institution for which a North–South NGO alliance is crucial, because of its unique structure in which the producer and consumer nations have equal voting power. Groups from both North and South are participating, but the campaign has not

[61] Many Southern groups now call upon NGOs from other countries for assist-ance in stopping disastrous development projects even if no international fund-ing is involved. Similarly, Northern groups are seeking help from Southern NGOs to pressure their governments and international institutions to take stronger measures to deal with loss of biological diversity, especially the destruc-tion of remaining primary forests within the industrialized countries.

[62] See Marcus Colchester and Larry Lohmann, *The Tropical Forestry Action Plan: What Progress?* (Penang, Malaysia: World Rainforest Movement, 1990).

yet borne fruit. This is mostly a function of the lack of leverage, but the lack of a common position among NGOs of different regions may also be proving detrimental.

The difficult issues for UNCED and beyond are the development ones, in which Northern states ought to confront their own wasteful patterns of consumption of natural resources and respond positively to demands for more equitable international economic relations (for example, debt relief and terms of trade).

The experience of the last ten years shows how a North–South coalition should work in their field:

- The NGOs in the North can build the political will to take action on certain issues, through education, specific campaigns, and the media.
- The information and proposals the Northern NGOs bring to their members can be shaped by Southern NGOs through the process of dialogue and working together over time. In the run-up to UNCED over the period 1990–2 there were over a dozen major NGO conferences where controversial development and environment questions could be hammered out.
- This North–South dialogue may prove to be an alternative forum to the intergovernmental committees, to produce proposals for eventual official negotiation.
- If there is no North–South accommodation, there is no chance for building a sustainable world.

However, the North–South NGO alliances are vulnerable. Most are relatively new with little history of personal trust. In the North the majority of the groups are basically environmental in orientation, whereas in the South many of the groups focus on social justice, or represent grass-roots movements or unions. This leads to divergent priorities and may cause fundamental splits in the future.

The Southern and Northern groups have radically different styles of dealing with governments, media, industry, etc. Many more Northern groups are pragmatists, and in the Southern view lack a set of basic principles. The language barriers still cause frustration and anger, especially when English is the language often forced upon a meeting if no money is available for translation. The ignorance of many Northerners (particularly US groups) about other countries, and the impacts of our government and industry upon their citizens, causes old resentments to rise; memories of past oppression come out when Northern groups dominate the speakers' platforms and information sources.

Everyone is equally frustrated at the lack of solid, detailed alternatives to current economic models that all could support. Even the best of the alternatives, the extractive reserves, are still a stopgap measure. They need to be implemented in practice to demonstrate that they could support future populations in their aspirations for education and a better quality of life.

There are also a series of real issue conflicts among NGOs, although the split is not clearly along North–South lines. Can trade liberalization be modified or should it be opposed? Can, or should, structural adjustment be turned into 'green conditionality'? Should the MDBs be abolished or can they be reformed? Should debts be cancelled on moral grounds, or should we institute debt-for-nature swaps? What do we do about national parks and biological reserves that are the homelands of indigenous peoples?

These issues are enough to split any coalition apart, much less the new coalitions with communication problems. But these are among the fundamental questions facing the world in the next decade. The NGO alliances are at risk just when they are most needed.

3. *Complementarity of NGOs*

The complementary roles played by different types of NGOs can add more to a campaign than mere numbers of participating groups. For example, in the MDB campaign early in the 1980s NGOs took widely different approaches to dealing with the World Bank. The World Wildlife Fund US tried to ameliorate the expected impacts of the Polonoroeste project by suggesting tough environmental control measures for inclusion as loan conditions. But neither the Bank nor the Brazilian government implemented them. In 1986, when the first wave of Congressional hearings had run their course (with testimony from EDF, NWF, NRDC, FOE/EPI, and experts from various countries) the Rainforest Action Network made headlines around the world by scaling down from the roof of a building across the street from the Bank and hanging a giant banner reading 'WORLD BANK DESTROYS TROPICAL RAINFOREST'. While none of these groups could have carried out one of the other actions, each type of activity was needed.

The ozone case was similar. The NRDC took the pivotal role of providing information and analysis and a legal approach to the negotiations. Friends of the Earth organized boycotts and media campaigns. Neither would have sufficed alone.

A fairly low-key lobbying approach has so far characterized the NGO work on ITTO. It is increasingly clear that to be effective it should be complemented with something more visible.

4. *Role of the media*

Obviously, press and electronic coverage of environmental issues is one of the best ways of achieving the public awareness and pressure that impel governments and industry to take needed action. But the MDB campaign illustrates that there can be too much of a good thing.

Only a few serious articles on the banks and particularly Polonoroeste were published in the US press before 1988; in addition, *The Decade of Destruction* was broadcast in Europe and Japan, and a piece appeared on '60 Minutes'. These put pressure on the World Bank, and by virtue of having come out in the North, they received attention in Brazil. But after the assassination of Chico Mendes in December 1988, press and TV coverage of Brazilian rainforest destruction became almost hysterical. The year 1988 saw heat waves and drought throughout the United States; new evidence of ozone layer depletion emerged; the giant forest fire in Yellowstone National Park raged for weeks; and controversial satellite data revealed how much of Brazil's Amazon forest had already been destroyed. The crescendo of criticism focused on Brazil as the environmental villain at the end of that year of ecological disasters world-wide. This was probably because of the symbolic importance of Chico Mendes, that modest, quiet coalition builder, who became a martyr. Although much of the criticism was deserved, Brazil was probably no worse than Indonesia, Malaysia, the Philippines, Ecuador, or the United States, which still subsidizes the destruction of the remnants of its primary forests in the North-West.

The avalanche came when the NGOs already had the attention of the MDBs, so it was of little use at that phase of the campaign. In fact it alienated World Bank staff who were implementing some of the changes the NGOs had sought. In Brazil the effect was mixed. The federal and state governments took some needed actions in response to international pressure, so in that sense it was effective. But the feeling of being unfairly singled out caused resentment that will last for years. There is reason to fear that many of the responsive government actions have been just for show. But it will be up to the greatly strengthened NGO movement in Brazil to keep up the domestic pressure for progress.[63]

Conclusion: The Shifting Political Context of Global Environmental Issues

The future of global environmental politics—and the potential for NGOs to influence international environmental policy—will be determined in part by the nature of the issues and the international forums considering them, as illustrated by the cases examined above. But it will also be constrained by larger factors, such as fiscal and budgetary conditions in major donor states and the impact of international security politics. The major global issues now under negotiation (climate change, world forest management, technology transfer) all involve the expenditure of significant financial resources by the industrialized countries, especially the United States, Japan, and Germany. NGO influence on those issues will turn on the elaboration of acceptable funding mechanisms, and the strength of the political will in major donor states.

[63] See further Andrew Hurrell's chapter in this volume.

13

Japan's Global Environmental Policies

Hanns W. Maull

JAPAN'S international environmental reputation is abysmal: it is widely seen as one of the worst offenders against the protection of nature and the global environment. *Time* and *Newsweek* in 1989 ran major stories about 'Putting the Heat on Japan', and other international media soon joined the chorus of criticism.[1] The list of accusations is long and familiar. Whaling, driftnet-fishing, smuggling of endangered species, and wholesale destruction of tropical rainforests are but the most prominent items. As a result Japan has been singled out by transnational groups such as Greenpeace and the World Wildlife Fund as a prime target. On one such occasion during the IMF/World Bank meeting in Berlin in 1988, Japanese bureaucrats and bankers were exposed to a barrage of demonstrations and heckling. Clearly, Japan was beginning to have a major international image problem.

At the same time, this bad reputation appears somewhat surprising in light of Japan's domestic environmental policy record. There Japan can point to a whole range of environmental laws and practices which are among the most advanced in the world. Air pollution in particular has been very effectively reduced, and environmental pollution control has become a major and booming business, attracting a great deal of attention from Japanese industry. Thus the *Mainichi Daily News* reported on

The author would like to gratefully acknowledge the generous financial support from the Japan Foundation which made possible field research in Japan in September and October 1990, and the invaluable assistance provided by staff members of the National Institute of Research Advancement and the Japan Centre of International Exchange, Tokyo.
[1] Thus the title of the *Time* story (*Time*, 10 July 1989). The cover included the headline: 'Japan—Environmental Predator?'. *Newsweek* referred to Japan as an 'Eco-outlaw' (quoted in Jonathan Hollimand, 'Environmentalism with a Global Scope', *Japan Quarterly* (July–Sept. 1990), 284–90).

30 October 1990 that Mitsubishi Heavy Industries, Ltd.—the leading Japanese producer of pollution control equipment—expected the annual turnover of its environmental business to breach the 100 billion Yen barrier in 1990, three years earlier than predicted. Although this represented only 3.6 per cent of its total business, growth rates in this sector have been very high and have attracted fierce competition from other manufacturers.

There thus seems to be a striking discrepancy between Japan's domestic environmental policy achievements and its international reputation. This gap may well partly reflect psychological elements in foreign perceptions such as an aversion to Japan's past, its post-war economic successes, and its lack of international empathy. Overall, however, Japan's image problem has very real foundations, and reflects the substantial differences that exist between domestic and international environmental policies in Japan. This chapter seeks, first, to explain these differences and, second, to argue that they are likely to narrow as international environmental policies follow the same sequence of phases as Japan's domestic environmental policies: from ignorance to symbolic steps and then to substantive but essentially technocratic efforts to remedy environmental problems.

A. Environmental Policies in Japan: The Setting

Japan's environmental policy process has reflected a number of peculiarities. In the first place, public awareness of, and interest in, environmental issues, is low in Japan when compared with other developed countries, and international environmental issues in particular attract very little public attention. According to a survey by the United Nations Environment Programme of public and élite opinion in fourteen countries, Japan ranked last in terms of environmental awareness.[2] This has been confirmed by other opinion polls. A comparison of the level of concern about such global environmental issues as the extinction of animal and plant species, deforestation, and climatic change in

[2] UNEP, *What the Countries Think: National Highlights, Public and Leadership Attitudes to the Environment in 14 Countries* (Nairobi: UNEP, 1989).

Japan and the EC countries shows persistently lower figures for the former.[3]

Second, although grass-roots environmental organizations have sometimes been quite influential at the local level, they have traditionally been comparatively weak and—with a few notable exceptions—ineffective at the national level.[4] In addition, transnational environmental organizations have encountered difficult problems in trying to establish a presence in Japan. Thus international environmental issues have had a particularly weak domestic lobby at the grass-roots.[5] The top ten national environmental organizations in the US have a combined membership of about 5.2 million people and a combined annual budget of $200 million. In 1989 Friends of the Earth had about 250,000 members in the UK alone and an annual income of £2.2 million—about the same number of members and a higher level of funding than the total of all Japanese environmental organizations (broadly defined).

Third, there is no real tradition for independent charity or independent public policy research in Japan. This contributes significantly to the weakness of grass-roots organizations and effectively entrusts the protection of the environment to government and business. From the inception of its modernization under the emperor Meiji in the late nineteenth century, government has taken the lead in shaping economic—and thus, by extension, environmental—policies, in close co-operation with business. The result has been a persistent priority for economic growth, with other concerns and social objectives in a subordinate position. While the Japanese experience with environmental policies clearly shows that effective pollution control need not be detrimental to economic performance—and indeed, may stimulate economic growth—specific conflicts of interest are bound to arise between the objectives of economic growth and environ-

[3] See Helmut Weidner, 'Japanese Environmental Policies in an International Perspective: Lessons for a Preventive Approach', in Shigeto Tsuru and Helmut Weidner (eds.), *Environmental Policy in Japan* (Berlin: Edition Sigma, 1989), 479–552.

[4] See Shigeto Tsuru, 'History of Pollution Control Policy', in Tsuru and Weidner (eds.), *Environmental Policy in Japan*, 15–42; and Jun Ui, 'Anti-Pollution Movements and Other Grassroot Organisations', in ibid. 109–22.

[5] Hollimand ('Environmentalism') provides comparative data on environmental movements in Japan, the USA and the UK, and details the specific problems faced by such organizations in Japan.

mental protection, and between industries and government departments.[6]

Fourth, bureaucratic rivalries and conflicts between various ministries and government agencies and their respective business clienteles have been endemic in Japan. Thus responsibility for environmental policy rests with at least three major government agencies—the Environment Agency, the Ministry of Construction, and the Ministry of International Trade and Industry (MITI). The Environment Agency bears primary responsibility for environmental policies but in fact has accounted for only a few per cent of annual budget outlays on environmental protection. The Agency is bureaucratically weak. While its head holds a cabinet position, the organization itself is designated as an 'Agency' rather than a 'Ministry' and, technically, is a special department of the Prime Minister's Office. Most of its staff are seconded for relatively short periods from other ministries and thus carry conflicting loyalties.

Fifth, environmental policies in Japan have basically reflected the need to accommodate the strong pressures that have emerged when groups outside government (mostly local grass-root movements organized by victims of pollution) have been able to mobilize politically. Government policies have therefore been essentially reactive, pragmatic, and technocratic. Problems have been dealt with as they arose politically, without any effort to define environmental policy philosophies and concepts in a systematic way. Policymakers have been imbued with a profound confidence in the ability of technology to produce adequate responses to any given challenge. Lastly, Japan, by virtue of its geographic position, shape, and climatic conditions, has until now by and large been naturally sheltered from cross-border environmental problems (although this is beginning to change). There has been a lag in the internationalization of Japan in this regard, particularly if we compare its position with that of the European countries, which have long been exposed to transnational environmental issues. In other words the division between national and international environmental policies has until now been considerably more clear-cut in Japan than in Western Europe.

[6] On the relationship of pollution control to economic performance see Helmut Weidner, Eckhard Rehbinder, and Rolf-Ulrich Sprenger, 'Die Umweltpolitik in Japan: Ein Modell für die EG?', IFO-Schnelldienst, 16–17 (1990), 40 ff.

Against these essentially negative trends, which have tended to impede or at least constrain Japan's environmental policies, there are three factors which have worked toward more effective environmental policies. First, Japan's social cohesion, pragmatism, and adaptability enable it to move very rapidly and thoroughly once problems have been recognized and responses agreed. The speed of social learning in Japanese society is remarkable. Thus, within a few years in the late 1960s and early 1970s, domestic environmental policies moved from ignorance or, at best, symbolic steps, to a comprehensive set of environmental laws which in some areas continue to set world-wide standards of excellence. It is precisely the very effectiveness of this response to growing environmental pressures inside Japan which contributes to the present, relatively low level of public concern about environmental issues. Domestically, then, there has been very significant progress over the last two decades, demonstrating that Japan is able to respond effectively to environmental issues once the necessary will coalesces.

Second, the superior adaptability of Japanese industry and its impressive technological base give it considerable flexibility to develop alternatives to environmentally detrimental forms of economic activities. To some extent environmental improvements and benefits have emerged as the by-product of industrial restructuring. As energy- and raw-material-intensive industries have given way to advanced high-technology industries with a high information content, the adverse ecological impact of industrial activity on Japan has changed and, at least to some degree, lessened. Some of the traditional polluting industries were, of course, only relocated abroad in the process of internationalization of Japanese corporate activities, and new types of industrial activities have produced new environmental burdens within Japan itself. Nevertheless, the flexibility and adaptability of Japanese corporations to changing circumstances and their rapidly expanding technological base must be seen as major assets for Japan.

Third, Japan's international environmental policies will be pushed forward by the internationalization of the Japanese economy and its enterprises. Many major Japanese companies are in the process of 'globalizing' their activities along the lines of their big model, IBM. Japan's economic weight has become such that its activities reverberate around the globe and profoundly affect the lives of people in distant countries. But the internationalization of the Japanese economy and corporations is a two-way process. It will produce pressures for adjustment that feed back into Japan itself, forcing Japanese companies, Japanese society, and ultimately Japanese politics to change (probably in that order).

B. Japan, the Eco-Predator

Japan's contribution to international environmental degradation and destruction basically comprises two different dimensions: the impact of the Japanese economy itself on the world environment, and the 'ecological shadow' of its global economic activities, which include a number of environmentally detrimental or at least dubious practices. Japan's relatively good performance with regard to the first category explains the genuine sense of irritation with which many Japanese react to foreign criticism of Japan's environmental policies. In comparison with other countries, Japan can point to very substantial achievements related to its domestic environmental policies. The core of the problems with Japan as an environmental predator, however, lies in the second category—Japan's 'shadow ecology' of environmental destruction and degradation.[7] Let us look at those two dimensions of the problem in turn.

1. *Japan's direct impact on the global environment*

The first dimension concerns Japan's contribution to global environmental destruction and degradation, such as the depletion of the ozone layer, global warming, acid rain, and the destruction of the world rainforests. Japan's domestic economy now represents around 10 per cent of gross world product, and thus inevitably has a major impact on the global environment.

(i) *Global warming.* Over the last 100 years, the average tem-

---

[7] It may be noted in passing that this point nicely illustrates the growing deficiencies of the traditional nation-state-centred concepts of international relations. Focusing solely on Japan's national economy produces a misleading impression of Japan's real contribution to the global environmental problems.

perature of the atmosphere has risen by about 0.4–0.7 °C. Assuming a continuation of present trends in emissions, temperatures could rise by anything between 2.0 °C and 5.8 °C over the next hundred years, with 3.0–3.3 °C as the best estimate. This would imply a rise in sea levels of about 50–60 cm, and could cause major changes in the world climate and hence in social and economic conditions.[8] The marked energy efficiency of the Japanese economy and its strict emission regulations help Japan to limit its contribution to the problems of global warming quite effectively. Thus, in terms of emission of CO_2 per unit of GDP, Japan shows the best performance of any country, while its CO_2 emission per capita (2 tonnes in 1987) compares favourably with that of the UK (2.8 t.) or the USA (5.078 t.)—but not with that of France or Italy (1.7 t. and 1.84 t., respectively). Given the size of its economy, Japan nevertheless comes fourth in the list of major CO_2 polluters (with 4.7 per cent) after the USA, the USSR, and China (which, however, with 23.7 per cent, 18.6 per cent, and 10.1 per cent respectively represent an altogether different league of polluters).[9] Overall, in relation to the size of its economy, Japan can point to a very impressive record of lowering its emissions of CO_2 over the last two decades. While this was largely the by-product of efforts at enhancing energy efficiency through industrial modernization and restructuring, the positive contribution to the global environment has been real. It is therefore understandable that Japan is irritated by policy proposals which do not reflect Japan's superior efforts in the past.

(ii) *Acid rain.*   Japan's performance with regard to emissions of sulphur and nitric oxides (SOx and NOx), which are major causes of acid rain (as well as—in the case of N_2O—global warming), also compares very favourably with that of other industrialized countries. Japanese SOx emissions represent about 1.1 per cent of the world total, NOx emissions about 2.1 per cent. In terms of SOx

---

[8] See the report of UN Intergovernmental Panel on Climate Change, as reported in the *Financial Times*, 24 May 1990, and the *International Herald Tribune*, 26 May 1990. For a different (higher) estimate by Japanese experts see *Asahi Evening News*, 7 Feb. 1990. A good description of our knowledge—and its uncertainties—can be found in Stephen H. Schneider, 'The Changing Climate', *Scientific American* (Sept. 1989), 70–9. For an assessment of possible implications see Jim Mac-Neill, Pieter Winsemius, Taizo Yakushiji, *Beyond Interdependence: The Meshing of the World's Economy and the Earth's Ecology* (Oxford: Oxford UP, 1991), 10 ff.

[9] Environment Agency, 'Japanese Performance of Energy Conservation and Air Pollution Control' (Tokyo, Aug. 1990).

this means that Japan's contribution to atmospheric pollution comes to about one-twentieth of that of the USA, and to little more than one-fourth of that of the UK, while for the N_2O emissions, the figure for Japan corresponds to about half of the quantities emitted by Western Germany. Japan scores the lowest figures among all major industrialized countries with regard to absolute quantities, as well as to pollution per unit of GDP and per capita. [10]

(iii) *Depletion of the stratospheric ozone layer.*   Human releases of chlorofluorocarbons (CFCs) and other gases are consuming the stratospheric ozone layer, which protects the surface of the planet from harmful ultraviolet radiation. According to UNEP estimates, every 1 per cent reduction of ozone in the stratosphere results in a 4 to 6 per cent increase in skin cancer. Between 1919 and 1986, the average global concentration of ozone in the stratosphere fell by 2 per cent, with higher values for the major industrialized regions in the northern hemisphere. Those changes not only endanger human health, but also crops and the oceanic life-support systems since phytoplanktons are very sensitive to ultraviolet rays. CFCs, which are used as refrigerants, aerosol sprays, foams, and detergents, reside for very long periods (60–100 years) in the atmosphere and slowly drift upwards to the higher strata, where they are broken up by ultraviolet rays. The components then catalyse the formation of oxygen from ozone. In 1986 Japan accounted for about 170,000 tons of annual consumption. About 133,000 tons was used by industry. By 1988 consumption had risen to about 159,000 tons. [11] Seventy-six per cent of demand was accounted for by the use of CFCs in cleaning electronic components and in the production of foam and refrigerants. Japan's comparative environmental performance with regard to CFCs until now has been undistinguished. In 1986, it consumed 10 per cent of the world total, which corresponded closely to its share of overall world economic activity.

Taken together, Japan's contributions to global environmental degradation are at the same time substantial and relatively small. They have become substantial simply as a result of Japan's large

[10] OECD, *Environmental Data 1989* (Paris: OECD, 1989). The comparisons are even slightly biased against Japan due to the fact that Japanese figures are for 1983 while those of the other countries are for 1986 or 1987.
[11] Environment Agency, *Quality of the Environment in Japan 1988* (Tokyo, 1990); *Financial Times*, 16 Mar. 1990 (Survey: Industry and the Environment, p. vii).

and rapidly growing share of world economic activity. Japan's efforts to reduce the impact of its domestic economy on the global environment do therefore matter. At the same time, Japan's record as a polluter of the world environment compares—with the exception of CFC use—quite favourably with that of the other major economies. Japan's bad reputation on that score appears to be undeserved.

2. Japan's ecological shadow

The second major category of Japan's contribution to global environmental degradation concerns what has been aptly called the 'shadow ecology' of Japan's global economic activities.[12] Japan exports pollution—directly through such activities as dumping waste, but more importantly indirectly through its global trading and direct investments activities. To quote MacNeill et al.:

> Today . . . the major urban/industrial centers of the world are locked into complex international networks for trade in goods and services of all kinds . . . these nations . . . draw upon the ecological capital of all other nations to provide food for their populations, energy and materials for their economies, and even land, air, and water to assimilate their waste by-products. This ecological capital, which may be found thousands of miles from the regions in which it is used, forms the 'shadow ecology' of any economy. The oceans, the atmosphere (climate), and other 'commons' also form part of this 'shadow ecology'. In essence, the ecological shadow of a country is the environmental resources it draws from other countries and the global commons. . . . Third World economies seek to be drawn into these trading networks.[13]

To measure Japan's 'shadow ecology' exactly is obviously difficult, if not impossible. Its importance can be gauged, however, by reference to Japan's share of world imports of primary commodities and its explosively growing foreign direct investments. In 1986, Japan imported some 13 per cent of world trade in the four major cereals, corn, wheat, barley, and soybeans—a quantity which needed about four times the agricultural area of Japan's total cultivable land.[14] And in 1987 Japan accounted for about 20 per cent of OECD energy (and 37 per cent of OECD coal) imports, 39 per cent of total OECD iron ore imports, and 29 per

[12] MacNeill et al., Beyond Interdependence, 58 ff.   [13] Ibid. 58–9.
[14] Environment Agency, Quality of the Environment in Japan 1988, 50.

cent of OECD nonferrous metal imports.[15] Japan's total foreign direct investment over the period 1951 to 1988 came to $186 billion—of which $47 billion was invested in the single year 1988! The global reach of Japan's corporations and economic activities thus impinges in a myriad of ways and places on the global environment. As the Japanese economy continues along the trajectory of internationalization on which it now seems firmly set, the importance of Japan's shadow ecology will also expand. The size of this shadow will be determined by the number of people it envelops, their consumption or level of economic activity, and the efficiency with which this activity uses material resources and energy. Of these, the third area may be politically the most important: the degree to which Japan will—or will not—develop and transfer technologies to improve the resource efficiency of economic activities could have critical importance for the future sustainability of growth.

Perhaps the most conspicuous example of Japan's shadow ecology has been the Japanese role in destroying tropical forests in South-East Asia. Tropical rain-forests today disappear at a rate conservatively estimated at 20 million hectares per year—an area roughly the size of the United Kingdom. Japan's total consumption of lumber is the third largest in the world, and that of plywood the second largest. In terms of per capita consumption, Japan comes third, after the US and Canada, with regard to plywood, and tenth with regard to lumber consumption. Its self-sufficiency in timber has declined steeply, from about 90 per cent in 1970 to less than 30 per cent in 1988, making Japan the largest importer of tropical broadleaf logs (49.6 per cent of world imports) and tropical broadleaf sawn wood (9 per cent—with Singapore accounting for 19.0 per cent, much of which presumably was re-exported to Japan).[16] Worldwide annual wood production from tropical forests amounts to about 1,820 million cubic metres annually, of which nearly 80 per cent is consumed locally for firewood. Wood exports account for only about 4 per cent of total wood production, and exports to Japan—whose overall share of world imports corresponds to 28 per cent—for only 1 per cent. However, the causes of deforestation vary from

---

[15] *Japan 1990, A Statistical Comparison* (Tokyo: Keizai Koho Center, 1990).
[16] Environment Agency, *Quality of the Environment in Japan 1990, Executive Summary* (Tokyo: Environment Agency, 1990), 34 ff.

region to region. In the case of the island nations of South-East Asia, logging for commercial export represents the most important element in the rapid destruction of tropical rain-forests. Most of Japan's imports of tropical wood (which, however, account for less than half of total wood imports) are used to make concrete forms and materials.[17] These are uses for which, by and large, substitutes could easily be found.

Japan's heavy reliance on timber from tropical regions basically reflects short-term price advantages. It does not take into consideration the massive 'externalities' associated with the wholesale slashing of tropical forests and represents a stark example of putting narrow and short-term national interests first. The shift from domestic supplies of wood to tropical timber allows Japan to husband (expensive) domestic forests to the detriment of forests abroad, which are destroyed by cheap but highly destructive methods of exploitation.

While the destruction of tropical forests is the most dramatic, it is certainly not the only activity which contributes to Japan's bad international environmental image. Japan's reluctance to join international efforts to protect endangered species (notably, but not only, whales), environmentally destructive practices of exploiting natural resources such as driftnet-fishing, and its environmentally dubious official development assistance all illustrate the problem of Japan's ecological shadow. Yet those well-known and heavily criticized practices are only the tip of the iceberg represented by the impact of Japan's global economic activities on the world environment.

To illustrate the ramifications of this shadow, let us look briefly at Japan's official development assistance from an environmental perspective. Japan's ODA has recently become the world's largest and can be expected to continue its rapid growth. But the distinction between government assistance and commercial activities of Japanese corporations has in the past been consistently blurred. ODA has thus often contributed to environmentally damaging projects of resource extraction and the

[17] Keidanren, 'Basic Views of the Global Environment Problem: A Report by the Environment Subcommittee submitted to the Committee on Environment and Safety' (Apr. 1990), 6; Environment Agency, *Quality of the Environment in Japan 1988*, 51 ff.

relocation of polluting industries. A careful analysis of Japanese ODA practices has concluded:

It is becoming increasingly apparent that Japan's foreign economic co-operation programmes not only cause the same problems as those of other aid agencies, but that the particular emphases of Japan's system lie in projects that are socially and environmentally disruptive.[18]

One such example of the catastrophic neglect of environmental considerations was the Japan International Co-operation Agency's development survey for the Greater Carajás Development Programme in Brazil, which covered 1.1 million km²—three times the area of Japan, half of it covered with tropical rain forest. JICA proposed a $62 billion integrated natural resource development with export processing activities, including expansion of farmland. Forrest concludes his analysis of this project as follows:

If a significant number of the pig iron plants will be built, forest surrounding the Carajás region will be destroyed in less than 20 years. Interestingly, this will threaten the economic viability of the pig iron facilities, because charcoal is expensive to haul over long distances. . . . Catastrophic environmental destruction is thus occurring in the Carajás region in Brazil, having been largely planned in offices in Tokyo by a Japanese consulting company, implemented by a Japanese development agency, specializing in technical expertise, and funded in large part by Japanese banks. . . . Because the area affected is larger than Japan, and with much greater biological diversity and importance for the global environment and regional climate, the unsustainable development encouraged by Japan's advice will be likely to result in greater ecological destruction than any number of projects within Japan ever could.[19]

C. Moving Towards Symbolic Action—and Beyond?

It has been argued that Japan's international environmental policies have evolved along the lines of domestic environmental policies, which, in response to political pressures reflecting accu-

[18] Richard A. Forrest, *Japanese Economic Assistance and the Environment: The Need for Reform* (Washington, DC: National Wildlife Federation, Nov. 1989). For a general analysis of Japan's ODA, see Bernhard May, *Japans neue Entwicklungspolitik* (Munich and Vienna: Oldenbourg, 1989), and Robert M. Orr, *The Emergence of Japan's Foreign Aid Power* (New York: Columbia UP, 1990).

[19] Forrest, *Japanese Economic Assistance*, 35.

mulating problems, have moved from abstention to symbolic
actions and then toward technocratic efforts to tackle the problems. With a time lag of about twenty years, political pressures
have been building up on the Japanese government over global
environmental issues in the second half of the 1980s. These
pressures have not primarily come from domestic constituencies.
As we have seen, the environmental lobby in Japan is comparatively weak and parochial in its outlook. Rather, they have come
from abroad, from three directions: transnational environmental
groups and organizations such as Greenpeace and Friends of the
Earth; Japan's transnational corporations, which have had to
confront environmentalist pressures abroad and which have
begun to suffer from Japan's bad image as an environmental
predator; and, perhaps most important, peer pressure from other
governments.

(i) *Transnational environmental groups* have for some time
targeted Japan's bad environmental practices. The fierce protests
against Japan's lack of concern for the global environment at the
1988 World Bank/IMF meeting in Berlin visibly shook some of the
government representatives and contributed to a change of attitude within the Japanese government. More recently transnational environmental groups have been trying to establish
themselves in Japan and to link up with domestic environmental
groups. On one occasion they were successful in halting
Japanese funding for a World Bank-sponsored development project in India, the Narmada Dam project. However, such an effort
to foster transnational environmental co-operation at the grass-
roots level between Japan and other countries has been exceptional.

(ii) *Business attitudes* towards environmental issues are
changing rapidly in response to their exposure to environmental
concerns abroad. A study by the Dentsu Institute for Human
Studies—a think tank set up by Japan's largest advertising corporation—of the attitudes of 700 chief executives found that environmental concerns were ranked as the fifth highest priority
and were expected to move up the list of priorities in the future.
In the case of large companies, executives expected environmental concerns to vie for first place with Research and Development.[20] Large Japanese companies have begun to undertake

[20] *The Economist*, 25 Aug. 1990.

public relations efforts to improve their environmental image. For example, Toyota recently ran a major advertising series featuring essays by prominent Japanese scientists on environmental issues, and two foundations established by Japanese companies (Toyota and Hitachi) in the US have made their first (tentative) moves into environmental grant making.[21] More importantly, Japanese industry has moved quickly and energetically in specific areas such as the substitution of CFCs. Nissan, for example, was the first automobile company to announce its decision to completely abolish the use of CFCs by 1993. Others then followed.

The Keidanren (the Japanese employers' federation) has also begun to move on global environmental issues. The Committee on Energy and Safety (headed by Nissan Motor Company President Kume) initiated a study of global environmental issues in July 1989 by a working group chaired by Nissan Managing Director Miura. This working group presented its findings and recommendations in April 1990. These recommendations went considerably further than Keidanren guidelines originally issued in 1973 and revised in 1987, which only requested companies to preserve the living and natural environment of the host countries. The new principles call for, among other things, making environmental protection a priority at overseas sites, treating host country standards as the minimum required (and using Japanese standards in the management of harmful substances), making a full environmental assessment before starting overseas business operations, consulting and co-operating with all concerned local parties, and establishing environmental management systems. The report also demanded stronger action by the Japanese government through steps to improve the administrative apparatus in global environmental decision-making as well as substantive policy efforts in a number of identified areas (such as support for the development and transfer of environmental technologies to developing countries).[22]

(iii) *Other governments.* The most important pressures, however, have probably come from other governments, particularly those of the major industrialized countries. Global environ-

---

[21] Theodore M. Smith, 'Japan, The Environment and Developing Countries', MS, 1989.
[22] See Keidanren, 'Basic Views of the Global Environmental Problem'.

mental issues have been on the agenda of all Economic Summits since 1981, and played a major role at the Summit of the Arche in Paris in 1989. This reportedly convinced the then Japanese Prime Minister Takeshita to make global environmental issues a major policy concern during his period in office. There have also been a number of international conferences (both governmental and non-governmental) on global environmental issues in recent years. The United States has repeatedly pushed Japan to make concessions during such meetings, and Japan has also been pressured by the positive shift that has occurred in recent years in European Community attitudes towards global environmental issues.[23]

Japan's reaction to these international pressures has been a predictable mixture of symbolic and substantive steps, with a hopeful trend towards the latter. The real importance of measures and programmes announced is not always easy to establish, and steps taken originally to defuse or pre-empt pressure without substantive changes may develop their own dynamic. The distinction between symbolic and effective technocratic action may therefore at times be blurred. Nevertheless, there have been a number of environmental programmes whose substantive contribution towards reducing global environmental damage has been marginal at best. Examples include the financial support provided for international environmental efforts such as the World Commission on Environment and Development (the Brundtland Commission), the hosting and support of the International Tropical Timber Organization (ITTO), and the organization of a major international conference in Tokyo in September 1989 in co-operation with UNEP. Environmentalist NGOs were not invited to this latter meeting, which, according to one press report, was 'marked by vagueness'.[24] A further example concerns the numerous announcements of bureaucratic and organizational changes, national action programmes, and declarations. These have included a programme worked out by the Japanese Council of Ministers for Global Environment, a cabinet committee set up in 1989 and chaired by the Director-

---

[23] Richard Elliot Benedick, 'Ozone Diplomacy', *Issues in Science and Technology* (Fall 1989), 43–50; *RAMSES 91, Rapport annuel mondial sur les systèmes économiques et les stratégies* (Paris: Dunod, 1990), 353 ff; and Benedick, *Ozone Diplomacy* (Cambridge, Mass.: Harvard UP, 1991).

[24] *The Daily Yomiuri*, 15 Sept. 1989.

General of the Environment Agency, a bureaucratically weak department;[25] the proposal for a 'Green Revolution' in Africa submitted to the Economic Summit in 1985; and the announcement of a 300 billion Yen three-year ODA programme for environmental conservation, whose definition of 'environmental' left much to be desired and which has been troubled from the start by the organizational and structural weaknesses of Japan's ODA. An intriguing example of a possibly irrelevant but potentially significant government programme is 'Earth 21', which outlines a 100-year global action programme to reverse the damages to the global climate caused by 200 years of industrialization and to lay the foundations for sustainable development.[26]

In some areas, however, Japan has responded to international pressures by implementing effective technocratic measures to contain environmental damage. Those areas include the legislation passed in 1987 to curtail the import of endangered species banned by the 1973 Convention on International Trade in Endangered Species (CITES), which Japan joined in 1980. The new legislation allows effective implementation of the ban, although it should be noted that Japan has registered 11 reservations to the Convention, one of the largest numbers of any country. Japan has also moved to ban the import of ivory to help conserve the African elephant population, and announced in 1990 that it would end driftnet-fishing in the South Pacific. Further examples include the efforts to phase out CFCs and to stabilize CO_2 emissions by the year 2000. These moves to eliminate the production and use of CFCs to protect the ozone layer reflect the interaction between commercial and political pressures: Japanese industry was put under pressure by American CFC producers, who began to develop substitutes, while at the same time the Japanese government was confronted with policy shifts and pressures from the US and some of the European countries. During the negotiations for the Montreal Protocol, Japan showed consider-

[25] The establishment of this committee in itself does not suggest real movement. Indeed it only institutionalizes bureaucratic conflicts between ministries. The fact that the EA was put in charge of the committee underlines this since the Agency has limited bureaucratic clout and depends on decisive leadership being exercised by the Prime Minister or senior LDP politicians.

[26] A short description of this programme can be found in Japanische Botschaft, *Neues aus Japan*, 329 (July/Aug. 1990), 12 ff.

able reluctance to move and only fell into line under pressure. By the time of the London agreement of June 1990, which widened the scope of the Montreal Protocol and accelerated the timetable of abolishing the CFCs, Japan had moved from the position of laggard into the mainstream, and had agreed to co-finance conversion from CFC use in developing countries. Lastly, measures to combat global warming were actively promoted by the Action Programme to Prevent Global Warming, adopted by the Japanese government in October 1990. In this programme, the Japanese government committed itself to stabilizing Japanese per capita emissions of CO_2 at the 1990 level. Again, Japan moved during the course of a few months from the position of laggard into the mainstream. Although at the 1990 Economic Summit meeting in Houston, Texas, Japan—together with the USA and the UK—held out against firm commitments to limit CO_2 emissions, the October 1990 Action Programme represents a major step forward. This is all the more remarkable in the light of, first, Japan's good record on CO_2 emissions; second, the recalcitrant attitude of the US government (whose lead Japan often tends to follow); and third, the traditional strengths of the contestants in the fierce bureaucratic infighting in Tokyo about this decision. The split between the Environment Agency (which favoured a freeze at 1990 emission levels) and the powerful Ministry of International Trade and Industry (MITI), which felt Japan's economy needed some further leeway in CO_2 emissions before they could be frozen, was widely aired in the Western press.[27] The EA eventually won—with the help of pressure from abroad.[28]

Conclusions

Japan's global environmental policies have thus been changing. There has been a clear trend away from neglect, towards symbolic expressions of concern and even action to halt environmental degradation. As perhaps best typified by the grandiose project 'Earth 21' to halt global warming, the Japanese government has followed its inclination to seek technological

[27] See *Financial Times*, 29 May 1990; *Far Eastern Economic Review*, 25 Oct. 1990.
[28] See *Asia Technology*, Dec. 1990, p. 33.

breakthroughs as a way to remove environmental constraints on economic development, an inclination well established in Japanese domestic environmental policies. Although this approach has its limitations, it has produced impressive results in some areas and can be expected to do so again as Japanese industry rapidly moves its substantial resources towards the development of less environmentally damaging products and production processes.

Pressures on Japan to move in this direction can only intensify in the future, for three major reasons. First, the traditional insulation of Japan from international environmental problems such as acid rain has already been broken and will become more and more meaningless in the future. For example, the environmental impact on Japan of a China heavily industrializing itself with traditional disregard for environmental side-effects could well be disastrous. Second, the globalization of the Japanese economy, and more particularly of Japanese corporations, will continue. This will lead to a proliferation of pressures on Japanese companies and on Japanese society to show consideration for the global environment. The corporate sector is already beginning to show itself as an effective transmission belt of global environmental concerns into Japanese politics, and this role is likely to be accentuated in the future. And third, peer pressure from other industrialized countries is likely to intensify as Japan continues to achieve better economic performances than its rivals and partners in the Group of Seven.

The world can therefore expect more Japanese money and technological resources flowing into efforts to cope with environmental degradation. But for the time being the process will be driven by external pressures, rather than by genuine domestic concern or domestic pressure. The Japanese environmental movement has a long way to go. This poses problems of political management, because external pressures could produce a domestic backlash which could endanger support for the right policies. The government and industry will thus have to foster domestic awareness and support for costly and sometimes painful adjustments.

There will also have to be a learning process of 'internationalizing' Japan's environmental policy debate at home. Japan will have to respond to new global constraints by adjusting its own society and economy. But there will also have to be a second thrust in efforts to internationalize Japan's environmental policies focused on measures to halt and reverse environmental degradation that takes place within Japan's shadow ecology. This means, above all, the development and the effective transfer of technologies to facilitate more sustainable forms of economic growth in the developing world. This is a tall order and one which Japan obviously cannot be expected to meet alone. Yet Japan in some sense will be in a natural position to exert leadership, due to its extensive involvement in East and South-East Asia, its dynamic technological base and economy, and its superior economic performance. To fill this role effectively will require a very real internationalization of Japan's economy, politics, and society. And while 'internationalization' has become something of a mantra in Japan, the reality still lags behind.

14

The Unavoidability of Justice

Henry Shue

IN the end this chapter is about justice, specifically the justice of
the international allocation of the costs of dealing with a global
environmental problem like global warming. In the beginning it
looks briefly and informally at what kinds of allocations of costs
between rich nations and poor nations it would be reasonable for
a poor nation to accept. The later comparison of what would be
acceptable to a poor nation and what would be just to a poor
nation turns out, I think, to be instructive.

A. Two Tracks

Perhaps questions about international justice would not have to
be considered by negotiations aimed at producing international
accords concerning global climate change. One thing at a time,
experts on negotiation will suggest. Lawrence Susskind and
Connie Ozawa, for example, observe: 'This underlying North–
South conflict is a serious impediment to concerted action, and it
is aggravated by the traditional approach to environmental diplomacy that emphasizes the gap between the haves and the have-
nots'.[1] They go on to caution against the making of unnecessary

Many hands have tried to help me untangle the threads here. First and most
important, I sorted through them with Jeremy Waldron. For written comments
on various versions I am grateful to John Carbonell, David Miller, and Andrew
Williams, in addition to the editors. For oral comments I am indebted to insightful
audiences at the original seminar at Oxford as well as at subsequent presentations
at Pittsburgh, Berkeley, and Cornell. The time to work on this topic was made
available by support from the Division of Arts and Humanities of the Rockefeller
Foundation.

[1] Lawrence Susskind and Connie Ozawa, 'Environmental Diplomacy: Strategies for Negotiating More Effective International Agreements' (MIT–Harvard
Public Disputes Program, 1990), 1.

'linkages'. Similarly, James K. Sebenius has recently warned that 'issues should be linked with caution' and recalled that as the regime for the sea-bed contained in the Convention on the Law of the Sea 'took on more of an NIEO-like character, industry opposition grew'.[2]

In the end, I shall argue, some issues of justice need not come up now, but others are unavoidable. In order to see why, we will later need to distinguish different issues about justice from each other. For now let us pursue the suggestion that we leave aside 'the gap between the haves and the have-nots', that is, leave aside all issues about international justice.

Negotiators could, then, say to each other: 'We acknowledge that some parties to these climate negotiations believe that the current international situation is unjust and that this pre-existing injustice might infect and corrupt our negotiations here. Nevertheless, we all agree to set aside within this forum all doubts about the circumstances from which we begin and agree simply to negotiate with scrupulous fairness from this point forward.' Let us, the suggestion could be, have two negotiating tracks unlinked to each other: a climate track and a justice track.

From the point of view of poor nations, who might have been expected to favour always keeping injustice on the agenda, the two-track approach has at least two strong considerations in its favour. First, assuming that what the elimination of injustice would turn out to require, in the crudest terms, is transfers of wealth from rich nations to poor nations, one can see that even negotiations that were merely rational bargaining about how to divide the costs of slowing the rate of global climate change, even if they left considerations of justice entirely to one side, might quite independently require that rich nations bear a far higher proportion of the costs than poor nations. Fundamentally, this could be because, with much more to lose materially from increases in the rate of climate change, rich nations could spend much more on co-operative action to slow the rate of climate change and still be better off than they would have been

---

[2] James K. Sebenius, 'Designing Negotiations Toward a New Regime: The Case of Global Warming', *International Security*, 15 (1991), 126 and 128. The New International Economic Order (NIEO), he has explained, 'involved a series of proposals advocated by LDCs during the 1970s which included significant wealth

if co-operative action had not been taken to slow the rate. Those with more to lose from inaction can rationally choose to pay more to bring about action, even when they are basing their choices exclusively upon their own national interest.[3] Therefore, while it may be that proper consideration of international injustices would lead to the conclusion that rich nations ought to transfer large sums to poor nations, simple rational consideration of national interest, based upon *de facto* holdings, may in any case lead to the conclusion that rich nations are well advised to contribute the vast preponderance of whatever is needed to prevent severe damage to, if not destruction of, those very holdings by rapid climate change. If what poor nations want from negotiations about global climate is for rich nations to pay most of the bill for action, they may be able to get it, even if justice does not come into the discussions. The rich nations have the most to lose—and, given current holdings of the world's wealth and resources, are the only ones able to pay the amounts probably required—so either they pay most of the freight or no co-operative effort will be undertaken. So it may not in fact be in the interest of the poor nations to complicate and embitter the negotiations by insisting upon keeping the issue of injustice on the agenda, however serious the injustices may actually be.

The second step of this defence of the two-track approach—climate now, justice later—from the poor nations' point of view builds upon the first. It may be in the material interest of the rich nations to reach accords to deal with global climate change even if those accords will be quite expensive for those rich nations (because rising temperatures and thinning ozone will be far more expensive still). Even from negotiations that are nothing but narrow rational bargaining, the poor nations are likely to receive substantial transfers to avoid future problems concerning climate.

It is, on the other hand, presumably not in the material interest of the rich nations over the short term, nor perhaps even the medium term, to correct international injustices if that simply

---

redistribution, greater LDC participation in the world economy, and greater Third World control over global institutions and resources' (p. 128).

[3] This is convincingly demonstrated in Jeremy Waldron, 'Bargaining and Justice: A Simple Model', in *Ethical Guidelines for Global Bargains* (Ithaca, NY: Cornell Program on Ethics and Public Life, 1990), photocopy.

requires substantial additional transfers of wealth to the poorest nations, with no additional quid pro quo. If one is profiting from injustice, it is hardly going to be in one's interest to pursue justice. Consequently, while rich nations could be expected to accept an accord that dealt strictly with climate change, they might bridle at an accord that, in effect, added the bill for the elimination of international injustices to the bill for the prevention of climatic disaster and demanded payment of both with, so to speak, one cheque. The poor nations are not likely to receive substantial transfers to correct *past* problems of injustice. Better for the poor nations to put climate on a fast track (and secure the transfers called for on that track), one might reckon, even at the price of leaving justice on a slower one (since those transfers are unlikely to occur in any case).

B. Double-or-Nothing

One consideration against the two-track approach, from the point of view of the poor nations, is the following. The growing political crises about the atmosphere and the climate may provide unprecedented leverage for the most populous of the poor nations on non-environmental issues, including justice, on which the rich nations have already proved beyond all doubt to be recalcitrant, and the poorest of the poor nations may be desperate enough to want to see this leverage used. I assume that while it may be in the material interest of the rich nations to foot most of the climate bill (because they may have so much more to lose materially from rapid climate change than the poor nations do), the rich nations must have the thorough going co-operation of the most populous of the poor nations—because so much of what needs to be done must be done inside the borders of the most populous nations that are yet to develop. The mountains of coal that must not be burned in future with the same technology with which the US and the UK burned most of their own coal in the past are in China; and while only nations as wealthy as the United States and Japan can afford to underwrite alternative technologies, the large poor nations like China, India, and Indonesia must agree to use the improved but more expensive technologies within their own respective territories if their emissions are not to add enormously to whatever magnitude the problem would otherwise have. Thus, the problem of global climate is one of the very few on which the rich nations actually need the co-operation of major groups of the poor in the implementation of a solution.[4]

If the rich do in fact need the poor, the populous poor nations may have leverage on the issue of global climate to an unusual, if not unique, degree. They would be sorely tempted to make political linkages of the kind that Susskind and Ozawa seem to advise against, even if there were no ethical linkages of the kind that I hope eventually to show. And James K. Sebenius, who himself advises in the end against such moves, nevertheless reluctantly judges that 'especially given current levels of distrust, as well as the steep energy requirements of vital development, a threat by key developing nations not to co-operate with an emerging climate regime—although it might ultimately be mutually destructive, and its effects more severe in the developing world—could have a clear rationale and a measure of credibility'.[5]

For poor nations have no particular reason to believe that any progress would in fact ever be made on a politically unlinked justice track. A separate international justice 'track' has, after all, been available for a long time without any movement having occurred along it, in spite of loud and urgent cries from the South to the North in support of a New International Economic Order and various other proposals, none of which have ever been taken seriously by any of the richest nations (in spite of the endorsements by a few of the Willy Brandts and Olaf Palmes of the North). How do we imagine the de-linked justice track is to be activated? Can those who pride themselves upon being 'realists' about climate negotiations consistently assume that the wealthy nations will one day be seized by a spontaneous desire to do justice? Since the rich nations have so far been unwilling to redistribute voluntarily when there was not known to be an urgent and expensive global climatic crisis, what reason is there to believe that they will—without exceptionally strong presssure—step forward to do justice in the midst of an ongoing crisis? If the

[4] Terrorism may be one of the few other problems on which the rich need the poor—and it is not going particularly well so far, in spite of doing almost infinitesimal harm compared to the potential catastrophes that the alteration of the global climate may hold in store.

[5] Sebenius, 'Designing Negotiations', 129.

rich would not agree to pay both the climate bill and the justice bill in order to get a climate accord they badly need, when the two subjects were politically linked, why should anyone expect that they will spontaneously volunteer to deal with injustice later, after they have already secured co-operation in protecting their own holdings against a threatening disaster that may continue to require expensive countermeasures throughout the next millennium?

Negotiations that were no more than rational bargaining intended to advance narrowly construed national interests might indeed yield some transfers of wealth or technology from rich to poor. Those transfers, however, would merely be calculated to cover some of the additional costs resulting from an agreement to take action to deal with some threat like global warming. The transfers from rich to poor nations would be calculated, perhaps, to guarantee that the poor nations would not have to bear much of the additional expense of the additional efforts to slow climate change. This might leave at least some poor nations little or no worse off from having co-operated with the climate initiative than they would have been from refusing to co-operate. No reason at all has been given, however, to think that the transfers produced by the single-track agreement about climate would exceed the additional costs produced by the agreement. These 'transfers of wealth' would be wholly distinct from any 'transfers of wealth' that might be required for the elimination of injustice. If the transfers required to undo existing injustices are ever to occur, leverage will need to be employed to bring them about. Poor nations should not fail, according to this counter-argument to the two-track approach, to use their leverage in this rare situation in which they actually have some. The strategy for poor nations being considered is double-or-nothing: demand from the richest nations redress of the grievances of injustice as well as performance of a fair share of the task of slowing destructive environmental changes, and, by that very linkage, risk securing neither. This is a gambler's strategy, but the poorest of the poor are in precisely the kind of circumstances that can encourage the adoption of such strategies.[6]

---

[6] Indeed, one of the genuinely self-interested reasons for the wealthiest nations to correct injustices is to remove desperate situations specifically in order not to have to deal with such daring strategies.

C. Poor Nations with the Least Leverage

Unfortunately, the alternative of double-or-nothing is, upon a second look, a less promising alternative for the poor nations than it initially seems. First, the poorest of the poor nations and the most populous of the poor nations are by no means all the same.[7] The prospect of the Indians and Indonesians all installing refrigeration using CFCs, or of the Chinese burning all their coal in an industrialization process as polluting as the one that occurred in Europe and North America (*and* installing refrigeration using CFCs), is a monumental threat to the value of the material holdings, not to mention the health and safety, of the people of the wealthy nations. That threat might provide considerable bargaining leverage to these large nations, whose development could produce far more emissions of dangerous gases than the wealthy nations can possibly eliminate from their own economies without virtually eliminating the economies themselves. But how would all this help Ethiopia, Sudan, Chad, Mali, Haiti, or any of the rest of the very poorest nations whose populations (and consequent potential for emissions) are relatively insignificant? If there were some sort of general Third World solidarity stretching across the continents, the leverage of the most populous nations might be mobilized politically on behalf of justice for the poorest nations. Yet I see no such solidarity between the poor with leverage, and the poor without it.

Further, even the poorest nations with populations too small to have significant leverage of their own might be split among themselves. Desperation produces radically divergent reactions: the desperately poor may either anxiously grasp the least they are offered or, reckoning that they have next to nothing to lose in any case, hold out for the most they believe they might get.[8] Some might do each, further undermining any potential Third World solidarity. Consequently, the prospects of a general double-or-nothing strategy appear dubious at best for all but the most populous nations whose potential emissions provide them with the greatest leverage.

One must be careful about what is taken to constitute

[7] I am grateful to Andrew Hurrell for impressing the significance of this fact upon me.
[8] See Waldron, 'Bargaining and Justice'.

bargaining strength or leverage in this case. Wealth provides bargaining strength because it constitutes resources that can be drawn upon in the absence of any agreement, making the wealthy bargainer willing to pay relatively less in order to reach agreement. The wealthy party can draw upon her wealth to survive non-agreement. In this case, however, non-agreement means 'dirty development' rather than 'clean development' by some very large countries that have a lot of developing still to do. That is, if there is no agreement between wealthy nations and poor nations upon a plan under which the wealthy subsidize, to some extent, the choice by the most populous poor nations of a relatively less polluting, but therefore more costly, strategy of development, the largest of the poor nations will presumably proceed with what they would have done anyway: the most cost-effective available development strategy in which the costs of, for example, emissions of greenhouse gases are ignored ('externalized'), as they were during the development of the now wealthy countries. This means that without necessarily intending anyone else any harm and without engaging in any non-standard economic calculations, the most populous poor nations would on the option of non-agreement add gigantic increments to the gases that cause global warming by simply proceeding with their own economic development. Accordingly, while the wealthy nations might have sufficient wealth to protect themselves against the effects of any climate changes caused by the choice of 'dirty development' over 'clean development', the additional expense would presumably be huge—and probably incalculable in advance. The costs that the most populous poor nations might unintentionally impose on the wealthy nations with a relatively 'dirty' development strategy (even one less dirty than those the wealthy nations followed in their own times) would provide these poor nations with considerable bargaining strength, even while questions of justice were being ignored. Because of the leverage provided by the threat of 'dirty' development, the most populous of the poor nations might be able to negotiate fairly favourable terms for themselves in any international environmental agreement.

For the even poorer but smaller nations, as we have already noted, no such threat is available. Haiti can emit all the carbon dioxide it can afford to emit for a very long time before it creates any increase in the rate of global warming; I would think the same would be true even if all the poorest nations without large populations, which would include much of the continent of Africa, acted in (improbable) concert. They cannot pollute enough to gain any bargaining power.

That the double-or-nothing strategy faces difficulties does not, of course, establish that the pure two-track approach is a good idea. A third alternative is that rich nations should, contrary to the two-track approach, take some aspects of justice into account from the beginning but, unlike the use of the double-or-nothing strategy, without having to be forced to consider justice by the poor nations with leverage. This would involve approaching climate negotiations, not as rational bargaining in the narrow sense, but as a process constrained all along by some consideration of justice. It is this third alternative for which I shall in the end argue. Meanwhile, it is useful to return to the two-track approach, on which negotiations are rational bargaining unconstrained by justice, to see what it would be reasonable for a poor nation populous enough to have a great deal of leverage to agree to.

D. Poor Nations with the Most Leverage

To make the issue more concrete, suppose that if the Chinese co-operate on an unlinked climate track, on which the United States (simply because it is rationally in its interest to do so) foots many times as much of the bill as China does by developing and transferring pollution-abating technology that China then implements, global warming can at best be held to a temperature that produces only a 'moderate' rise in sea level. Suppose further that a nation with the wealth then still remaining to the United States can, in one way or another, provide for its coastal inhabitants so that their lives are not ruined (or taken) by the expanding seawater, but that a nation with only the wealth that China can by then expect to have, in spite of having been able to continue developing as rapidly as possible thanks to the subsidization of its environmental efforts by the US technology transfers, will not be able to save Shanghai and other seaports. Is it clear that China could live with a co-operative global environmental initiative that was *successful*? For the two-track option is implicitly assuming a future in which each nation handles *its own* problems with *its own* resources.

For, consider the question that China confronts after any international environmental agreement has been carried out by all sides. It seems evident that some destructive climate changes have already today been set in motion and can no longer be prevented; for example, it seems likely that average global temperatures are going to rise during the next century because of (among other things) carbon dioxide that we have already released into the atmosphere by burning fossil fuels, so that all that the best possible accord upon international action can possibly accomplish now is to slow the rate of an already inevitable temperature rise of unknown magnitude. A poor nation's agreeing to proceed on the climate track without any pre-conditions about what happens on the justice track means, then, its agreeing to try to ameliorate the effects upon its own citizens of the climate changes that can no longer be prevented even by implementation of the concerted action agreed to in the climate negotiations, with only the wealth and resources that would be left to that nation after the performance of its share as specified in the agreement emerging from the climate negotiations. The nation must live with the results of even the full implementation of the best attainable climate accord entirely within whatever then happen to be its own assets.

Agreeing to a climate accord is certainly going to entail, at least for rich nations, making economic sacrifices in the sense of putting wealth and resources that might have been invested otherwise into less polluting but not necessarily more productive (perhaps even less productive) technology. What about poor nations? Suppose the rich nations will agree to no climate accord that does not also require (no doubt smaller but) genuine sacrifices by the poor nations as well. Continue to think of China as the case in point in order to make matters slightly more concrete. A proposed final agreement might specify that every year from 2000 to 2050 China was to divert $n billion dollars out of its own economic development and into the production and installation of pollution abatement technology. Fifty years of diverting significant sums away from increased production and into reduced carbon dioxide emissions would leave China considerably less wealthy in 2050 than it otherwise could have been entirely with its own resources, although a much smaller contributor of carbon dioxide to the greenhouse effect than it otherwise would have been. Let us call China's choices 'Co-operation' (with such a proposed climate accord) and 'Isolation' (which means proceeding with its own development at the maximum sustainable rate, ignoring the effects on global climate that do not undermine the sustainability of its own strategy). Now obviously no determinate answer to the question whether Co-operation or Isolation is more in China's interest is available, because a strategic interaction between China's choice and the choices made by other nations would determine the outcomes. And clearly there are various quite different possibilities. All that we need to notice, however, is uncertainty—on one specific issue. The issue is whether it might be in China's national interest to choose Isolation, even if its own defection from the proposed accord would doom the accord and prevent concerted action to slow climate change, rather than to choose Co-operation and enable the accord to be implemented at the price of reducing the level of its own wealth in 2050 by the amount that its compliance with the accord would require. And the critical factor is that China has no guarantee that it would be better off by co-operating irrespective of the amount represented by n billion per year. On the contrary, there is surely some number n such that if China were required to divert n billion per year from development to pollution abatement, it would be worse off by choosing Co-operation than by choosing Isolation. And there is no *a priori* guarantee that there is any number m such that if China were required to divert m billion per year from 2000 to 2050, it would be better off in 2050.

The fundamental difficulty is that what matters is a ratio. What counts is the ratio of China's wealth in 2050 to China's cost for dealing with the climatic effects the Chinese people face in 2050. We may call the two possibly quite different ranges of levels of wealth 'Co-operation Wealth' and 'Isolation Wealth', and we may similarly label the two ranges of levels of costs of dealing with greenhouse effects 'Co-operation Costs' and 'Isolation Costs'. We may readily grant that the Isolation Costs for China (or any other nation except an extremely small one) would be more severe than the Co-operation Costs, on the reasonable

assumption that the international effort would be more successful with China's participation. Consider, however, that Isolation
Wealth would be considerably greater than Co-operation Wealth
on the equally reasonable assumption that China can develop
further if it does not divert resources away from development.[9]
The critical information that we do not have is whether the ratio
of Co-operation Wealth to Co-operation Costs is better or worse
than the ratio of Isolation Wealth to Isolation Costs. This uncertainty means, unfortunately, that a populous poor nation has
no guarantee that Co-operation with an agreement on the climate
track is more in its interest than Isolation from the agreement.
Obviously it matters how costly the terms of Co-operation are,
and, other things being equal, the more costly Co-operation is,
the more reason to suspect that Isolation would be in its national
interest as normally construed.

E. Two Kinds of Compound Injustice

This fundamental uncertainty about whether it would be in the
interest of a populous poor nation to co-operate in international
attempts to prevent harmful climate change in the absence of any
complementary agreement for international co-operation in
coping with the harms that turn out not in fact to have been
prevented means, it is clear, that it would not be reasonable for
such a poor nation to agree to a two-track approach according to
which the climate track covered only prevention and did not
cover coping as well. Any such nation should insist that any
agreement include co-operative coping with the harms that in
fact occur later, as well as earlier co-operative attempts to prevent
harm. I do not see how anyone could show that it would be
reasonable for a populous poor nation to agree to the combination of co-operative prevention and non-co-operative coping.
Since a populous poor nation whose 'dirty' development will

---

[9] I realize that one strategy for co-operators to take against defectors in desperate circumstances would be economic warfare designed to guarantee that no
nation does better by refusing to co-operate. Indeed, given the awful magnitude
of the social consequences of even some of the intermediate climatic disasters, I
think we must seriously contemplate nuclear blackmail, nuclear attack, and mas-
sacre of refugees fleeing disaster. I am simply trying to deal with less horrible
cases at this point.

involve extensive emissions of greenhouse gases has considerable leverage, it might well be able to insist in fact upon a fairly
favourable agreement covering coping as well as prevention, at
least for itself. On the other hand, as we have already noted, a
poor but not very populous nation—say, Haiti or Mali—would
lack the leverage to insist upon such a complementary agreement
for dealing with the harms that will occur and so could easily be
left to fend for itself, as far as its bargaining strength goes.

This, of course, is where justice comes in. Justice is about not
squeezing people for everything one can get out of them, especially when they are already much worse off than oneself. A commitment to justice includes a willingness to choose to accept less
good terms than one could have achieved—to accept only agreements that are fair to others as well as to oneself. Justice prevents
negotiations from being the kind of rational bargaining that
maximizes self-interest no matter what the consequences are for
others. There are some bargains too favourable for a just person
to accept. Justice means sometimes granting what the other party
is in no position to insist upon. In this case, it means sharing the
costs of coping with the Haitis and Malis of the world, which
cannot insist, as well as with the Chinas and Indias, which probably can insist. Or so I shall now try briefly to show.

Three general reasons would be worth considering, although I
shall rely upon the third. The first reason involves the first of two
kinds of what I shall be calling compound injustice. I have
referred above to the situation in the absence of a complementary
agreement about how to share the costs of coping with the
unprevented harmful effects of climate change as 'a future in
which each nation handles *its own* problems with *its own* resources'. If 'its own' merely means 'those it happens to have',
this description is unobjectionable: each nation would handle the
problems it happened to have with the resources it happened to
have. This description, however, has no moral force; and, in
particular, it provides no basis for concluding: 'and so things are
arranged as they should be'. That conclusion would be supported only if 'its own resources' meant 'the resources to which it
is entitled' or 'what really belongs to it'. Since *all* questions of
justice would be left unexamined by the pure two-track
approach, it would be totally groundless to assume that each
nation miraculously just happens to have exactly what it would

turn out to be entitled to if the justice of holdings were ever discussed and settled. So, we should not comfort ourselves by misreading 'Haiti has whatever Haiti has' as if it meant 'Haiti has received its due [and so is entitled to nothing else]'. Until the justice of the national holdings that happen to exist today is discussed, there would be no basis for assuming that, without even trying, we had inadvertently arrived at the most just of all possible worlds, in which each nation has exactly the wealth and resources it ought to have.

So far I have put the point negatively: that it is groundless simply to assume that whatever international distribution turns up over the course of history is fully just. I would think, although I shall not argue for it here, that, quite to the contrary, we have lots of good reasons to think that the existing international distributions of wealth and resources are morally arbitrary at best and the result of systematic exploitation at worst. Insofar as the existing distribution is unjust toward, say, Haiti, it may turn out that some of Haiti's 'own' resources are elsewhere (for example, in France). If we are a little more precise about some of the varieties of justice, we can formulate and assess more positive assertions.

Issues of justice arise, of course, in more than one way, and it is an open question whether the standards of justice applicable to the various different contexts in which questions of justice arise are the same; and if they are not the same, how the standards for one kind of case relate to the standards for other kinds of cases and whether, in particular, some standards refer back to the fulfilment or violation of other standards.

When two or more parties agree to work together toward the solution of a common problem, we often want to ask whether the terms of their agreement are fair to all the parties concerned, even in cases in which all parties have in fact accepted, or would in fact accept, the agreement. We believe that a party may in fact acquiesce in an unfair agreement for any of several different reasons: for example, through a failure to understand how unfair the arrangements really are, or through a lack of any good alternative. The lack of any good alternative might itself reflect a different case of injustice: an injustice in the background conditions within which the agreement is being made. I shall refer to the justice of the terms of the agreement itself—the justice among the parties inside the agreement—as *internal justice*; and I shall refer to the justice of the circumstances within which the agreement is being made as *background justice*.

I believe that it is uncontroversial to note that, in general, it is perfectly possible for an instance of internal injustice to be the result of a background injustice: someone may in fact accept unconscionable terms in an agreement because an independent background injustice has, for example, left her with no good alternative to the agreement. [10] Without the agreement she would be even worse off than she will be with the agreement—in this specific sense, she may even be rational, in the circumstances, to accept the unfair terms of the agreement—but the reason she would be worse off without the agreement is a prior injustice, independent of the agreement in question.

It is an open question, of course, whether any of the parties to a particular agreement was a perpetrator of a relevant background injustice; *ex hypothesi* the victim of the background injustice is a party to the agreement. If Wrong is a beneficiary of the internal injustice against Right *and* a perpetrator of the background injustice against Right as well, the plot thickens. One then confronts the first kind of compounded injustice. Any attempt to avoid taking up any questions of justice in negotiations over future action creates, generally speaking, the ideal situation for inflicting this kind of compound injustice. Some parties are liable to press for the acceptance of internally unjust agreements using bargaining strength that results from background injustice against the very other parties now being pressed.

One would of course have to look at cases to establish when and where injustice is being compounded: for example, is the reason why Haiti has so little bargaining strength on environmental issues its level of poverty (and if so, is that in turn the result of background injustice in the form of, say, land-holdings shaped by French colonialism?)? I shall not pursue any case here. Whatever the truth about, say, French colonialism in Haiti, I have already made clear that I think the main reason for Haiti's having

---

[10] One can, of course, argue about whether in that case the acceptance of the agreement is voluntary or about whether the case would embody genuine consent. I suspect that those matters are less completely independent from the question of fairness than one might hope. Be that as it may, I think we sometimes consider even a consensually or voluntarily accepted agreement to be unfair to one or more of the parties who in fact accepted it.

so much less leverage on environmental matters than, say, China is not in fact its (undeniable and appalling) poverty, but its relatively small population and consequent relatively small potential for pollution (even if it somehow finds the resources with which to develop). In a perverse way, the more of a nation's development that lies ahead of it—that is, the poorer it is now—the greater the threat of future pollution it can bring to bargaining about the terms for preventing environmental damage. Accordingly, the fact that Haiti cannot offer much of a positive threat if the terms of an agreement do not accommodate Haitian requirements must be blamed less on any past colonial exploitation than upon the small size of Haiti's population compared to China, India, and Indonesia.

Nevertheless, Haiti's position is also weak on the other side of the bargaining coin, namely its poverty gives it so little capability itself for coping with the harmful results of climate change that it might have no better alternative than to grasp at any terms that would leave it even only slightly better off than it would be with no agreement. This is not a lack of an ability to make non-agreement worse for others (like the lack of a capability to pollute during the 'dirty' development of a country with a large population), but a lack of an ability to survive non-agreement oneself. But it still makes one's bargaining position weak relative to those in a better position to survive. In sum, Haiti can neither threaten to make non-agreement worse for others nor deal well with non-agreement itself. The former is more the result of population size than of poverty, but the latter is the result of poverty. Insofar as that poverty can be shown to be, in turn, the result of a background injustice (like colonial exploitation), the potential for compound injustice during climate negotiations exists. For any rich nation which has benefited from exploitation to insist that poor nations which have suffered from exploitation must cope with unsolved problems using only 'their own resources' would constitute this first kind of compounded injustice.

The second reason for thinking that the Haitis of the world should receive more assistance in coping with unprevented harms than they are in a position to insist on involves the second of the two kinds of compound injustice. This kind will become clear through a progression of examples. Suppose, first, that you agree to help me wash my car even though I make a point of announcing in advance that I have no intention of helping you to wash your car (or in any other way repaying the favour). This would be a totally one-sided arrangement, and it is not at all obvious why you would choose to assist me instead of someone else who at least might possibly reciprocate. In general, I think we would have some doubts about the character of anyone who consistently offered only such one-sided arrangements. In a specific case, however, we might accept that if you actually had agreed to help me with my car knowing that I was intending not to help you with yours, you had no grounds on which later to insist upon my help (although at least some grounds to wonder about the character of someone who seemed unmoved by any notion of reciprocity). The conclusion that you had no grounds to insist upon reciprocal assistance is, of course, supported by the triviality of the whole business: cars can go for years without being washed and do not seem to rust much faster than shiny cars (so you do not lose much by not getting your car washed), and the example implicitly suggests that you were not making any great sacrifice to help me wash mine—presumably you had nothing better to do anyway.

Now consider a second example. An arsonist has set fire to my house, and you agree to help put out the fire. While you are away from your house helping to fight the fire in my house, the arsonist sets fire to your house. You then ask me to help you to fight your fire. I say: 'You know me—do I wash your car just because you wash my car? No way.' This would of course be outrageous. For a start, the case is no longer trivial: whether cars get washed does not matter, but whether fires get put out does; and fighting fires is dangerous, while washing cars is not. In addition, this time you need assistance only because you had chosen to provide assistance to me. If you had simply stayed at home to watch me fight my fire, the arsonist would not (let us assume) have been able to set fire to your house. It may be that my lack of reciprocity in car-washing is tolerable—partly because trivial—if unadmirable. The lack of reciprocity in fire-fighting is inexcusable, however, because the favour from you that I fail to return is the cause of your needing it returned: it is only because you did what you could to help me to fight my fire that you now have a fire of your own to fight.

In the third example there is no evil arsonist to cause the problems. I myself am innocently burning brush in a field that seems to be a safe distance from all houses. Unexpectedly the wind shifts and stiffens, and the fire gets away from me and begins moving through the tall dry grass toward the houses. You and I agree to do what we can to stop the fire from reaching the houses, and we each do our best. My house is saved, but yours burns. I say: 'Thanks for helping to save my house.' You say: 'What about my house?' I reply: 'Our agreement was about preventing houses from burning, not about coping with burnt ones.' The absurdity of my response partly results from the implicit assumption built into the example that during the prevention phase you did not restrict your efforts exclusively to protecting your own house but did your part in the general enterprise of trying to protect all the houses. Perhaps you could have saved your own house if you had restricted your efforts to keeping the flames away from it and had ignored the edge of the fire near my house. The primary reason my response is outrageous, however, is that I started the fire that burned down your house. I did not intend to burn it, or any other house—this was an accident—but I did cause it. At a minimum, then, I cannot simply wash my hands of the actual consequences of my own action.

Since the analogy with prevention of, and coping with, climate change like global warming is built explicitly into the third example, there is no need to belabour it. I chiefly want to note that a second kind of compounding of injustice occurs here. If, in the second example, it would already have been unfair of me to ignore difficulties of yours that arose from your assisting me with my difficulties caused by a third party, this is compounded in the third example by the fact that I myself am the cause of everyone's difficulties. No one doubts that the overwhelmingly preponderant cause so far of ozone depletion, which is certainly occurring, is the activity of the rich nations. One can doubt whether global warming is already occurring, but if it is, the industrial activity of the now rich will again have been the principal cause.[11] Any harms caused were unintentional, but it has

---

[11] For extraordinarily specific calculations, see Yasumasa Fujii, 'An Assessment of the Responsibility for the Increase in the CO_2 Concentration and Inter-generational Carbon Accounts', Working Paper WP-90-55 (Laxenburg, Austria: IIASA, 1990), processed. Fujii has calculated cumulative carbon emissions per capita by region back to 1800. Fujii's calculations suggest that North America and Western Europe are responsible for, respectively, 35% and 26% of the total cumulative

surely been the same industrial activity that has made the rich nations rich that will have been the source of the most serious climate problems, even if it is not sure how seriously the gases added to the atmosphere will affect the climate at ground level. We built the fires of industrialization, doubtless ignorant in the beginning of the damage they might do, but they are our fires and we continue to benefit from them.

About specific alleged instances of the first kind of compound injustice controversy continues: to what extent is the poverty that contributes to the weak position of Haiti the result of French colonialism? what extent is the poverty that contributes to the weak position of Indonesia the result of Dutch colonialism? and so forth. These are important but intractable debates about causal mechanisms. Concerning the second kind of compound injustice, in contrast, there are far fewer debates about the causal mechanism. The rich nations have indisputably so far caused most of whatever problems there are in the cases of ozone depletion and global warming. Consequently, any attempt by rich nations to wash their hands of any resultant harms that are not prevented would be doubly unfair.

F. Vital Interests

Before we turn to the third, and strongest, reason for rejecting the separation of prevention and coping, let us look back over what has been argued so far. The first half of the chapter attempted to show that it cannot be established to be in the interest of a poor nation—even so populous a poor nation that its co-operation with a climate agreement might be essential to the success of the agreement—to co-operate with an agreement that covers only the attempted prevention of climate changes that will be harmful and

---

man-made increases in atmospheric CO_2 since 1800 (Fig. 9, p. 20). For this reference I am grateful to Dale Rothman. However, causal responsibility does not translate smoothly into moral responsibility. Peyton Young has observed: 'There is also a theoretical difficulty: Not only did producers benefit from unregulated past emissions, so did consumers and investors—including consumers and investors in the nonindustrialized world. ... Indeed, the entire economic order has been based on a regime of free CO_2 disposal. The accumulated benefits (and blame) are widely diffused, so past emissions are *not* a measure of liability.' See H. P. Young, *Sharing the Burden of Global Warming* (College Park, Md.: School of Public Affairs of the University of Maryland, 1990), 8.

fails to cover coping with the harms that do occur. This does not show that, from the point of view of poor nations, the two-track approach *per se* is objectionable but only that it is objectionable if it is arbitrarily restricted exclusively to the terms of co-operative prevention and ignores the terms of co-operative coping. This is a point not directly about justice but about interest, and it is a point about national interests, not about the interests of specific persons taken individually. Justice, on the other hand, is ultimately, I think, about the interests of specific human individuals (even if some principles concerning justice are stated in terms of nations or other groups).

When in the second half of the chapter we turned directly to questions of justice, we asked, in effect, whether, given that it would be in the interest of a poor nation not to agree to be deserted by its erstwhile partners when the time came to cope with unprevented problems, it would be fair to demand the sacrifice of this interest by those nations with too little bargaining strength to resist the demand. Negotiators often ask each other to sacrifice some of their interests—there is nothing in principle wrong with that, and there would be little to negotiate about without it. The question of justice is: is there anything special about the interest in question, or about the circumstances in which its sacrifice is demanded, which makes a specific demand unfair? The first two reasons for thinking that the demand by the rich nations for the sacrifice of this interest on the part of poor nations is unfair have been based upon the circumstances in which the demand is made, rather than upon the nature of the interest that would have to be sacrificed in order to satisfy the demand. These have been the two points about compound injustice: first, that if background injustices have produced the weak bargaining position of the poor nations, it is doubly unfair to exploit that bargaining weakness in order to insist that the poor nations sacrifice the interest in question; and second, that if the rich nations have caused, albeit unintentionally, the impending harms that co-operation would attempt to prevent, it is doubly unfair to leave poor nations that have pitched in on the prevention effort to cope on their own with what the effort fails to prevent. I have not tried to show that background injustices have in fact produced the weak bargaining position of the poor, because I consider that much too controversial to deal with in a single chapter; and I have not tried to show that the rich nations have caused any impending harms, because that is conceded on all sides. So far I have also said nothing about the inherent nature of the interest of a poor nation that it would be asked to sacrifice if asked to cope with '*its own* problems with *its own* resources' once the prevention effort had achieved whatever it can from this point forward still achieve. I would now like to correct this last omission.

The third reason for thinking that the exclusion of problems of coping with unprevented harms from the agreement to try to prevent harms is unjust turns upon the nature of the interests ignored if coping is ignored. 'Coping' has so far been given no concrete content. What would 'coping' with the unresolved problems actually amount to? Clearly, a genuinely concrete account would depend upon exactly which problems remained, and we do not know exactly which problems will remain after our best prevention efforts. However, since we are talking about very poor nations, we do know some things about the general charac-ter of the 'unresolved problems', most notably that they are highly likely to be life-threatening. Why? Because in very poor nations almost all big problems are life-threatening. This is what it means to be 'very poor': it means having no cushion to fall back upon, no rainy-day fund, no safety-net, no margin for error. Being very poor means living on the edge, and having a big problem—sometimes, even, having a small problem—means going over the edge: losing one or two of the children, for example. In spring 1991 the Kurds in Northern Iraq and the Bangladeshis near the Bay of Bengal have each just provided another demonstration of the meaning of being very poor: one big disruption to the normal routine and people start starving left and right. For such a group, dealing with '*its own* problems with *its own* resources' means: sitting and watching loved ones while they die.

Climate changes mean problems for agriculture, and problems for agriculture mean that, even if there are no aggregate shortages, food is in the wrong place at the wrong time. Everyone understands by now that climate changes need not produce cyclones or droughts to disrupt agriculture severely; a shortening of the growing season by a week or two, or a modification of the average temperature by a degree or two, can produce a local crop failure. The sort of thing that 'unprevented' climate changes are most likely to produce are local crop failures of a kind that rich nations can easily adjust to and that poor nations cannot. In rich nations like the USA and the countries of the EC, food routinely travels hundreds and thousands of miles from field to table— there are virtually no local crops; in large areas of poor nations, where transportation is inadequate, the local crops are all there is.

So, what is the nature of the individual interests that the poorest nations would be asked to sacrifice if they were asked to ignore provisions for coping? They are, in a word, vital inter-ests—survival interests. This means, I think, that it is unfair to demand that they be sacrificed in order to avoid our sacrificing interests that are not only not vital but trivial. If this is correct, we are now in a position to see a little about what justice may actually require in our case of international climate agreements.

G. A Modest Practical Implication for the Negotiating Agenda on Global Warming

I have been arguing that justice requires that coping, not merely prevention, be part of any package negotiated. This does not mean that no variant of a two-track approach to negotiations could be used. Issues about justice that are truly extrinsic should, perhaps, not be given purely political linkages to unrelated climate issues. The point, however, has been that a number of considerations about justice are intrinsic, not extrinsic, to any negotiations that are not simply going to create new injustices, in some cases compounding old ones. These aspects of justice are unavoidable, except at the price of committing fresh injustices.[12]

Far short of taking the positive action needed to allow the poorest nations to cope fully with the climate changes that will occur despite everyone's best efforts—positive action that I assume would involve considerable international transfers of wealth and resources from rich to poor nations—rich nations could begin by adopting a far weaker, but still significant, guideline that is, I would suggest, an absolutely minimal require-ment of justice. Poor nations ought not to be asked to sacrifice in

---

[12] The measures to enable the poorest nations to cope with climate changes might rectify some, but certainly not all, background injustices.

any way the pace or extent of their own economic development in order to help to prevent the climate changes set in motion by the process of industrialization that has enriched others. 'Their own' resources for coping later should be the most that they can sustainably develop between now and then.

It is not unusual, even on the part of writers relatively sensitive to the concerns of developing nations, for it to be taken for granted that development must be to some extent slowed or diverted. Durwood Zaelke and James Cameron assume interference with development and urge subsequent compensation:

A central issue for many developing states will be how to obtain compensation for the opportunity costs they will incur from forgoing or altering their development. This compensation must include the transfer of more efficient industrial technologies and sufficient financial aid and debt relief to allow developing states to achieve sustainable development.[13]

I suggest, on the contrary, that any technology transfers and financial relief ought to be sufficiently timely and substantial that no opportunity costs are incurred by the poor nations. All the economic cost of co-operative action by poorer nations should be borne by wealthier nations. This requires what is called in UN circles 'additionality'.[14] The external funds for 'clean' development should be in addition to whatever funds already ought for other reasons (including other aspects of justice genuinely external to climate agreements) to be provided for development, so that sustainable development is neither forgone nor altered. If, for example, Chinese coal or Brazilian rainforests must not be burned, then co-operation means not burning them. But Chinese and Brazilian development—and, I must say, internal redistribution in the case of Brazil—should not be set back as a result.[13] International transfers of wealth and/or technology should subsidize co-operation by poorer nations with environmental actions, as was already to some degree recognized explicitly in the London amendments to the Montreal Protocol on Substances

[13] Durwood Zaelke and James Cameron, 'Global Warming and Climate Change: An Overview of the International Legal Process', *American University Journal of International Law and Policy*, 5 (1990), 283.

[14] See Peter S. Thacher's chapter in this volume.

[15] The precise relationship between domestic injustice, like the extremes of wild affluence and crushing poverty in Brazil, and international justice obviously requires further discussion.

that Deplete the Ozone Layer in June 1990; and to some extent was acknowledged, for the case of the Brazilian rainforests, by the summit meeting of the Group of Seven in Houston in July 1990.

I want to underline the extreme modesty of the weak minimum guideline proposed here for climate negotiations. There are, I believe, other completely independent reasons why affluent nations like the United States, Japan, Germany, and Saudi Arabia ought to transfer quite separate resources to poor nations like China and Haiti so that they can not only develop as rapidly as possible but also act as decisively as possible against pollution of the earth's atmosphere.[16] It is being maintained here, by contrast, only that it surely ought not to be demanded—as part of any international agreement for co-operation in dealing with global climate—that such poor nations *divert resources already in their possession* from their own development as their contribution to the common effort to save the atmosphere. If, as a matter of rational self-interested choice, rich nations can spend large sums (smaller than the amount they stand to lose if the common effort fails), and if, as a matter of efficiency, large portions of those sums are most effectively spent in developing nations, the funds for pollution abatement within the poor nations can reasonably come from outside their borders. These transfers would, however, merely be what is necessary to avoid committing fresh injustice in future if the effort to protect the atmosphere is to go forward in the places where, as a matter of efficiency, some of the biggest differences can perhaps be made: in the poor but developing countries.

If unprevented climate changes eventually become rapid enough to destroy world agriculture as we know it, everyone,

---

[16] I have argued elsewhere—and continue to believe—that the fulfilment of at least some of people's most basic needs entitles them, if necessary, to the use of some resources currently held by *other* people. The judgement put forward in the text is far, far weaker (although, of course, not in any way inconsistent), yet has quite powerful implications for the case at hand. Since the weaker thesis is presumably acceptable to more people, it is worthwhile to endorse it, and explore its implications, even though it is not the most that one might reasonably defend. For the stronger thesis, see Henry Shue, *Basic Rights: Subsistence, Affluence, and U.S. Foreign Policy* (Princeton, NJ: Princeton UP, 1980), ch. 5, although the argument there failed to take up the important issue of the significance of the difference between situations of full, or strict, compliance, and situations of only partial compliance.

rich and poor, could in the end starve to death. The question is where to begin in order to see to it that the human threat never becomes that severe, and the answer being suggested is that justice requires that one not begin by slowing the economic development of the countries in which considerable numbers of people are already close to the edge of starvation just so that the affluent can retain more of their affluence than they could if they contributed more and the poor contributed less. Poor nations, therefore, ought not to be required to make sacrifices in their sustainable development. Even in an emergency one pawns the jewellery before selling the blankets. The weak guideline being proposed as a start merely reflects that, whatever justice may positively require, it does not permit that poor nations be told to sell *their* blankets in order that rich nations may keep *their* jewellery.[17]

[17] The most explicit recognition of a version of this modest guideline in the London amendments to the *Montreal Protocol* came in the new Article 10, which was adopted in June 1990 and begins: 'The Parties shall establish a mechanism for the purposes of providing financial and technical co-operation, including the transfer of technologies, to Parties operating under paragraph 1 of Article 5 of this Protocol [poor states] to enable their compliance with the control measures set out in Articles 2A to 2E of the Protocol. The mechanism, contributions to which *shall be additional* to other financial transfers to Parties operating under that paragraph, *shall meet all agreed incremental costs* of such Parties in order to enable their compliance with the control measures of the Protocol.' [emphasis added]. See *Montreal Protocol on Substances That Deplete the Ozone Layer*, as amended, Article 10, para. 1.

15

Brazil and the International Politics of Amazonian Deforestation

Andrew Hurrell

FOR most of the 1980s official Brazilian attitudes and policies towards the Amazon provided a clear example of the traditional emphasis placed by developing countries on the twin imperatives of economic development and political autonomy. Indeed there was a striking similarity between the strident environmental nationalism of the Sarney government (1985–90) and the influential language and positions adopted by Brazilian spokesmen at the time of the 1972 Stockholm Conference. But the case of Brazil also highlights the fact that attitudes towards the environment in the developing world have not been static.[1] The Brazilian government of President Collor de Mello which came into office in March 1990 announced a major change of policy towards both the Amazon in particular and the country's stance on international environmental issues in general. This was symbolized by the appointment of the prominent environmentalist José Lutzenberger as head of a newly created Secretariat for the Environment and was followed by a number of significant policy initiatives.

This chapter analyses the evolution of Brazilian attitudes and policies towards the Amazon and, in particular, seeks to explain the nature, causes, and limits of the move away from the hard-

I would like to thank David Pearce, Margaret Keck, and Benedict Kingsbury for their detailed comments on an earlier version of this chapter.

[1] The shift in Brazilian attitudes is not an isolated one. See e.g. the development of the attitudes of the North African countries to the Mediterranean Action Plan described in Peter Haas, *Saving the Mediterranean: The Politics of International Environmental Co-operation* (New York: Columbia UP, 1990); or the evolution of Indian policy towards the ozone question analysed by Richard Benedick, *Ozone Diplomacy. New Directions in Safeguarding the Planet* (Cambridge, Mass.: Harvard UP, 1991), esp. ch. 12.

line environmental nationalism of the mid-1980s. It considers the impact of the growth of environmentalism within Brazil but argues that international factors have been critical. Three sets of international factors are explored: first, the emergence of transnational coalitions of pressure groups, economists, and ecologists and the process of externally induced 'environmental learning' to which they contributed; second, the successful imposition of external pressure on Brazil which raised the costs of continuing with its previous policies and which came increasingly to interfere with the pursuit of other, more important, foreign policy goals. And third, the growing awareness in the Brazilian government that the environment issue could provide large developing countries such as Brazil with new international opportunities and with a new, if problematic, source of potential leverage.

Yet, if the case of the Amazon provides some grounds for believing that external action can be effective, it also illustrates very clearly the limits to such action. In part these limits have to do with international factors and with the difficulty of constructing a viable inter-state regime that combines equity, substantial external assistance, and an acceptable compromise on the questions of sovereignty and intervention, and which also represents a stable and viable trade-off between the environment and the broader pattern of Brazil's foreign policy objectives. But, equally importantly, the limits result from the strength of the underlying social, economic, and political forces pressing for the development of the Amazon and from the limited institutional and political capacities of the Brazilian state.

A. Amazonian Deforestation an International Political Issue

In one sense Amazonian deforestation has become an issue because of its global ecological impact in terms of the loss of biodiversity and its contribution to global climate change.[2] The

---

[2] For an overview of these problems, see the chapter by Norman Myers in this volume and Kenton R. Miller, Walter V. Reid, and Charles V. Barber, 'Deforestation and Species Loss', in Jessica Tuchman Matthews (ed.), *Preserving the Global Environment* (New York: W. W. Norton, 1991), 78–111.

biological resources of the tropical rainforests are extraordinary and the natural life of the rainforests is the richest and most diverse on earth. Covering only 6 per cent of the earth's land area, tropical forests are estimated to contain at least 50 per cent and perhaps up to 90 per cent of the world's species. In the next twenty years tropical deforestation may result in the extinction of between 5 and 15 per cent of the world's species. In addition to their aesthetic and ethical value, forests and forest products have great potential (although still very uncertain) scientific and medicinal value: as genetic material for plant breeding, as natural insecticides, or as pharmaceutical or medicinal products. Tropical forests also have a global impact in terms of their role in the global carbon cycle and the effect of deforestation on the global climate. After fossil fuel consumption, deforestation is the second most important human source of atmospheric carbon dioxide. Of the 8 billion tonnes of carbon dioxide accumulating per year in the global atmosphere, one estimate suggests that around 2.4 billion tonnes comes from forest burning, or around 30 per cent.[3] Tropical deforestation also releases two other, potent greenhouse gases (methane and nitrous oxide). Although estimates vary, tropical deforestation probably contributes around 10–15 per cent of total greenhouse gas emissions.

Brazil is the single most important actor in the international politics of the deforestation. Although the Amazon is not limited to Brazil, Brazilian Amazonia is the largest rainforest on earth. It covers some 58 per cent of Brazil's total land area and accounts for around 33 per cent of the world's surviving tropical forests, larger than the combined forested areas of Colombia, Indonesia, Peru, and Zaire. The exact contribution of Amazonian deforestation to total greenhouse gas emissions is disputed. According to the World Resources Institute, Brazil ranked third in the world in terms of net greenhouse gas emissions in 1987 (with 10.5 per cent of the total), after the USA (17.6 per cent) and the USSR (12.0 per cent). However, these estimates have been criticized, and the overall Brazilian contribution is perhaps nearer 4–5 per cent.[4]

[3] R. A. Houghton, 'The Future Role of Tropical Forests in Affecting the Carbon Dioxide Concentrations of the Atmosphere', *Ambio*, 19 (1990), 294–309.

[4] The WRI estimates are given in World Resources Institute, *World Resources 1990–1991* (New York: Oxford UP, 1990), 15, and disputed by Anil Agarwal and Sunita Narain, *Global Warming in an Unequal World* (New Delhi: Centre for Science

Nevertheless, the combination of deforestation and the country's actual and potential industrial development make Brazil a major actor in the international politics of the environment.

Yet, as other chapters in this volume have emphasized, the political problem does not emerge directly from the global impact of deforestation but rather from the incongruence between the international legal and political boundaries of the state system and the boundaries of ecological causal networks. Deforestation raises particularly difficult issues because of the fact that the forests are wholly located within a particular country—in this case Brazil—and that their preservation or destruction lies within the sovereign jurisdiction of the Brazilian state. This raises the important question as to whether and to what extent rainforests are in fact part of the 'global commons' and represent a collective good.[5] On the one hand, the situation is similiar to the environmental impact of the destruction of other resources over whose use states have sovereign jurisdiction. Thus the use of CFCs or the burning of fossil fuels has a direct impact on the atmosphere, which clearly is a global common and provides collective goods from which all benefit. Tropical forests, like the ozone layer or the atmosphere, provide benefits for all and are in this sense a collective good. They are therefore characteristic of commons in terms of the functions that they perform. On the other hand, unlike the ozone layer, the oceans, or Antarctica, forests are located firmly within particular sovereign states and do not share the typical characteristics of collective goods: indivisibility and non-excludability.[6] They are clearly divisible given that they are divided between states and are the 'property' of those states. Although no one can be excluded from the benefits, individual states claim the right to exclude others from the forests and from decisions affec-

---

and Environment, 1991), 4–5; and by Latin American and Caribbean Commission on Development and Environment, *Our Own Agenda* (New York: IDB/UNDP, 1990), 35–8.

[5] For a strong claim that they do form part of the global commons, see Edith Brown Weiss, *In Fairness to Future Generations: International Law, Common Patrimony, and Intergenerational Equity* (Dobbs Ferry, NY: Transnational Publishers, 1989), esp. ch. 7.

[6] On this question see Jeffrey Pentland, 'International Theory and the Environment: Tropical Deforestation as a Case Study', M.Phil. thesis (Oxford University, 1989), 28–35.

ting the future of the forests. Forests are thus both a 'global commons' providing a collective good from which all benefit and the 'property' of an individual state.

This dual focus means that the problem of sovereignty arises in a sharper and more intractable form than in the case of Antarctica or the ozone layer, and arguments that resources of the rainforests should be considered the common patrimony of mankind raise extremely difficult political and moral questions. Precisely which resources should be so classified and who should decide on their definition and fate? What does a right of access to such resources mean? Should it be on the basis of a free market? If not, how and by whom should markets in forest resources be managed? To what extent do duties to conserve such resources legitimize outside political intervention?

To a very significant extent deforestation became an actual, as opposed to potential, international political issue because pressure groups and NGOs succeeded in convincing governments and public opinion both of the globarel impact of deforestation and of the unwillingness or inability of the Brazilian government to take effective steps to address the problem. The particular salience of rainforest preservation within the campaigning priorities of the environmental movement needs to be emphasized. In part this reflected the intrinsic importance of the issue, the potentially catastrophic consequences of uncontrolled deforestation, and the sharp increases that occurred in the mid-1980s in both the rate of deforestation and the accompanying social violence. In part it became a priority because the external funding of some aspects of Amazonian development provided scope for effective lobbying in Washington and other capitals of the industrialized world.[7]

Deforestation also achieved international prominence because it lent itself to dramatic and extremely effective media presentation. On the one hand, there was the drama and visibility of the process itself, with huge palls of smoke, bulldozers at work, vast areas of jungle being flooded. On the other there were seemingly clear villains (military governments, multinational companies, international banks) and tragic victims (above all Indians but also the rural poor). Indeed the murder of Chico Mendes in December 1988 and the impending destruction of Indian peoples (especially

[7] See the chapter by Bramble and Porter in this volume.

the Yanomani) became particularly powerful and emotive catalysts for international protest. Amazonian deforestation, then,
provides a particularly powerful example of the role of the media
in setting the foreign policy agendas of states and in helping to
shape political responses to environmental issues.

B. The Growth of External Pressure and Brazilian Responses

The dominant international response to the problem of
Amazonian deforestation in the 1980s was the growth of external
pressure on the Brazilian government. Such a response was logical, given the central role played by the Brazilian state in the
post-war development of the Amazon and its apparent susceptibility to outside pressure. It was, after all, the Brazilian state that
had provided the initiative and dominant drive behind the
opening up of Amazonia, and it is important to view events in the
Amazon against the broader pattern of state-led development
that has been so characteristic of post-war Brazil, and especially
of the period of military rule.[8] The period after 1964 saw the
expansion and strengthening of a large state apparatus in the
region in order to encourage other groups—both national and
foreign—to participate. The various categories of state involvement have been extensively described in the literature and can be
summarized briefly:[9] first, the road-building programme, which
dated from the 1950s but which was expanded dramatically as
part of the military government's National Integration Plan. This
both facilitated large-scale movements of population and had an
important impact on patterns of land tenure. Second, the state-
organized colonization schemes which played an important role

[8] Anthony Hall, *Developing Amazonia. Deforestation and Social Conflict in Brazil's
Carajás Programme* (Manchester: Manchester UP, 1989); Stephen Bunker, *Under-
developing the Amazon. Extraction, Unequal Exchange and the Failure of the Modern
State* (Chicago: University of Chicago Press, 1985); and M. Schmink and C. Wood,
'The "Political Ecology" of Amazônia', in P. Little, M. M. Horowitz and A. E.
Nyerges (eds.), *Lands at Risk in the Third World* (Boulder, Colo.: Westview, 1987).

[9] For useful overviews: Dennis J. Mahar, *Government Policies and Deforestation in
Brazil's Amazon Region* (Washington, DC: World Bank, 1989); and Philip
Fearnside, 'Environmental Destruction in the Brazilian Amazon', in David Good-
man and Anthony Hall (eds.), *The Future of Amazonia: Destruction or Sustainable
Development* (London: Macmillan, 1990), 179–225.

in official thinking on Amazon development in the late 1960s and early 1970s. Third, large-scale development projects, symbolized by the Grand Carajás mining complex, the construction of hydroelectric plants, and extension of road and railway links. This reflected the important shift that took place around 1974/75 away from small-scale settlement projects and towards large-scale export-oriented development projects. And fourth, the wide-ranging system of government incentives for Amazonian development, which totalled some $1.5 billion in the period between 1967 and 1988 and which included investment tax-credits, subsidized rural agriculture, and low rates of tax on agricultural income (thereby encouraging the purchase of land for speculation).[10]

Brazil also appeared to be readily susceptible to outside pressure. It was in the grips of the most severe economic crisis since the 1930s and had become the largest debtor in the developing world. The external financing of many aspects of Amazonian development opened up the possibility of effective influence on multinational companies and financial institutions in the industrialized world. The overall role of foreign capital in Amazonian development has been exaggerated in much of the literature; it was, in fact, secondary to that of the Brazilian state.[11] Nevertheless, there were various external financial linkages to specific projects, the best known being the role of the World Bank, the Japanese government, and the EC in the financing of Grand Carajás, the role of the World Bank in the development of Rondônia, and the well-publicized multinational investment in cattle ranching.

Yet mounting external pressure met with great resistance in Brazil and provoked a nationalist reaction that reached its peak during 1988 and 1989. In one of his most hard-line speeches to a

[10] See Hans Binswanger, 'Fiscal and Legal Incentives with Environmental Effects on the Brazilian Amazon', World Bank Working Paper (Washington, DC: World Bank, 1987).

[11] For accounts that stress the role of foreign capital see Jaime Sautchuk et al., Projeto Jari: A Invasão Americana (São Paulo: Editora Brasil Debates, 1980); L. F. Pinto, Carajás: O Ataque ao Coração da Amazônia (Rio de Janeiro: Editora Marco Zero, 1982); and R. G. Cota, Carajás: A Invasão Desarmada (Petrópolis: Editora Vozes, 1984). For a more balanced view of the role of foreign capital see Hall, Developing Amazonia, 253–4; and David Cleary, Anatomy of the Amazon Gold Rush (London: Macmillan, 1990), 204.

military parade in March 1989, Sarney spoke of 'an insidious, cruel and untruthful campaign' against Brazil:

Brazil is being threatened over its sovereign right to use its own territory . . . With each day there are new forms of intervention containing veiled or explicit threats, designed to force us to take decisions not constructed by us in the defence of our own interests.[12]

This nationalist reaction involved a variety of themes which illustrate, albeit in an extreme form, many of the core concerns of the developing world. The first concerned the emphasis on economic growth and the role of developing the Amazon in that growth. The priority of economic growth was restated by the foreign minister Abreu Sodré in early 1989: 'Brazil does not want to transform itself into an ecological reserve for humanity. Our greatest duty is with our economic development.'[13]

A second theme was the suspicion that the developed world was using the environment to 'keep Brazil down' and to prevent it from developing. As Sarney put it: 'We cannot accept the developed world's manipulation of the ecology issue to restrict Latin America's autonomy and progress.' Or, to quote Paulo Tarso, the Secretary-General of *Itamaraty* (the Brazilian foreign ministry), there was an international 'campaign to impede the exploitation of natural resources in order to block Brazil from becoming a world power'.[14] Indeed much of the Brazilian debate of the late 1980s focused on the idea that the developed world was seeking to impose a new 'ecological order' that would work to the detriment of the developing world and that would legitimize external intervention in its affairs.[15]

Third, Brazilian reactions reflected the historical sense of the vulnerability of the region and the deep-rooted fear that predatory foreign interests were seeking to 'internationalize' it. The continuity of foreign attitudes was forcefully asserted by the Minister of the Interior, João Alves, in a statement to a congressional inquiry in April 1989:

Today we are facing an economic war disguised in terms of a noble quest for ecological protection, but with very old roots and very clearly defined objectives. . . . The nations, which in the past occupied or threatened to

[12] *Jornal do Brasil*, 18 Mar. 1989, p. 5.   [13] *Jornal do Brasil*, 25 Jan. 1989, p. 5.
[14] Both quotations as reported in *The Times*, 8 Mar. 1989.
[15] For an example of this perspective, see Bernardo Pericás Neto, 'Meio Ambiente e Relações Internacionais', *Contexto Internacional*, 9 (Jan./June 1989), 9–17.

occupy and take Amazonia from the Brazilians in order to exploit it in the name of the 'good of humanity', now say that Brazil must give up its sovereignty in this area so that it may be preserved as a kind of 'Garden of Eden'.[16]

Fourth, Brazilian statements stressed various aspects of Northern hypocrisy: in having devastated their own environment and having grown rich in the process; and in singling out Brazil as a particularly guilty environmental villain whilst themselves contributing far more to global environmental degradation. As Sarney put it during a visit to Guyana in March 1989: 'It is the developed countries which should be giving explanations for the destruction of the environment.'[17] They also pointed to the extremely one-sided nature of external interest and the lack of concern for Brazil's many other environmental problems. Finally, there were frequent speeches, especially from the military, restating the importance of the national security imperative of national integration.[18]

As part of this nationalist response, Brazilian policy-makers consistently rejected the growing number of proposals that would link debt reduction to environmental improvements (for instance, the suggestions made during a visit to Brazil in early 1989 by the US Senator Tim Wirth). President Sarney refused to participate in the summit conference at The Hague in March 1989 on the protection of the global atmosphere. The Brazilian delegation at The Hague argued forcefully against any reference to the Amazon in the final communiqué and against President Mitterand's suggestion for a strengthened environmental role for the United Nations that would carry with it an increased capacity to intervene.[19] Brazilian policy-makers also rejected any talk of environmental conditionality (as, for instance, in the series of proposals in the US Senate during 1989 that would link World Bank

[16] The full report contained a detailed history of foreign attempts to dominate the region, including the much-cited Hudson Institute proposals of the late 1960s to flood much of the Amazon basin. See *Correio Brasiliense*, 21 Apr. 1989, p. 4.

[17] Quoted in *Estado de São Paulo*, 4 Mar. 1989, p. 5.

[18] See e.g. the comments by the Head of the President's Military Household, General Bayma Denys, reported in *Correio Brasiliense* 8 Mar. 1989, p. 17; or the reactions to external pressure by the military commander of Amazonia, General Mario Sampaio, *Correio Brasiliense*, 9 Mar. 1989, p. 15.

[19] For a detailed account of Brazilian statements at The Hague see *Folha de São Paulo*, 11 Mar. 1989, p. C-3.

funding to tighter environmental conditionality).[20] According to Paulo Tarso, such moves would 'only increase bitterness and delay important works which, with or without aid, will be realized'.[21] The Brazilian position was forcefully restated during the Amazon Pact summit in May 1989, and Brazil was instrumental in the rejection by the Group of Eight Latin American countries of all forms of non-economic conditionality on economic or financial assistance.[22]

The environmental nationalism of the Sarney government did not occur in a vacuum and is closely related to other developments that were taking place in the country's foreign policy. The mid-1980s witnessed a number of points of friction between Brazil and the United States particularly over economic issues. There was much resentment in Brazil over US policy towards the Latin American debt crisis, and the two countries became involved in a series of clashes (both bilaterally and within the Uruguay Round) over a wide range of trade-related issues: the liberalization of services, intellectual property rights, and US criticism of Brazil's attempt to develop an autonomous computer industry. The informatics issue, in particular, generated a considerable nationalist backlash and, when seen together with external pressure on the environment, fuelled the widespread belief that the US was attempting to exploit Brazilian weakness in order to reassert its hegemony over the country.[23] International friction over the Amazon was therefore not an isolated case, and Brazil's reactions to external pressure over the Amazon need to be understood within this broader context.

There are significant and interesting elements of continuity between the arguments of the late 1980s and the positions adopted by Brazil and other developing countries during the first wave of international concern over the environment which led to the convening of the Stockholm Conference in 1972. At Stockholm Brazil argued strongly for the primacy of economic development. As the influential Brazilian ambassador to the United Nations, João de Araújo Castro, put it:

[20] *Estado de São Paulo*, 15 Feb. 1989, p. 12.
[21] *Estado de São Paulo*, 14 Jan. 1989, p. 12.
[22] See *Folha de São Paulo*, 23 May 1989.
[23] On the growth of these frictions see Andrew Hurrell and Ellene Felder, *The U.S.-Brazilian Informatics Dispute* (Washington, DC: SAIS/University Press of America, 1989).

Two thirds of humanity are far more threatened by hunger and misery than by the evils of pollution. . . . These developing countries work from the premiss that any adequate programme for the preservation of the environment must take into account the basic factors of development, since underdevelopment represents in itself one of the worst forms of environmental pollution.[24]

Not only had the developed countries destroyed their own forests and despoiled their environment, but that process had been central to the generation of their wealth and to the consequent inequality that existed between North and South. Brazilian representatives argued that the environment issue was being used by the North to maintain their political dominance, to 'freeze the structure of world power', and justify intervention in the affairs of the developing world. For Brazil, the balance between the environment and development was totally a matter for the individual sovereign state to decide, and outside intervention in the name of environmental management was wholly illegitimate. Together with other developing countries, Brazil was influential in ensuring that these kinds of arguments were reflected in the Final Declaration of the 1972 Stockholm Conference on the Human Environment.[25]

Brazil's language at Stockholm reflected very clearly the developmentalist ideology of the post-1964 military government, with its plans to forge an economic miracle propelling Brazil towards First World status and with its need to build political legitimacy on continued economic success. Such thinking has not, however, been limited to military governments, and there is no straightforward relationship between regime type and environmental policy. All Brazilian governments since 1930 have been concerned to promote rapid, industrially based development and there is a clear continuity between President Kubitschek's construction of Brasilia in the 1950s and his promise of

[24] João de Araújo Castro, 'O Congelamento do Poder Mundial', in Rodrigo Amado (ed.), *Araújo Castro* (Brasilia: Editora Universidade de Brasilia, 1982); and Araújo Castro, 'Environment and Development: The Case of the Developing Countries', *International Organization*, 26 (1972), 401–16.

[25] On the evolution of developing country attitudes see Lawrence Juda, 'International Environmental Concern: Perspectives of, and Implications for, Developing States', in David Orr and Marvin Soroos (eds.), *The Global Predicament: Ecological Perspectives on World Order* (Chapel Hill: University of North Carolina Press, 1979), 90–107; and John McCormick, *The Global Environmental Movement* (London: Belhaven Press, 1989), esp. chs. 5 and 8.

fifty years' growth in five years and the military government's promotion of rapid economic development in the post-1964 period. Such thinking has also reflected a deep-rooted cultural tradition (common to both Americas) in which European colonists became accustomed to the idea that land and natural resources were virtually limitless and so need not be cherished.

C. The Move Away from Hard-Line Environmental Nationalism

Gradually, however, Brazilian policy began to change.[26] This process began under Sarney. The subsidy element of rural credit was eliminated in 1987 and many of the fiscal subsidies that encouraged deforestation were ended in October 1988 (although only for new projects). In October 1988 Sarney also made his first major speech on the environment and established six working groups to study the problem. In April 1989 he launched the *Nossa Natureza* (Our Nature) programme as a major response to external pressure. This involved the creation of IBAMA (the Brazilian Environment and Renewable Resources Institute), which was charged with more effective ecological zoning, speeding up the demarcation of Indian lands, and establishing a more effective monitoring and fire-prevention scheme. In January 1990 Sarney created a system of 'extractive reserves' designed to formalize and protect the sustainable exploitation of forest resources by local groups.

The pace of change accelerated significantly with the declaration of a radical reshaping of Brazil's environmental policies by Sarney's successor as president, Fernando Collor de Mello, who took office in March 1990. The new policy was characterized by several dramatic gestures clearly intended to court international public opinion. Thus he appointed an internationally renowned

[26] It would be wrong to suggest that Brazilian policy did not change at all between Stockholm and the mid-1980s. For example, the Special Secretariat for the Environment was established in 1973 and a National Council for the Environment (CONAMA) was created in 1981. But such bodies exercised little influence over decision-making during the period of military rule, particularly over the formulation of economic policy. For an analysis of the evolution of Brazil's environmental policy see Roberto Guimarães, *Politics and the Environment in Brazil* (Boulder, Colo.: Lynne Rienner, 1991).

environmentalist, José Lutzenberger, as Secretary of the Environment. Collor's first official visit outside Brasilia was to Roraima, where he announced the launching of Operation Amazonia to counter illegal forest burning, together with plans to blow up 80 illegal airstrips used by gold-diggers (*garimpeiros*). On 5 June (International Environment Day) Collor he made a further well-publicized visit to the Pantanal. Similarly, the president pressed forcefully, and ultimately successfully, for the prosecution and conviction of the murderers of Chico Mendes. Other measures included the creation of a new Secretariat for the Environment (SEMA); the establishment of a National Environment Programme (PNMA); the creation of a new working group to review environmental zoning in the Amazon; the appointment of a new director to IBAMA and the promise to address the resource problems that had crippled the organization since its creation; the creation of a Research Centre for Tropical Forests to study the problem of sustainable development in the Amazon; and the establishment of environment sections in all the major government departments. In addition there was the significant decision to impose an effective system of income tax on agricultural land.

Although many of the changes were aimed primarily at international opinion and many others have remained rhetorical, some progress has been achieved. The pace of demarcation of Indian lands has increased somewhat, as has the government's willingness to evict gold-diggers from Indian territories. More importantly there has been a marked slowdown in the rate of deforestation: Brazilian government figures showed a decline of 65 per cent in the number of fires from 1989 to 1990 and a preliminary estimate suggested that $13.818 \, km^2$ of forest had been destroyed in 1990, some 27 per cent lower than in 1989.[27] It remains unclear, however, how much of this decline was due to specific government policies and how much was the result of unusually wet weather, the gradual shift in the pattern and pace of migration to the region, and, most important, the severity of the economic crisis and the drying up of agricultural credit.

Significant shifts also occurred in international environmental

[27] Other figures suggest a clearance rate for 1990 of around $20,000 \, km^2$, as against an average annual rate between 1980 and 1988 of $59,227 \, km^2$. See David Pearce, 'Deforesting the Amazon: Toward an Economic Solution', *Ecodecision*, 1 (1991), 42.

policy. In March 1990 Brazil decided to sign and ratify the Montreal Protocol. More generally, government rhetoric moved away from denunciations of outside interference and towards demands for external assistance. In particular Brazil argued that international economic pressures, especially the debt crisis, had exacerbated the problem, acting to force both the state and individuals to develop Amazonia. The government stressed that the country did not have the resources for the effective management of the forests. Thus if the industrialized countries were serious about saving the forests, they should dramatically increase foreign aid: to fund research into sustainable development; to create the institutions for the effective monitoring and control of forest areas; and to facilitate the transfer of environmentally efficient technology.

In line with these arguments, Brazil responded positively to the decision of the Group of Seven industrialized countries at the Houston summit in July 1990 to support the preservation of the Brazilian rainforest.[28] It agreed to draw up detailed plans for the Amazon in discussion with both the EC and the World Bank.[29] These plans called for external aid of $1.56 billion and were presented to the Group of Seven at the London summit in July 1991.[30] The summit agreed an initial aid package of $50 million but did not approve the Brazilian proposals, calling instead for further work on the identification of appropriate environmental projects. Lastly, in June 1991 Brazil reversed its long-standing opposition to debt-for-nature swaps.

D. Explaining the Shift in Policy

One explanation for the evolution of Brazilian policy might lie in the growth of environmentalism inside Brazil, either in the form of a broad-based environmental movement across the country, or in the form of protest and social mobilization specifically focused around Amazonian deforestation. There is some evidence for such an argument. The Brazilian environmental movement has

[28] See *Folha de São Paulo*, 12 July 1990, p. C-4.
[29] These were published in mid-1991. Government of Brazil, World Bank, EC Commission, *Programa piloto para a proteção das florestas tropicais do Brasil* (Brasilia: May 1991).
[30] See *Gazeta Mercantil*, 17 July 1991, p. 7.

grown steadily since the early 1970s and has gradually helped to increase national awareness of environmental issues.[31] What one might call rather loosely the Brazilian environmental 'movement' emerged out of three principal sources. The oldest was the conservation movement, whose roots lie in the nineteenth century and whose thinking can be seen in the creation of national parks in the 1930s. This became more organized in the post-war period with the formation of such groups as the Union of Protectors of Nature and the Brazilian Foundation for the Conservation of Nature, founded in 1955 and 1958 respectively. Second, the 1970s saw the growth of grass-roots organizations in and around the cities in the form of neighbourhood associations and Church groups. These groups developed as a response to the appalling poverty and inequality that has characterized Brazilian economic development and were also related to the growth of political protest against the military government that gathered pace after 1974. They were not self-consciously 'ecological' but their demands were a direct reaction against the ecological degradation of Brazil's urban environment: the lack of clean water and sanitation, the uncontrolled industrial pollution, and the lack of housing and basic amenities. Finally, the period since the early 1970s has seen the emergence of specifically ecological groups, whose membership is largely middle-class and which are based mostly in the industrialized south of the country. Perhaps the two most important and well-established environmental groups of the 1980s were the Atlantic Rainforest Foundation and the Funatura Foundation for Nature, both created in 1986.

These diverse activities have undoubtedly helped to stimulate a shift in attitudes towards the environment in Brazil. There have been numerous successful local campaigns, several of which have attracted a good deal of publicity and financial backing (including from abroad). The campaign to save the Atlantic forests (*SOS Mata Atlantica*) is a good example. There has also been a gradual seepage of environmentalism into the political arena with the growth of vocal environmental groups within several of the major political parties. Environmental issues have also been

[31] On environmentalism in Brazil see José Augusto Padua (ed.), *Ecológia e Política no Brasil* (Rio de Janeiro: Editora Espaço e Tempo, 1987); and Eduardo Viola, 'The Ecologist Movement in Brazil', *International Journal of Urban and Regional Research*, 12 (June 1988), 211–27.

given increased prominence as, with the return to civilian rule after 1985, opposition parties have come into office at the state or municipal level. Finally, the highly developed Brazilian media and advertising industries have been very quick to latch on to the commercial advantages of environmentalism.

Yet, whilst these developments are significant (particularly in what they might mean in the longer term), the political weaknesses of the environmental movement (especially as regards the Amazon) need to be noted. First, the impact of the movement has been limited by the fact that it grew out of concern for a very wide range of mostly local issues and has been unable to develop a clear ideology and a consistent political stance. Second, there has been a major division between the concerns and priorities of the mostly middle-class environmental groups and the priorities of the urban poor and the political organizations that represent them. Third, the influence of the environmental movement within the mainstream of Brazilian party politics and, perhaps more importantly, within the economic ministries, has remained limited. The environment has not become a major domestic political issue, as the 1989 presidential campaign clearly showed. Finally, although opinion polls do provide evidence of growing environmental awareness, its overall salience as an issue remains limited.[32] Thus, whilst the growth of environmentalism inside Brazil needs to be noted, the shift in Brazilian policy towards the Amazon was not principally a reaction to such pressure.

What, then, of political protest and mobilization focused specifically around the issue of the Amazon by the peoples most directly affected by the process of deforestation? As has been well chronicled, the process of development in the Amazon has generated intense social conflict. The late 1980s witnessed an intensification of conflict over access or title to land, fraudulent land sales and peasant evictions, and the invasion of Indian lands by the military, gold prospectors, and small farmers.[33] This led in

[32] One survey in São Paulo in June 1991 found that 86% of those polled believed Indian lands should be protected and 77% that the preservation of the rainforest was more important than developing its economic potential. However, on a list of important issues, the environment came well below security, health, education, inflation, and corruption. See *Folha de São Paulo*, 28 and 29 June 1991.

[33] The human costs of Amazonian development are well catalogued in several of the papers in Goodman and Hall (eds.), *The Future of Amazonia*. See also Amnesty International, *Brazil: Authorised Violence in Rural Areas* (London: Amnesty International, 1988).

turn to increased political mobilization by the victims, visible in the formation of rural trade unions (the most famous of which was the Rubber Tappers Union led by Chico Mendes), the growth of Church groups, and the creation of Indian groups such as the Indigenous Peoples Union, founded in 1980. Significant ties developed between these groups and the major Brazilian opposition parties (for example, the links between the rural union movement and the Workers Party (PT)). Leading Brazilian environmentalists campaigned against government policies in the Amazon, as for example in the 'condemnation' in 1989 of the Brazilian state for ecological crimes by the Amazonian Nature Tribunal, chaired by José Lutzenberger.[34] But whilst political mobilization and the extent of social violence did increase the salience of the Amazon as an issue in Brasilia, its direct impact on the evolution of Brazilian government policies was small.

What is far more striking are the very close links that have grown up between the victims of Amazonian deforestation and the international NGO community. Many groups, such as the National Council of Rubber Tappers, have received significant funding from abroad. The work of groups such as Survival International, Oxfam, and Amnesty International has been critical in publicizing the scale of the violence and thereby offering an albeit fragile degree of support and protection. The direct participation of Indian groups, rural unions, and Brazilian environmentalists such as Lutzenberger in the lobbying process in the US and Europe formed a central part of the NGO rainforest campaigns.[35] Indeed the threat to the Yanomani and the murder of Chico Mendes were far more extensively publicized abroad than in Brazil. The density and range of these transnational linkages has thus been a very important characteristic of the politicization of the Amazon question. The political impact of social mobilization in the Amazon was largely the result of these transnational ties and their contribution to the international campaign against Brazilian government policies, rather than the result of direct pressure on the government in Brasilia.

[34] See *Jornal do Brasil*, 23 Feb. 1989.

[35] The density of these transnational linkages is brought out very well by Kenneth Maxwell, 'The Mystery of Chico Mendes', *New York Review of Books*, 28 Mar. 1991, pp. 37–46. See also Susanna Hecht and Alexander Cockburn, *The Fate of the Forest* (London: Verso, 1989), esp. ch. 8; and Dave Treece, *Bound in Misery and Iron* (London: Survival International, 1987).

If the growth of domestic environmentalism was only a marginal factor behind the shift of government policy, what has been the role of international factors? One increasingly popular explanation places emphasis on the growth of knowledge, the possibility of externally induced 'environmental learning', and the formation of transnational epistemic communities. It seems clear that the growth of external concern and the explosion of debate and the increase in research did lead gradually to a growing reappraisal within the Brazilian government of its policies towards the Amazon. In other words there was a discernible process of environmental learning. Increasing numbers of officials and politicians came to accept much of the scientific case against previous policies. Not only was Brazil being adversely affected by the global impact of deforestation on the world's climate, but it would be still more directly affected locally and regionally: locally by the degradation of soils, regionally by the predicted changes in rainfall patterns.

The degree of consensus has not been as clear-cut as, say, over the ozone debate. Arguments over the relative importance of Amazonian deforestation to global climate change have continued, as have disagreements over the data on the rate and scope of deforestation. Similarly, the question of who controls the relevant data and appropriate technology has remained a focus of debate and disagreement. Nevertheless a significant degree of convergence is clearly evident. Statements from Brazilian officials denying the whole scientific validity of the case against deforestation have all but disappeared.[36] In addition, from 1989 onwards there were an increasing number of *Brazilian* reports of ecological destruction in the Amazon, for example over the impact of mercury poisoning, and domestic discussion of the heavy social costs of rapid and largely uncontrolled development in the region.[37]

Furthermore, much (but by no means all) of the economic case against previous policies has come to be accepted. The evidence of the economic idiocy of the massive range of government subsidies (especially for cattle ranching) appeared virtually irrefut-

[36] For such a statement by the Army Minister, General Leônidas Pires Gonçalves, see *O Globo*, 14 Apr. 1989.

[37] See e.g. the report of the National Department for Mineral Production (DNPM), which spoke of a 'silent ecological tragedy' resulting from the use of mercury by *garimpeiros*, reported in *Folha de São Paulo*, 27 May 1989, p. C-3.

able. Previous levels of government subsidies were not only contributing to an increasingly unsustainable fiscal crisis, but were supporting activities that were uneconomic as well as ecologically destructive. Moreover, if the costs were rising, then awareness was also growing that the economic benefits of traditionally conceived Amazonian development were far more limited than the mythology suggested and that the country was failing to profit from some of the most important potential benefits (for example, the commercialization of the forest gene pool). Indicative of this shift, editorials in leading newspapers came to focus less on outrage against external interference and more on the legitimacy of outside concern, on the damage to Brazil of increased deforestation, on the need for more research, and on the possibility of deriving sustainable, and more significant, economic benefits from alternative forms of Amazonian development.[38]

These changes appear to owe much to the formation of transnational coalitions of ecologists and economists as well as to the international publicity given to Amazonian deforestation by NGOs and scientists in the industrialized world. They provide some evidence to confirm Peter Haas's arguments about the importance of epistemic communities in explaining how environmental learning occurs:

Epistemic communities may introduce new policy alternatives to their governments, and depending on the extent to which these communities are successful in obtaining and retaining bureaucratic power domestically, they can often lead governments to pursue them. In the case of the Mediterranean . . . governments learned about the complexity of the pollution problems and accepted the need for more comprehensive and co-ordinated policies to accomplish state and regional goals.[39]

In the case of the Amazon, the formation of transnational links between scientists, policy-makers, and pressure groups helped the development of consensus about the nature of the problem of deforestation and about the major reforms that had to be taken to deal with it.

Yet notions of environmental learning and the role of epistemic communities are insufficient to explain the evolution of Brazilian

[38] See e.g. editorials in *Jornal do Brasil*, 9 July 1989, *Folha de São Paulo*, 18 Aug. 1989, *Estado de São Paulo*, 4 Aug. 1989.

[39] Peter M. Haas, 'Do regimes matter? Epistemic Communities and Mediterrean Pollution Control', *International Organization*, 43 (1989), 402.

policy towards the Amazon. Such factors have been over-shadowed by the role of external pressure and by consequent changes in Brazil's calculations of the international costs and benefits of continuing with its previous Amazonian policies.

By 1989 the growth of external criticism had begun to cause Brazil significant problems. Many of these costs were related specifically to the Amazon. Thus NGO campaigning began to limit Brazilian access to multilateral finance. European NGOs mounted a campaign against the role of the EC in financing the Grand Carajás project. In Washington criticism of the World Bank and calls for greater environmental conditionality became more strident and helped to undermine a $500 million World Bank loan to the Brazilian energy sector and to complicate other Bank lending programmes in Brazil. The Inter-American Development Bank decided not to proceed with a planned $65 million loan for the extension of the BR364 road in Rondonia. Several large multinational companies abandoned their involvement in large-scale ranching, partly due to the end of fiscal subsidies but also to avoid adverse publicity.

But the most significant costs were more general and concerned the impact of the Amazon issue on Brazil's broader foreign policy goals. As Collor discovered during his pre-inauguration visits to Europe and the United States in early 1990, negotiations over far more important economic issues were increasingly being obstructed and overshadowed by the wave of foreign criticism of Brazil's Amazon policy. Thus it was not simply the direct political and economic costs of external pressure, but rather their impact on Brazil's broader foreign policy objectives that was decisive in helping to shift Brazilian policy. The Collor government came into office determined to reorient Brazilian foreign policy away from what it perceived to be an outdated and counter-productive 'third worldism' and to improve relations with the industrialized countries, especially the United States. To this end Brazil moved to try and defuse the outstanding sources of friction with Washington: over Brazil's nuclear policy, over its missile development programme and its policy on arms exports, and over a range of trade-related issues, such as the Brazilian informatics regime, intellectual property rights, and restrictions on foreign investment.

In part these foreign moves reflected a belief that the disputes with the United States of the 1980s had been counter-productive. But more importantly, they were the natural corollary to the reorientation of Collor's economic policy, which, in common with most of Latin America, came to lay increasing emphasis on economic liberalization and integration into world markets. A direct parallel may thus be traced between the decline of Brazil's strident economic nationalism (for example, over computers) and the move away from Sarney's environmental nationalism. Brazil's change of stance on the environment was not aimed solely—or perhaps even principally—at the environment but rather reflected a broader range of political objectives. It was designed to remove the constant criticism of Brazil that had come to dominate Brazil's contacts with its major partners and that threatened negotiations over what were the far more important issues of trade, debt, and development.

In addition to the costs imposed by external pressure there was also growing awareness in the Brazilian government of the potential benefits and opportunities provided by environmental issues. From late 1989 an increasing number of Brazilian spokesmen came to argue that the country should seek to exploit the environmental concerns of the industrialized world in order to further Brazil's foreign policy goals. In an early and eloquent statement of this position, Collor's future Secretary of Science and Technology, José Goldemberg, argued that Brazil 'should adopt a position of international leadership in the case of atmospheric CO_2 and not adopt the defensive position that it has been taking up to now'.[40] In June 1989 the former ambassador to the GATT and the UN, Paulo Nogueira Batista, called for the creation of a UN fund of $2 billion a year to help developing countries deal with environmental problems.[41] By early 1990 the Brazilian foreign minister was stressing the need for increased foreign economic assistance: 'For the preservation of the tropical forest it is necessary to have financial and human resources from all the developed nations concerned with the problem.'[42]

The idea that the environment might be turned to Brazil's advantage fitted with similar moves in other developing countries

[40] José Goldemberg, 'A Destruição da Amazonia', *Folha de São Paulo*, 23 Apr. 1989, p. A-3.
[41] *Jornal do Brasil*, 25 June 1989, p. 19.
[42] See *Estado de São Paulo*, 27 Jan. 1990.

and also reflected the extent to which the international environmental debate was moving towards an at least partial and rhetorical acceptance of the developing countries' case. The concept of sustainable development and the imperative of continued economic growth in the developing world was a central theme of the influential report, *Our Common Future*. The Toronto Conference of the World Meteorological Organisation in June 1988 called explicity for the transfer of financial resources and relevant technologies to the developing world and proposed the creation of a World Atmosphere Fund financed by a tax on fossil fuel consumption in the developed world. In September 1989, at a Non-Aligned Summit in Belgrade, India called for the creation of a $18 billion Planet Protection Fund. Such themes were repeated at the Commonwealth Summit in Malaysia in October 1989 and at the Noordwijk conference on climate change in November 1989. The principle of financial and resource transfers to the developing world achieved concrete results in the ozone negotiations and the creation of a multilateral fund at the London Conference in June 1990. By the time of the Group of Seven summit at Houston in July 1990, which explicitly recognized the need for external assistance to preserve the Amazon, there were therefore good reasons for believing that the environment could be turned to Brazil's advantage.

The need to exploit international interest in environmental questions was strengthened by the belief that Latin America was becoming increasingly marginalized. The late 1980s witnessed growing concern in Latin America that developments in the Soviet Union and Eastern Europe would divert attention and resources from the developing world, and that, within the developing world, Latin America would be unable to match either the geopolitical importance of the Middle East or the humanitarian pull of Africa and Asia. There was awareness that many of the factors that had helped underpin earlier ideas of North–South interdependence were losing much of their force. On many indicators, North–South interdependence had declined since the heady days of the 1970s: the North traded less with the South; the South had become relatively less important as a target for Northern investment; the North had less need of most Southern minerals and commodities; and Northern banks had gradually reduced their crippling exposure to developing-country debt.[43] The emergence of global environmental inter-dependence was seen to represent an important exception to this trend and one which the developing world could ill afford to ignore. It is therefore not surprising that Brazil should have come to consider the possibility of exploiting the Amazonian issue. The need to include large developing countries in any effective global climate or deforestation regime and the multiple contributions to mankind provided by the rainforest have increasingly placed Brazil in the position of potentially being able to 'trade' the conservation of the forest or to export 'environmental public goods' to the rest of the world in return for financial and technological assistance from its international partners or for support on other issues.

E. The Limits to External Pressure and the Scope for Effective International Action

Whilst the internationalization of the issue and the growth of external pressure have been successful in persuading Brazil to shift its policy, there are clear limits to what such strategies are likely to achieve. In the first place, external pressure does not adequately address questions of justice and equity. Seeking to counter Amazonian deforestation primarily by means of external pressure on Brazil ignores the fundamental distributional questions that dominate environmental negotiations between the industrialized and developing countries: the balance between environment and development, the need to ensure a fair distribution of the costs of effective management of the global environment, and the importance of treating the wide range of factors which contribute towards global warming in an equitable manner.[44] Moreover, the distribution of costs cannot be perceived solely in economic terms. If an effective deforestation regime is going to involve legal constraints on state autonomy, there has to be a belief that such constraints and the political costs

---

[43] See John Ravenhill, 'The North-South Balance of Power', *International Affairs*, 66 (1990), 731–48.

[44] For Brazilian examples of these arguments see Goldemberg, 'A Destruição da Amazônia', p. A-3; and G. E. do Nascimento e Silva, 'A Amazônia e a poluição do mundo', *Jornal do Brasil*, 4 Aug. 1990.

that they involve are being distributed equitably between all the states concerned.[45]

External pressure over deforestation also ignores the problem of finding a fair distribution of priorities between different environmental issues inside Brazil. There has been much legitimate Brazilian criticism that the rest of the world concerns itself solely with the rainforests, whilst ignoring the depth and seriousness of Brazil's other environmental problems. In particular, very little international attention has been paid to the extent of environmental degradation in and around Brazil's urban centres: the pollution, lack of clean water and sanitation, insecurity, overcrowding. These problems have grown dramatically through the years of rapid economic growth and have been intensified by the enormous social inequalities that have come to characterize Brazilian society. Indeed it is often forgotten that Brazil's environmental problems and perspectives are those of a predominantly urban and industrial society.[46] During a forty-year period of economic growth (around 7 per cent p.a.) the urban component of population increased from 36 per cent to 68 per cent and the share of non-agricultural employment rose from 40 per cent to 70 per cent. This is an important factor distinguishing Brazilian (and Latin American) environmental concerns from those in some other parts of the developing world. Lastly, external pressure does nothing to address the question of procedural equity or the question of how decisions over the management of the global environment should be taken. These questions of equity are, for most people, important in their own right. But they are also important for political reasons, given the role that perceptions of fairness play in explaining successful bargaining outcomes. Even if a solution is some sense economically or ecologically

[45] Even if environmentally related resources are forthcoming from the industrialized countries, there are other important distributional questions that are likely to prove rather more problematic for Brazilian policy-makers: first, the distribution of environmentally related assistance *between developing countries*; and second, the question of whether the outside world should concern itself over the distribution of such resources *within Brazil*.

[46] For details of Brazil's social and economic conditions which do so much to shape the country's environmental attitudes, see Edmar L. Bacha and Herbert S. Klein (eds.), *Social Change in Brazil 1945–1985. The Incomplete Transition* (Albuquerque: University of New Mexico Press, 1986); and Helio Jaguaribe *et al.*, *Brasil 2000* (Rio de Janeiro: Editora Paz e Terra, 1986).

'efficient' it will not be accepted if it is perceived to be manifestly unjust.[47]

Secondly, external pressure is unlikely to ensure the continued willingness of the Brazilian government to improve environmental management in the Amazon. For many officials and policy-makers in Brasilia the shift of policy over Amazonia has been at least partially tactical: a means of eliminating an internationally divisive source of friction that was obstructing the management of far more important and immediate issues; and a way of increasing the international salience of Brazil's problems and of seeking to secure concessions from the industrialized countries. The possible 'pay-off' for this shift in policy might be related directly to the Amazon or other environmental questions, or it could involve a favourable trade-off between the Amazon and some wholly unconnected issue.

For many others in Brasilia, the moves toward environmental reform are genuine but the implications of this for the country's economic development remain unclear. Although the rhetoric of sustainable development has become all but universal, there continue to be very deep divisions between those who favour a radical recasting of Brazil's development strategy and those who want a continuation of the push for rapid industrialization but with a greater degree of ecological rationality.[48] External assistance will play an important role in deciding how this balance is played out. Lastly, significant flows of external aid will be important in countering the still vociferous arguments of what might be called the unreconstructed developmentalists, within the military and traditional political forces in Amazonia.[49]

[47] On the role of perceptions of equity in environmental negotiations, see Oran Young, 'The Politics of International Regime Formation: Managing Natural Resources and the Environment', *International Organization*, 43 (1989), 368–9.

[48] The public disagreements between Lutzenberger and Goldemberg over future hydro-electric projects in the Amazon illustrate these broader divisions (see *Folha de São Paulo*, 14 Apr. 1990), as do the clashes between Lutzemberger and the powerful Secretary for Regional Development, Egberto Baptista, over the reintroduction of government subsidies for the Amazon in Jan. 1991 (see *Jornal do Brasil*, 24 June 1991).

[49] On the continued strength of such views see the leaked report of the *Escola Superior de Guerra* (Higher War College) which reiterated the importance of developing and settling the region and of countering the 'subversive' threat posed by environmental NGOs (reported in *Folha de São Paulo*, 29 May 1990, p. A-5); the statement by the military commander of Amazonia that 'The presence of the *garimpeiro* has strategic importance for the occupation of territory' (quoted in *Istoé*,

Third, the focus solely on external pressure ignores the question of the ability of Brazil to implement effective environmental policies in the Amazon. Whilst the causes of deforestation have received a great deal of attention, the ability of the Brazilian state to modify and manage these pressures has received less attention.[50] The bombing of *garimpeiro* airstrips was largely symbolic and has not been followed up. Progress on the politically sensitive task of demarcating Indian lands has been extremely slow. Much of the decline in deforestation rates can be attributed to the weather and the impact of the economic crisis. The ability to enforce new regulations on the ground remains limited and many of the fines imposed by IBAMA remain uncollected. Many of these problems are the result of economic and institutional weaknesses. There are many projects that the government is unable to undertake. Both IBAMA and SEMA remain chronically under-funded and underequipped and are extremely weak compared to other parts of the bureaucracy. The inefficiency of the bureaucracy remains a serious difficulty, and environmental policy under Collor has been the subject of protracted bureaucratic in-fighting. These problems have been made worse by the economic and financial crisis that has racked Brazil since the early 1980s and by the consequent determination to reduce public spending.

There is clearly scope for effective international assistance in helping to solve these problems. Institutional weaknesses have been identified by the World Bank as a major priority, whilst external financial assistance can help provide the resources to fund research into sustainable development strategies and to help create effective bureaucratic structures. Technological co-operation agreements and relatively low-level environment-related funding have been increasing steadily over the past year. Thus there has been a $117 million World Bank loan for Brazil's National Environment Programme; the negotiation of a $150 million environmental aid programme with Germany; the signature in July 1989 of a $3 million bilateral environment programme with Britain; and moves to increase the environ-

---

4 Apr. 1990); or the denunciation of a foreign conspiracy to internationalize the rainforests by the Governor of Amazonas in June 1991 (see *Correio Brasiliense*, 21 June 1991, p. 4).

[50] See Andrew Hurrell, 'The Politics of Amazonian Deforestation', *Journal of Latin American Studies*, 23 (1991), 197–215.

mental component of both Canadian and, more significantly, Japanese bilateral aid. Moreover, as mentioned earlier, the Group of Seven has agreed in principle to significant transfers of resources.

Yet it has to be recognized that many of the most pressing constraints on effective environmental policies are not institutional, but are related to the structural economic and political problems that Brazil has faced since 1985 and to the character of the Brazilian state. By their very nature these problems are far less susceptible to outside influence. Brazil's environmental policy has been, and will remain, hostage to the restoration of financial stability and economic growth. Various quite specific linkages can be identified. First, the severity of the economic crisis has totally dominated the agenda of both the president and the major policy-makers and has reinforced the crippling 'short-termism' of economic policy-making. For successive economic ministers, surviving from week to week has often been a major achievement. Second, without price stability at the macro-economic level, the problem of getting prices and incentives right at the regional and local levels (which forms the central thrust of, for example, World Bank policy) is unlikely to be effectively addressed. Third, although overshadowed by more specific economic incentives, the widespread rural poverty of many parts of Brazil has been an important factor encouraging the migration of small farmers to the region.[51]

The ability of the outside world to solve Brazil's economic crisis is limited. Many have argued that there is a direct link between deforestation and Brazil's large foreign debt and that this represents the most efficient way of tackling the problem.[52] Without the burden of the developing world's largest external debt, it is argued, Brazil would be able to eliminate the large-scale development projects in the Amazon that are devoted to generating the export revenues needed to service the foreign debt, and could channel more resources into investment into sustainable development.

[51] For a discussion of the relationship of poverty to deforestation, see Pearce, 'Deforesting the Amazon', 40–5.

[52] The link between deforestation and debt was popularized by the Brundtland Report. For more specific arguments see Elmar Altvater, 'Falência e Destruição', *Contexto Internacional*, 10 (July/Dec. 1989), 7–42; John Cartwright, 'Conserving Nature, Decreasing Debt', *Third World Quarterly*, 11. 2 (Apr. 1989), 114–27.

Moreover, the overall improvement in the economy that would follow from debt reduction would undercut the economic pressures on both the state and individuals that encourage deforestation. There are, however, difficulties with this argument. The relationship between international economic pressures and Amazonian deforestation is much looser than the popular rhetoric would suggest. It is true that successive Brazilian governments since 1974 have looked to the export potential of the Amazon (especially in the form of mineral exports from the Grand Carajás project) as an increasingly stopgap solution to the imbalances in the Brazilian economy. Yet the main policy decisions facilitating large-scale development in the Amazon were taken well before the emergence of the debt crisis. The overall economic importance of the Amazon has remained limited, with the region accounting for only around 6.4 per cent of GNP and less than 5 per cent of Brazilian exports, which are now dominated by manufactured products. Furthermore, primary sector production and exports declined in relative terms both through the borrowing years of the 1970s and the debt crisis of the 1980s. There are a number of technical problems that complicate large-scale linkage between debt-relief and deforestation.[53] Finally, it has to be recognized that Brazil's economic problems are the result of a complex mixture of domestic and international factors and are certainly not reducible to the resolution of the foreign debt or to any other magic key held by the outside world.

Effective environmental management is also critically hindered by political constraints and by the difficulty of putting together a stable political coalition behind the new environmental policy. Brazilian responses to international pressure cannot be understood except with reference to the changing nature of the Brazilian state and to the policies, values, and attitudes of the contending political forces within the country. The definition of Brazilian interests will change according to institutional context, to the degree of organization of the various groups, and to the leadership capacities of the major actors.

During the Sarney years the balance of political interests does a

[53] For an assessment of the scope of debt-for-nature swaps see Stein Hansen, 'Debt for Nature Swaps: Overview and Discussion of Key Issues', World Bank Environment Department Working Paper No. 1; and Stephen van R. Winthrop, 'Debt-for-Nature Swaps: Debt Relief and Biosphere Preservation', *SAIS Review*, 9. 2 (Summer/Fall 1989), 129–46.

great deal to explain both the continuity of official development policies in the Amazon and the nationalist reaction against external pressure.[54] Sarney's own effective political authority was extremely limited, and the period saw an increase in the political power of those groups which were most strongly in favour of continuing the unrestricted development of the Amazon. First, there was the emergence of powerful lobbies, such as the São Paulo based Association of Amazonian Entrepreneurs (AEA), the Amazonian Association of Agriculture and Ranching, and, most importantly, the UDR (*União Democrática Ruralista*) which was formed in July 1985 and which successfully crippled the land reform proposals in the final 1988 debates in the Constituent Assembly. Second, the period saw the strengthening of the position of many of these same interests within the major party structures. And third, there was the continued central political role of the military, visible both in the drafting of the 1988 constitution and in the direct impact of the military on the direction and implementation of policy towards the Amazon.

Much of the potential significance of Collor's shift on environmental policy has depended on his ability to resolve, or at least effectively manage, Brazil's long-standing political crisis. His early period of office was characterized by the cultivation of a strong presidential style: centralizing decisions within a narrow group of policy-makers; basing his authority on a direct populist appeal to the people; bulldozing a radical economic stabilization programme through both a hesitant Congress and the courts; and achieving a significantly greater degree of autonomy from the military. Yet by early 1991, much of this impetus had been lost due largely to the failure of Collor's first two economic stabilization packages, disarray and infighting within the administration, and the limits and fragility of his political base within Congress and the established parties. This has once more raised doubts about the government's political capacity to implement effective changes in the Amazon and about the extent to which Collor may be pressed towards political alliances with precisely those groups least likely to favour radical reform in the Amazon.[55]

[54] For a more detailed analysis, see Hurrell, 'The Politics of Amazonian Deforestation', 205–10.

[55] Thus far most of Collor's environmental initiatives have taken the form of short-term 'provisional measures' that must be subsequently agreed to by Congress. Sustained Congressional backing is particularly critical because of the need for a major revision of Brazil's Forest Code.

Moreover, whatever the degree of political stability at the centre, the scale of Amazonian development has led to an erosion of the capacity of the state to implement effective control in the region. The evolution of state policies created or consolidated powerful groups able to resist state authority and to use the instruments of state power (state finance, the bureaucracy, the army, the police) for their own purposes.[56] The process of development subverted previous land tenure systems, displacing traditional social and economic structures and replacing them with groups better able to exploit new opportunities—for example, by being able to establish legally registered title to lands or to buy the support of local police and bureaucrats.

If the potential for effective international assistance in resolving Brazil's structural economic problems is limited, the scope for outside influence on the balance of political forces is still more constrained. The Brazilian political system is a very closed one.[57] The most important exception concerns the possible expansion of ties between the international NGO community and Brazilian environmental groups. But the role for external involvement here is likely to be long-term, diffuse, and indirect.

F. Conclusion

This chapter has sought to analyse the nature of Amazonian deforestation as an international political issue and to identify the role of international factors in the evolution of recent Brazilian policy towards the Amazon. It has argued that international action has played an important role in altering Brazilian attitudes and policies towards the region: through assisting a process of environmental learning, through raising the costs of continuing with existing policies, and through fostering an international environment in which a shift in policy might be expected to lead to future benefits. Of these the role of external pressure needs to be stressed. Indeed, the case of deforestation is a useful reminder

[56] This theme is well developed by Stephen Bunker. See *Underdeveloping the Amazon*, 52–3.

[57] This is explored in greater depth in Andrew Hurrell, 'International Support for Political Democracy: The Case of Brazil', to appear in Laurence Whitehead (ed.), *International Political Support for Political Democracy in Contemporary Latin America* (forthcoming, Johns Hopkins UP).

that, although the environment is often seen as a natural arena for co-operation, power and coercion are also likely to play an important role in global environmental management.

The chapter has also pointed to the critical issues that will need to be addressed in any future international regime which seeks to manage the problem of Amazon deforestation. If Brazilian support is to be maintained, such a regime will have to take on board many of the Brazilian arguments over justice and equity. There will have to be awareness of continuing sensitivities over sovereignty and intervention. And, most important, it will need to contain a substantial degree of external assistance, both in the form of resources directly relevant for sustainable Amazonian development, and as a more general 'side payment'.

This chapter also suggests that the idea of a deforestation regime should not be conceived too narrowly. On the one hand, continued NGO activity is likely to remain extremely important in ensuring the continued politicization of the issue, in monitoring developments on the ground, in supporting Brazilian environmental groups, and in maintaining the pressure on the Brazilian government and in pressing the industrialized world to increase environment-related aid. On the other, this chapter has repeatedly stressed the extent to which environmental policy has to be seen within the broader pattern of Brazilian foreign policy and the Brazilian political system. Calculations of advantage will not be limited to a deforestation regime, nor even to an international agreement on global climate change, but will depend crucially on trade-offs and linkages between the environment and the many other issues on Brazil's foreign and domestic political agenda.

The final conclusion to emerge is that ensuring some degree of international understanding over the importance of Amazonian deforestation and over the broad steps that need to be taken to address the problem is only half the task, and perhaps the easier half. As this chapter has argued, a sustained shift towards ecologically rational policies in the Amazon is very closely related to the structural economic and political problems, problems that are only tangentially and indirectly susceptible to amelioration from outside. Effective environmental management of the Amazon will certainly involve international co-operation and inter-state agreements. But it will also depend on some improvement in

Brazil's overall economic situation and the existence of both a sufficiently powerful domestic political coalition and a sufficiently effective administrative apparatus to ensure compliance with whatever international norms and agreements may be entered into.

16

The Anatomy of Environmental Action: The Case of Tropical Deforestation

Norman Myers

TROPICAL deforestation has recently emerged as a major issue in the international political arena. We have already lost half of the original forests, and the present rate of deforestation, 1.8 per cent per year, implies the remainder will last little more than another half-century. But because the amount of annual destruction has increased by almost 90 per cent during the 1980s and shows every prospect of increasing still further, virtually all remaining forests could well be eliminated within just a few decades.

This all supposes there will be no enhanced efforts to prevent the ultimate débâcle. Fortunately there is emergent hope that tropical forest countries, together with the rest of the global community, are growing more aware of what is at stake. Already new measures are under way to do a better management job with the remaining forests, albeit through a policy approach that is far too restricted. What hope is there that we can get to grips with the problem while we still enjoy a modicum of manœuvring room for incisive action? This chapter reviews the causes and consequences of tropical deforestation, and assesses the opportunity for remedial measures.

The problem is far from unresolvable. While it grew steadily worse throughout the 1980s, the prospects for amelioration have been enhanced more recently by supportive responses from a broad array of interested parties. These include a number of governments both within the tropical forest zone and outside, several international agencies, and a spectrum of non-governmental bodies. It is this recent recognition of interest that offers the prospect of slowing and eventually halting deforestation in much of the biome. But success will ultimately depend on a policy approach of a scope and scale to match the problem itself. To date, such an approach has been sorely deficient. It is this policy challenge that forms the main focus of this chapter.

The chapter opens with a brief review of deforestation rates and patterns, looking at how we all contribute (sometimes unwittingly) to deforestation. It goes on to consider what is at stake, not only for tropical forest countries themselves but for the entire community of nations: just as we all contribute to the problem, we shall all lose by it too. This argues, as is postulated in the next section, that we should all engage in a collective campaign to safeguard remaining forests—a response that should be facilitated by a new-found interest on the part of the global community. The chapter then examines the principal cause of deforestation, the 'shifted cultivator', before asking what should be done to address the particular needs of this person. In turn, this entrains the imperative of an expanded policy framework for tropical forests, possibly in the form of a Global Forests Convention together with a World Forests Agency. The chapter concludes with an assessment of the scope for grand-scale tree planting in the humid tropics, an initiative that would not only serve to counter the greenhouse effect but would surely transform the prospect for tropical forestry.

A. Tropical Deforestation: Rate and Patterns

In 1979 tropical deforestation was estimated by the Food and Agriculture Organization and the National Academy of Sciences[1] to be around 75,000 km^2 per year. A recent survey by this writer,[2] updated to the end of 1990, reveals that the annual amount has soared to 120,800 km^2, an area equivalent to half the British Isles. (These estimates derive largely from remote-sensing assessments, which constitute an objective and comprehensive mode of documentation.) There is good reason to believe that in the absence of much more vigorous and urgent safeguard measures, the deforestation rate will continue to accelerate into the fore-

[1] FAO, *Tropical Forest Resources* (Rome: FAO, 1981); N. Myers, *Conversion of Tropical Moist Forests*, Report to the National Academy of Sciences (Washington, DC: National Research Council, 1980).

[2] N. Myers, *Deforestation Rates in Tropical Forests and Their Climatic Implications* (London: Friends of the Earth, 1989).

seeable future, if only because of the phenomenon of the shifted cultivator (see section E below).[3]

Current deforestation is due to several causes apart from the shifted cultivator. The commercial logger is affecting roughly 45,000 km² per year, an expanse no greater than in 1979. Of this total, some 30,000 km² in South-East Asia feature such heavy and destructive logging that most of the residual forest is damaged beyond recovery for decades,[4] and so must be counted for present purposes as forest destruction. The cattle rancher, almost entirely confined to Central America and Amazonia, is eliminating roughly 15,000 km² per year, less than the 20,000 km² of 1979. A number of subsidiary factors, such as road building (with associated infrastructure), mining, dam construction, and plantations (for example, rubber, oil palm, and coffee), are accounting for roughly another 10,000 km² per year. The remainder, more than 65,000 km², is attributable to the slash-and-burn farmer. Admittedly, this last figure has not been documented with the accuracy that applies to the other causes of deforestation. The true figure could be a little less. But even if it is as low as 60,000 km², it still means the shifted cultivator is accounting for as much deforestation as all the other factors together, and his forest destruction is expanding rapidly.

The pattern of deforestation is not evenly spread throughout the tropical forest zone comprising more than 70 countries (Table 1). Ten countries, namely Brazil, Burma, Colombia, India, Indonesia, Malaysia, Mexico, Nigeria, Thailand, and Zaïre, are each losing more than 4,000 km² of forest per year, while others, including such sizeable countries as Guyana, Suriname, Gabon, and Congo, are losing 800 km² or less. There may be better

[3] G. W. Jones and H. V. Richter, *Population Mobility and Development: Southeast Asia and the Pacific* (Canberra: Development Studies Centre, 1981); W. J. Peters and L. F. Neunschwander, *Slash-and-Burn Farming in Third World Forests* (Moscow, Idaho: University of Idaho Press, 1988); W. Schulte, *Report on Population Data in Slash-and-Burn Forestry Communities in Asia* (Rome: FAO, 1981); D. A. Schumann and W. L. Partridge (eds.), *The Human Ecology of Tropical Land Settlement in Latin America* (Boulder, Colo.: Westview Press, 1989); R. Sinha, *Landlessness: A Growing Problem* (Rome: FAO, 1984); W. C. Thiesenhusen (ed.), *Searching for Agrarian Reform in Latin America* (Boston, Mass.: Unwin Hyman, 1989).

[4] J. Ewel and L. F. Conde, *Potential Ecological Impact of Increased Intensity of Tropical Forest Utilization* (Bogor, Indonesia: BIOTROP (Regional Centre for Tropical Biology), 1989); K. Kartawinata, S. Adifoemarto, S. Riswan, and A. P. Vayda, 'The Impact of Man on a Tropical Forest in Indonesia', *Ambio*, 10 (1981), 115–19.

TABLE 1. Tropical Moist Forests: Present Status in Select Countries.

Country (with area, km²)	Original Extent of Forest Cover (km²)	Extent of Forest Cover in 1989 (km²)	Extent of Primary Forests in 1989 (km²)	Amount of Deforestation in 1989 (km² per year; %)	
Bolivia (1,098,581)	90,000	70,000	45,000	1,700	2.4
Brazil (8,511,960)	2,860,000	2,200,000	2,000,000	30,000	1.4
Cameroon (475,442)	220,000	164,000	60,000	2,300	1.4
C. America (522,915)	500,000	90,000	55,000	3,300	3.7
Colombia (1,138,891)	700,000	278,500	180,000	6,500	2.3
Congo (342,000)	100,000	90,000	80,000	800	0.9
Ecuador (270,670)	132,000	76,000	44,000	3,000	4.0
Gabon (267,670)	240,000	200,000	100,000	800	0.4
Guyanas (French Guiana, Guyana, and Suriname) (469,790)	500,000	410,000	370,000	500	0.12
India (3,287,000)	1,600,000	165,000	70,000	4,300	2.6
Indonesia (1,919,300)	1,220,000	860,000	530,000	12,000	1.4
Ivory Coast (322,463)	160,000	16,000	4,000	2,500	15.6
Kampuchea (181,035)	120,000	67,000	20,000	500	0.75
Laos (236,800)	110,000	68,000	25,000	1,100	1.6
Madagascar (590,992)	62,000	24,000	10,000	2,000	8.3
Malaysia (329,079)	305,000	157,000	84,000	4,800	3.1
Mexico (1,967,180)	400,000	166,000	110,000	7,000	4.2
Myanmar (Burma) (696,500)	500,000	245,000	80,000	8,500	3.5
Nigeria (924,000)	72,000	28,000	10,000	4,000	14.3
Papua New Guinea (461,700)	425,000	360,000	180,000	3,500	1.0
Peru (1,285,220)	700,000	515,000	420,000	3,700	0.7
Philippines (299,400)	250,000	50,000	8,000	2,700	5.4
Thailand (513,517)	435,000	74,000	22,000	6,000	8.1
Venezuela (912,050)	420,000	350,000	300,000	1,600	0.5
Vietnam (334,331)	260,000	60,000	14,000	3,500	5.8
Zaïre (2,344,886)	1,245,000	1,000,000	700,000	4,200	0.4
	13,626,000	7,783,500	5,521,000	120,800	1.6
	= 97% of estimated total original extent of tropical forests, around 14 million km²	= 97.5% of present total extent of tropical forests, viz. 8 million km²	= 69% of total remaining tropical forests, viz. 8 million km²		

Source: N. Myers, *Deforestation Rates in Tropical Forests and Their Climatic Implications* (London: Friends of The Earth, 1989).

survival prospects, however, for large blocks of forest in western Brazilian Amazonia, the Guyana Highlands, the Zaïre basin, and New Guinea. By contrast, the next decade could see the virtual end of forest in most of South-East and Southern Asia, East and West Africa, and Central America.

It is important to note that deforestation is not altogether the responsibility of tropical-forest nations. Other nations contribute as well by virtue of international trading linkages. In Central America deforestation has stemmed much more from the spread of cattle ranching on the part of a relatively small number of large-scale cattle ranchers than from population pressures in a region that is conventionally perceived to experience pronounced population problems. In turn, the spread of cattle ranching has reflected the demand from North America for artificially cheap beef—the so-called hamburger connection.[5] There has been a parallel phenomenon of developed-world consumerism driving deforestation in Thailand by way of the cassava connection with the European Community. Similar linkages operate with respect to the developed world's demand for tropical timber, again at prices that do not reflect the full deforestation costs of timber extraction.[6] Yet another exogenous factor lies with international debt, that induces tropical-forest countries to exploit their timber resources in unsustainable fashion. These countries in question now owe well over $500 billion, or roughly three-fifths of all developing-world debt. As long as they endure a debt burden of this size, there is less prospect of them allocating adequate investment to improved forestry. In this context too, it is pertinent to recall that when all forms of foreign aid and development loans are considered, there is currently a net flow of funds totalling around $50 billion from the South to the North each year.

B. Emergent Recognition of the Problem: What Is At Stake

As indicated, the 1980s have been marked by a rising awareness of the problem. But it has been slow in coming, despite the 1980 and 1981 reports referred to above that indicated a rate of deforestation

[5] N. Myers, 'The Hamburger Connection: How Central America's Forests Become North America's Hamburgers', *Ambio*, 10 (1981), 3–8.

[6] N. Myers, 'Economics and Ecology in the International Arena: The Phenomenon of "Linked Linkages"', *Ambio*, 15 (1986), 296–300.

much higher than had been supposed. It is revealing to trace the emergence of this recent awareness.

In the mid-1970s the author served as a full-time staffer with the Forestry Department of the Food and Agriculture Organization, this being the United Nations agency with chief responsibility for tropical forests. Forestry was a Cinderella sector of FAO, with only a 6 per cent share of the overall budget (a proportion that has since declined). This was largely because forestry's importance received scant recognition by contrast with agriculture. As a senior agriculturalist once put it to me: 'There is only one thing wrong with deforestation, and that is that it is not proceeding fast enough: where else are we going to get the additional croplands required to feed a hungry world?'—a reaction that was perhaps not surprising in an agency that is primarily devoted to food production.

Fortunately not all organizations viewed the situation that way. In 1979 the US State Department convened an International Conference on Tropical Forests, followed by a US Office of Technology Assessment appraisal of the issue. In 1980 the United Nations Environment Programme organized a Conference of Tropical Forest Experts.

In the wake of these 'consciousness raising' exercises, various analysts began an assessment of the full range of values associated with tropical forests. It soon transpired that the main modes of exploitation, or rather over-exploitation, of tropical forests were focused on only a very few of the many products available from forest ecosystems, resulting in degradation if not destruction of the rest. Yet it was apparent that through systematic screening of raw materials such as phytochemicals and genetic resources for agriculture, medicine, and industry, there were exceptional opportunities to make expanded use of tropical forests—and the harvesting of these low-volume products need cause little disruption of forest ecosystems. In addition, tropical forests were supplying many environmental services, whose value was becoming all the more apparent as deforestation proceeded. In short, the forests were being over-exploited while under-utilized. Hence the premium on a fundamental shift to a forest-development strategy that would emphasize the many goods and services available without degradation of forest ecosystems.[7]

Some of the specific benefits available from tropical forests merit

[7] N. Myers, *A Wealth of Wild Species* (Boulder, Colo.: Westview Press, 1983).

particular attention. First, hardwood timber. Annual timber exports were worth $8 billion as recently as 1980, or as much as cotton, twice as much as rubber, and almost three times as much as cocoa exports. Due largely to deforestation, the timber figure has already dropped to $6 billion, and is projected to slump to $2 billion by the year 2000, with marked impact on the economies of major exporter countries.[8]

Also important are non-timber products. In Indonesia the export of these products, such as essential oils, exudates, waxes, tannins, and medicinals, earned $200 million in 1982 or almost one-quarter the value of timber exports.[9] In India they have been worth at least 40 per cent of forestry-sector products.[10] As forests disappear, so there is a decline in these non-timber revenues.

Much the same applies to the forests' environmental services. Deforestation of upland catchments leads to disruption of watershed systems, causing year-round water flows in downstream areas to give way to flood-and-drought regimes. In the Ganges Valley with its 500 million small-scale farmers in India and Bangladesh, the costs in India alone are estimated to exceed $1 billion per year.[11] A similar decline of watershed services is becoming apparent in the densely populated valleylands of the Irrawaddy, Salween, Chao Phraya, and Mekong Rivers in South-East Asia. There is also evidence that deforestation sometimes results in reduced rainfall.[12] This can be unusually significant for agriculture. In Peninsular Malaysia, the Penang and Kedah States have experienced disruption of rainfall regimes to the ex-

[8] N. P. Sharma, R. Rowe, R. A. Kramer, and M. Jacobson, *Forestry Sector Policy Paper, Revised Version* (Washington, DC: Office of the Forestry Adviser, The World Bank, 1990). F. Nectoux and Y. Kuroda, *Timber from the South Seas: An Analysis of Japan's Timber Trade and its Environmental Impact* (Gland: Switzerland: WWF International, 1989).

[9] M. Gillis, *Non-Wood Forest Products in Indonesia* (Chapel Hill: Department of Forestry, University of North Carolina, 1986).

[10] T. Gupta and A. Guleria, *Non-Wood Forest Products in India* (New Delhi: IBH Publishing Company, 1982).

[11] High Level Commission on Floods, *Report on the Emergent Crisis* (New Delhi: Ministry of Irrigation, Government of India, 1983).

[12] V. M. Meher-Homji, 'Disasters of Deforestation: Desertification or Deluge?', in *Proceedings of the Conference on Forest Resources Crisis in the Third World* (Penang: Sahabat Alam Malaysia, 1985); N. Myers, 'Tropical Deforestation and Climate Change', *Environmental Conservation*, 15 (1988), 293–8; E. Salati and P. B. Vose, 'Amazon Basin: A System in Equilibrium', *Science*, 225 (1984), 129–38; J. Shukla, C. Nobre, and P. Sellers, 'Amazon Deforestation and Climate Change', *Science*, 247 (1990), 1322–5.

tent that 20,000 hectares of paddy ricefields have been abandoned and another 72,000 hectares have registered a marked fall in production in this 'rice bowl' of the Peninsula.[13] Similar deforestation-associated changes in rainfall have been documented in the Philippines, India, The Ivory Coast, and Panama.

In addition to these deforestation-related losses confined to tropical-forest countries, there are other adverse repercussions, much more important in the long run and affecting all nations. The depletion of biological resources is among the most serious of these. Tropical forests can be considered the greatest celebration of nature to grace the face of the planet in four billion years of life's existence. While covering only 6 per cent of Earth's land surface, they are estimated to contain at least 70 per cent and possibly even 90 per cent of Earth's species.[14] Half a square kilometre of Malaysia's forests can feature as many tree and shrub species as the whole of the United States and Canada.[15] A single bush in Peruvian Amazonia has revealed as many ant species as in the British Isles.[16]

As the forests go, so do their species. In just 4 per cent of tropical forests' expanse and 0.2 per cent of Earth's land surface, at least 15 per cent of Earth's plant species are threatened with extinction by the year 2000 or shortly thereafter, together with hundreds of thousands (possibly millions) of animal species.[17] By the year 2025 we could well lose one-quarter of all Earth's plant species in these forests,[18] again accompanied by the elimination of large numbers of animal species. The mass extinction overtaking the planet's biotas is occurring almost entirely within tropical forests. Lasting just a few decades, it could have an impoverishing impact on the course of evolution for at least one million years.[19]

[13] N. W. Chan, 'Drought Trends in Northwestern Peninsular Malaysia: Is Less Rain Falling?', *Wallaceana*, 44 (1986), 8–9.

[14] T. L. Erwin, 'The Tropical Forest Canopy: The Heart of Biotic Diversity', in E. O. Wilson (ed.), *Biodiversity* (Washington, DC: National Academy Press, 1988), 123–9.

[15] S. Hubbell, Personal communication, conversation Jan. 1991. Dept. of Zoology, Princeton University.

[16] B. Holldobler and E. O. Wilson, *The Ants* (Berlin: Springer-Verlag, 1990).

[17] N. Myers, 'Threatened Biotas: "Hot Spots" in Tropical Forests', *The Environmentalist*, 8 (1988), 187–208; N. Myers, 'The Biodiversity Challenge: Expanded Hot Spots Analysis', *The Environmentalist*, 10 (1990), 243–56.

[18] P. H. Raven, *We're Killing Our World: The Global Ecosystem in Crisis* (Chicago: MacArthur Foundation, 1987).

[19] N. Myers, 'The End of the Lines', *Natural History*, 94 (1985), 2, 6, 8, 12.

Apart from the scientific, aesthetic, and ethical values of bio-diversity, these losses affect the immediate material welfare of people throughout the world. One in four products sold by pharmacies, whether medicinal or pharmaceutical, is manufactured from materials taken from tropical-forest plants.[20] These products include antibiotics, antivirals, analgesics, tranquillizers, diuretics, and laxatives, among many other items. The contraceptive pill is based upon forest-plant materials from Mexico and West Africa. Two potent drugs against leukaemia and Hodgkin's disease derive from the Madagascar periwinkle. Commercial sales of these diverse products are now worth around $20 billion a year world-wide.

We enjoy these contributions to our health after pharmacologists have taken a cursory look at only one plant species in ten, and an intensive look at only one plant species in one hundred, to assess their economic value. We can surely look forward to entire pharmacopoeias of new products provided the forests and their species survive. One of the promising responses to AIDS could stem from a plant of Queensland's forests.

The most numerous species by a long way are insects. One might suppose that if we are losing perhaps fifty insect species in these forests every day,[21] it hardly matters: what have creepy-crawlies ever done for us? But consider the oil-palm plantations of Peninsular Malaysia. Until 1980, pollination of the palm trees was undertaken by human hand, an inefficient and expensive process. The plantation owners asked themselves how the palm got itself pollinated in its native habitat of Cameroon's forests. It turned out the task was performed by a tiny weevil. The plantation owners brought back a stock of weevils to Malaysia for release into the plantations, where they performed admirably. The savings are reckoned to be $120 million a year.[22]

We enjoy a still greater benefit from tropical forests by virtue of their role in the global carbon cycle. They constitute a larger stock of vegetation-stored carbon than all other ecological zones put together. When forests are burned (as is the case with cattle

[20] N. Myers, *The Primary Source: Tropical Forests and Our Future* (New York: W. W. Norton, 1984); see also P. P. Principe, *The Economic Value of Biological Diversity Among Medicinal Plants* (Paris: OECD, 1987).

[21] E. O. Wilson, 'Threats to Biodiversity', *Scientific American*, 261 (1989), 108–16.

[22] D. J. Greathead, 'The Multi-Million Dollar Weevil That Pollinates Oil Palm', *Antenna* (Royal Entomological Society of London), 7 (1983), 105–7.

ranching and small-scale agriculture), they release their carbon. Of the 8 billion tonnes of carbon dioxide accumulating per year in the global atmosphere, and contributing half of greenhouse-effect processes, around 2.4 billion tonnes (30 per cent) comes from forest burning,[23] almost all the rest coming from fossil-fuel combustion. (Forest burning also releases two other greenhouse gases, methane and nitrous oxide, much more potent as global-warming agents than carbon dioxide; but their amounts are largely unknown.) Moreover the forest-burning component is increasing more quickly than the fossil-fuel component; it grew by 75 per cent during the 1980s. From this standpoint alone, the entire community of nations has a strong interest in curtailing tropical deforestation.

C. Enhanced Efforts to Safeguard Remaining Forests

Tropical forests make multiple contributions to the welfare of people throughout the tropical forest zone, of people throughout the nations concerned, and of people throughout the world. Similarly their survival depends on factors arising throughout the forests themselves, throughout the nations concerned, and throughout the world.

This new recognition has been matched by growing awareness of the worsening outlook for tropical forests. A number of tropical-forest countries now recognize control of deforestation as a critical factor for their development prospects, and several, such as India, Thailand, and the Philippines, describe deforestation as a 'national emergency'. Some governments have already taken significant steps, such as the decision of the Collor government in Brazil to end state subsidies for new cattle ranches in Amazonia.[24]

There have been numerous grass-roots initiatives within tropical-forest countries in support of the forests. In India, for instance, the Chipko and Silent Valley campaigns have achieved signal successes in preserving local tracts of forest. In Kenya and Colombia the Greenbelt Movements have engaged in extensive

[23] R. A. Houghton, 'The Future Role of Tropical Forests in Affecting the Carbon Dioxide Concentrations of the Atmosphere', *Ambio*, 19 (1990), 204–9.
[24] See Andrew Hurrell's chapter in this volume.

tree planting, thus relieving exploitation pressures on remaining forests. In Indonesia and Ecuador the non-governmental organizations (NGOs) have expanded so fast that environmental-activist groups have become an appreciable political factor, with access to the highest levels of government. Similar stories can be told of grass-roots activism in Malaysia, Madagascar, Cameroon, Costa Rica, and Brazil, among at least two dozen tropical-forest countries where the NGO movement is starting to have a marked impact on government activities.

This increased attention by tropical-forest nations has been matched by a highlighting of the issue on the part of outsider nations. We have already noted the pioneering initiatives of the United States government a full ten years ago, an effort that has been replicated by vigorous measures in support of forests on the part of the Netherlands, Sweden, Australia, Canada, and the United Kingdom. The Western leaders' summit meetings from 1989 onward cited the issue in their communiqués, the 1990 Houston communiqué declaring that 'the destruction of tropical forests has reached alarming proportions'. The Intergovernmental Panel on Climate Change laid emphasis on the linkages between tropical deforestation and global warming.

NGO activity has blossomed in developed nations. As Bramble and Porter note with respect to the United States, Friends of the Earth, Greenpeace, the World Wide Fund for Nature, and other environmental organizations have seen their membership and revenues increase several times over during the 1980s, and they have focused a good part of their new-found strength on tropical forests. It has been due in large measure to this citizen activism that a number of developed-world governments have been persuaded to play a more substantive part in the global campaign to safeguard the forests.

Tropical deforestation became firmly established during the 1980s on the agendas of governments, international agencies, and NGOs in many parts of the world. There have been renewed efforts to get to grips with the problem, most prominently through an initiative begun in 1985 when the World Bank, in conjunction with the World Resources Institute and the United Nations Development Programme, convened a Tropical Forestry Task Force (to which this writer contributed). The result was a Tropical Forestry Action Plan (TFAP), proposing greatly expanded action to foster sustainable logging, tree planting, watershed rehabilitation, research and education, species protection, and enhanced forestry management all round. The planned budget was to be $1.6 billion a year, or three times as much as all funding going into tropical forestry at that time. It is a measure of the broad support for the Plan that funding eventually rose to $1.3 billion in 1990. Subsequently more than 70 countries comprising 60 per cent of tropical forests completed or started to prepare National Forestry Action Plans.

Regrettably TFAP did not live up to expectations when it was put into practice. The largest responsibility for this must lie with FAO. Ironically FAO had refused to collaborate with the World Bank's Task Force on the grounds that there was no tropical forest problem that warranted further effort, and that FAO, as the leading UN agency in the field, would take care of any problem that arose. But when FAO saw the Plan was to go ahead anyway, it swiftly moved to joined in the exercise. The result was that FAO was appointed the chief executive agency, despite its less than satisfactory record in the tropical forestry field over a period of decades.

TFAP's overriding purpose was to stem deforestation by promoting sustainable forestry through a number of cross-sectoral strategies, including in particular a programme to assist subsistence farmers outside the forests and so deter them from becoming 'shifted cultivators' (for a detailed treatment of this predominant factor, see below). But FAO was inclined to view TFAP as a means to enhance support for traditional forestry activities, despite the essentially innovative character of the Plan with its major new proposals. In its execution of the Plan, FAO offered scant regard for non-forestry activities, despite the Plan's original intent to integrate forestry with agriculture and thereby to address root causes of deforestation.[25] It did not even direct much attention to forestry-associated issues such as biodiversity and climate change. Worst of all, it did next to nothing to instigate policy reform, especially concerning the factors that generate the

[25] FAO, *Report of the Independent Review of the Tropical Forestry Action Plan* (Rome: FAO, 1990); C. J. Lankester, *Address to 'Men of the Trees' in London, UK* (New York: UNDP, 1989); J. S. Spears, *A Reappraisal of Past and Future TFAP Objectives* (Washington, DC: Consultative Group on International Agricultural Research, World Bank, 1989); and R. Winterbottam, *Taking Stock: The Tropical Forestry Action Plan After Five Years* (Washington, DC: World Resources Institute, 1990).

shifted cultivator. In short, the central deficiency of TFAP was that, in practice at least, it was essentially oriented toward traditional forestry—a case of 'the same as before, only more so'. As the discussion below will show, the overriding need is for fresh responses that address forestry issues within a context of rural development generally, hence responses that address non-forestry sources of deforestation.

Another broad-scale initiative was the establishment of the International Tropical Timber Organization in 1986. It is intended as a forum where both producer and consumer countries, accounting for 70 per cent of tropical forests and 95 per cent of international trade in tropical timber, can make common cause by ensuring that timber harvesting is conducted in sustainable fashion. But less than half of one per cent of all logging areas are managed on a self-renewing basis, and ITTO has done little to improve the situation—let alone to promote other objectives under its mandate such as conservation of exceptional-value forest ecosystems. ITTO has recently accepted new guidelines for certain environmental activities and biodiversity protection. But the organization's record in its area of purported expertise, sustainable logging, must raise severe questions about its capacity to implement the new proposals.

During the period of the existence of TFAP and ITTO, deforestation has been proceeding faster than ever.

D. Additional Measures to Save the Forests

A number of other positive measures have been taken on a smaller scale. One is the debt-for-nature swaps, notably in Ecuador, Costa Rica, Madagascar, and the Philippines. While they certainly help, and we need many more such imaginative ideas, they have hitherto been on too small a scale to make much difference to the problems overall. An expansion of the concept has been proposed by the British entrepreneur Sir James Goldsmith,[26] envisaging an international company which would finance deals as large as $50 billion, writing off tropical-forest countries' debts at less than face value against undertakings for

[26] Sir James Goldsmith, *The Adam Smith Lecture* (London: The Adam Smith Institute, 1989).

forest protection. Lending governments have also become involved, as with the decision of the German government to write off DM850 million of debt in support of reforestation measures in Kenya. The debt-for-nature concept has been opposed by some tropical-forest countries on the grounds that it infringes sovereignty. But this obstacle could perhaps be surmounted if the initiatives were taken by tropical-forest countries themselves.

Another initiative appraises ways for tropical-forest countries to reduce the covert subsidies and other inducements that foster runaway deforestation.[27] When some of these forestry supports were first introduced two decades or more ago, they played a valid role in promoting investment. But they have long outlived their purpose. In the Philippines the government has persisted with reduced royalties and fees on timber harvests, tax-free holidays for logging concessionaires, and restricted export taxes on processed timber, to the extent of forgoing revenues five times greater than those it actually collected. In Indonesia the government has been losing more than $1 billion a year in stumpage fees, royalties, rents, and other harvest revenues that it should have derived from the recent timber boom.

The subsidies problem has been particularly acute in Brazil, where much deforestation has occurred through the establishment of cattle ranches in Amazonia. The government has spent $2.5 billion in subsidizing ranchers' investments through long-term loans, tax credits and other fiscal incentives, monetary inducements, and duty-free imports of capital equipment. This support has meant that many ranches, no matter how inefficient, have made a quick killing by courtesy of the government's give-away inducements—to the extent that hardly any ranchers have bothered to sell the timber felled to make way for their pasturelands, collectively torching $5 billion worth of timber. Virtually every ranch has been a financial success for the individual entrepreneur, while an economic disaster for the national economy.[28] Fortunately the Brazilian government decided in 1989 that there would be no subsidies for new ranches,

[27] R. Repetto, 'Deforestation in the Tropics', *Scientific American*, 262 (1990), 36–42; R. Repetto and M. Gillis (eds.), *Public Policies and the Misuse of Forest Resources* (Cambridge: Cambridge UP, 1988).
[28] J. O. Browder, 'The Social Costs of Rain Forests Destruction', *Interciencia*, 13 (1988), 115–20.

though such supports continue for established ranches covering a total of 120,000 km^2.

Further measures include encouraging, and eventually requiring, the logger to take his harvest from secondary or disturbed forests, and from tree plantations established on already deforested lands. If recent patterns and trends of deforestation persist, he will shortly have no other option anyway. Similarly the cattle rancher could be persuaded to engage in management practices that demonstrably enable an increased flow of beef to be produced from established pasturelands, thus eliminating the urge to clear more forest for new ranches. But all these potential advances, however productive, would be overtaken within just a few years by fast-spreading deforestation at the hands of the 'shifted cultivator'.

E. The Special Case of the Shifted Cultivator

The shifted cultivator finds himself squeezed out of traditional farmlands in areas many horizons away from his country's forests, whereupon he feels compelled to head for the only unoccupied lands available, the forests. This applies in dozens of countries, from the Philippines and Thailand to Madagascar and The Ivory Coast, and to Mexico and Brazil. Being powerless to resist the factors that drive him into the forests, the shifted cultivator is no more to be 'blamed' for deforestation than a soldier is to be held responsible for fighting a war. But he advances on the forest fringe in ever-growing throngs, pushing deeper into the forest year by year.[29] Behind him come more multitudes of displaced peasants. By contrast with the shifting cultivator of tradition, who made sustainable use of forest ecosystems, the shifted cultivator is unable to allow the forest any chance to restore itself.

The factors driving the shifted cultivator into the forest include the obvious pressure of population growth,[30] and also the maldistribution of farmlands in established agricultural areas. In

[29] See e.g. J. S. Spears, *Containing Tropical Deforestation: A Review of Priority Areas for Technological and Policy Research* (Washington, DC: World Bank, 1988).

[30] N. Myers, 'The World's Forests and Human Populations: The Environmental Interconnections', *Population and Development Review*, 16 (1991).

Brazil, 5 per cent of farmers occupy 70 per cent of arable lands, and 70 per cent occupy 5 per cent. Some of the larger holdings amount to thousands of hectares, too large for the owner to cultivate more than half, while the small-scale farmer over the fence has to make out with just a few hectares. Equally important, there is often scant attention by national planners to subsistence agriculture (as opposed to Green Revolution agriculture) in order to help the impoverished peasant make more intensive and permanent use of his smallholding outside the forests. Worst of all, there is generally an inadequate policy emphasis on rural development overall, favouring manufacturing over agriculture and hence cities over the countryside.

At the level of the national economy, this situation is aggravated by external factors such as international debt and inequitable trade-and-aid patterns. To this extent, many outsiders have their hands on the chainsaws at work in tropical forests. Efficient deforesters are to be found among the banker creditors and trade protectionists in developed countries.

There are two factors which will tend to increase the stream of shifted cultivators heading toward the forests. First, tropical-forest countries will account for the bulk of population growth projected for the foreseeable future, meaning an extra three billion people in the next forty years (for some country-by-country projections, see Table 2). Moreover the numbers of shifted cultivators have recently been growing far faster than national populations, usually at rates between 4 and 16 per cent per year, meaning that they double in anything from 17.25 to 4.3 years.[31] Secondly, alternative forms of livelihood for landless peasants are becoming still more limited by the unemployment problem. Developing countries need to generate 600 million jobs (or as many as all jobs in the developed world today) during the next twenty years in order to accommodate new entrants into the work-force.

The issue has been recognized for at least a decade,[32] yet it has been largely ignored, reflecting the tremendous difficulties for policy-makers in tackling the shifted-cultivator problem. Throughout the 1980s the deforestation focus has been almost entirely confined to the logger and the rancher. We do not even

[31] Ibid.
[32] Myers, *Conversion of Tropical Moist Forests* and *The Primary Source*.

TABLE 2. Population Growth in Select Tropical Forest Countries.

Country	Population in 1950 (millions)	Population in 1990 (millions)	Growth of Population 1989 (%)	Population in Rural Areas (%)	Population Projected in 2000 (millions)	Population Projected in 2020 (millions)	Projected Size of Stationary Population (millions)	Per-Capita GNP 1988 (US$)
Latin America								
Bolivia	3	7	2.6	51	9	13	25	570
Brazil	53	150	2.0	26	180	234	280	2280
Central America	9	29	2.8	54	37	54	88	1250
Colombia	12	32	2.0	32	38	49	57	1240
Ecuador	3	11	2.5	46	14	20	24	1080
The Guyanas	n/a	1.6	2.1	52	2	3	n/a	1050
Mexico	27	89	2.4	34	107	142	170	1820
Peru	8	22	2.4	31	26	35	46	1440
Venezuela	5	20	2.3	17	24	33	42	3170
Asia								
India	362	853	2.1	74	1042	1374	1766	330
Indonesia	77	189	1.8	74	224	287	430	430
Kampuchea	4	7	2.2	89	8	12	n/a	n/a
Laos	n/a	4	2.5	84	5	7	180	180
Malaysia	6	18	2.5	65	21	27	37	1870
Myanmar (Burma)	18	41	2.0	76	50	68	97	n/a
Papua New Guinea	2	4	2.7	87	5	8	12	770
Philippines	20	66	2.6	58	83	117	127	630
Thailand	20	56	1.5	82	64	78	98	990
Vietnam	24	70	2.5	80	88	119	168	n/a
Africa								
Cameroon	5	11	2.6	58	14	23	67	1010
Congo	1	2	3.0	60	3	5	17	930
Gabon	n/a	1	2.2	59	1.6	2.6	6	2970
Ivory Coast	3	13	3.7	57	18	35	83	740
Madagascar	5	12	3.2	78	17	30	49	180
Nigeria	41	119	2.9	69	161	273	500	290
Zaire	14	37	3.3	60	50	90	200	170

have a basic idea of how numerous the shifted cultivators have become; we have only broad estimates that range from 200 to 500 million people. If the latter figure is correct, they account for almost one in ten of humankind. Yet as margin dwellers they remain a largely forgotten phenomenon.

F. An Expanded Policy Framework

The shifted cultivator reflects a failure of overall development, in that half a billion people endure landlessness and absolute poverty in tropical-forest countries. Hence the survival of the forests depends on a range of policy interventions to help the subsistence farmer make an acceptable living in established farmlands outside the forests, and thus to forestall his compulsion to head for the forests. This requires measures to promote efficient agriculture and agrarian reform, plus a variety of rural-infrastructure measures such as extension services, marketing networks, and credit facilities. In short, the shifted cultivator constitutes a challenge that can be confronted only by a restructuring of macro-level policies on the part of tropical-forest governments and international development agencies. This is a far cry from current highly restricted approaches to the deforestation problem.

In essence, we must broaden our understanding of what is needed to save remaining forests. Primarily we should recognize that for the most part it is no longer a forestry problem. While much can still be achieved through traditional forestry practices (also through more protected areas within forests, plus other 'defensive' measures), these activities often do no more than tackle symptoms of deeper problems. We must address the source problem of shifted-cultivator encroachment. Anything less is akin to building around tropical forests a fence that would be speedily overrun by multitudes of land-hungry farmers.

As countries move to safeguard forests at the level of national planning, benefits at the national level will also accrue. The welfare of the forests is intimately tied up with the welfare of human communities throughout tropical-forest countries, notably by way of timber and non-wood revenues, climate linkages, and watershed functions. Regular river flows from forested watersheds are critically important for valleylands agriculture. The same flows support public health: without sufficient supplies of domestic water, there can be little hope of reducing the many developing-world diseases that are related to dirty water. Forests protect watershed soil, preventing the silting up of hydropower dams: recent sedimentation rates are projected to cause a loss of electricity worth $6 billion in the year 2000.[33]

Thus tropical forests contribute to several key sectors of development. This insight should engender a basic change in our perception of the forests and their contributions to human welfare. During the 1970s the standard forestry approach was 'How can we best (i.e. most rapidly) exploit the forests?' During the 1980s there was an advance to 'How can we best develop the forests?', an approach that took account of more of the forests' goods and services, but was still centred only on the forests, leaving them marginal to numerous national sectoral concerns. During the 1990s we must move on to 'How can we best enable forests to make their full contribution to development overall?', expanding the focus to the arena of national planning in which the forests play several pivotal roles.

The first step of policy reappraisal is thus to develop an enlarged view of what is driving the forests ta o their demise, and of what they can increasingly supply if they survive. It implies a seismic shift in our understanding of tropical forests and their part in the human enterprise.

Three areas of priority activity emerge. The cfirst, a within-forests measure, is a full-scope evaluation of the forests' outputs. We urgently need a better g frasp of all goods and services available—genetic resources, watershed systems, climate controls, the entire spectrum of non-wood products and environmental functions. While the forests are much more than so many board feet of timber, our market-place mechanisms tend to deny this by highlighting what can be readily bought and sold, with disregard for the multiple benefits that cannot be 'voted for' by consumers' dollars (where can one purchase a watershed output?). This applies especially to the forests' function in support of climate stability. Precisely because climate benefits carry no price tag, they have been entirely overlooked in economic planning for

[33] A. Sfeir-Younis, *Soil Conservation in Developing Countries: A Background Report* (Washington, DC: World Bank, 1986).

forests. We should not get hung up with what can be counted, to the detriment of what also counts.

The second area of priority activity lies with grass-roots contributions. More than is the case with development sectors such as energy and industry, forestry policy is critically dependent on the support of people living within the forests or their immediate environs. Without their active involvement, there is far less hope of implementing an array of on-ground safeguards for the forests, or for reforestation measures to relieve further forest exploitation. Moreover local people, especially indigenous forest-dwelling communities, often have keener insights into what makes forests tick, and how to keep them ticking, than do dash-in/dash-out experts. Yet the potential contributions of local people have generally been disregarded. We should systematically bring them into efforts to safeguard the forests right from the start of planning processes. In the jargon of the trade, there is need for a bottom-up approach to complement the usual top-down one. The 1989 decision of the Colombian government to assign 180,000 km^2 of Amazonian forest to the care of tribal peoples provides a welcome illustration.

Activities in these two areas will avail little, however, without attention to the third and highest priority, namely confronting the challenge posed by the shifted cultivator. Some institutional initiatives are under consideration that would go far to address this key factor, notably in the form of a Global Forests Convention.

G. A Global Forests Convention

Fundamental policy reform and a visionary approach are required to turn the profound problems of tropical forests into a splendid opportunity. For all its professional skills and decades-long experience as the leading United Nations agency in tropical forestry, the Food and Agriculture Organization hardly matches up to the challenge: it has failed to respond to the opportunity for remedial action available under the Tropical Forestry Action Plan.

One possibility which has attracted attention is subsuming the tropical forestry issue under the proposed Global Climate Convention. A Convention Protocol on World Forest Conservation seems appropriate in light of the forests' role in planetary climate systems generally and in global-warming processes in particular. But there are several drawbacks. An effective Climate Convention may not enter into force for some years. A number of tropical-forest nations, notably Brazil, are reluctant to support a forests protocol unless the main agents of global warming, the industrialized nations, commit themselves to doing much more to limit their fossil-fuel emissions of greenhouse gases. Most important of all, a protocol would not supply an institutional response in terms of capacity to actually safeguard the forests, especially as concerns the shifted cultivator: it could turn out to be no more than a pious expression of intent, with scant institutional support.

The best option may be a Global Forests Convention, leading to a World Forests Organization backed by a Tropical Forests Fund. The communiqué of the Group of Seven summit in Houston in July 1990 declared: 'We are ready to begin negotiations . . . on a global forests convention or agreement, which is needed to curb deforestation, protect biodiversity, stimulate positive forestry actions, and address threats to the world's forests.' This goal was reaffirmed at the London summit in July 1991: 'We aim to achieve the following by the time of UNCED: . . . Agreement on principles for the management, conservation and sustainable development of all types of forest, leading to a framework convention.' However, by August 1991 negotiations to prepare a forest convention had run into serious difficulties.

The essential objective of any convention would be to reflect the common global interest in tropical forests (in all other forests too, though others are not so widely and immediately threatened as are tropical forests). This would not mean, of course, that tropical-forest nations would lose their sovereign rights to use their forest resources for their own purposes. But tropical forests are now seen to serve global purposes too (not only through their climate connection but through their biodiversity stocks). As currently envisaged, a Global Convention with accompanying institutional mechanisms would promote the entire array of the forests' benefits for people everywhere and forever. It would supply a conceptual framework to deal with all aspects of the management, conservation, and development of the forests, including threats from agricultural encroachment. It would mobilize a critical mass of intersectoral expertise in all areas related to tropical forests; it would be much more than an assemblage of foresters. It would offer a forum for continuous contributions from non-governmental bodies, especially those that promote environmental values and grass-roots interests, such as those representing indigenous peoples.

There is what may be a marked disadvantage in that the Convention would produce yet another international agency. Many observers protest that there are enough of them already: why not spend the same effort on making the existing ones work better? But the main existing agency, the Food and Agriculture Organization, seems unable to tackle the challenges of intersectoral endeavour. In fact its operational make-up fosters precisely those sectoral divisions that have helped generate the deforestation crisis in the first place. This deficiency is not confined to the Food and Agriculture Organization; many international agencies are set up for single-sector purposes (food, health, energy, population, trade, and the like). A worthwhile World Forests Organization, by contrast, would have to be specifically intersectoral from the start.

H. Grand-Scale Tree Planting in the Humid Tropics: A Proposal

Finally, the most salient aspect of tropical deforestation—the linkage to global warming—may soon open up the prospect of utilizing deforested lands to mount a substantial counter to global warming. In turn, the financial and technical contributions entailed could transform the outlook for tropical forests. An initiative on this front could be an immediate and central concern of a World Forests Organization.

As indicated already, half of the greenhouse effect is caused by build-up of carbon dioxide in the global atmosphere. A full 30 per cent of this build-up now stems from burning of tropical forests. Just as a burning tree releases carbon, a growing tree absorbs it through photosynthesis: a tree is half made up of carbon. This opens up the option of a grand-scale tree-planting programme to sequester carbon dioxide from the global atmosphere.[34] By far the best place to plant trees for carbon-absorption purposes is the humid tropics with their year-round warmth and moisture that foster rapid growth. Of course a tree-planting programme would work only if it were accompanied by greatly increased efforts to reduce deforestation. It is at least conceivable, however, that such an idea could generate precisely the type and scale of outside support that would finally provide the incentive for tropical-forest governments to get to grips with the deforestation problem.

One hectare of fast-growing trees in the humid tropics can absorb roughly 10 tonnes of carbon per year throughout its twenty to thirty years of major growth.[35] So one million square kilometres of plantations would absorb one billion tonnes of carbon. We could hardly hope to plant enough trees to take care of all the carbon dioxide accumulating in the atmosphere. But enough land is available out of 8 million km^2 already deforested (i.e. it has not been taken for permanent human occupation),[36] for us to think in terms of two million square kilometres assigned for reforestation forthwith—enough to knock a solid dent in the carbon dioxide problem. True, it would not be a permanent solution in so far as the trees would eventually stop growing. But it would gain us a breathing space of several decades while we find energy sources other than fossil fuels.

What would the tree-planting campaign cost? Suppose—as has been the experience with many agroforestry and social-forestry projects—that land and labour were supplied free, in light of the many local benefits of reforestation such as watershed functions and other environmental services. Suppose too that the average cost of planting and maintenance of trees is $400 per hectare.[37] Then two million square kilometres would cost $80 billion. This sum is to be compared with some costs of living in a greenhouse-affected world, for example $73–111 billion just to safeguard the

[34] N. Myers, 'The Greenhouse Effect: A Tropical Forestry Response', *Biomass*, 18 (1989), 73–8; see also G. Marland, *The Prospect of Solving the CO$_2$ Problem Through Global Reforestation* (Washington, DC: Carbon Dioxide Research Division, United States Department of Energy, 1988); and S. Postel and L. Heise, *Reforesting the Earth* (Washington, DC: Worldwatch Institute, 1988).

[35] Myers, 'The Greenhouse Effect', 73–8.

[36] R. A. Houghton and G. M. Woodwell, 'Global Climate Change', *Scientific American*, 260 (1989), 36–44.

[37] See Myers, 'Threatened Biotas'.

eastern seaboard of the United States from sea-level rise, and $150–300 billion to adapt irrigation systems world-wide.[38] Moreover, were the tree-planting programme to be spread over ten years, i.e. at a cost of $8 billion a year, it would work out at five times more than the annual budget of the most ambitious programme to date, the Tropical Forestry Action Plan. The principal sources of funding should presumably be the developed nations, on the grounds that they have been the main cause of the greenhouse effect, and could often be the ones to suffer most from it.

The proposal need not entail horizon-to-horizon expanses of single-species plantations as the dominant form of reforestation. While there would be a place for commercial-scale projects, vast monocultures would be more expensive to establish and maintain, and more vulnerable to pests and diseases, than would localized and community-based projects. Indeed the major emphasis should be on small plantings with multiple species, such as are standard practice with agroforestry and social forestry, and also on village wood-lots and farm plantings. While grand-scale reforestation represents a single large challenge, it will best be met by millions of mini-responses, tailored to local conditions and opportunities.

The basic idea was supported in principle by the Intergovernmental Panel on Climate Change, which proposed the planting of 120,000 km^2 of trees a year for twenty years, making a total of 2.4 million km^2, in unspecified parts of the world. If the idea were to be centred on the humid tropics, it would transform the prospect for tropical forests. Already the Netherlands government is engaged on a 25-year programme to finance reforestation projects covering 2,500 km^2 in South America, in order to offset carbon emissions from two new 600-megawatt coal-fired power stations.

I. Conclusion

Although the new interest in tropical forests is encouraging, there is still a danger that enhanced support for tropical forests will miss the crucial target. Thus, for instance, Prime Minister Thatcher's

[38] L. R. Brown *et al.*, *State of the World 1990* (New York: W. W. Norton, 1990).

pledge of an additional £100 million over a period of three years was almost all directed to problems within the forests, leaving aside the source problems of deforestation in areas outside. It is only by comprehending the proper scope of the tropical deforestation issue—and also by recognizing the full measure of benefits available from tropical forests if they survive—that we shall get to grips with the challenges ahead. Much of the policy programme proposed will be difficult. But it will not be nearly so difficult as living in a world bereft of its tropical forests.

NOTES ON CONTRIBUTORS

WILFRED BECKERMAN has been Fellow and Tutor in Economics, Balliol College, Oxford, since 1975. He was previously Professor of Political Economy at the University of London. He is a member of Council of the Royal Economic Society and was a member of the Royal Commission on Environmental Pollution, 1970–3. His publications include *In Defense of Growth*, 1974, and *Pricing for Pollution*, second edition 1990.

PATRICIA BIRNIE is Director of the IMO International Maritime Law Institute in Malta. She is a non-practising barrister and was formerly lecturer in public international law at the University of Edinburgh and Senior Lecturer at the London School of Economics, specializing in the law of the sea and international environmental law. She has published widely in both fields, including (with R. Barston) *The Maritime Dimension*, 1980, and *The International Regulation of Whaling*, 1985.

BARBARA BRAMBLE is Director of International Programs at the National Wildlife Federation which she established in 1982. She is an environmental lawyer and worked for six years in private practice representing national and local conservation groups. She then joined the Council on Environmental Quality as legal counsel handling domestic and international environmental matters and mediating disputes among US government agencies.

RICHARD N. COOPER is Boas Professor of International Economics at Harvard University. During 1989–91 he served as a member of the US National Academy of Sciences panel on the policy implications of greenhouse warming. He also served as Under-Secretary of State for Economic Affairs, US State Department, 1979–81, and as chairman of the Federal Reserve Bank of Boston, 1990–2. His publications include *The Economics of Interdependence*, 1968 and (with Barry Eichengreen, C. Randall Henning, Gerald Holtham, and Robert D. Putnam) *Can Nations Agree?*, 1989.

NIGEL HAIGH is Director of the Institute for European Environmental Policy, London. He is an Honorary Research Fellow at the Faculty of Laws, University College London, and Visiting Research Fellow at the Imperial College Centre for Environmental Technology. He has frequently acted as specialist adviser to the House of Lords Select Committee on the European Community. His publications include *EEC Environmental Policy and Britain*, second edition 1990.

ANDREW HURRELL is University Lecturer in International Relations at Oxford University and a Fellow of Nuffield College. He taught previously at the Johns Hopkins School of Advanced International Studies in Bologna, Italy. He has written on the theory of international relations and the international relations of Latin America, including (as editor and contributor) *Latin America in Perspective*, 1990, and *The Quest for Autonomy: Brazil in the International Sytem*, forthcoming.

BENEDICT KINGSBURY is University Lecturer in Law at Oxford University and a Fellow of Exeter College. He has jointly edited and contributed to *United Nations, Divided World*, 1988, and *Hugo Grotius and International Relations*, 1990, and is the author of a forthcoming book on *Indigenous Peoples and International Law*. A specialist in international law, he has also taught recently at Cornell and Duke Law Schools.

MARTIN LIST is Assistant Professor of Political Science at the University of Hagen. He received his doctorate in Social Science from Tübingen University and was previously Research Associate at the Institute of Political Science in Tübingen. He recently published *Unweltschutz in zwei Meeren. Vergleich der internationalen Zusammenarbeit zum Schutz der Meeresumwelt in Nord- und Ostsee*, 1991.

HANNS MAULL holds the Chair for Foreign Policy and International Relations at the University of Trier and is Co-Director of the Research Institute of the German Society for Foreign Policy in Bonn. He has also taught at the universities of Munich and Eichstätt and served as European Secretary of the Trilateral Commission. Since 1979 he has represented the Japan Center for International Exchange in Europe. His publications include *Raw Materials, Energy and Western Security*, 1984.

NORMAN MYERS is an independent scientist and consultant in environment and development. He has been serving as Senior Adviser to Maurice Strong, Secretary-General of the UN Conference on Environment and Development. He has published widely on environmental matters, including *The Primary Source: Tropical Forests and Our Future*, 1984.

CONNIE OZAWA is an associate at the Program on Negotiation at Harvard University and Visiting Assistant Professor at the Sloan School of Management, MIT. Her research focuses on negotiations in public policy and she is the author of *Recasting Science: Consensual Procedures in Public Policy Making*, 1991.

KENNETH PIDDINGTON was appointed as the first Director of the Environment Department at the World Bank in 1988 and is currently Special Adviser (Environment). He was previously New Zealand's Commissioner for the Environment and the first Director-General of the New Zealand Conservation Department. He is currently working with the team preparing the 1992 *World Development Report* which focuses on the linkages between environment and development.

GARETH PORTER is Director of the International Program and Co-Director of the Climate Program at the Environmental and Energy Study Institute. He has taught at the Johns Hopkins School of Advanced International Studies, the City College of New York, and the School of International Service at The American University, Washington. He is the author of four books on South-East Asian politics and is now co-authoring a book on global environmental politics.

ELLIOT L. RICHARDSON has held many senior posts in the US government, including Under-Secretary of State, Secretary of Defense, and US Attorney-General. From 1977 to 1980 he was the Special Representative of the US President to the Law of the Sea Conference. He is a partner of Millbank, Tweed, Hadley, and McCloy.

VOLKER RITTBERGER has been Professor of Political Science at the University of Tübingen since 1973. He received an MA and PhD in Political Science from Stanford University and has held various visiting appointments in Germany and abroad. His recent publications include *International Regimes in East–West Politics*, 1990, and *Theorien der Internationalen Beziehungen*, 1990.

HENRY SHUE is the Wyn and William Y. Hutchinson Professor of Ethics and Public Policy at Cornell University. He was a founding member of the Institute for Philosophy and Public Policy at the University of Maryland from 1976 until moving to Cornell in 1987. He is the author of *Basic Rights* (1980) and a number of articles on international justice, including 'Exporting Hazards', *Ethics* (1981) and 'Mediating Duties', *Ethics* (1988).

KEVIN STAIRS joined Greenpeace International's Convention and Treaties Division as a practising lawyer from the United States. He has been chief advocate for Greenpeace in its role in the development of new conventions and in the implementation of policy within various ocean protection treaties.

LAWRENCE SUSSKIND is Professor of Urban and Environmental Planning at MIT and Director of the MIT–Harvard Public Disputes Program. He is also Secretary of the International Environmental Negotiation Network and author of *Environmental Diplomacy: Negotiating More Effective International Agreements*, 1992.

PETER TAYLOR was, until 1991, director of The Political Ecology Research Group, an Oxford-based science consultancy. He has been an independent adviser to Greenpeace on ocean science issues for 12 years. He is currently working on questions relating to the global carbon cycle and environmental change.

PETER S. THACHER is Senior Counsellor at the World Resources Institute (WRI) and Senior Adviser to the Secretary-General of the UN Conference on Environment and Development. He joined the United Nations in 1971 as Program Director on the secretariat preparing for the 1972 Stockholm Conference on the Human Environment. From 1973 to 1977 he ran the European Office of the United Nations Environment Programme (UNEP), before moving to Nairobi as Deputy Head of UNEP, a post which he held until 1983.

BIBLIOGRAPHY

Books

Adams, W. M. *Green Development: Environment and Sustainability in the Third World*. London and New York: Routledge, 1990.

Agarwal, Anil, and Narain, Sunita. *Global Warming in an Unequal World: A Case of Environmental Colonialism*. New Delhi: Centre for Science and Environment, 1991.

Axelrod, Robert. *The Evolution of Cooperation*. New York: Basic Books, 1984.

Barbier, Edward B., Burgess, J., Swanson, T., and Pearce, D. W. *Elephants, Ivory and Economics*. London: Earthscan Publications, 1990.

Barde, Jean-Phillipe, and Pearce, David (eds.). *Valuing the Environment: Six Case Studies*. London: Earthscan Publications, 1991.

Barrett, Brendan F. D., and Therivel, Riki. *Environmental Policy and Impact Assessment in Japan*. London and New York: Routledge, 1991.

Bartelmus, Peter. *Environment and Development*. Boston, Mass.: Allen & Unwin Inc., 1986.

Benedick, Richard Elliot. *Ozone Diplomacy. New Directions in Safeguarding the Planet*. Cambridge, Mass.: Harvard University Press, 1991.

―― et al. *Greenhouse Warming: Negotiating a Global Regime*. Washington, DC: World Resources Institute, 1991.

Birnie, Patricia, and Boyle, Alan. *International Environmental Law*. Oxford: Oxford University Press, 1992.

Biswas, Asit K., Khoshoo, T. N., and Khosla, Ashok (eds.). *Environmental Modelling for Developing Countries*. London and New York: Tycooly Publishing, 1990.

Brickman, Ronald, Jasanoff, Sheila, and Ilgen, Thomas. *Controlling Chemicals: The Politics of Regulation in Europe and the United States*. Ithaca: Cornell University Press, 1985.

Brownlie, Ian. *Principles of Public International Law*, 4th edn. Oxford: Oxford University Press, 1990.

Caldwell, Lynton Keith. *Between Two Worlds: Science, the Environmental Movement, and Policy Choice*. Cambridge and New York: Cambridge University Press, 1990.

―― *International Environmental Policy: Emergence and Dimensions*, 2nd edn. Durham, NC: Duke University Press, 1990.

460 Bibliography

Carroll, John E. (ed.). *International Environmental Diplomacy: The Management and Resolution of Transfrontier Environmental Problems.* Cambridge: Cambridge University Press, 1988.

Carter, Barry E., and Trimble, Philip R. *International Law: Selected Documents.* Boston, Mass.: Little, Brown, 1991.

Charney, Jonathan I. (ed.). *The New Nationalism and the Use of Common Spaces: Issues in Marine Pollution and the Exploitation of Antarctica.* Montclair, NJ: American Society of International Law, 1982.

Churchill, Robin R., and Freestone, David. *International Law and Global Climate Change.* London: Martinus Nijhoff, 1991.

Cleveland, Harlan. *The Global Commons: Policy for the Planet.* Lanham, Md.: University Press of America, 1990.

Commoner, Barry. *Making Peace with the Planet.* New York: Pantheon Books, 1990.

Dryzek, John. *Rational Ecology.* Oxford: Blackwell, 1987.

Efinger, Manfred, Rittberger, Volker, and Zürn, Michael. *Internationale Regime in den Ost-West-Beziehungen.* Frankfurt: Haag & Herchen, 1988.

Engel, J. R., and Engel, J. G. *Ethics of Environment and Development. Global Challenge and International Response.* London: Belhaven, 1990.

Falk, Richard. *This Endangered Planet. Prospects and Proposals for Human Survival.* New York: Vintage Books, 1971.

Fantechi, R., and Ghazi, A. (eds.). *Carbon Dioxide and Other Greenhouse Gases: Climatic and Associated Impacts.* Dordrecht and Boston, Mass.: Kluwer Academic Publishers, 1989.

Firor, John. *The Changing Atmosphere: A Global Challenge.* New Haven, Conn.: Yale University Press, 1990.

Fisher, D. E. *Fire and Ice: The Greenhouse Effect, Ozone Depletion and Nuclear Winter.* New York: Harper and Row, 1990.

Fisher, Roger, and Ury, William. *Getting to Yes: Negotiating Agreements Without Giving In.* Boston, Mass.: Houghton Mifflin, 1981.

Fowler, Cary, and Mooney, Pat. *Shattering: Food, Politics, and the Loss of Genetic Diversity.* Tucson, Ariz.: University of Arizona Press, 1990.

Francioni, F., and Scovazzi, T. (eds.). *International Responsibility for Environmental Harm.* London: Graham and Trotman, 1991.

Franck, Thomas M. *The Power of Legitimacy Among Nations.* New York: Oxford University Press, 1990.

Friedmann, Wolfgang. *The Changing Structure of International Law.* New York: Columbia University Press, 1964.

Fujii, Yasumasa. *An Assessment of the Responsibility for the Increase in the CO_2 Concentration and Inter-Generational Carbon Accounts.* Laxenburg [Austria]: IIASA, 1990.

Goodman, David, and Hall, Anthony (eds.). *The Future of Amazonia: Destruction or Sustainable Development.* London: Macmillan, 1990.

Grubb, Michael (ed.). *Energy Policies and the Greenhouse Effect,* Volume i: *Policy Appraisal.* Brookfield: Dartmouth Publishing Company, 1990.

—— *Energy Policies and the Greenhouse Effect,* Volume ii: *Country Studies and Technical Options.* Brookfield: Dartmouth Publishing Company, 1991.

Gupta, Joyeeta. *Toxic Terrorism.* London: Earthscan Publications, 1990.

Haas, Peter. *Saving the Mediterranean: The Politics of International Environmental Cooperation.* New York: Columbia University Press, 1990.

Haigh, N. *EEC Environmental Policy and Britain,* 2nd edn. London: Longman, 1990.

Hakapää, K. *Marine Pollution in International Law: Material Obligations and Jurisdiction with Special Reference to the Third United Nations Conference on the Law of the Sea.* Helsinki: Suomalainen Tiedeakatemia Distribution, 1981.

Harf, James E., and Trout, B. Thomas. *The Politics of Global Resources. Population, Food, Energy, and Environment.* Durham, NC: Duke University Press, 1986.

Jacobson, Jodi L. *Environmental Refugees: A Yardstick of Habitability.* Washington, DC: Worldwatch Institute, 1988.

Jessup, Philip C. *The Price of International Justice.* New York: Columbia University Press, 1971.

Johnson, Stanley P., and Corcelle, Guy. *The Environmental Policy of the European Communities.* London and Boston, Mass.: Graham and Trotman, 1989.

Juma, Calestous. *The Gene Hunters: Biotechnology and the Scramble for Seeds.* Princeton: Princeton University Press, 1989.

Keohane, Robert O. *After Hegemony: Co-operation and Discord in the World Political Economy.* Princeton: Princeton University Press, 1985.

—— *International Institutions and State Power.* Boulder, Colo.: Westview, 1990.

——, and Nye, Joseph S. *Power and Interdependence: World Politics in Transition,* 2nd edn. Boston, Mass.: Little, Brown, 1989.

Kish, John. *The Law of International Spaces.* Leiden, Sijthoff, 1973.

Kiss, Alexandre, and Shelton, Dinah. *International Environmental Law.* London: Graham and Trotman, 1991.

Krasner, Stephen D. (ed.). *International Regimes.* Ithaca: Cornell University Press, 1983.

Lammers, J. G. *Pollution of International Watercourses: Search for Substantive Rules and Principles of Law.* Boston, Mass.: Nijhoff, 1984.

Leggett, Jeremy (ed.). *Global Warming: The Greenpeace Report.* New York: Oxford University Press, 1990.

List, Martin. *Umweltschutz in zwei Meeren. Vergleich der internationalen Zusammenarbeit zum Schutz der Meeresumwelt in Nord- und Ostsee.* Munich: Tuduv, 1991.

462   Bibliography

Lunde, Leiv. *The North/South Dimension in Global Greenhouse Politics.* Lysaker, Norway: Fridtjof Nansen Institute, 1990.

McCormick, John. *The Global Environmental Movement. Reclaiming Paradise.* London: Belhaven Press, 1989.

McHale, John, and McHale, Magda. *Basic Human Needs: A Framework for Action.* New Brunswick: Transaction Books, 1978.

MacNeill, Jim, Winsemius, Peter, and Yakushiji, Taizo. *Beyond Interdependence: The Meshing of the World's Economy and the Earth's Ecology.* Oxford: Oxford University Press, 1991.

Managing a Common Resource. Washington: World Bank and the European Investment Bank, 1990.

Mathews, Jessica Tuchman (ed.). *Preserving the Global Environment: The Challenge of Shared Leadership.* New York: W. W. Norton and Co., 1991.

Medvedev, Zhores A. *The Legacy of Chernobyl.* New York: W. W. Norton and Co., 1990.

Mitchell, James K. (ed.). *Global Environmental Change: Human and Policy Dimensions.* Guildford: Butterworth-Heinemann, 1990.

Molitor, Michael (ed.). *International Environmental Law: Primary Materials.* Deventer: Kluwer, 1991.

Nardin, Terry. *Law, Morality, and the Relations of States.* Princeton: Princeton University Press, 1983.

National Research Council. *Ozone Depletion, Greenhouse Gases, and Climate Change.* Washington, DC: National Academy Press, 1988.

OECD. *The State of the Environment*, 3rd edn. Washington, DC: OECD, 1991.

Ophuls, William. *Ecology and the Politics of Scarcity.* San Francisco: W. H. Freeman, 1977.

Ostrom, Elinor. *Governing the Commons: The Evolution of Institutions for Collective Action.* New York: Cambridge University Press, 1990.

Oye, Kenneth A. (ed.). *Cooperation Under Anarchy.* Princeton: Princeton University Press, 1986.

Pearce, David W., Barbier, Edward, and Markandya, Anil. *Sustainable Development: Economics and Environment in the Third World.* London: Edward Elgar, 1990.

—— (ed.). *Blueprint 2: The Greening of the World Economy.* London: Earthscan Publications, 1991.

Pierce, John C. *Public Knowledge and Environmental Politics in Japan and the United States.* Boulder, Colo.: Westview Press, 1989.

Renner, Michael. *National Security: The Economic and Environmental Dimensions.* Washington, DC: Worldwatch Institute, 1989.

Rittberger, Volker (ed.). *International Regimes in East–West Politics.* London and New York: Pinter Publishers, 1990.

Sand, Peter H. (ed.). *Marine Environment Law in the United Nations Environment Programme: An Emergent Eco-Regime*. New York: Tycooly Publishing, 1988.

Schachter, Oscar. *International Law in Theory and Practice*. Boston, Mass.: Martinus Nijhoff, 1991.

—— *Sharing the World's Resources*. New York: Columbia University Press, 1977.

Schneider, Jan. *World Public Order of the Environment: Towards an International Ecological Law and Organization*. Toronto: University of Toronto Press, 1979.

Schramm, Gunther, and Warford, Jeremy J. (eds.). *Environmental Management and Economic Development*. Baltimore: Johns Hopkins University Press, 1989.

Shue, Henry. *Basic Rights: Subsistence, Affluence, and U.S. Foreign Policy*. Princeton: Princeton University Press, 1980.

Soroos, Marvin S. *Beyond Sovereignty: The Challenge of Global Policy*. Columbia: University of South Carolina Press, 1986.

Sprout, Howard, and Sprout, Margaret. *Toward a Politics of the Planet Earth*. New York: Van Nostrand Reinhold, 1971.

Starke, Linda. *Signs of Hope: Working Towards Our Common Future*. New York: Oxford University Press, 1990.

Stein, Robert E., and Johnson, Brian. *Banking on the Biosphere? Environmental Procedures and Practices of Nine Multilateral Development Agencies*. Lexington, Mass.: Lexington Books, 1979.

Streeten, Paul. *First Things First: Meeting Basic Human Needs in the Developing Countries*. New York: Oxford University Press, 1981.

Susskind, Lawrence. *Environmental Diplomacy: Negotiating More Effective International Agreements*. New York: Oxford University Press, 1992.

——, and Cruikshank, Jeffrey. *Breaking the Impasse: Consensual Approaches to Resolving Public Disputes*. New York: Basic Books, 1987.

——, Siskind, Esther, and Breslin, J. William (eds.). *Nine Case Studies in International Environmental Negotiation*. Cambridge, Mass.: Program on Negotiation at Harvard Law School, 1990.

Tolba, Mostafa Kamal. *Development Without Destruction: Evolving Environmental Perceptions*. Dublin: Tycooly International, 1982.

—— *Sustainable Development: Constraints and Opportunities*. London and Boston, Mass.: Butterworths, 1987.

United Nations Environment Programme. *Register of International Treaties and Other Agreements in the Field of the Environment*. Nairobi and New York, UNEP: 1991.

Vig, Norman J., and Kraft, Michael E. (eds.). *Environmental Policy in the 1990s*. Washington, DC: Congressional Quarterly Press, 1990.

Ward, Barbara, and Dubos, René. *Only One Earth: The Care and Maintenance of a Small Planet*. New York: W. W. Norton and Co., 1972.

Weiss, Edith Brown. *In Fairness to Future Generations: International Law, Common Patrimony, and Intergenerational Equity*. Dobbs Ferry, NY: Transnational Publishers, 1989.

Wettestad, J., and Andresen, S. (eds.). *Science and North Sea Policy-Making: Organization and Communication in the North Sea*. London: Graham and Trotman, 1990.

World Bank. *Our Common Future*. New York: Oxford University Press, 1987.

—— *The World Bank and the Environment: First Annual Report, Fiscal 1990*. Washington, DC: World Bank Publications,

World Commission on Environment and Development, *Environmental Protection and Sustainable Development: Legal Principles and Recommendations. Adopted by the Experts Group on Environmental Law of World Commission and Development*. London: Graham and Trotman, 1987.

—— (The Brundtland Report). *Our Common Future*. London: Oxford University Press, 1987.

Young, H. P. *Sharing the Burden of Global Warming*. College Park: School of Public Affairs of the University of Maryland, 1990.

Young, Oran R. *International Cooperation: Building Regimes for Natural Resources and the Environment*. Ithaca: Cornell University Press, 1989.

Articles

Agarwal, Anil. 'The North–South Perspective: Alienation or Interdependence?', *Ambio*, 19 (1990), 94–6.

Allott, Philip. 'Power Sharing in the Law of the Sea', *American Journal of International Law*, 77 (1983), 1–30.

Anderson, Christopher, and Aldhous, Peter. 'Third World Muscles in on Climate Treaty', *Nature*, 28 (Feb. 1991), 28.

Barbier, Edward B., *et al.* 'The Economics of Tropical Deforestation', *Ambio*, 20 (1991), 55–8.

Barrett, Scott. 'The Problem of Global Environmental Protection', *Oxford Review of Economic Policy*, 6 (1990), 68.

Bertrand, Maurice. 'Can the United Nations Be Reformed?', in *United Nations, Divided World*, ed. Adam Roberts and Benedict Kingsbury (Oxford: Oxford University Press, 1988), 193–208.

Birnie, Patricia W. 'Delimitation of Maritime Boundaries: Emergent Legal Principles and Problems', in *Maritime Boundaries and Ocean Resources*, ed. Gerald Blake (Totowa, NJ: Barnes & Noble, 1987), 15–37.

—— 'Legal Techniques of Settling Disputes. The "Soft Settlement" Approach', in *Perestroika and International Law*, ed. William E. Butler (Dordrecht: Martinus Nijhoff, 1990), 177–95.

Bruhl, Christoph, and Crutzen, Paul J. 'Ozone and Climate Changes in the Light of the Montreal Protocol: A Model Study', *Ambio*, 19 (1990), 293–301.

Caldwell, Lynton Keith. 'Beyond Environmental Diplomacy: The Changing Institutional Structure of International Co-operation', in *International Environmental Diplomacy: The Management and Resolution of Transfrontier Environmental Problems*, ed. John E. Carroll (Cambridge: Cambridge University Press, 1988), 13–28.

Caron, David D. 'Protection of the Stratospheric Ozone Layer and the Structure of International Environmental Lawmaking', *Hastings International and Comparative Law Review*, 14 (1991), 755–80.

Chafee, John H., and Shimberg, Steven J. 'Supplementing the Montreal Protocol: The Need for Domestic Legislation', *Ambio*, 19 (1990), 310–12.

Chinkin, C. M. 'The Challenge of Soft Law: Development and Change in International Law', *International and Comparative Law Quarterly*, 38 (1989), 850–66.

Cooper, Richard. 'International Co-operation in Public Health as a Prologue to Macroeconomic Co-operation', in *Can Nations Agree? Issues in International Economic Co-operation*, ed. Richard Cooper, *et al.* (Washington, DC: Brookings Institution, 1989), 178–254.

D'Amato, Anthony, *et al.* 'Agora: What Obligation Does Our Generation Owe to the Next? An Approach to Global Environmental Responsibility', *American Journal of International Law*, 84 (1990), 190–212.

Deudney, Daniel. 'The Case Against Linking Environmental Degradation and National Security', *Millennium*, 19.3 (Winter 1990), 461–76.

Dixon, John A., and Sherman, Paul B. 'Economics of Protected Areas', *Ambio*, 20 (1991), 68–74.

Dupuy, Pierre-Marie. 'The International Law of State Responsibility: Revolution or Evolution?', *Michigan Journal of International Law*, 11 (1989), 105–28.

Fraenkel, Amy. 'The Convention on Long-Range Transboundary Air Pollution: Meeting the Challenge of International Co-operation', *Harvard International Law Journal*, 30 (1989), 447–76.

Gaillard, Jacques. 'Science in the Developing World: Foreign Aid and National Policies at a Crossroad', *Ambio*, 19 (1990), 348–53.

Gaines, Sanford E. 'International Principles for Transnational Environmental Liability: Can Developments in Municipal Law Help Break the Impasse?', *Harvard International Law Journal*, 30 (1989), 311–49.

Gilbert, Geoff. 'The Criminal Responsibility of States', *International and Comparative Law Quarterly*, 39 (1990), 345.

Goldie, L. F. E. 'Liability for Damage and the Progressive Development of International Law', *International and Comparative Law Quarterly*, 14 (1965), 1189–264.

Gray, C. Boyden, and Rivkin, David B., Jr. 'A "No Regrets" Environmental Policy', *Foreign Policy*, 83 (1991), 47–65.

Grieco, Joseph M. 'Anarchy and the Limits of Co-operation: A Realist Critique of the Newest Liberal Institutionalism', *International Organization*, 42 (1988), 485–507.

Gruchalla-Wisierski, Tadeusz. 'A Framework for Understanding "Soft Law"', *Revue de Droit de McGill*, 30 (1984), 37–88.

Gundling, Lothar. 'The Status in International Law of the Principle of Precautionary Action', *International Journal of Estuarine and Coastal Law*, 5 (1990), 23–30.

Haas, Peter M. 'Do Regimes Matter? Epistemic Communities and Mediterranean Pollution Control', *International Organization*, 43 (1989), 377–403.

—— 'Epistemic Communities and International Policy Co-ordination'. *International Organization*, 46 (1991–2). Special Issue on *Knowledge, Power and International Policy Co-ordination*, ed. Peter M. Haas.

Haggard, Stephan, and Simmons, Beth A. 'Theories of International Regimes', *International Organization*, 41 (1987), 491–517.

Hahn, Robert W., and Richards, Kenneth R. 'The Internationalization of Environmental Regulation', *Harvard International Law Journal*, 30 (1989), 421–46.

Handl, G. 'Liability as an Obligation Established by a Primary Rule of International Law', *Netherlands Yearbook of International Law*, 16 (1985), 49–79.

—— 'The Principle of Equitable Use As Applied to Internationally Shared Natural Resources: Its Role in Resolving Potential International Disputes over Transfrontier Pollution, *Revue Belge de Droit International*, 14 (1977–8), 40–64.

Hartshorn, Gary S. 'Key Environmental Issues for Developing Countries', *Journal of International Affairs*, 44 (1991), 393–402.

Jenks, C. Wilfred. 'Liability for Ultra-Hazardous Activities in International Law', *Recueil des Cours*, 117 (1966), 99–200.

Jennings, R. Y. 'What Is International Law and How Do We Tell It When We See It?', *Annuaire Suisse de Droit International*, 37 (1981), 59–88.

Jervis, Robert. 'Co-operation Under the Security Dilemma', *World Politics*, 30 (1978), 167.

Kamieniecki, Sheldon. 'Political Mobilization, Agenda Building and International Environmental Policy', *Journal of International Affairs*, 44 (1991), 339–58.

Kasoulides, George. 'Paris Memorandum of Understanding: A Regional Regime of Enforcement', *International Journal of Estuarine and Coastal Law*, 5 (1990), 180–92.

Kelson, John M. 'State Responsibility and the Abnormally Dangerous Activity', *Harvard International Law Journal*, 13 (1972), 197–244.

Keohane, Robert O., and Nye, Joseph S., Jr. 'Power and Interdependence Revisited', *International Organization*, 41 (1987), 725–53.

Kindt, John Warren, and Menefee, Samuel Pyeatt. 'The Vexing Problem of Ozone Depletion in International Environmental Law and Policy', *Texas International Law Journal*, 24 (1989), 261–93.

Kiss, A., and Brusasco-MacKenzie, M. 'Les Relations Extérieures des Communautés Européennes en Matière du Protection de l'Environment', *Annuaire Français de Droit International*, 35 (1989), 702–10.

Koehler, Jamison, and Hajost, Scott A. 'The Montreal Protocol: A Dynamic Agreement for Protecting the Ozone Layer', *Ambio*, 19 (1990), 82–6.

Lachs, Manfred. 'The Challenge of the Environment', *International and Comparative Law Quarterly*, 39 (1990), 663–9.

Lowe, A. V. 'A Move Against Substandard Shipping', *Marine Policy*, 6 (1982), 326.

—— 'Reflections on the Water: Changing Conceptions of Property Rights in the Law of the Sea', *International Journal of Estuarine and Coastal Law*, 1 (1986), 9.

Mäler, K. G. 'International Environmental Problems', *Oxford Review of Economic Policy*, 6 (1990), 80–108.

Mann, Dean E. 'Environmental Learning in a Decentralized Political World', *Journal of International Affairs*, 44 (1991), 301–38.

Mathews, Jessica Tuchman. 'Redefining Security', *Foreign Affairs*, 68 (1989), 162–77.

Millennium, 19 (1990), Special Issue on International Environmental Politics.

Morgenstern, Richard D. 'Towards a Comprehensive Approach to Global Climate Change Mitigation', *American Economic Review*, 81 (1991), 140–5.

Müller, Harald. 'Internationale Ressourcen- und Umweltproblematik', in *Einführung in die Internationale Politik*, ed. Manfred Knapp and Gert Krell, (Munich, 1990), 350–82.

Myers, Norman. 'Environment and Security', *Foreign Policy*, 74 (1989), 23–41.

Nanda, Ved P. 'Stratospheric Ozone Depletion: A Challenge for International Environmental Law and Policy', *Michigan Journal of International Law*, 10 (1989), 482–525.

Nollkaemper, A. 'The European Community and International Environmental Co-operation: Legal Aspects of External Community Powers', *Legal Issues of European Co-operation*, 2 (1987), 55–91.

Nordhaus, William D. 'A Sketch of the Economics of the Greenhouse Effect', *American Economic Review*, 81 (1991), 146–50.

—— 'The Cost of Slowing Climate Change: A Survey', *Energy Journal*, 12 (1991), 37–65.

Pearce, David, and Mäler, Karl-Goran. 'Environmental Economics and the Developing World', *Ambio*, 20 (1991), 52–4.

Petsonk, Carol Annette. 'The Role of the United Nations Environment Programme (UNEP) in the Development of International Environmental Law', *American University Journal of International Law and Policy*, 5 (1990), 351–92.

Ramakrishna, Kilaparti. 'North–South Issues, Common Heritage of Mankind and Global Climate Change', *Millennium*, 19 (1990), 429–46.

Randall, Alan. 'The Value of Biodiversity', *Ambio*, 20 (1991), 64–8.

Rehbinder, Edward. 'U.S. Environmental Policy: Lessons for Europe', *International Environmental Affairs*, 1 (1989), 3–11.

Rose-Ackerman, Susan. 'Tort Law as a Regulatory System: Regulation and the Law of Torts', *American Economic Review*, 83 (1991), 54–8.

Rosemarin, Arno. 'Some Background on CFCs', *Ambio*, 19 (1990), 280.

Rosencranz, Armin, and Milligan, Reina. 'CFC Abatement: The Needs of Developing Countries', *Ambio*, 19 (1990), 312–17.

Rowland, F. Sherwood. 'Stratospheric Ozone Depletion by Chlorofluorocarbons', *Ambio*, 19 (1990), 281–92.

Ruggie, John Gerard. 'International Responses to Technology: Concepts and Trends', *International Organization*, 29 (1975), 557–83.

Sandbrook, Richard. 'Development for the People and the Environment', *Journal of International Affairs*, 44 (1991), 403–20.

Sands, Philippe J. 'The Environment, Community and International Law', *Harvard International Law Journal*, 30 (1989), 393–420.

Schachter, Oscar. 'The Emergence of International Environmental Law', *Journal of International Affairs*, 44 (1991), 457–93.

Schiel, Carl-Heinz. 'Promoting Indigenous Research Capacities in Developing Countries—The International Foundation for Science (IFS) and Its Work', *Ambio*, 19 (1990), 346–8.

Schreiber, Helmut. 'The Threat from Environmental Destruction in Eastern Europe', *Journal of International Affairs*, 44 (1991), 359–92.

Sebenius, James K. 'Designing Negotiations Toward a New Regime: The Case of Global Warming', *International Security*, 15 (1991), 110–48.

Seidel, Stephen R., and Blank, Daniel P. 'The Montreal Protocol: Pollution Prevention on a Global Scale', *Ambio*, 19 (1990), 301–4.

Singh, Nagendra. 'The United Nations and the Development of International Law', in *United Nations, Divided World: The UN's Roles in International Relations*, ed. Adam Roberts and Benedict Kingsbury (New York: Oxford University Press, 1988), 159–91.

Skolnikoff, E. 'The Policy Gridlock on Global Warming', *Foreign Policy*, 79 (1990), 77–93.

Smith, Kirk R. 'Allocating Responsibility for Global Warming: The Natural Debt Index', *Ambio*, 20 (1991), 95–6.

Somers, E. 'The Role of the Courts in the Enforcement of Environmental Rules', *International Journal of Estuarine and Coastal Law*, 5 (1990), 193–200.

Stolarski, R. S., et al. 'Nimbus 7 Satellite Measurements of the Springtime Antarctic Ozone Decrease', *Nature*, 322 (1986), 808.

Strong, Maurice F. 'ECO '92: Critical Challenges and Global Solutions', *Journal of International Affairs*, 44 (1991), 287–300.

Thacher, Peter S. 'Multilateral Co-operation and Global Change', *Journal of International Affairs*, 44 (1991), 433–55.

Virally, Michel. 'Panorama du droit international contemporain', *Recueil des Cours de l'Académie de Droit International*, 183 (1983), 9–382.

Von Weizsacker, Ernst U. 'Sustainability: A Task for the North', *Journal of International Affairs*, 44 (1991), 421–32.

Weidner, Helmut. 'Japanese Environmental Policies in an International Perspective: Lessons for a Preventive Approach', in *Environmental Policy in Japan*, ed. Shigeto Tsuru and Helumt Weidner (Berlin: Edition Sigma, 1989), 479–552.

Weiss, Edith Brown. 'The Planetary Trust: Conservation and Intergenerational Equity', *Ecology Law Quarterly*, 11 (1984), 495.

Westing, Arthur H. 'Environmental Security and Its Relation to Ethiopia and Sudan', *Ambio*, 20 (1991), 168–71.

—— 'Environmental Component of Comprehensive Security', *Bulletin of Peace Proposals*, 20 (1989), 129–34.

Wirth, David A., and Lashof, Daniel A. 'Beyond Vienna and Montreal —Multilateral Agreements on Greenhouse Gases', *Ambio*, 19 (1990), 305–10.

Young, Oran R. 'The Politics of International Regime Formation: Managing Natural Resources and the Environment', *International Organization*, 43 (1989), 349–75.

—— 'Political Leadership and Regime Formation: On the Development of Institutions in International Society', *International Organization*, 45 (1991), 281–308.

Zaelke, Durwood, and Cameron, James. 'Global Warming and Climate Change: An Overview of the International Legal Process', *American University Journal of International Law and Policy*, 5 (1990), 249–90.

INDEX

References to policy, politics, legislation, and the environment are omitted as qualifiers due to their ubiquity.